Enterprise Resource Planning Models for the Education Sector:

Applications and Methodologies

Kanubhai K. Patel
Ahmedabad University, India

Sanjaykumar Vij
Sardar Vallabhbhai Patel Institute of Technology, India

Managing Director:	Lindsay Johnston
Editorial Director:	Joel Gamon
Book Production Manager:	Jennifer Romanchak
Publishing Systems Analyst:	Adrienne Freeland
Development Editor:	Myla Merkel
Assistant Acquisitions Editor:	Kayla Wolfe
Typesetter:	Erin O'Dea
Cover Design:	Nick Newcomer

Published in the United States of America by
Information Science Reference (an imprint of IGI Global)
701 E. Chocolate Avenue
Hershey PA 17033
Tel: 717-533-8845
Fax: 717-533-8661
E-mail: cust@igi-global.com
Web site: http://www.igi-global.com

Library of Congress Cataloging-in-Publication Data

Enterprise resource planning models for the education sector : applications and methodologies / Kanubhai K. Patel and Sanjaykumar Vij, editor.
   p. cm.
 Includes bibliographical references and index.
 Summary: "This book is a comprehensive collection of research that highlights the increasing demand for insight into the challenges faced by educational institutions on the design and development of enterprise resource planning applications"--Provided by publisher.
 ISBN 978-1-4666-2193-0 (hardcover) -- ISBN 978-1-4666-2194-7 (ebook) -- ISBN 978-1-4666-2195-4 (print & perpetual access) 1. Universities and colleges--Business management--Computer programs. 2. Enterprise resource planning. 3. Educational technology. I. Patel, Kanubhai K., 1970- II. Vij, Sanjaykumar, 1950-
 LB2341.92.E58 2013
 378.1'01--dc23
                                  2012019285

British Cataloguing in Publication Data
A Cataloguing in Publication record for this book is available from the British Library.

All work contributed to this book is new, previously-unpublished material. The views expressed in this book are those of the authors, but not necessarily of the publisher.

Editorial Advisory Board

Table of Contents

Section 2
Knowledge Management

Section 3
ERP Adoption and Implementation

Section 4
Customer Relationship Management

Detailed Table of Contents

Section 1
Learning Management and Administration

Chapter 1

José Luis Sánchez de la Rosa, University of La Laguna, Spain
Silvia Alayón Miranda, University of La Laguna, Spain
Carina Soledad González, University of La Laguna, Spain

The importance of the evaluation of the transversal competences in engineering studies is explained in this chapter. Transversal competences are of great importance to enterprises that like to recruit students after their graduation. They look for trained professionals, thoroughly prepared not only to solve practical problems but also to be successfully integrated in a team work. Transversal competences are not directly related to the theoretical content of the curricula, and the assessment of the level of transversal competences developed through the university studies is not an easy task. A methodology for evaluating transversal skills during the Final Year Project (FYP) assessment is proposed. And a new modality of FYP to improve the acquisition of transversal skills is presented.

Chapter 2

Agnes Chigona, Cape Peninsula University of Technology, South Africa
Rabelani Dagada, Witwatersrand University, South Africa

Tertiary institutions in the developing countries are investing a lot in equipping their institutions with Information Communication Technologies (ICT) for teaching and learning. However, there is still a low adoption rate in the use of the new technologies among many academics in these countries. This chapter aims at analysing the factors that impact on the academics' effective use of ICTs for teaching and learning in the new education paradigm. Sen's Capability Approach was used as a conceptual lens to examine the academics' phenomena. Data was collected through in-depth interviews. The analysis of the findings has shown that individual, social, and environmental factors are preventing some academics from realising their potential capabilities from using the new technologies. It is recommended, therefore, that institutions in the developing countries should look into, and deal with accordingly, the conversion factors that are impacting on the academics' capabilities when utilising the new technologies.

Chapter 3

P. Srinivas Subba Rao, Maharajah's Post Graduate College, India
P. Suseela Rani, TRR College of Engineering & Technology, India

Virtual and Interactive Learning (VIL) is one of the new directions for education. It aims at using the WEB, being a networked, anytime, interactive, high-capacity, and content-rich environment, to enhance and facilitate independent learning and teacher-student communication. It would eventually lead to a paradigm shift of learning style, from teacher-centered to student-centered. It is bringing hope to millions who had abandoned the dream of continuing education due to paucity of time and money. It makes learning much easier as one need not be physically present in the classrooms all the time. Through VIL students are anticipated to learn to analyse the problem situation, devise the problem solving strategies, solve the problems and evaluate the consequences, all of which are considered as high-order abilities required in this new era. VIL should be facilitated by the provision of real-life experience so as to bridge the gap between classroom learning and real-life experiences by enabling students to learn in a simulated situation similar to the real ones.

Chapter 4

Knut Arne Strand, Sør-Trøndelag University College, Norway
Arvid Staupe, Norwegian University of Science and Technology, Norway
Tor Atle Hjeltnes, Sør-Trøndelag University College, Norway

Instructional design is a process that in many cases requires multidisciplinary collaboration among several stakeholders. Domain experts, pedagogues, technical experts, economists, administrative personnel, customer representatives, instructors, and learners may have very different preferences, and sometimes it is a great challenge to coordinate them all. In this chapter, the authors present the principles of concurrent e-learning design. Concurrent e-learning design is a novel approach to computer supported and cooperative instructional design where several stakeholders actively participate in the design process. The results from a concurrent e-learning design project can typically be a comprehensive design document containing details regarding how higher education e-learning courses should be developed and delivered. The authors have worked to codify this methodological approach for several years and conducted a qualitative analysis of data collected during this period. This analysis has yielded sixteen principles, which are grouped into five categories and presented in this chapter. The chapter describes each principle in detail, discusses whether ERP systems can be of assistance in the instructional design process, and outlines a plan for testing ERP systems in connection with the concurrent e-learning design approach.

Section 2
Knowledge Management

Chapter 5

Elena Railean, Informational Society Development Institute, Republic of Moldova

This chapter aims to describe a new knowledge management (KM) model, which can be considered an enterprise resources planning model proved in Electronic Textbook in Electronic Portfolio technology. The model comprises a dynamic and flexible instructional strategy which allows constructing the personalized digital content through development of core structure of competence. This strategy allows bidirectional transitions from tacit to explicit knowledge and hermeneutic dialogues. The KM model can be described using adjacency matrix and optimized knowledge graphs techniques. The target audience of this chapter is expected to be consisted of educational management students, professionals and researchers working in the field of education including policy makers, consultants, and agencies. Applications and methodologies validate the educational efficiency of KM model for electronic textbook design. The affordance of the KM model for education relies on informational / communicational processes, cognitive processes, and computerized assessment processes.

Chapter 6

An Institutional Knowledge Repository (IKR) is "a digital archive of intellectual product created by the faculty, research staff, and students of an institution and accessible to end users both within and outside of the institution, with few if any barriers to access." This chapter discusses the growing trend in Open Access Repositories, Institutional Repositories worldwide. It throws light on the concepts of enterprise resource planning and enterprise content management and then explores academic institutions in India who have already initiated the use of Institutional Knowledge Repositories, as an enterprise content management system for knowledge sharing & management with regard to content, access, and other factors.

Chapter 7

Research in the integration of technology and content knowledge using problem-based learning (PBL) is a challenge. Thus, the aim of this chapter is to describe experiences and lessons learned from integrating ERP-systems (enterprise resource planning systems) into economic topics course using PBL and cases created for the integration of technology and content knowledge in a business school setting. The mission was to develop the economic students' analyzing abilities using a ERP-system as a pedagogical tool. A summary table describes how problem-based learning and cases were developed and used within collaboration among universities, colleagues, businesses, and students to accomplish integration of both technology and content knowledge. The experience was that students developed abilities to analyze technology from both theory and a deeper understanding of theory by analyzing technology. The lessons learned were that integration of technology and content knowledge using problem based learning and cases is a never-ending cooperative and learning process.

Chapter 8

Nowadays in higher education, we create lots of documents and datasets for every activity. We have to maintain course, program, and syllabus information, and also the connections between the course themes. We can download some documentation for this information, but there are many questions difficult to answer. Also we can find some HR related or organizational issues. The authors are working for an ontology which is able to picture the connections between the actors of a higher education system. Their ontology is built with integrating some existing one, for example AIISO (Academic Institution Internal Structure Ontology), FOAF (Friend of a Friend) and DC (Dublin Core). The ontology has four connected parts. These can describe an organization with its internal structure, the program and courses of a University, the people connected with the organizations, the courses or some documents. The authors can also characterize course materials, such as documents, books, or multimedia contents and can connect the knowledge base with ERP systems also.

Section 3
ERP Adoption and Implementation

Chapter 9

Jorge A. Romero, Towson University, USA

Enterprise Resource Planning (ERP) has been a major investment for most companies since the early nineties. ERP is a type of investment that has an integrated approach, and has been widely adopted, but there is little empirical evidence about how ERP implementation affects company performance. This chapter begins with the discussion of ERP investment and its role as a commodity or as a strategic investment. Then follows a discussion of an industry in which companies have invested enormous amounts of money on ERP. Finally, in spite of the growing dominance of ERP systems, there is still little empirical evidence on the type of benefits that companies get from an ERP implementation. Therefore, it is important to understand the effects of ERP in cross-functional systems.

Chapter 10

Y. Callero, University of La Laguna, Spain
R. M. Aguilar, University of La Laguna, Spain
V. Muñoz, University of La Laguna, Spain

In light of the proliferation of information technology in every area of society/business, its adoption by academia seems like a natural extension of this trend. What the authors find, however, is that few examples exist of the use of Business Process Management to improve processes in academia. This chapter presents simulations as a necessary mechanism for understanding and overseeing organizations as they undergo a continuous process of change. Enterprises, their organization, business processes, and supporting information technology must be understood as socio-technical systems that consist of people (human actors) and technical subsystems and their complicated relationships. In designing, redesigning, and improving such systems, modeling and simulation methods are not only relevant, but essential.

Section 4
Customer Relationship Management

Chapter 11

Viral Nagori, GLS Institute of Computer Technology, India

"Keep your customers happy and satisfied to create value in the long run for the firm." The statement is the motto of all business organisations to become a successful enterprise. Customer relationship management is mainly used to identify the buying habits of the customers, analyse trends and patterns, and market the product to the targeted customers. Academic institutions and universities are considered as a service industry, so the scope and role of CRM would be drastically different compared to manufacturing industries. In the Indian context, the main customers of the institutions or universities are parents of the students who spend significant amount on their children's education. The companies that recruit graduate students are also considered as the customer for academic institutions and universities. The chapter discusses the fundamentals of CRM, its uses and application in academic environment, and technology supporting CRM. The major emphasis of the chapter is on how to automate communication among the students, parents, and faculties. The chapter also focuses on streamlining and providing the details of the performance of students for the campus interview and final placements to the companies. The chapter also throws light on the role of technology in CRM implementation in academic institutions and universities. Advantages offered by CRM in academic environment are also discussed. The chapter provides guidelines for successful implementations of CRM in academic environment. To narrow down the scope of the study, it is confined to CRM for academic institutions universities offering higher education (graduate/post graduate courses) in Indian environment.

Chapter 12

P. A. Khatwani, Sarvajanik College of Engineering Technology, India
K. S. Desai, Sarvajanik College of Engineering Technology, India

Industry-institute interaction, training, and placement are very important aspects to be considered while designing any system to improve the methodologies for the education sector. This chapter deals with the different modules related to industry institute management, training and placement, alumni database, and management to be covered while designing an ERP system for improving these most important areas for any academic institution. Some of the modules to be covered in industry-institute management are as follows: database of industries, industrial visits for enhancing knowledge of students as well as faculty, regular lectures from speakers from industry, providing technical training to staff from industry by means of workshop/seminar/small term courses, and providing technical/consultancy services to industry. Some of the modules to be covered in training and placement management are as follows: database of industries, vocational training to students for enhancing their knowledge, database of students and their academic performance, arrangement of programmes for soft skill development, guidance to students for written exam, group discussions, and personal interviews. Some of the modules to be covered in alumni management are as follows: database of alumni, networking of alumni, interaction with alumni for different issues like industrial visits, placement, guest lectures, institutional developments, et cetera.

Section 5
Course and Curriculum Development

Chapter 13

Theodosios Tsiakis, Alexandrian Technological Educational Institute of Thessaloniki, Greece
Theodoros Kargidis, Alexandrian Technological Educational Institute of Thessaloniki, Greece

Contemporary organizations rely on ERP systems to implement their business processes. Moreover, there is a high demand from companies for ERP systems because it is an effective management system that optimizes productivity. It is important for next generation managers to understand what ERP systems are as well as the impacts for an organisation to implement an ERP system. This reliance on ERP indicates the importance of studying security issues and requirements in an ERP Environment. Information Security is both a theoretical and practical discipline and can vary from a technical aspect to the management aspect. Educational institutions must educate students to concepts, strategies, and tools that promote security of ERP systems so that after studying the certain course students understand technical, technological, management, and human security problems, identify and respond to information security challenges in ERP systems, evaluate and implement security solutions and tools to protect ERP systems against risks, and finally design information security policies, and evaluate and apply organizational security objectives. This chapter examines how universities and educational institutions are responding to current educational needs by integrating an enterprise resource planning (ERP) security course to current curriculum programs and propose a course framework.

Chapter 14

Colla J. MacDonald, University of Ottawa, Canada
Martha McKeen, University of Ottawa, Canada
Donna Leith-Gudbranson, University of Ottawa, Canada
Madeleine Montpetit, University of Ottawa, Canada
Douglas Archibald, University of Ottawa, Canada
Christine Rivet, University of Ottawa, Canada
Rebecca J. Hogue, University of Ottawa, Canada
Mike Hirsh, University of Ottawa, Canada

In response to the challenges faced by rapid expansion and curriculum reform, the Department of Family Medicine (DFM) at the University of Ottawa (U of O) developed a Faculty Development Conceptual Framework (FDCF) and companion plan as a first step toward meeting the challenges of providing quality opportunities for the continuing professional development of preceptors in Family Medicine. The FDCF outlines the processes, opportunities and support structures needed to improve preceptors' teaching skills and effectively deliver a newly revised "Triple C" competency-based curriculum. The FDCF acts as a quality standard to guide the design, delivery, and evaluation of a vibrant Faculty Development (FD) Program. It further provides a structure for implementing Enterprise Resource Planning (ERP) web applications to facilitate the flow of information between seven teaching sites, provide consistency among programs, and play a tactical role in the sharing of academic resources.

Preface

Enterprise Resource Planning (ERP) is seamlessly integrated computer-based application used to manage internal and external resources, including tangible assets, financial resources, materials, and human resources covering all the functions and processes of an enterprise/institution. Education institutions and universities all over the world are facing challenges in designing robust Enterprise Resource Planning applications and methodologies to align themselves with the expectations of students and other stakeholders. The existing standard Enterprise Resource Planning solutions are proprietary, inflexible, and expensive to implement in academia. Thus, there is a growing demand for action-oriented research to provide insights into the challenges, issues, and solutions related to the design, development, implementation, and management of education institutions' resources through Enterprise Resource Planning applications. Education sector, being a huge service sector and having a high social and economic impact value with its unique set of challenges, has a high potential for using ERP application. Hence, the editors gathered the recently completed and ongoing research in this field and shared them with other researchers. Each researcher has brought some fresh insights and experiences to ERP applications for the education sector. All the chapters were peer-reviewed before they were accepted. This book suggests Enterprise Resource Planning frameworks for the academic sector along with their applications and methodologies to improve effectiveness and efficiency of processes including teaching-learning processes, and to enhance student-centric and stakeholders related services. This book helps the reader in gaining a good insight into various aspects of (a) process automation, (b) reduction of process cycle time, and (c) prompt and better service to all stake-holders.

THE BOOK'S ORGANIZATION

This book consists of five sections. Section 1, "Learning Management and Administration," opens with José Luis Sánchez de la Rosa, Silvia Alayón Miranda, and Carina Soledad González's chapter Evaluation of Transversal Competences of the Engineering Students and their Relation to the Enterprise's Requirements. This chapter describes the importance of and methodology for the evaluation of the transversal competences of engineering students during their final year project assessment. Transversal competences are of great importance to enterprises which like to recruit students after their graduation. Chapter 2, Academics' ICT Capabilities in a New Educational Paradigm in Developing Countries: A Capability Approach by Agnes Chigona and Rabelani Dagada, focuses on analysing the factors that impact on the academics' effective use of ICTs for teaching and learning in the new education paradigm. P. Srinivas Subba Rao and P. Suseela Rani describe characteristics and essential requirements along with current practices, web resources, and tools and technology for Virtual and Interactive Learning (VIL) in their chapter Virtual and Interactive Learning (VIL) in Transformation and Imparting Education in the Digital Era (Chapter 3). Chapter 4, Principles of Concurrent E-Learning Design by Knut Arne Strand, Arvid Staupe, and Tor Atle Hjeltnes, presents the sixteen principles of concurrent e-learning design that are grouped into five categories, in detail.

Section 2, "Knowledge Management," focuses on knowledge and content management for institutions and universities. Chapter 5, Knowledge Management Model for Electronic Textbook Design by Elena Railean, describes a new knowledge management (KM) model for electronic textbook design which comprises a dynamic and flexible instructional strategy in order to construct the personalized content through development of core structure of competence. Gayatri Doctor throws light on the concepts of Enterprise Resource Planning and Enterprise Content Management and then explores academic institutions in India who have already initiated the use of Institutional Knowledge Repositories as an enterprise content management system for knowledge sharing & management with regard to content, access and other factors in her chapter Institutional Knowledge Repositories: Enterprise Content Management in Academics (Chapter 6). Chapter 7, Learn to Learn to Integrate ERP-Systems and Content Knowledge Using Problem Based Learning and Cases: A Swedish Business School's Experiences by Annika Andersson, describes experiences and lessons learned from integrating ERP-systems into economic topics course using problem-based learning (PBL) and cases created for the integration of technology and content knowledge in a business school setting. Chapter 8, Towards an Ontology-Based Educational Information System by Erika Nyitrai, Balázs Varga, and Adam Tarcsi, presents an ontology which is able to picture the connections between the actors of a higher education system.

Section 3, "ERP Adoption and Implementation," showcases two chapters that examine ERP investment and its role as a commodity or a strategic investment for institutions. Chapter 9, ERP Adoption: Is it Worth the Investment? by Jorge A. Romero, discusses previous research on ERP and how much we know about the effects of ERP investments. Y. Callero, M. Aguilar, and V. Munoz present example of a possible use of BPS in academia with SIGHOS along with simulation tests and results in their chapter Business Process Simulation in Academia (Chapter 10).

Section 4, "Customer Relationship Management," examines the scope and role of CRM for academic institutions and universities. Chapter 11, CRM for Academic Institutions and Universities by Viral Nagori, describes the fundamentals of CRM, its uses and application in academic environment, and technology supporting CRM. Chapter 12, ERP Modules for Industry-Institute Interaction, Training and Placement, and Alumni Management by P. A. Khatwani and K. S. Desai, describes the different modules related to industry-institute interaction management, training & placement, and alumni database & management.

Section 5, "Course and Curriculum Development" focuses on course and curriculum development not only for students but also for faculty development. Chapter 13, Design, Development and Implementation of an ERP Security Course by Theodosios Tsiakis and Theodoros Kargidis, explains how universities and educational institutions are responding to current educational needs by integrating ERP security course to current curriculum programs. The last chapter (Chapter 14), University of Ottawa Department of Family Medicine Faculty Development Curriculum Framework by Colla J. MacDonald, Martha McKeen, Donna Leith-Gudbranson, Madeleine Montpetit, Douglas Archibald, Christine Rivet, Rebecca Hogue, and Mike Hirsh, presents a Faculty Development Conceptual Framework (FDCF). This framework outlines the processes, opportunities and support structures needed to improve preceptors' teaching skills and effectively deliver a newly revised 'Triple C' competency-based curriculum.

We hope that these chapters open up a sense of possibilities of use of ERP and point the way to new directions for the design and development of ERP applications for the academic sector. We anticipate this book will benefit management and engineering students; professionals and researchers working in the field of education including policy makers, ICT vendors, consultants, and implementing agencies, and top-management of institutes and universities.

Kanubhai K. Patel
Ahmedabad University, India

Sanjaykumar Vij
Sardar Vallabhbhai Patel Institute of Technology, India

Section 1
Learning Management and Administration

Chapter 1
Evaluation of Transversal Competences of the Engineering Students and their Relation to the Enterprise Requirements

José Luis Sánchez de la Rosa
University of La Laguna, Spain

Silvia Alayón Miranda
University of La Laguna, Spain

Carina Soledad González
University of La Laguna, Spain

ABSTRACT

The importance of the evaluation of the transversal competences in engineering studies is explained in this chapter. Transversal competences are of great importance to enterprises that like to recruit students after their graduation. They look for trained professionals, thoroughly prepared not only to solve practical problems but also to be successfully integrated in a team work. Transversal competences are not directly related to the theoretical content of the curricula, and the assessment of the level of transversal competences developed through the university studies is not an easy task. A methodology for evaluating transversal skills during the Final Year Project (FYP) assessment is proposed. And a new modality of FYP to improve the acquisition of transversal skills is presented.

DOI: 10.4018/978-1-4666-2193-0.ch001

INTRODUCTION

A complete Engineering study program must allow students to acquire essential knowledge to become capable and competent in the professional fields associated to the qualification. In the framework of the European Higher Education Area (EHEA), universities are responsible for creating good professionals. Therefore they are aware of the importance of the study program design and its relation to the professional profiles and the competences or skills needed.

The evaluation of the knowledge acquisition process when this study program is developed in practice is of paramount importance. This evaluation is usually carried out through theoretical and/or practical exams. These tests quantify the achievement in the acquisition of the established knowledge and the specific competences for each subject. However they scarcely take the transversal competences skills into account.

Transversal competences are not directly related to the theoretical content of the curricula. They are related to attitudes and values (know how to be) and to procedures (know-how). They can be transferred outside of the specific professional field. For example: capacity to structure information, team work, decision-making, capacity to analyse and synthesise, command of a foreign language, among others. These competences are skills or attitudes that could be instilled into students. Although some competences are innate, others can be developed through different subjects of the curricula.

Transversal competences are of great importance to enterprises which like to recruit students after their graduation. They look for trained professionals, thoroughly prepared not only to solve practical problems but also to be successfully integrated in a team work. It is not enough to have good grades, an impressive intelligence quotient or a smart appearance. Nowadays, enterprises give precedence to other features like interpersonal skills. The assessment of the trans-versal competences allows evaluating the extent to which the curricula has been successful in the global education of students.

The transversal skills of the engineering graduates are inadequate. Universities need to identify these skills and then incorporate processes to fine tune/impart those skills in the students. This would require additional resources and the universities would need to plan for such resources. In this chapter a model to identify and measure these skills to help in revising the programs at Universities is proposed. This is the relation between ERP in education sector and the transversal skills.

Although the evaluation of transversal competences could be carried out in other periods of the student's life, we propose to do it at the final year. Since all engineering students must complete a final year project (FYP), this is the ideal subject for assessing these skills. Through their FYP students must demonstrate that they are able to put into practice the theoretical knowledge acquired during their studies. This assessment can be considered a simple task. However the problem is the objective determination of the level of the transversal competences developed through their university studies. Therefore a procedure to evaluate a subset of skills of high interest for entrepreneurs using the FYP will be presented in this chapter.

BACKGROUND: THE EUROPEAN HIGHER EDUCATION AREA AND THE TRANSVERSAL COMPETENCES

Generic skills are usually forgotten and neglected in the education system. Fortunately, the Bologna process (official Bologna Process website, 2007) has rescued them by giving a more important role.

The EHEA (European Higher Education Area) has been developed through various arrangements of the European countries education ministers, among which we mention the 1999 Bologna Declaration (official Bologna Process website, 2007), the 2001 Prague Declaration (European ministers, 2001), the 2003 Berlin Communiqué (European ministers, 2003), the 2005 Bergen Communiqué (European ministers, 2005), the 2007 London Communiqué (European ministers, 2007) and the 2009 Leuven Communiqué (European ministers, 2009). The rules generated at European level were adopted by each country, developing its own standards. In the case of Spain, some of the relevant regulations are the RD1125/2003 (2003), Royal Decree 1509/2005 (2005), the 2514 order / 2007 (2007) and the RD1393/2007 (2007).

It was stated in Bergen Communiqué that the frame for European Higher Education must include generic descriptors for each cycle based in learning outcomes and competences. The Project Report (Haug et al., 1999) reflects that the general movement is to give more importance to employment prospects and to the acquisition of transversal core skills. That makes necessary to redefine the curricula to take into account professional partners and to reach a minimum level for each principal component.

It is a requirement that the degrees must be considered not only as a training for a particular and well defined profession, but also to include several skills needed for nearly any future professional activity. Moreover grades must describe the realized job, the level of competence and the profile (European ministers, 2003).

A group of experts, in the context of the "Joint Quality Initiative (JQI)" developed the well known "Dublin Descriptors" (Joint Quality Initiative Group, 2004). Those were proposed as a base of the different national accreditation frames and state generic expectation regarding achievement and skills. They were approved in the 2005 Bergen Communiqué (European ministers, 2005) and in 2009 Leuven Communiqué (European ministers, 2009). It was highlighted that regarding employability, labour market demands higher level of transversal competences and skills:

With labour markets increasingly relying on higher skill levels and transversal competences, higher education should equip students with the advanced knowledge, skills and competences they need throughout their professional lives. Employability empowers the individual to fully seize the opportunities in changing labour markets. We aim at raising initial qualifications as well as maintaining and renewing a skilled workforce through close cooperation between governments, higher education institutions, social partners and students. This will allow institutions to be more responsive to employers' needs and employers to better understand the educational perspective. Higher education institutions, together with governments, government agencies and employers, shall improve the provision, accessibility and quality of their careers and employment related guidance services to students and alumni. We encourage work placements embedded in study programmes as well as on-the-job learning. (European ministers, 2009).

Therefore Higher Education must provide advanced knowledge, skills and competences that students need for their professional life. But how has this been carried out by each European country? We will analyse the case of Spain.

In Spain, the 2003 MEC framework document (Spanish Ministry of Education, Culture and Sport, 2003) states that official degrees must have, in general, a professional orientation. That is, they must provide a university level education in which basic general competences, transversal competences related with well-rounded development and specific professional competences will be integrated. It is also stated that generic, transversal and specific competences must be specifically mentioned in any title to be designed. Royal Decree 1393/2005 (2005) mentions the following generic competence descriptors:

1. Systematic understanding of a field of study and mastery of the skills and methods of research associated with that field
2. Ability to conceive, design, implement and adopt a substantial process of research with scholarly integrity
3. Ability to make a contribution through original research
4. Critical analysis, evaluation and synthesis of new and complex ideas
5. Ability to communicate with their peers, the larger scholarly community and with society in general about their areas of expertise
6. Ability to promote, within academic and professional contexts, technological, social or cultural advancement in a knowledge-based society

As it can be observed there is a legislative framework governing degrees and the competences that must be acquired by students in each one. Some research has been done in Spain about which competences are the most relevant and how to assess them (Mérida et al., 2011) (Márquez et al., 2009) (Montes-Berges et al., 2011) (Sicilia, 2009). However, most efforts are still concentrated in the identification and assessment of professional skills or specific content. There is no clear idea of how to implement the teaching of these transversal skills, so much less about assessing them.

The research study presented in this chapter was born in this background to find solutions for the engineering studies. Therefore the main body of the chapter will offer answers to the following questions:

1. Which transversal competences are more important and more appreciated by engineering enterprises?
2. When is the best moment to evaluate them?
3. How can the assessment of these transversal skills be developed?

This work has determined a subset of skills of high interest for entrepreneurs and the descriptors for each one. A procedure to ensure the evaluation of these skills is presented, and the best moment to carry out the evaluation is also proposed: in the final year project (FYP) of the engineering students.

EVALUATION OF TRANSVERSAL COMPETENCES IN ENGINEERING STUDENTS

Transversal Competences Required by Engineering Enterprises

The determination of the transversal competences preferred by enterprises is a key issue in our research study. Our main objective is to improve the quality of the teaching process in order to facilitate the acquisition of the transversal skills to our students, and therefore increase their job opportunities.

There are some interesting previous works related to this problem. For example, the Organisation for Economic Cooperation and Development (OECD) has a Programme for International Student Assessment (PISA project, 1997). The main objective of the PISA project is to analyse if students from different countries are well prepared for future challenges, if they can reason and communicate effectively or if they have the capacity to continue learning throughout life, among others. This project found some important transversal competences:

1. **Use tools interactively:** Use language, symbols, texts, knowledge, information and technology interactively.
2. **Interact in heterogeneous groups:** Relate well to others, cooperate, work in teams, manage and resolve conflicts.

3. **Act autonomously:** Form and conduct life plans and personal projects, defend and assert rights, interests, limits and needs.

Annus (2004) presented an identification of transversal competences and qualifications. One of the final conclusions of this study is that people with a low level of skills can become skilled by opening learning opportunities, flexibility and adaptability and through good interpersonal skills, all developed by a combination of formal and non-formal work-based and situational learning. This fact has been the main motivation of our research.

With all this information in mind we have designed and carried out a survey among our local engineering companies, in order to establish the transversal competences of high interest for them. The survey was done through 3 clusters which represent 60 local companies. As a result, the most important transversal competences for the Canarian business (our geographical region) are:

1. Written and oral communication skills in foreign language (English)
2. Capacity for drafting documentation and reports in native language (Spanish)
3. Effective oral communication in native language (Spanish)
4. Interpersonal skills
5. Basic entrepreneurial culture.

On the other hand, information from OPSIL has been taken into account. OPSIL (Observatorio Permanente para el Seguimiento de la Inserción Laboral, 2010 – Permanent Observatory for Tracking the Labour Insertion, in English) is the name of a project developed by the Canary Employment Service (Canary Government) that has carried out an exhaustive study about the employment of the students of the University of La Laguna. Some recommendations about the competences of interest for Canarian engineering business

were extracted from these studies (García and Díaz, 2008).

Mastering in foreign languages has become an institutional primary objective (The Commission of the European Community 2003). The relative importance associated with mastering in foreign languages by university graduates is growing. Additionally, this competence is the one that shows the highest perceived deficit in university graduates. Most of the engineering companies in Canary Islands are small-medium enterprises that do not demand high levels of foreign language to their employees. However, English language knowledge has a great impact on engineering companies due to:

1. Manuals and documentation are usually written in English, and
2. Companies are increasing their links to other enterprises at European and African level using English as a common language.

A very similar situation happens regarding basic entrepreneurial culture. It is often not taken seriously enough. Although this knowledge is usually acquired by our graduated students after starting to work in the companies and it can vary depending on the business organization, there is a lack of a minimum level of knowledge about that topic before entering in the labour market.

The next competence with higher perceived deficit is oral communication. Although the need for oral communication differs significantly between academic and working environments, a fluent oral communication in the academic environment could help both the entrance in the labour market and in the career progression.

Interpersonal skills are often neglected by students in general, but highly appreciated by employers. The employee must communicate at three different levels. Firstly, he/she must maintain a close contact with his/her colleagues as a member of a team. Secondly, he/she must convince to his/her supervisors about the suitability of his proposals. Thirdly, he/she must be friendly enough to attract customer's interest.

Finally, the capacity for drafting documentation and reports in native language (Spanish) is not perceived as a deficit of the students at University level, because these students are used to write reports for their practical work. However, producing reports, drafting research proposals and responding to tenders require a mastering in written language.

Taking into account suggestions from employers, the head of the faculty and the management team can determine the subjects more appropriate to fit the competences demanded and get in touch with the responsible teachers to ensure the correct training and evaluation of such competences.

Final Year Project Assessment in Engineering

The evaluation of transversal competences in Engineering could be carried out in other periods, but we propose to do it at the final year, through the evaluation of the Final Year Project (FYP), a very important milestone in the student's life. This FYP represents the culmination of the student learning process; where he/she must put into use their previously learned engineering and personal skills. The FYP is a complex work, and its assessment has a major influence on decisions regarding the student's readiness to graduate (Valderrama et al., 2009).

Some research has been done about the process of assessment for the Final Year Project. In that sense, Valderrama et al (2009) propose a 6 stages procedure. Those stages together with some recommendations are:

1. **Learning outcomes definition for the FYP and assignment of a set of objective descriptors to each one:** From the set of 28 competences suggested in the Tuning Proyect (Beneitone and Meer, 2000), they did a poll and obtained 135 replies of Universities, 107 from Spain and 28 from the rest of Europe. The top five scored abilities were:
    a. To put into practice the acquired knowledge,
    b. Written and oral communication skills in their native language,
    c. Inception, design and implementation of projects using engineering tools,
    d. Organization and planning,
    e. Knowledge about their study field.

2. **Definition of assessment milestones:** Who and what will assess each descriptor. Valderrama et al. (2009) recommends to make a soon assessment in the first weeks of the Project to check that the student has analyzed the state of the art and has a clear approximation to it. Moreover, it is necessary to make several assessments through the project development and a final assessment at the end.

3. **Descriptors assignment to each assessment action:** The descriptors assigned in that case were:
    a. **Descriptor 1:** Student presents a diagram of the Project planning.
    b. **Descriptor 2:** Student is able to monitor the level of compliance regarding the initial plan and take into account deviations from it.
    c. **Descriptor 3:** The student analyzes the level of compliance regarding the initial plan, the causes of deviations from the original plan and their consequences.

4. **Definition of level of compliance for each descriptor establishing a clear and objective level of compliance to be satisfied by the student:** The levels of compliance are:
    a. 0- Student do not comply,
    b. 1- Superficial compliance,
    c. 2- Proper compliance,
    d. 3- Excellent compliance

5. **Assessment report:** The assessment report must include descriptors, the level of compliance and the level of demand for each descriptor. They also propose an overall assessment report organized by skills.
6. **Qualification:** The faculty or college must define the criteria to be followed in order to provide the students with qualifications.

On the other hand, Cruz et al. (2008) propose a take-home exam, within a subject, to assess competences which are very difficult to evaluate in a normal exam. Students solve this exam in a long period of time (e.g. one week) so they are not bounded by time or lack of information resources. The competences under evaluation are:

1. Entrepreneurial spirit,
2. Sustainability and Social Commitment,
3. Effective written and oral communication skills,
4. Team working,
5. Efficient use of information resources,
6. Autonomous learning,
7. Work attitude,
8. Way of thinking.

Regarding how to assess the final year project, Kim (2010) proposes a qualification based in a weighted sum of each one of the evaluated items.

$$M = \sum_{i=1}^{N} F_i * X_i \qquad (1)$$

Where Fi=weight and Xi=Qualification of descriptor i.

On the other hand, Teo and Ho (1998) introduce five assessment components:

1. Interim assessment with a weight of 15%, named S1,
2. Report and final assessment with a weight of 50%, named S2,
3. Oral presentation with a weight of 5%, named S3,
4. Report and demonstration with a weight of 25%, named M1 and
5. Oral presentation with a weight of 5%, named M2.

Each one of the 5 components is divided in topics. For example, Final report is divided in

1. Introduction,
2. Structure,
3. Theory, design and implementation
4. Results,
5. Conclusions and
6. Presentation.

These previous works will serve us as a frame of reference to elaborate our own assessment procedure for the final year project. In addition we will consider what local enterprises demand from the engineering students to adapt our procedure to assess such competences.

Competences Assessment through the Final Year Project

A mixed model that combines the previously discussed models is proposed to assess the transversal competences required by enterprises. This assessment is carried out during the evaluation of the Final Year Project. Taking into account that the weight traditionally assigned to practical works is around 30% of the total qualification, we decided to assign a 28% to the transversal competences in the FYP.

The first four most valued transversal skills for the Canary engineering companies mentioned before are considered for assessment:

1. Written and oral communication skills in foreign language (English)
2. Capacity for drafting documentation and reports in native language (Spanish)

3. Effective oral communication in native language (Spanish)
4. Interpersonal skills.

In addition it is necessary to add some technical competences:

1. Theoretical knowledge.
2. Practical knowledge.
3. Information search and management.
4. The use of advanced software for document processing.
5. The use of advanced software presentation tools.

The final score of the FYP is an exclusive competency of the evaluation panel that judges the project. Some evidences must be collected by the project supervisor during the whole project to be evaluated by the evaluation panel. Regarding the competences which are evaluated at the final examination, some of them are related to the written project and the oral presentation.

Four levels of compliance are considered: Fail, Pass, Good and Excellent. Requirements to be satisfied in each level must be clearly specified. These basic objectives are qualified and the overall score will be obtained as a weighted sum of these factors.

Additionally, we consider three different kinds of reports (see Tables 1 to 3). The first set of reports (Table 1) is done by the supervisor to provide evidence, throughout the life of the project, about long term skills to the evaluation panel. It includes mastering in foreign languages (S1), interpersonal skills (S2) and competence in the use of information resources (S3). Regarding foreign languages, it will be evaluated only the writing and reading capacity, because in Spain the project must be defended in Spanish, by law. Interpersonal skills will be evaluated on the basis of the relation with the supervisor and with a peer (if a team approach is used).

Table 1. Supervisor reports (S1, S2, and S3) providing evidence throughout the life of the project

Report	Competence	Descriptor
S1	1) Written communication skills in foreign language.	- Capacity to look for information in foreign language (English) sources. - Capacity to extract information from those sources. - Capacity to write reports in foreign language (English) about those sources - Capacity to explain some parts in foreign language (English)
S2	4) Interpersonal Skills	- Social Skills - Emotional intelligence - Empathy
S3	7) Information search and management	- Capacity to look for information by itself - Capacity to determine the importance of each piece of information. - Classification and organization of information - Relevant information extraction from the search results

The second set of reports (Table 2) must be filled by the evaluation panel taking into account the written report presented by the student. They have to inform about the capacity for drafting reports and documentation in native language (Spanish) (M1), the use of advanced software for written documents (Latex, graphics, etc…) (M2), Theoretical knowledge (M3) and practical knowledge (M4). Altogether, those four reports account for 70% of the overall score.

Finally, the third set of reports must also be filled by the evaluation panel based on the oral presentation basis. It has to be informed about the use of advanced software for presentations (Beamer + latex, multimedia, etc…) and the effective oral communication in native language (Spanish). Each assessment report must include the objectives, descriptors and competences evaluated together with the evidences in which

they are based. The overall score is a weighted sum of each one of the competences.

Each descriptor is assessed according to its level of compliance: Not compliance, Pass, Good and Excellent. Qualification for each competence is obtained as an average of its descriptors. The overall score is obtained as:

$$FYP\_mark = A*(S1 + S2 + S3 + M1 + M2 + P1 + P2) + B*M3 + C*M4 \quad (2)$$

Where A = 0.28, B = 0.22 y C = 0.50 (theoretical knowledge mark represents 22% of the overall score and practical knowledge mark is 50%, remaining a 28% for transversal competences). These weights have been discussed and agreed by several teachers that are used to be part of the FYP evaluation panels in our Engineering

Table 2. Evaluation panel reports (M1, M2, M3, and M4) based on the written report presented by the student

Report	Competence	Descriptor
M1	2) Capacity for drafting written reports and documentation in native language	- Absence of spelling errors. - Document organization - Clear and impersonal explanations. - Document format.
M2	8) The use of advanced software for document processing	- Document processor for editing (Latex or other publishing software) - Graphics resources (Graphics, figures, tables, schemes,) - Level of compliance with an author style guide.
M3	5) Theoretical knowledge	- Well structured theoretical knowledge. - Clear explanations about theoretical concepts. - Large bibliography
M4	6) Practical knowledge	- The object of the FYP works properly. - Proposed solution belongs to current technology. - Well documented technical solution. - Well structured technical solution.

Table 3. Evaluation panel reports (P1and P2) based on the oral presentation

Report	Competence	Descriptor
P1	9) The use of advanced software presentation tools	- Document processor for presentation (Latex+Beamer, etc…) - Advanced software as HTML 5, concept maps, flash, etc. - Organization of presentation - Multimedia resources in the presentation
P2	3) Effective oral communication in native language.	- Not weaver. - No use of fillers. - Clear explanation. - Capacity to defend his arguments.

schools. According to their experience practical knowledge is very important in the Engineering field; therefore it is highly valued in the final mark. But these weights could be changed in order to adapt other kind of FYP assessments (FYP of disciplines not related to the Engineering field).

The evaluation panel must provide the overall score and the evidences and acquired level for each one.

FUTURE RESEARCH DIRECTIONS

The Final Year Project in the Enterprise: A New Model for the Future

In previous sections we have analysed which transversal skills are more attractive for engineering enterprises, proposed to assess the student's skills during the Final Year Project evaluation, studied different existing methodologies for developing this assessment, and finally, we have proposed a new FYP evaluation procedure where transversal competences are taken into account.

The following questions are relevant when thinking about the future: How can students improve the acquisition of the transversal competences required by enterprises? Until now the FYP has been considered a tool for evaluating the student's transversal competences, but could it be used as an acquisition tool of such competences? Can enterprises collaborate with university in the teaching process of these special competences?

In order to achieve these objectives we have started in 2005 a pilot scheme that involves the creation of a new FYP modality: the "FYP in the enterprise". The methodology is based on sending our engineering students to develop their FYP to local enterprises. It is not a closed research line; we are still studying how to improve the methodology.

We have started from this premise: if the student could carry out his/her FYP under supervision of the enterprise's technical staff, he/she would be able to acquire the more important transversal skills for that enterprise. Without a well-established teaching methodology, enterprise's staff can teach these skills because they need them in practice.

Following this premise we have sent several students to develop their FYPs to local engineering enterprises. The experience has been so positive for students and for enterprises that the number of students that choose this FYP modality and the number of enterprises that require our students for developing their FYPs have increased in the last years (see Figure 1).

With this scheme students finish their studies with an additional acquisition of technical knowledge and important transversal skills, and enterprises have an opportunity to "know" the worker before hiring him/her. We must add in this point that enterprises accept students without hiring them (students go to enterprises covered by the scholar insurance and without salary) but there are some contracts of employment at the end of the FYP.

At this moment the methodology is not finished and some points must be well researched and established:

1. Improve the legal aspects of the collaboration university-enterprise for development of FYPs.
2. Adapt the FYP assessment procedure: if enterprises take part in the teaching process of the students they should take part in the evaluation of the FYP.
3. Analyse why some students are hired by enterprises when they finish their FYPs there, and why others students are not hired in the same conditions.
4. Search of strategies for recruit enterprises.

CONCLUSION

This chapter has been written with the idea of helping other engineering schools to face the problem of the acquisition and assessment of transversal competences in the engineering studies, but the contents of the chapter and the methodology explained could be extrapolated to other university studies.

The engineering schools have a fundamental role in the improvement of the engineer's capacities. The Engineering schools of the University of La Laguna (Spain) are aware of their responsibility for the training of the students and for their integration in the engineering sector of its geographical region (Canary Islands). Consequently we consider that theoretical and practical contents of the engineering study program are important. But

Figure 1. Number of students that have carried out the FYP in enterprises in 2005-2011 years

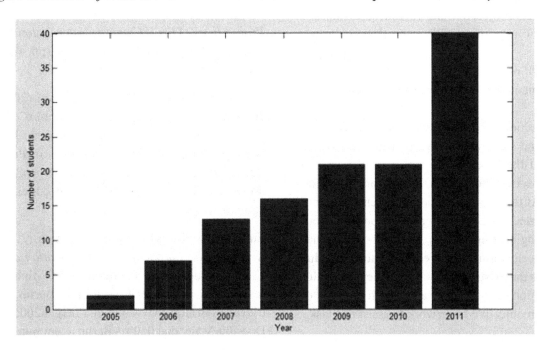

after our collaborative experience with enterprises we consider that the acquisition of transversal competences is of paramount importance.

A communication framework among engineering companies, engineering schools at University of La Laguna and students in their last year of studies has been established in this work. The main objective is to improve the acquisition and assessment process of the most important transversal competences for enterprises. This will improve the students' formation and therefore their job opportunities.

To achieve this goal we have presented the following actions:

1. A methodology for finding out which transversal competences are considered positive by enterprises.
2. A model for assessing transversal competences through the Final Year Project: learning outcomes, descriptors and milestones for assessment have been defined. Moreover, descriptors assignment to competences, their level of compliance, reports for assessment and evaluation criteria has also been clarified.
3. A new modality for developing the Final Year Project that allows students to improve the acquisition of transversal competences.

With regard to how these actions have been implemented in our engineering schools:

1. Action 1 has been already finished. Teachers and students are aware of the importance of these key transversal competences and advised about how to teach or acquire them.
2. At this moment action 2 is being incorporated into the FYP evaluation process in our engineering schools. The methodology has been warmly received by the teachers, due to the existing difficulties in the FYP evaluation process. They agree with the need of an objective framework to assist this task.

3. The FYP modality called "FYP in enterprise" is more popular every year between students, teachers and enterprises. We are really proud of this methodology and the obtained results. But this contribution constitutes our future research work because, as commented in previous section, there are several aspects to improve.

REFERENCES

Annus, T. (2004). *Identification of transversal competences and qualifications*. Office for Official Publications of the European Communities. Cedefop Reference series, 52. Retrieved from http://www.cedefop.europa.eu/EN/Files/3037_EN27.pdf

Beneitone, P., & Meer, I. V. D. (2000). *Tuning educational structures in Europe*. University of Deusto, University of Groningen. Retrieved from http://tuning.unideusto.org/tuningeu

Cruz, J. L., López, D., Sánchez, F., & Fernández, A. (2008). Evaluación de competencias transversales mediante un examen no presencial (A take-home exam to assess transversal competences). *Proceedings of the V Congreso Internacional de Docencia Universitaria e Innovación* (pp. 1-25). Lleida, Spain.

European Ministers for Higher Education. (2001). *Towards the European higher education area*. Communiqué of the meeting of European Ministers in charge of Higher Education in Praga. Retrieved from http://www.bologna-bergen2005.no/Docs/00Main_doc/010519prague_communique.pdf

European Ministers for Higher Education. (2003). *Realising the European higher education area*. Communiqué of the Conference of Ministers responsible for Higher Education in Berlin. Retrieved from http://www.bologna-bergen2005.no/Docs/00-Main_doc/030919Berlin_Communique.PDF

European Ministers for Higher Education. (2005). *The European higher education area -Achieving the goals.* Communiqué of the Conference of European Ministers Responsible for Higher Education in Bergen. Retrieved from http://www.bologna-bergen2005.no/Docs/00-Main_doc/050520_Bergen_Communique.pdf

European Ministers for Higher Education. (2007). *Towards the European higher education area: Responding to challenges in a globalised world.* London Communiqué. Retrieved from http://webarchive.nationalarchives.gov.uk/20100202100434/dcsf.gov.uk/londonbologna/uploads/documents/londoncommuniquefinalwithlondonlogo.pdf

European Ministers for Higher Education. (2009). *The Bologna Process 2020. The European higher education area in the new decade.* Communiqué of the Conference of European Ministers Responsible for Higher Education, Leuven and Louvain-la-Neuve. Retrieved from http://www.ond.vlaanderen.be/hogeronderwijs/bologna/conference/documents/Leuven_Louvain-la-Neuve_Communiqu%C3%A9_April_2009.pdf

García, L. A., & Díaz, C. (2008). *Las competencias para el empleo en los titulados universitarios. Observatorio permanente para el seguimiento de la inserción laboral.* Ed. Sedicana.

Haug, G., Kirstein, J., & Knudsen, I. (1999). *Trends in learning structures in higher education.* Copenhague, Denmark: Danish Rectors' Conference Secretariat.

Joint Quality Initiative Group. (2004). *Shared Dublin descriptors for short cycle, first cycle, second cycle and third cycle awards.* Retrieved from http://www.jointquality.org/content/descriptors/CompletesetDublinDescriptors.doc

Kim, H. S. (2010). An assessment model and practical rubric design for thesis assessment. *Proceedings of the International Conference on Engineering Education*, Gliwice, Poland.

Márquez, R. D., Moreno, R. A., González, C., Espejo, R., & Herruzo, E. (2009). An experience to define the enterprising attitude as a transversal competence in the European higher education area. In Mendez-Vilas, A. (Eds.), *Research, reflections and innovations in integrating ICT in education* (*Vol. 1*, pp. 3–677). Badajoz, Spain: Ed. Formatex.

Mérida, R., Angulo, J., Jurado, M., & Diaz, J. (2011). Student training in transversal competences at the University of Cordoba. *European Educational Research Journal*, *10*(1), 34–52. doi:10.2304/eerj.2011.10.1.34

Montes-Berges, B., Castillo-Mayén, M. R., Rodríguez-Espartal, N., López-Zafra, E., & Augusto, J. M. (2011). Transversal competence for nursing and physiotherapy students. *Proceedings of the 5th International Technology, Education and Development Conference* (pp. 3345-3351). Valencia, Spain.

OPSIL Project. (2010). *Observatorio Permanente para el Seguimiento de la Inserción Laboral.* Retrieved from http://www.feu.ull.es/es/proyecto/opsil/28/

Order 2514/2007. (2007). Retrieved from http://www.boe.es/boe/dias/2007/08/21/pdfs/A35424-35431.pdf

PISA project. (1997). *OECD Programme for International Student Assessment (PISA project).* Retrieved from http://www.pisa.oecd.org/pages/0,3417,en_32252351_32235731_1_1_1_1_1,00.html

Royal Decree 1125/2003. (2003). Retrieved from http://www.boe.es/boe/dias/2003/09/18/pdfs/A34355-34356.pdf

Royal Decree 1393/2007. (2007). Available at; http://www.boe.es/boe/dias/2007/10/30/pdfs/A44037-44048.pdf

Royal Decree 1509/2005. (2005). Available at; http://www.boe.es/boe/dias/2005/12/20/pdfs/A41455-41457.pdf.

Sicilia, M. A. (2009). How should transversal competence be introduced in computing education? *ACM SIGCSE Bulletin Archive, 41*(4).

Spanish Ministry of Education. Culture and Sport. (2003). *La integracion del sistema universitario español en el espacio europeo de enseñanza superior.* Retrieved from http://www.uab.es/iDocument/IntegracioSistemaUniversitariEspanyolEnEEES,0.pdf

Teo, Y., & Ho, D. J. (1998). A systematic approach to the implementation of final year project in an electrical engineering undergraduate course. *IEEE Transactions on Education, 41*(1), 25–30. doi:10.1109/13.660783

The official Bologna Process website. (2007). Retrieved from http://www.ond.vlaanderen.be/hogeronderwijs/bologna

Valderrama, E., Rullán, M., Sánchez, F., Pons, J., Mans, C., & Giné, F. … Peig, E. (2009). Guidelines for the final year project assessment in engineering. *Proceedings of the 39th ASEE/IEEE Frontiers in Education Conference*, M2J-1. San Antonio, Texas.

ADDITIONAL READING

Ahmad, R. R., Suradi, N. R. M., Majid, N., Shahabuddin, F. A., Rambely, A. S., Din, U. K. S., & Ali, Z. M. (2011). The role of final year project in the school of mathematical sciences in human capital development. *Procedia-Social and Behavioral Sciences, 18*, 450–459. doi:10.1016/j.sbspro.2011.05.066

Anderson, D. (2008). Productivism, vocational and professional education, and the ecological question. *Vocations and Learning, 1*(2), 105–129. doi:10.1007/s12186-008-9007-0

Buchberger, F. (1994). Teacher education in Europe – Diversity versus uniformity. In Galton, M., & Moon, B. (Eds.), *Handbook of teacher training in Europe* (pp. 14–51). London. doi:10.2753/EUE1056-4934300144

Capano, G., & Piattoni, S. (2009). *Building up the European higher education area: The struggle between common problems, 'shared' goals and national trajectories.* Lisbon: ECPR Joint Sessions of Workshops.

Civcisa, G., Janauska, J., Mezinska, I., Mazais, J., Mikelsons, J., Rudnevs, J., & Salenieks, N. (2010). Engineering education--New approach and new style. *Proceedings of the 9th International Scientific Conference Engineering for Rural Development*, (pp. 7-12).

Cleary, L., Graham, C., Jeanneau, C., & O'Sullivan, I. (2009). Responding to the writing development needs of Irish higher education students: A case study. *AISHE-J: The All Ireland Journal of Teaching and Learning in Higher Education, 1*(1).

Crosier, D., Purser, L., & Smidt, H. (2007). *Trends V: Universities shaping the European higher education area.* European University Association Brussels.

Elen, J., & Verburgh, A. (2008). *Bologna in European research-intensive universities: Implications for bachelor and master programs.* Garant Uitgevers NV.

European Association for Quality Assurance in Higher Education. (2005). *Standards and guidelines for quality assurance in the European higher education area.* Brussels, Belgium: European Commission. Retrieved from http://www.ond.vlaanderen.be/hogeronderwijs/bologna/documents/Standards-and-Guidelines-for-QA.pdf

European Commission. (1995). *Teaching and learning: Towards the learning society*. Luxemburg. Retrieved from http://europa.eu/documents/comm/white_papers/pdf/com95_590_en.pdf

European Commission. (2009). *Key data on education in Europe 2009*. Retrieved from http://eacea.ec.europa.eu/education/eurydice/documents/key_data_series/105EN.pdf

Fargion, S., Gevorgianiene, V., & Lievens, P. (2010). Developing entrepreneurship in social work through international education. Reflections on a European intensive programme. *Social Work Education, 30*(8), 964–980. doi:10.1080/02615479.2010.532206

Fraile Muñoz, R., Argüelles Alvarez, I., González de Sande, J. C., Gutiérrez Arriola, J. M., Benavente Peces, C., Arriero Encinas, L., & Osés del Campo, J. D. (2010). A proposal for the evaluation of final year projects in a competence-based learning framework. *Proceedings of the Education Engineering Conference (EDUCON),* Madrid, España

Garcia-Aracil, A., & Van der Velden, R. (2008). Competencies for young European higher education graduates: Labor market mismatches and their payoffs. *Higher Education, 55*(2), 219–239. doi:10.1007/s10734-006-9050-4

Garcia-Garcia, M. J., Gonzalez, C., & Argüelles, R. (2009). Methodological changes in technical teaching in order to the European higher education area comparison between countries: Italy and Spain. *Procedia-Social and Behavioural Sciences, 1*(1), 2701–2706. doi:10.1016/j.sbspro.2009.01.478

Gibb, A., Haskins, G., Education, D. E., & Robertson, I. (2009). *Leading the entrepreneurial university*. Birmingham: NCGE Policy Paper.

Holmberg, J., Svanstrom, M., Peet, D. J., Mulder, K., Ferrer-Balas, D., & Segalas, J. (2008). Embedding sustainability in higher education through interaction with lecturers: Case studies from three European technical universities. *European Journal of Engineering Education, 33*(3), 271–282. doi:10.1080/03043790802088491

Korka, M., & Spilling, O. (2008). Towards a comprehensive policy on entrepreneurship education in the european higher education. *Theoretical and Applied Economics, 11*(528), 3–16.

Littlefair, G., & Gossman, P. (2008). Final year project assessment--leaving out the subjectiveness. *Proceedings of the 2008 AaeE Conference,* Yeppoon, Queensland.

Malhotra, A. (2006). *Fundamentals of excellence in technical and other universities*.

Martinez, D., Mora, J. G., & Vila, L. E. (2007). Entrepreneurs, the self-employed and employees amongst young european higher education graduates. *European Journal of Education, 42*(1), 99–117. doi:10.1111/j.1465-3435.2007.00285.x

Miguel, V., Coello, J., Martínez, A., Manjabacas, M. C., & Calatayud, A. (2011). Learning strategies for deep-drawing processes in the European higher education area context. *Materials Science Forum, 692,* 74–82. doi:10.4028/www.scientific.net/MSF.692.74

Neuckermans, H. (2005). *European architectural education in motion* (pp. 6–10). ITU Journal of the Faculty of Architecture.

Novoa, A. (1996). The construction of the European: Changing patterns of identity through Europe. In Simola, H., & Popkewitz, T. (Eds.), *Professionalisation and education* (pp. 28–51). Helsinki.

Organisation for Economic Co-Operation and Development - OECD. (1999). *Classifying educational programmes. Manual for ISCED-97 implementation in OECD countries*. Retrieved from http://www.oecd.org/dataoecd/41/42/1841854.pdf

Rhoades, G., & Sporn, B. (2002). Quality assurance in Europe and the US: Professional and political economic framing of higher education policy. *Higher Education, 43*(3), 355–390. doi:10.1023/A:1014659908601

Ríos Carmenado, I., Díaz-Puente, J. M., & Blanco, J. L. Y. (2011). The integration of project competences within the post-graduate programme: a case study of the international masters in rural development agris mundus. *Procedia-Social and Behavioral Sciences, 15*, 96–110. doi:10.1016/j.sbspro.2011.03.058

Sánchez-Elvira, A., López-González, M., & Fernández-Sánchez, M. (2010). Análisis de las competencias genéricas en los nuevos títulos de grado del EEE en las universidades españolas. *Revista de Docencia Universitaria, 8*(1), 35.

Schwarz, S., & Westerheijden, D. F. (Eds.). (2004). *Accreditation and evaluation in the European higher education area*. Dordrecht, The Netherlands: Kluwer Academic Publishers. doi:10.1007/978-1-4020-2797-0

Siakas, K. V., Prigkou, A. A., & Draganidis, S. (2005). Key performance indicators for quality assurance in higher education--The case of the Department of Informatics at the Technological Educational Institute of Thessaloniki, Greece. *Proceedings of the 10th International Conference on Software Process Improvement-Research into Education and Training INSPIRE*, (pp. 21-23).

Szabo, A. (2008). Education for entrepreneurship from Kindergarden to adult learning. *Erenet Profile, 3*.

Teixeira, A. A. C. (2008). Entrepreneurial potential in engineering and business courses. *Innovation in Manufacturing Networks: 8th IFIP International Conference on Information Technology for Balanced Automation Systems*, (pp. 266-325).

UNESCO. (1998). *World declaration on Higher Education for the twenty-first century: Vision and action*. Retrieved from http://www.unesco.org/education/educprog/wche/declaration_eng.htm#world declaration

Wagenaar, R. (2008). *Learning outcomes a fair way to measure performance in higher education: The TUNING approach*. Organization for Economic Co-operation and Development (OECD). Retrieved from http://www.oecd.org/dataoecd/60/7/41203784.pdf

Witte, J. (2006). *Change of degrees and degrees of change. Comparing adaptations of European higher education systems in the context of the Bologna process*. Dissertation, University of Twente. Retrieved from www.che.de/downloads/c6jw144_final.pdf

KEY TERMS AND DEFINITIONS

Bologna Declaration: Declaration signed by Education Ministers from 29 European countries in 1999 for the creation of the EHEA.

Competence: Skill.

EHEA (European Higher Education Area): European cooperation program for ensuring more comparable, compatible and coherent systems of higher education in Europe.

Final Year Project (FYP): Final work that students must present at the last year of the engineering studies. Through their FYP students must demonstrate that they are able to put into practice the theoretical knowledge acquired during their studies.

Transversal Competence: Special skill that is not directly related to the theoretical content of the curricula. It is related to attitudes and values (know how to be) and to procedures (know-how) and can be transferred outside of the specific professional field. For example: capacity to structure information, team work, decision-making, capacity to analyse and synthesise, command of a foreign language, among others.

Chapter 2

Academics' ICT Capabilities in a New Educational Paradigm in Developing Countries:
A Capability Approach

Agnes Chigona
Cape Peninsula University of Technology, South Africa

Rabelani Dagada
Witwatersrand University, South Africa

ABSTRACT

Tertiary institutions in the developing countries are investing a lot in equipping their institutions with Information Communication Technologies (ICT) for teaching and learning. However, there is still a low adoption rate in the use of the new technologies among many academics in these countries. This chapter aims at analysing the factors that impact on the academics' effective use of ICTs for teaching and learning in the new education paradigm. Sen's Capability Approach was used as a conceptual lens to examine the academics' phenomena. Data was collected through in-depth interviews. The analysis of the findings has shown that individual, social, and environmental factors are preventing some academics from realising their potential capabilities from using the new technologies. It is recommended, therefore, that institutions in the developing countries should look into, and deal with accordingly, the conversion factors that are impacting on the academics' capabilities when utilising the new technologies.

INTRODUCTION

With the new millennium, came new educational paradigms due to dramatic technological revolutions. University institutions in South Africa like many other developing countries have responded to the paradigm by deploying Information Communication Technologies (ICTs) such as Learning Management Systems (LMS) e.g. Blackboard and other emerging technologies, e.g. face book, to enhance teaching and learning processes. Few institutions have gone as far as integrating Enterprise Resource Planning (ERP) Systems to an eLearning system. However, such few institutions find it difficult to integrate the ERP system to the proprietary LMS such as the Blackboard hence

DOI: 10.4018/978-1-4666-2193-0.ch002

the institutions are abandoning the proprietary LMSes; they are migrating to the Open Source LMSes such as Sakai and Moodle. Nevertheless, the adoption of the ERP systems in the South African universities is still at infancy. Anecdotal evidence shows that the institutions do not have capabilities to effectively integrate the systems into the LMSes. Elsewhere, researchers have argued that acquisition of knowledge is believed to be problematic within ERP-projects (Linderoth and Lundqvist, 2004).

While the deployment of the new technologies is recommendable, the actual benefit of the ICTs for teaching and learning in South Africa and the other developing countries is yet to be realised. Research and anecdotal evidence show that despite a commendable deployment of the new technologies, in particular LMS, into the tertiary institutions, there is a low adoption rate in the use of the technologies among many academics in South Africa (Madiba 2009, Chigona and Dagada 2011); however, the situation in other countries on the African continent is worse (Njenga 2011). It is argued that "the act of integrating ICT into teaching and learning is a complex process and one that may encounter a number of difficulties known as barriers i.e. any condition that makes it difficult to make progress or to achieve an objective" (Bingimlas 2009:237). Elliot (2010) concurs and notes that, although the new technologies in education since a decade ago have enabled higher education providers to expand and enrich teaching and learning opportunities and pedagogies, there is a concern about the professional learning of academics so that they have the confidence to exploit the new technologies to expand, extend and modify their pedagogies.

Other researchers (e.g. Madiba 2009; Mumtaz 2000) have also shown that there is a wide range of factors which influence academics' under-utilisation of new technologies in curriculum delivery. Among others, such factors include access to resources, quality of software and hardware, ease of use, incentives to change, support and collegiality available in the institution, computer self-efficacy, and perceived credibility of the platforms (BECTA 2003; Mumtaz, 2000). Recent research has shown that for many instructors who may have the capability to use the new technologies, lack of self-confidence in using the technology is noted to be a strong limiting factor of the domestication of the new technologies for curriculum delivery (Chigona & Dagada 2011; Madiba 2009; BECTA 2003). The barriers could be viewed as deprivation of the academics' capabilities. According to Zheng (2009) 'capability' in ICT research refers to abilities individuals have to use technology.

Therefore, this chapter aims to analyse the factors that impact on the academics' effective use of the technology, hence looking at the new technology implementers' capabilities to benefit from it in their teaching processes. The perspective of limited use of the new technologies as deprivation of capabilities provides a conceptual basis for the study. Sen's Capability Approach is used as a conceptual lens to examine the academics' phenomena regarding new technologies for curriculum delivery. The approach is concerned with the individuals' capabilities and freedom. This translates into effective opportunities that individuals have, to live a type of a lifestyle they have a reason to value. It is recommended that social arrangements should aim to broaden peoples capabilities (Sen 1999).

Research Questions

This chapter aims at analysing the factors that impact on the academics' effective use of ICTs for teaching and learning in the new education paradigm, in particular within the developing nations context. The following questions therefore, provided the focus and drive to the empirical study for this chapter:

- What capabilities do academics in a developing country realise from new technologies for teaching and learning?
- What factors impact on the academics' realization of their capabilities when using the technologies for teaching and learning at university level?

To answer these questions, a qualitative research approach was employed whereby data was collected through in-depth interviews with 26 random sampled academics from different universities in South Africa. The results of the study show that institutional, social and individual constraints are preventing some academics from realising their potential capabilities from using ICTs for teaching and learning. Among the factors is the instructors' lack of a complex, situated form of knowledge referred to as Technological, Pedagogical Content Knowledge (TPCK) (Mishra & Koehler 2006) to effectively integrate the new technology into the course delivery. Therefore, it is recommended that university lecturers, though in most cases today they may be familiar with technology in general, be equipped with TPCK for effective teaching and learning.

ICTs and Teaching and Learning

According to Elliot (2010), digital learning and ICTs are widely viewed as having the potential to enhance and customise teaching and learning opportunities and experiences, hence reshaping traditional learning worldwide. While earlier on Jung (2005) had a similar opinion by arguing that the new technologies are offering new possible ways of teaching, other authors are less optimistic about skills constituting digital literacy. According to Johnson et al (2011:4) the digital literacy skills are still not well defined nor universally taught; though universities are beginning to fold these literacy skills into coursework for students, progress is observed to be still slow. The authors believe the situation is worsened due to "the

fact that digital technologies morph and change quickly at a rate that generally outpaces curriculum development" (ibid).

Nevertheless, some believe that one of the reasons for embracing the new educational paradigm, which means adopting new technologies, is the shift from the traditional talk and chalk method of teaching towards a more interactive teaching style where instructors and students positively interact throughout the learning process as they are using the technologies (Chapman & Mahlk, 2004). South Africa, just like many other nations, has invested a lot in ICT resources in order to improve teaching and learning processes. Madiba (2009) posits that growing interest in such technologies like eLearning platforms to improve resource supply and support for students, prompted South African universities to invest in LMS to enable teaching staff to develop and manage online courses with little professional support.

Nonetheless, Hussein (2011: 43) cautions that "eLearning should not only be seen as a set of courses made on the websites, but it is rather a set of teaching and learning management processes, and thus the eLearning is based on computerized systems to manage learning processes." He further argues that LMS is an important tool for the development of courses and management of students' learning and their motivation to learn. Besides, teaching through eLearning platforms achieves effectiveness in the development of teaching practices, student learning development as well as the development of student assessment and course administrative processes (Hussein, 2011: 43). However, while there are many noticeable benefits of integrating new technologies for teaching and learning at higher learning institutions, there are also challenges faced when adopting and using the learning platforms (Chigona & Dagada 2011).

Murphy and Greenwood (1998: 415) argued that "research findings suggest that Information and Communication Technology is significantly under-used by students and teachers". Locally, studies have shown that instructors and students are slow in the eLearning platforms uptake (Madiba, 2009; Chigona & Dagada 2011). Elsewhere Elliot (2010) shows that, although the new technologies in education since a decade ago have enabled higher education providers to expand and enrich teaching and learning opportunities and pedagogies, there is a concern about the professional learning of instructors so that they have the confidence to exploit the ICTs to expand, extend and modify their pedagogies. Another challenge which involves students, is that for them to be able to use the new technologies, there is a need to have basic skills on how to use the platforms. This implies that students who do not have prior experience with the technology or have limited access are likely to lose out (Roblyer, 2003).

Nevertheless, recent research (Madiba, 2009; Elliot 2010) show that the actual integration of ICTs into curriculum delivery could pose challenges. Tennent, Becker and Kehoe (2005: 650) provide "a number of disadvantages including the potential technology failures, the lack of face-to-face and therefore interpersonal cues, and from the instructor's viewpoint, a great deal of time and effort in converting traditional text-based content to information suitable for online delivery. In their study (Johnson et al, 2011: 3), it was clear that behind the many challenges faced "was a pervasive sense that individual organizational constraints are likely the most important factor in any decision to adopt — or not to adopt — any given technology"

Results of a study into capabilities of academics when using new technologies for course delivery may provide insights to tertiary institutions as well as individual academics when deploying and adopting the technologies. Institutions need to look into the capabilities of the teaching staff when using new technologies if the new education paradigm is to be really beneficial to both the instructors and their students. Since we are interested in the capabilities of the academics, we employed a Capability Approach as a conceptual lens to examine the phenomenon.

CAPABILITY APPROACH AS FRAMEWORK

The framework was developed by Sen Amartya. The approach has widely influenced human development debates (UNDP, 1990) as it is directly concerned with what people are effectively able to do and to be, taking into account the commodities to which they have access (Sen, 1999). This chapter is very interested in the conversion between ICT resources/commodities and capabilities of academics at tertiary level in the developing nations. Nevertheless, Sen argues that social arrangements should aim to broaden individuals' capabilities – their freedom to achieve valuable beings and actions. He believes that focusing on freedom is a more accurate way to develop what individuals really value in their lives. The framework helps to focus on individual capabilities and freedom. Sen (1999) defines 'freedom' as effective opportunities individuals have to live the sort of lifestyle they have reasons to value.

According to Zheng and Walsham (2008) the Capability Approach focuses on the capabilities which individuals may fail to enjoy due to limited resources e.g. access to education, participation in economic life and autonomy in decision-making. The Capability Approach looks at the failure to derive meaningful benefits from new technologies as a deprivation of the academics' freedoms and is therefore in need of being addressed. Again, Zheng and Walsham (2008) show that the framework seeks to understand transformation of commodities into valuable beings and doings, i.e. vectors of functioning or capability sets (see Figure 1).

From the vectors of functioning, individuals choose capabilities or functioning which they would like to achieve. The choice of specific subsets of functionings creates a given level of well-being. According to Sen (1999: 75) functioning "reflects the various things a person may value doing or being" while capabilities are "the alternative combinations of functionings that are feasible for her to achieve. Capability is thus a

Figure 1. Conversion of commodities to capabilities

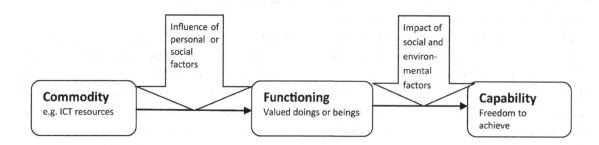

kind of freedom - the substantive freedom to achieve alternative functionings combinations (… the freedom to achieve various lifestyles)" (ibid). In other words, capabilities entail the actual opportunities open to an individual.

Gasper (2002) referred well-being to the evaluation which is focused on the individual's being. But, according to Zheng & Walsham (2008), 'well-being' refers only to one's own gratification and is distinct from the pursuit and fulfillment of one's ideals and commitments. Sen also defines agency as an individual's ability to pursue and realise what he/she values and has reason to value, or, in other words, the freedom to set and pursue one's own goals and interests (ibid). Well-being may be one of the goals and interests the individual is pursuing. The individual is viewed as an agent thus "someone who acts and brings about change" (Sen, 1999: 19).

Nevertheless, Zheng & Walsham (2008) show that achievement of functionings is a result of the individual's choice to select from the capabilities available, subject to the individual's preferences, social pressure and other decision-making mechanisms. It should be noted that these are again affected by individual, social and environmental factors. Putting it differently, Bass, Nicholson & Subrahmanian (2011) show that "the social context influences an individual's ability to create capabilities (freedom to achieve) from commodities". The objective being analysed in this chapter is the capabilities of academics to use

ICT resources for course delivery. The Capability Approach provides a set of concepts (as in Table 1) to unpack the relationship between new technologies and its limited use in course delivery as capability deprivation.

The assumption in relation to the framework is that academics are in the position of being able to use new technologies (commodity) deployed at their institutions for course delivery (functioning). If, however, the academician is unable to use the ICTs (e.g. due to lack of necessary skills), then the availability of the commodity at the institution would not result in the functioning i.e. using ICT for teaching and learning. However, the access to the new technologies coupled with the academics' individual characteristics (ICT training/knowledge etc), creates the capability for the instructors to integrate ICT in their course delivery whenever necessary. If, for example, the academician values this capability for enhancing teaching and learning – such capability would contribute to both the instructor's and students' happiness (self-fulfillment) or well-being.

RESEARCH DESIGNS

Interpretive studies like this one usually employ qualitative approaches whereby interviews and other ethnographic techniques are used to explore the meanings of the technology, the changing behaviours, and conflicts. Such data may not be

Table 1. Concepts for unpacking ICTs and its limited use as capability deprivation

Commodity/resource	New technologies (ICTs)
Conversion factors	Individual factors e.g. personal history Social factors e.g. social institutions, social norms, policy Environmental factors e.g. infrastructure, resources
Agents	Whose capabilities are deprived? e.g. students, academics
Capabilities	The capabilities instructors and students are deprived of Well-being freedom e.g. enhanced teaching and learning Agency freedom e.g. taking advantage of new technologies

accessible if using quantitative approaches. In this study, we want to understand academics', in particular those within a developing world, capability deprivation when using new technologies for teaching and learning as is expected in the new educational paradigm.

Sampling

Random sampling was used to select participants to take part in the data collection process. Twenty-five randomly selected academic staff from six universities in South Africa participated in the study. The reasons for choosing South Africa as a case study were twofold. First was for convenience as the researchers are based in South Africa. Secondly, evidence shows that South Africa is much further ahead regarding new technologies when compared with other nations on the African continent; and so we hoped to be well informed here regarding the capabilities when using the technologies for teaching and learning at tertiary level. However, it was noted that of all the selected institutions only one has tried to integrate ERP systems to it LMS but due to lack of competences the system is not used.

Data Collection and Analysis

Using a semi-structured interview questionnaire, we conducted one-on-one in-depth conversations with the 25 randomly sampled academics. Each interview was audio recorded and then transcribed verbatim. The transcription process helped us gain a deep understanding of the data. In the process we were be able to think about what the interviewee was saying and how this was said. Then we read each transcript several times while listening to the corresponding audio tape to ensure accuracy of the transcription and to come to a better overall understanding of each participant's narrative. The process of transcribing and listening to the interviews also prompted additional questions for subsequent sets of interviews, hence validating the data collected. After all the interviews were completed, we did a detailed systematic qualitative analysis, case by case. We read and examined each transcript over and over, each time annotating the text with initial comments pertaining to conversion factors (individual, social and environmental) and capabilities affected. Trustworthiness of the analysis was established through peer debriefing. A researcher trained in qualitative methodology compared the transcripts and the quality of the themes developed as well as critically looking at the analysis.

Ethical Considerations

Although we could not foresee any sensitive ethical issues in the course of conducting this study, we still complied with ethical measures whenever required. Participants were informed about the prevailing ethical consideration. We obtained informed consent from each participant. The first consent was obtained when the participants replied to the e-mail asking them to participate in this study. The second consent was obtained orally on the day of the interview after the participant had had the opportunity to carefully consider the risks and benefits and to ask any questions regarding the study as well as their participation. We tried as much as possible to adhere to privacy and confidentiality concerns which were given the deserved consideration (Cohen, Manion & Morrison, 2007). Participants were assured that participation was voluntary and so could withdraw from participating at any point without consequences on their part.

FINDINGS AND DISCUSSIONS

From the findings we noted that most academics were aware of the benefits of integrating new technologies in their teaching. Some are also aware of the advantages of integrating ERP systems to their LMSes. However, despite the awareness of the benefits, the integration of the new technologies is generally low. It may be argued at this point that, while the data analysed was obtained from South Africa which is considered as the leading economy on the continent, the situation in the other countries may be argued to be worse. Nevertheless, the analysis revealed a number of conversion factors that led to the capability deprivation of academics to effectively use the new technologies for teaching and learning. The conversion factors may be grouped into individual, social and environmental factors. Table 2 outlines the conversion factors noted in the study.

Individual Conversion Factors

Individual conversion factors represent the impact of personal influence on the individual's ability to convert the means to achieve service and/or goods into capabilities or freedom (Robeyns, 2005). Under this theme we identified two factors impacting on the conversion processes.

Skill for Integrating Technology into Pedagogy

Our analysis has shown that a lack of a complex skill or knowledge which every instructor intending to teach with technology is supposed to have, is negatively impacting the academics when using the ICTs for course delivery. The knowledge which Mishra & Koehler (2006) referred to as Technological, Pedagogical Content Knowledge (TPCK) is required for effective integration of the new technologies into the course delivery. According to Mishra & Koehler (2006:1029), "TPCK is the basis of good teaching with technology and requires an understanding of the representation of concepts using technologies; pedagogical techniques that use technologies in constructive ways to teach content; knowledge of what makes concepts difficult or easy to learn and how tech-

Table 2. Conversion factors impacting on academics' ICTs capabilities

Conversion factors	
Individual factors	-skill for integrating technology into pedagogy - personal experience and attitude towards new technologies
Social context	-fear that students will stop attending the face-to-face lecturer sessions - policies and regulations
Environment	- inadequate infrastructure and resources - insufficient technical support

nology can help redress some of the problems that students face; knowledge of students' prior knowledge and theories of epistemology; and knowledge of how technologies can be used to build on existing knowledge and to develop new epistemologies or strengthen old ones."

Though, almost all academics in the study would be familiar with technology in general, many are not in a position to make informed judgments on when and how the technologies could be effectively integrated in their pedagogy to enhance the teaching and learning. On the argument of effectively integrating ICTs in pedagogy, one participant commented:

You've got to look at the nature of the content that you're dealing with because there's some content that just does not lend itself to being taught interactively with a computer. But there's other content that does, so for example, if you've got three dimensional stuff and you've got visual simulations those can be very helpful to students. If you've got processes that are happening like in physics; diffusion of molecules or you're doing a simulation of what happens if you heat this thing what happens to the pressure and there are fantastic simulations where you can adjust the volume and get the readings for the pressure and all those are well and good but the computer then plots the graph for you and records the data. And the students come out of those pracs, they've got all the answers because the computer has done it for them. And they might know that volume is inversely proportional to pressure but they cannot draw graphs and they do not know how to draw graphs and they struggle to interpreted graphs. ... I'm not against using computers; I'm for using computers but the person who uses it they've got to know what they're doing...

The data shows that there are challenges regarding actual use of the new technologies for teaching and learning. At this point, it could be argued that mere deployment of new technologies into the tertiary institutions could not automatically result in enhanced teaching and learning. One of the participants bemoaned:

One of the biggest problems with computers, people think that it's a "magic pen is here" that you just "now we've got computers" suddenly all the problems we have are gonna go away and that is not gonna happen. It doesn't happen, it doesn't depend on the computer, it depends on the effective use of the software.

Another respondent so concerned about inappropriate use of the technology for teaching and learning argued:

...lack of relevance or rather comprehensiveness of online course material; you don't just load information on the internet. The lectures must be of high quality, they must have relevance. You must tailor the course towards what they are going to do .... Lack of instructional intimacy associated with face to face conventional delivery systems in traditional classrooms.

The concerns show that there is a need for a pedagogical familiarization on the side of the academics if they are to realize their capabilities when using the technologies for teaching and learning. The lack here is resulting in curtailment of the academics' well-being and freedom in that, despite the availability of ICT resources, they cannot effectively integrate the technologies in their pedagogies to enhance their teaching. Students as well are disadvantaged in that, though most of them are digital citizens, they could not learn using the new technologies because their instructors are not in a better position to deliver content with the support of ICTs. Nevertheless, it is argued that, "with personal access to the Internet from mobile devices on the rise, the growing set of resources available as open content, and a variety of reference and textbooks available electronically, students' easy and pervasive access to information outside of formal campus resources continues to encourage educators to take a careful look at the ways we can best serve learners" (Johnson et al 2011:4). However, the lack of capabilities on the academics side translates to negative impact on the agency freedom of both the academics and their students in that they are failing to take advantage of the new technologies to make their teaching and learning interesting.

Personal Experience and Attitude towards New Technologies

Personal experience as well as the attitude towards new technologies play a big role as to whether one would use ICTs for curriculum delivery or not. The data shows that many academics who were exposed to learning with technologies when they were students feel confident to teach with the ICTs; while those who did not have prior experience with the same do not see much benefit of teaching with technology. The latter usually do not want to change their mind set. They say it has been the norm for them teaching without the new technologies and things worked well, so why should they change now. On this issue, one participant said:

I haven't really seen a need to get as involved as I possibly could and I suppose because the way I structured the courses seems to work well. So you know I would probably need to sit with the e-learning specialist in order to see what I could add to the course to potentially make it more beneficial.

Meta analysis shows that there are some who do not want to change their old ways of teaching and learning because they are technophobic. Narrating his observations on why some colleagues would not want to change their mind-set, one participant said:

...you have a lot of people in the staff who are hugely technophobic, who are not interested in using it because that is not the way things have been done. And I think they are going to resist whether you make it policy or not.

While such academics deprive themselves and their well-being from the new technologies, the students enrolled in their courses are also experiencing capability deprivations since they cannot take advantage of the new technologies to make their learning flexible.

While individual factors seem to be strong in preventing the academics realizing the capabilities from using ICTs for teaching and learning, there are other important challenges as well. The social and environmental factors are discussed below. However, the pervasive sense is that the individual institutional constraints are seen to be the most challenging among the identified factors impacting on converting ICTs to capabilities among academics in a developing country.

Social Conversion Context

Social conversional factors represent the impact of social influence on the individual's ability to convert the means to achieve service and/or goods into capabilities or freedom (Robeyns, 2005). Looking at the social context in the data, we identified two factors socially impacting on the conversion processes.

Fear that Students Will Stop Attending the Face-to-Face Sessions

While new technologies can enhance access teaching and learning opportunities through provision of access to information resources, most of the participants in the study prefer face-to-face teaching and learning situations. The preference is deterring many of the academics to integrate new technologies in their course delivery because they think if they do that many students will stop attending the face-to-face lecturer sessions. One respondent said:

I have an experience with people in the past that they do not want to put their lecture notes on WebCT or blackboard because they think that it tends to harm lecture attendance.

It is argued that the opportunities due to ICTs can enhance 'aspiration fulfillment' hence increasing capabilities and freedoms among the academics. The students and the academics as instructors here are failing to take advantage of the new technologies. There is lack of awareness of the benefits of ICTs; and this lack is depriving both the academics and their students from the opportunities to enhance capabilities from the new technologies (Madon, 2004; Johnstone, 2007).

Policies and Regulations

While in the market place people would join a bandwagon to adopting and using technology, with academics, lecturers would normally use the technology when they actually see the benefit of using the commodity, not just because it is fashionable to do so. Even if the institutions would make it a policy that the academics should use technology in their teaching, some academics would still resist until they are assured of the benefits of integrating the technology in their instructions. One participant said:

...I use technology and I teach my students technology when it is going to promote learning. But technology for technology's sake you can forget it. It's not gonna have any long term impact. You've got know what exactly what you're doing and you've got to use it...

Nevertheless, there are some academics who wish to use emerging technologies like Facebook to enhance their teaching and learning. The argument given by such academics is that many stu-dents are already familiar with such platforms and therefore it would be a nice environment for both the lecturers and the students to use for academic purposes. However, in most institutions accessing Facebook in the university computer laboratories was not allowed, as this respondent narrates:

We had a restriction ..., I think they put it on from 5 o'clock so that students don't go on Facebook during the day and spent lots of time and energy and bandwidth on Facebook. But if you would like to integrate that into your teaching and learning environment, which I think is a great idea, then you [the institution] can't restrict it. That is something that need to evolve and see what comes out of it. I am very for the idea though, of using MXit in class for example. It is excellent.

While the restriction to access and use some emerging technologies as a policy or regulation in the institutions curtails the freedoms of the users (lecturers and students), such restriction can also be seen as an environmental factor preventing the users from realizing their capabilities regarding the use of the technologies. The users could not take advantage of the ICTs.

ENVIRONMENTAL CONVERSION FACTORS

According to the American Heritage Dictionary (2000), environment in ICTs means, "the entire set of conditions under which one operates a computer, as it relates to the hardware, operating platform, or operating system". Under the environment theme, we identified two factors.

Inadequacy of Infrastructure and Resources

Some academics in the study have indicated that due to some environmental factor like inadequate infrastructure and resources in their institution, they cannot use the technology for assessment in their courses of teaching. Some also indicated that they feel discouraged to use the new technologies because they usually experience internet problems and so they do not find it reliable for teaching and learning. One lecturer said:

The most common challenge is technical problems including bandwidth limitation and browser problems. Sometimes this goes down even here at the university, many times. And maybe if you live in an area where there is no electricity or where the electricity goes off from time to time it damages your electrical gadgets. And how much can you download from the internet? That is bandwidth limitation.

Insufficient resources here are impacting on the academics that have the confidence and ability to use the technology. Hence both the students and academics are deprived of their capability to use the technology. With regard to insufficient resources, one respondent narrated how tricky it is to use computer facilities at his university considering the number of students he has to teach:

So that becomes tricky because the classes are huge and out of a class of about 400 I get maybe between 70 and 100 who start coming to lessons so it means to fit them in our computer lab with 40 computers, I've got to do it for six weeks in the whole of the first block every single lunch time I go because lunch time is their only free time. So it becomes…the logistics of getting them to come is very tricky.

In most cases the inadequate infrastructure and resources in their institution are coupled with insufficient technical support and this makes the environment complex.

Insufficient Technical Support

Insufficient resources here are impacting on the lecturers who have the confidence and ability to use the technology. Hence both the students and instructors are deprived of their capability to use the technology. Our analysis has shown that while some academics really want to use the new technologies for teaching and learning, they feel they do not have sufficient technical support when it comes to use the ICTs. One respondent said:

If you have excited and enthusiastic people and you don't have the supporting infrastructure, all the stars in their eyes will die. The second thing that's also important is, if you have infrastructure, and you have exciting people, but you don't have a hand to hold on for them, it will also fail.

Because, in some cases, the support is not there, the academics and students' agency freedom to make effective use of ICT in their work was curtailed. Inadequate technical support and being denied access, (e.g. when using Facebook) to an extent, discouraged some academics from taking advantage of the new technologies for their teaching.

IMPLICATIONS OF THE RESEARCH

This study intends to make a practical contribution to university institutions to ensure the maximum benefits of using new technologies for teaching and learning are fully realized by both academics and institutions. From the results of the study, we can see that there is a need for institutions to look into conversion factors that are influencing some academics to fail to derive meaningful benefits from the new technologies. While the academics have the agency i.e. the ability to pursue and realise what they value and have reason to value, the institutions have the responsibility to aid the academics to bring about change that would result in both the academics and students enjoying the benefits of using the new technologies. The study helps in identifying conversion factors that are influencing academics in the developing countries to fail to derive meaningful benefits from new technologies.

CONCLUSION

This chapter focused on the factors that impact on academics capabilities when integrating new technologies in their teaching and learning activities. Using Capability Approach as a framework, we have analysed the factors. Our analysis has shown that there is limited use of the new technologies in the universities in the developing countries. Integration of ERP systems is even rarer in the countries. Academics are failing to realise their capabilities due to unfavorable conversion factors which are influencing on the academics' abilities to convert the means to achieve service or goods into capabilities or freedom.

Identified conversion factors that are influencing the academics not to derive meaningful benefits from ICTs include:

- Individual factors which are manifested as
  ◦ Lack of skills to effectively integrate the new technologies into pedagogy; and
  ◦ Insufficient personal experience and negative attitude towards the new technologies.
- Social context which, in the study, has been seen as being manifested through the fear of the academics that if they use the ICTs for teaching and learning then their students will stop attending lectures - which

to them are very important. Policies and regulations have also negatively impacted some academics that they feel restricted to integrate the technologies in their work.
- Environment has impacted on the capabilities of the academics in that in most cases there is inadequate infrastructure and resources, as well as insufficient technical support

Looking at the identified conversion factors, it may be concluded that academics need to change their mindset to want to teach with the technologies but at the same time the institutions need to take a lead by making sure that the academics are equipped with the skills they need to effectively integrate the technologies in their work. Mishra & Koehler (2006) call that skill Technological, Pedagogical Content Knowledge. Again, it is the responsibility of the institutions to ensure that there is adequate infrastructure and resources for their population. The adequacy is also a factor if ERP systems are to be integrated. Institutions should also ensure that there is adequate and readily available technical support for the technology users, otherwise they will feel de-motivated to use the ICTs available.

ACKNOWLEDGMENT

This chapter is the revised and extended version of our paper which we presented at the World Conference on Educational Multimedia, Hypermedia & Telecommunications in June 2011. Some of the revisions are based on the critical comments provided during presentation; others were due to new data collected on the topic as it was extended to cover the academics' ICT capabilities in developing nations.

REFERENCES

BECTA. (2003). *What the research says about using ICT in maths*. British Educational Communications and Technology Agency. Retrieved from http://partners.becta.org.uk/page_documents/research/wtrs_maths.pdf

Bingimlas, K. A. (2009). Barriers to the successful integration of ICT in teaching and learning: A review of the literature. *Eurasia Journal of Mathematics. Science and Technology Education*, *5*(3), 235–245.

Chapman, D. W., & Mahlk, L. O. (Eds.). (2004). *Adapting technology for school improvement: A global perspective*. Paris, France: UNESCO and International Institute for Educational Planning.

Chigona, A., & Dagada, R. (2011). Adoption and use of e-learning at tertiary level in South Africa: A qualitative analysis. *Proceedings of the Global Conference on Learning and Technology*, Melbourne, 27th March – 1st April 2011, (pp. 93-101).

Elliot, A. (2010). Equity, pedagogy and inclusion. Harnessing digital technologies to support students from low socio-economic backgrounds in higher education. *The Journal of Community Informatics*, *6*(3).

Gasper, D. (2002). Is Sen's capability approach an adequate basis for considering human development? *Review of Political Economy*, *14*(4), 435–461. doi:10.1080/0953825022000009898

Higgins, S. (2003). *Does ICT improve learning and teaching in schools?* Nottingham, UK: British Educational Research Association.

Hussein, H. B. (2011). Attitudes of Saudi universities faculty members towards using learning management system (JUSUR). *The Turkish Online Journal of Educational Technology*, *10*(2), 43–53.

Johnson, L., Smith, R., Willis, H., Levine, A., & Haywood, K. (2011). *The 2011 horizon report*. Austin, TX: The New Media Consortium.

Johnstone, J. (2007). Technology as empowerment: A capability approach to computer ethics. *Ethics and Information Technology*, *9*, 73–87. doi:10.1007/s10676-006-9127-x

Jung, I. (2005). ICT-pedagogy integration in teacher training: Application cases worldwide. *Journal of Educational Technology & Society*, *8*(2), 94–101.

Linderoth, H., & Lundqvist, A. (2004). Learn not to learn: Paradoxical knowledge creation and learning in ERP-projects. In *Proceedings IRNOP VI, 2004*, (pp. 409-422). Turku, Finland: Academy University Press.

Madiba, M. (2009). *Investigating design issues in e-learning*. Unpublished PhD Thesis, University of the Western Cape.

Madon, S. (2004). Evaluating the impact of e-governance initiative: An exploratory framework. *Electronic Journal on Information Systems in Developing Countries*, *20*(5), 1–13.

Mishra, P., & Koehler, M. J. (2006). Technological pedagogical content knowledge: A framework for teacher knowledge. *Teachers College Record*, *108*(6), 1017–1054. doi:10.1111/j.1467-9620.2006.00684.x

Mumtaz, S. (2000). Factors affecting teachers' use of information and communications technology: A review of the literature. *Technology, Pedagogy and Education*, *9*(3), 319–342. doi:10.1080/14759390000200098

Njenga, J. K. (2011). *eLearning adoption in Eastern and Southern Africa higher education institutions*. Unpublished PhD Thesis, University of the Western Cape.

Robeyns, I. (2005). The capability approach: A theoretical survey. *Journal of Human Development*, *6*(1), 93–114. doi:10.1080/146498805200034266

Sen, A. K. (1999). *Development as freedom*. Oxford, UK: Oxford University Press.

United Nations Development Programme (UNDP). (1990). *Human development report 1990.* New York, NY: Author. Retrieved from http://hdr.undp.org/en/report/global/hdr1990

Zheng, Y. (2009). Different spaces for e-development. What can we learn from the capability approach? *Information Technology for Development, 15*(2), 66–82. doi:10.1002/itdj.20115

Zheng, Y., & Walsham, G. (2008). Inequality of what? Social exclusion in the e-society as capability deprivation. *Information Technology & People, 21*(3), 222–243. doi:10.1108/09593840810896000

ADDITIONAL READING

Anderson, R. E., & Dexter, S. L. (2000). *School technology leadership: Incidence and impact.* Centre for Research on Information Technology and Organisations. University of California, Irvine and University of Minnesota. Retrieved from http://www.crito.uci.edu/tlc/html/findings.html

Chigona, A., Chigona, W., Kayongo, P., & Kausa, M. (2010). An empirical survey on domestication of ICT in schools in disadvantaged communities in South Africa. *International Journal of Education and Development using Information and Communication Technology, 6*(2).

Collis, B., & Jung, I. S. (2003). Uses of information and communication technologies in teacher education. In Robinson, B., & Latchem, C. (Eds.), *Teacher education through open and distance learning* (pp. 171–192). London, UK: RoutledgeFalmer.

Dagada, R. (2009). *Time space and pace: Computer integrated learning in corporate South Africa.* Pretoria, South Africa: Unisa Press.

Damoense, M. Y. (2003). Online learning: Implications for effective learning for higher education in South Africa. *Australian Journal of Educational Technology, 19*(1), 25–45.

Dawes, L. (2001). What stops teachers using technology? In Leask, M. (Ed.), *Issues in teaching using ICT* (pp. 61–79). London, UK: Routledge.

Felicetti, V. L. (2011). Teacher education: from education to teacher substance and practice. *Research in Higher Education Journal, 13,* 1–8.

Govindasamy, T. (2002). Successful implementation of e-learning pedagogical considerations. *The Internet and Higher Education, 4,* 287–299. doi:10.1016/S1096-7516(01)00071-9

Grainger, R., & Tolhurst, D. (2005). *Organisational factors affecting teachers' use and perception of information & communications technology.* Australian Computer Society.

Habib, L. (2004). *Domesticating learning technology in a higher education institution: A state of two virtual learning environments.* Centre for Educational Research and Development, Oslo University College.

Habib, L. (2005). Domesticating learning technologies in a higher education institution: A tale of two virtual learning environments. *ADIS Virtual Multi Conference on Computer Science and Information Systems 2005,* (pp. 83-88).

Haddon, L. (2006). The contribution of domestication research to in-home computing and media consumption. *The Information Society, 22,* 195–203. doi:10.1080/01972240600791325

Hung, D., & Khine, M. S. (2006). *Engaged learning with emerging technologies.* Dordrecht, The Netherlands: Springer. doi:10.1007/1-4020-3669-8

Kendall, K. E. (1999). *Emerging information technologies: Improving decisions, cooperation, and infrastructure.* Thousand Oaks, CA: Sage Publications.

Kinuthia, W., & Dagada, R. (2008). E-Learning Incorporation: An exploratory study of three South African higher education institutions. *International Journal on E-Learning, 7*(4), 623–639.

Lau, B. T., & Sim, C. H. (2008). Exploring the extent of ICT adoption among secondary school teachers in Malaysia. *International Journal of Computing and IT Research, 2*(2), 19–36.

Mapuva, J. (2009) Confronting challenges to e-learning in higher education institutions. *International Journal of Education and Development using Information and Communication Technology, 5*(3).

Ross, J. A., Hogaboam-Gray, A., & Hannay, L. (1999). Predictors of teachers' confidence in their ability to implement computer-based instruction. *Journal of Educational Computing Research, 21*(1), 75–97. doi:10.2190/CGXF-YYJE-47KQ-MFA1

Sen, A. K. (1987). *The standard of living: The Tanner lectures.* Cambridge, UK: Cambridge University Press.

Sen, A. K. (1992). *Inequality re-examined.* Oxford, UK: Clarendon Press.

Sen, A. K. (1993). Capability and well-being. In Nussbaum, M. C., & Sen, A. K. (Eds.), *The quality of life* (pp. 30–53). Oxford, UK: Clarendon Press. doi:10.1093/0198287976.003.0003

Sen, A. K. (2000). *Social exclusion concept, application and scrutiny. Social Development Papers. No. 1.* Tokyo, Japan: Asia Development Bank.

Sugar, W., Crawley, F., & Fine, B. (2004). Examining teachers' decisions to adopt new technology. *Journal of Educational Technology & Society, 7*(4), 201–213.

Vrasidas, C., & McIsaac, M. (2001). Integrating technology in teaching and teacher education: Implications for policy and curriculum reform. *Educational Media International, 38*(2/3), 127–132. doi:10.1080/09523980110041944

KEY TERMS AND DEFINITIONS

Academics: Lecturers at an academic institution.

Capabilities: One's ability to use, and enjoy new technologies.

Conversion Factor: Things impacting on the transformation of commodities or resources into well-being.

ICT: Any technology used for information retrieving or dissemination.

New Technologies: Traditional and emerging technologies believed to enhance teaching and learning.

Pedagogy: Art of teaching.

TPCK: Technological Pedagogical Content Knowledge required by any instructor to be able to teach with technology effectively.

Chapter 3
Virtual and Interactive Learning (VIL) in Transformation and Imparting Education in the Digital Era

P. Srinivas Subba Rao
Maharajah's Post Graduate College, India

P. Suseela Rani
TRR College of Engineering & Technology, India

ABSTRACT

Virtual and Interactive Learning (VIL) is one of the new directions for education. It aims at using the WEB, being a networked, anytime, interactive, high-capacity, and content-rich environment, to enhance and facilitate independent learning and teacher-student communication. It would eventually lead to a paradigm shift of learning style, from teacher-centered to student-centered. It is bringing hope to millions who had abandoned the dream of continuing education due to paucity of time and money. It makes learning much easier as one need not be physically present in the classrooms all the time. Through VIL students are anticipated to learn to analyse the problem situation, devise the problem solving strategies, solve the problems and evaluate the consequences, all of which are considered as high-order abilities required in this new era. VIL should be facilitated by the provision of real-life experience so as to bridge the gap between classroom learning and real-life experiences by enabling students to learn in a simulated situation similar to the real ones.

INTRODUCTION

Information and communication technologies are today playing a very important role in transforming the mode of imparting education. Virtual and Interactive learning (VIL) is one of the new directions for education. This approach aims at using the WEB, being a networked, anytime, interactive, high-capacity and content-rich environment, to enhance and facilitate independent learning and teacher-student communication. VIL would eventually lead to a paradigm shift of learning style, from teacher-centred to student-centred. It

DOI: 10.4018/978-1-4666-2193-0.ch003

is bringing hope to millions who had abandoned the dream of continuing education due to paucity of time and money. It makes learning much easier as one need not be physically present in the classrooms all the time. The traditional role of teachers as knowledge providers will be changed to that of learning facilitators, since students can learn from the wide repertoire of information enabled by the Internet.

Kiesler & McGuire, (1987) said that, "The result of interacting learning process will lead to internalized, long-term understanding."

Hong Kong Education and Manpower Bureau, (1998), "Students are expected to learn through communicating, either in a real environment requiring personal contact or on the Web, and then construct and reorganize their own knowledge."

According to Parker (1999), "The result of interactive learning can be new knowledge, reorganized knowledge, or simplify the awareness of a need for additional understanding."

Students should not be seen as empty vessels or sponges that absorb knowledge imparted by the teacher (Akyalcin, 1997). Therefore, VIL should be facilitated by the provision of real-life experience so as to bridge the gap between classroom learning and real-life experiences by enabling students to learn in a simulated situation similar to the real ones. Learning as it normally occurs, as argued by Lave (1988), is a function of the activity, context and culture in which it occurs (i.e., it is situated). The physical context is referred to as the situation and this kind of learning is called situated learning. Situated learning is usually unintentional rather than deliberate (Lave & Wenger, 1990). The modern web technology enables the creation of simulated situations for students to explore as well as the communication convenience for students to interact. It is therefore an ideal venue for students to construct their knowledge. This is what a web-based teaching environment is for. Learning, both outside and inside school, advances through collaborative social interaction and the social construction of knowledge (Brown, Collins & Duguid, 1989). Students need to learn by interacting with their peers so that knowledge can be constructed. Knowledge construction is a process of making sense of what the students are studying by synthesizing new information and experience into existing mental structures that they already possess. The modern WEB technology enables the creation of simulated situations for students to explore as well as the communication convenience for students to interact. It is therefore an ideal venue for students to construct their knowledge. This is what a WEB-based teaching environment is for. It is an enormous transformation, and as students discovers new ways to communicate and interact with the introduction of new technologies like interactive classroom teaching, online learning and virtual learning systems. Today's students must have 21st Century skills such as creativity, problem solving, communication and analytical thinking to compete in the increasingly digital global marketplace.

Through VIL students are anticipated to learn to analyse the problem situation, devise the problem solving strategies, solve the problems and evaluate the consequences, all of which are considered as high-order abilities required in this new era. VIL should be facilitated by the provision of real-life experience so as to bridge the gap between classroom learning and real-life experiences by enabling students to learn in a simulated situation similar to the real ones.

OBJECTIVES

- Virtual and Interactive Learning enhance and facilitate independent learning and teacher-student communication.
- VIL should be facilitated by the provision of real-life experience so as to bridge the gap between classroom learning and real-life experiences.

- VIL is bringing hope to millions who had abandoned the dream of continuing education due to paucity of time and money.
- Enabling students to learn in a simulated situation similar to the real ones.

CHARACTERISTICS OF VIL

- **As a repository of teaching materials:** Hyperlinks can be provided on the course WEB page so that students can conveniently download class notes, assigned reading materials, and class exercises, etc.
- **Class administration:** The course web page can be used to allow students to register for a course and the class list is maintained and published automatically on the web. This can be extended for other class administration exercises, such as taking attendance.
- **Information dissemination:** The course web page can be used to disseminate important course announcement, such as amendments to lecture materials and deadlines of assignments.
- **Student-Teacher interaction:** Email services can easily be integrated into the course web page to allow for efficient communication between teachers and students.
- **Email service:** The email services can be enhanced in such a way that emails on different topics are sorted and relevant emails are sent to only the relevant teachers.
- **Course Topics:** Threaded course discussion forums can also be set up and integrated into a course web page to facilitate students' discussion on particular course topics.
- **Broadcasting medium (anytime learning):** The course web page can also be used to deliver multimedia teaching materials and even broadcast live/stored video lectures.

- **Searching for information:** The web is an excellent medium for searching course-related information.
- **Examination medium:** The course web page can also be used to conduct assignments, quizzes, and examinations. Students are required to complete the exercises using the WEB interface. The collected submissions can then be sent to the teachers for manual or automated scoring. More intelligent systems should also be able to mark and give comments to the students, in addition to simply scoring the exercises.

ESSENTIAL REQUIREMENTS FOR VIL

- Ensure that you are well-versed in your web conference platforms interactivity tools.
- Plan to use polling, chat, annotation tools, and whiteboards creatively to achieve the same learning objectives as your face-to-face (f2f) classroom training.
- Don't eliminate interaction. "Repurpose" interactive, face-to-face classroom exercises with interactive, virtual classroom exercises.
- Apply adult learning principles to the web conference experience - talking heads don't work in the f2f classroom or the virtual classroom (no more than 3-5 minutes between participant interactions during your web conference training event).
- Don't upload the same slide presentation used in the classroom to the web conference platform.
- Don't send out the slide presentation prior to the web conference training.
- Avoid slide after slide with bullet points; instead, try visually-stimulating graphics.
- Encourage participants to share ideas and information using multiple modalities:

chat, polling, voice-to-voice and break-out rooms.

- If you are repurposing classroom content, allow 4-10 hours of design time for every hour of delivery. That means a 90-minute webinar requires a minimum of 6 hours of advance preparation and as much as 15 hours of work before your training event.
- Use both a Host and Presenter during the web conference training. The Host handles technical questions; sets up polls, chats, and break-out rooms behind the scenes; and banters with the Presenter to create lively conversation.
- Schedule a dry run prior to the event to test the design, practice the interactivity tools, and ensure that the Host and Presenter are on the same page.
- Create a link to an online, post-course evaluation and make it available at the end of the web training. Participants can click on the link within the web platform to give you immediate feedback.

QUALIFICATIONS OF A VIL TEACHER

- Good interpersonal skills.
- Strong internal student orientation.
- Awareness and receptivity to emerging global thought in school pedagogy.
- Highly developed sense of Personal Accountability.
- Strong ability to mentor the students.
- Excellent subject knowledge.
- Excellent communication skills - verbal and written.
- Creative thinking.
- Analytical skills.
- Sound computer and Internet knowledge.

CURRENT PRACTICES OF VIL

In class-room teaching and learning students are good only in paper talking and usually fail to put theory into practice. This greatly undermines students' problem-solving skills in real-life circumstances. So the aim of the VIL is:

- Helping students to learn from (near) real-life experience, and
- Supplementing classroom teaching.

VIL should typically be administered in the following manner:

- It provides an interactive and distributed virtual environment.
- It is Virtual since the environment is artificially created on the WEB-computer.
- It is Interactive in nature since the virtual world develops only as a result of user input.
- VIL is a student-oriented learning environment since it allows students to gain first-hand experience and learn directly from participation in the development of the virtual world.
- Participating students are divided into teams, each held responsible for a particular aspect of the virtual environment.
- The features of the system, the objectives of the topics being studied should be explained in details to the students concerned.
- Teachers serve only in a guidance role to ensure the smooth completion of a session and to lead class discussion on the proceedings of the session.
- It is a platform for teaching and learning, teaching research, and, to a certain extent, student evaluation.

- Students are free to experiment with ideas without having to bear any undesirable physical consequences and/or penalties.
- It is a multi-user (or multi-team) context and a realistic model.
- It is an advanced graphical and multimedia user-interface.
- User-feedback will be used to further improve the content and user-interface of the system.
- Perceptions of teachers and students using the system will be collected.
- Finally, self-developed pre- and post-tests will be administered to detect students' improvement in their high level abilities, namely application, integration, analysis and evaluation.

SOME SITES OF VIL COURSES

coMentor

coMentor is a software which can be used to create multi-user learning environments on the World Wide Web (WWW) that are accessible without the need for any special client-side software. The system provides a collaborative virtual environment in which students can take part in real-time and asynchronous discussion, along with a set of learning tools to support debate and collaborative work. coMentor is particularly aimed at arts, humanities and social science courses, where learning centres on discussion and textual resources.

System requirements

To run the coMentor server software, one needs a UNIX or a LINUX computer and a Web server. User can access coMentor from any computer connected to the WWW that supports Java (e.g. Macs/Win 95/98/NT plus Netscape/IE 3.0 or above).

Key Features

- Accessible over the World Wide Web without needing to download any special client software
- Visual and easy to use. It looks like a WWW site.
- Real-time discussion, recording and email
- Asynchronous discussion groups
- Students can easily set up groups and discussions lists and choose who has access.
- Concept mapping tools
- Student can leave and annotate work and choose who can read it.
- Role playing facility
- Users have their own home page to record interests and expertise
- Includes useful text resources
- Over time system grows into a repository of recourses
- Easy administration over web

The system proves popular with students as it is easy to use and they like the interface. Students learn from seeing each other's work and also from having to write and sharing their ideas with others. The students achieve high levels of deep and strategic learning.

coMentor can be downloaded from: http://comentor.hud.ac.uk/download.htm.

coMentor manual is available online or can be downloaded from: http://comentor.hud.ac.uk/manual.htm

Colloquia

It is a new kind of software system that supports group working. It allows any user to set up a working or learning group around a particular topic (a context), add people to it, add resources (web pages, documents etc) to it, set up group tasks, and then engage in group and personal "conversations" about the topic.

To support this way of working, users can continually build a library of resources they can use in different contexts, and have access to detailed information about the people they are working with. To use Colloquia every group member needs Colloquia installed on their machine, an E-mail Account, an Internet Connection. It is a user friendly software system and has simple functional methodology.

Resources in Colloquia are a bit like bookmarks or favourites. It can be viewed using Colloquia's built in Web browser. Web pages can also be pulled down and saved offline in their entirety.

Special Features

- By always displaying messages within the context of an activity, s/he always knows what context s/he is talking about, and what s/he has discussed previously.
- Unlike other groupware systems, one does not need to set up a complex central server.
- Any user can set up a group activity. In fact they can set up sub-activities to an activity set up by someone else. Any activity is managed by the initiator, who decides who participates, what resources are used, and sets tasks.

Colloquia is free for use within non-profit educational establishments - schools, colleges and universities.

It can be downloaded from: http://www.colloquia.net/install_main.html.

Skype: Learning through Internet Telephony

Skype, the software product provides telephone service through Voice over IP, allowing your personal computer to act like a telephone. A microphone attached to the computer is necessary and headphones are desirable (to prevent echoes of the voice of your conversation partner). It is not the only such tool, nor the first, but because it provides good quality (through highly efficient compression) and is free, it has become widely used. It is possible to link up to five people through Skype for conference calls. One member of the group acts as the convener and enters the Skype ids of call participants.

It can be downloaded from: http://www.skype.com/download/skype/windows/

iTunes U

It is a free, hosted service for colleges and universities that provides easy access to your educational content, including lectures and interviews 24 hours a day, 7 days a week. It's the most powerful way to manage a broad range of audio or video content and make it available quickly and easily to students, faculty, and staff. And it is the only application that supports the overwhelmingly popular iPod.

Main Features

- It provides easy access to educational content, 24 hours a day, 7 days a week.
- It is easy to learn, use, and administer as well as supports secure web-based standards for authentication and authorization.
- It is a fully integrated part of Apple's end-to-end solution for creating, managing, distributing, and accessing educational content.
- It's the only content management and distribution system that sets educational content free by delivering the best solution for the distribution of content that can be accessed by an iPod.
- It complements learning management systems, including Blackboard, WebCT, and Sakai. Students can access iTunes U content from within these systems with one click.

- Several leading Universities have seen potential in iTunes U service and have joined the programme such as University of Stanford, University of Michigan, Oregon State University, Duke University, University of California etc.

It can be downloaded from: http://www.apple.com/itunes/download/confirm/index.html

Claroline

Claroline is a free LMS, online learning management system developed in PHP/MySQL, which is an Internet based database programming language. It is originally developed in the IPM, Institut de Pédagogie universitaire et des multimedias of the UCL, Université Catholique de Louvain Claroline. It is a free General Public Licensing (GPL) software.

The teacher training philosophy of IPM is to develop the teacher autonomy concerning pedagogy and, furthermore the good use of technical tools in pedagogy. It is a course based educational tool allowing the teacher to create, admin and feed his courses through the web.

Main Features

- Claroline is translated in 32 languages and used by hundreds of institutions around the world.
- The software is released under Open Source license (GPL).
- Developed from teachers to teachers, Claroline is built over sound pedagogical principles allowing a large variety of pedagogical setup including widening of traditional classroom and online collaborative learning.
- It is a platform from teachers to teachers.

It can be downloaded from: http://www.claroline.net/download.htm

LearnITy: The Advanced Learning Engine

The adaptive assessment and e-learning tool LearnITy, is an online learning system that assesses a student's answers and gives the result within 10 minutes and also helps the student overcome any deficiency in knowledge. This has been developed by a team of researchers at Kolkata's Jadavpur University in India in collaboration with an American university.

Indian Space Research Organisation (ISRO) is using it to support the project assessment of EDUSAT, India's satellite exclusively for education. Sun Microsystems and IBM too have begun using it.

- **EkSathe:** This is an asynchronous collaboration module including Online Notice Boards, Online Forums (Threaded Discussion Groups), and Shared Calendar.
- **The LearnITy Assessor:** This is used to implement online testing and evaluation.
- **The LearnITy Virtual Classroom:** It is ideal for interactive and engaging learning in which the teacher wants to retain the human element of interaction while benefiting from delivering real-time multimedia communications.
- **The LearnITy Course Management System:** This is a software module that brings Web-based automation to many of the administrative aspects of teaching.
- **The LearnITy Training Management System:** It is a software module that facilitates tracking and management of training events and features automated collection, analysis, and interpretation of training data. A Skill Management System is used to define and manage the organisational skill sets, staff competence in those skills, providing top management with strategic inputs regarding staff development and hiring.

- **The LearnITy Digital Knowledge Library:** This is an innovative product that provides under a single umbrella all electronic library requirements like Digital Library, e-Journals, e-Books, Online Databases, etc.

Main Features

- LearnITy is not biased towards any particular learning theory or instructional strategy.
- Instead of hard-coding any particular strategy or implementing any particular theory in the source code, the unique feature of externalisation of the instructional strategies in XML notation enables the system to support an infinite variety of instructional strategies.
- Most organisations have a rich collection of content in various areas such as Sales Training, Management Training, etc., in various formats such as Microsoft Word files, PowerPoint presentations, etc. LearnITy makes it possible to make use of any existing source of content.
- It has been developed to work on any platform that supports Java.
- LearnITy has a much lower cost of ownership compared to other products.

A demo of the tool can be requested at: enq@aunwesha.com

More about LearnITy can be available at: http://www.aunwesha.com/

MORE USAGE OF VIL/WEB

- With powerful computer in the backend, it is possible to implement realistic and full-scale simulation.
- VIL environment provides a first-hand immersion experience for the students, which is otherwise impossible to provide in a typical classroom environment.
- VIL is fully automated.
- It saves teachers the tedious task to administer a complex class room culture.
- It inherits all advantages of the WEB architecture.
- It is anytime and anywhere, allowing students to be free from the time schedule and geographic constraints.
- It is interactive and multimedia, allowing students to visualize the results of their decision and strategies.
- Less cost of administration, infrastructure can be possible only through VIL.
- It enhances students' real-life problem-solving skills.
- VIL, being a WEB-based system, can benefit a large number of students, local and international, at the same time.
- It is user-friendly for users to operate.
- To help users to visualize, with the help of advanced computer graphics and multimedia techniques, the possibly complex state.

USEFUL AREAS

- **Virtual laboratory:** It is cost effective and flexible. It does not require instruments and there is no need for laboratory technicians. Problems of varying degree and complexity can be easily modeled and simulated using virtual instruments/laboratory concept. It is suitable for addressing student and faculty needs at a distance and as a result, more and more institutions are adding virtual laboratories to their curriculum.
- **Complex evolving systems:** It can be applied in subjects that involve complex evolving systems or organizations, such as
  - Ecosystems in biology,
  - City development in human geography,
  - Economics,

- Political sciences, etc.
- Financial markets in economics,
- Business organizations in management science, and so on.
- **Application domains:** The application domains of VIL include
  - Physical sciences,
  - Sociological sciences, and
  - Management sciences, etc.
- **Geography and Economics:** The students compete by achieving the best sustainable development of industry and environment, and at the same time, enrich their subject knowledge in geography and economics.
- **Environment Protection:**
  - Create a global concern of man-land-environment.
  - Provide a framework for integrating development and conservation.
  - Conserve the Earth's vitality and diversity.
  - Minimize the depletion on non-renewable resources.
  - Improve the quality of human life.
  - Enable communities to care for their environment.

DIFFERENT TOOLS AND TECHNOLOGY

- **On-line Learning:** Online education is that you can get an education according to your own schedule and can do it from the comfort of your own home. As technology progresses and the world becomes more reliant upon Internet functions, online learning has gained popularity and functionality. Online classes are offered by institutions ranging from major universities to junior and community colleges. You can get your AA, certification, and even pursue a doctoral degree without having to step foot into a classroom. Even some high schools offer online courses in certain situations. The flexibility of online learning is one of its greatest benefits. Most courses are specifically created in a manner that allows students to complete work at their own pace and convenience, whenever they have enough time to spare.

- **Home Study Courses:** There are so many home study courses are available on the Internet that can help the people to increase their jobs skills and earn a certificate of a degree, there are many opportunities that can simply help you become a more well-rounded person. This is a low-hanging fruit for any Adult to Succeed.

- **On-line Classes:** Online classes work the way you want them to work. By offering degree programs online, universities allow students to dictate their own work schedule within a given set of parameters. Additionally, you don't attend classes in a regular manner, but make your presence known to your instructor and fellow classmates by logging in to the system. Your syllabus and relevant study material are often distributed online, right to your computer, and exams are taken by logging in, filling out the test, and submitting it electronically. The benefits of online technology also allow for video presentations from instructors and live, interactive chatting with others in the program.

- **Adult Education courses:** This particular type of studying is designed with mature persons in mind, which is often extremely appealing to those who have already gained certification through higher learning institutions. While these programs are well-suited to those who have already obtained degrees from colleges, they are also made available to adults who may have developmental disabilities or who can only comprehend at a middle school grade level or lower. Whatever your particular education needs may be; the benefits of earning certification through adult learning programs are plenty.

- **Distance learning Courses:** Distance learning courses are designed to help busy individuals master the skills and education they need without having the restrictions of a traditional class schedule. This type of learning program can almost always be completed from the comfort of your own home and you can complete the course work whenever your schedule allows it. For working professionals, this can make the difference between earning their degree and never being able get a higher education.

- **Distance learning Programs:** Distance learning provides students with educational opportunities that are not readily available to them otherwise. The education received from an online school is just as good, and sometimes better, than one received in a classroom.

ADVANTAGES

- Helping students to learn from (near) real-life experience.
- It is a supplementing classroom teaching.
- Students learn by acting.
- It provides stimuli for learning.
- It gave problem-solving experience for the students.
- Students as decision-makers using information of the current state of the virtual world and observing the outcome as a result of their decisions.
- Students should learn to analyse the problem situation, devise the problem solving strategies, solve the problems and evaluate the consequences.

- Through VIL they gain high-order abilities required in this new era.
- VIL should be facilitated by the provision of real-life experience so as to bridge the gap between classroom learning and real-life experiences.
- Through VIL students should learn in a simulated situation similar to the real ones.
- It is more efficient and economical than traditional learning or 't-learning'.
- It enables the creation of simulated situations for students to explore as well as the communication convenience for students to interact.
- It is an ideal venue for students to construct their knowledge.
- Students learn by acting as decision-makers using information of the current state of the virtual world and observing the outcome as a result of their decisions and those of other participants combined.
- VIL is bringing hope to millions who had abandoned the dream of continuing education due to paucity of time and money.
- It makes learning much more easily as one need not be physically present in the classrooms all the time.
- It has in fact offered a whole new methodology of teaching and learning that is gaining ground very rapidly.
- Most institutes across the globe have today started their online education branches.
- Corporate houses today are utilizing the various e-learning tools to train their employees.
- Digital learning has covered the developments related to e-learning extensively.
- It enhances students' real-life problem-solving skills.
- VIL, being a WEB-based system, can benefit a large number of students, local and international, at the same time.

CONCLUSION

The interactive white boards are increasingly becoming common in the school classrooms, popularity of online courses are helping the countries in improving access and quality of education. Application of technology in the mode of imparting education is thus not only helping a lot in bridging the rural urban divide but also in improving the quality of life. So, VIL has in fact offered a whole new methodology of teaching and learning that is gaining ground very rapidly. Most institutes across the globe have therefore today started their online education branches. Even corporate houses today are utilizing the various e-learning tools to train their employees. Digital learning has covered the developments related to e-learning extensively.

REFERENCES

Akyalcin, J. (1997). *Constructivism: An epistemological journey from Piaget to Papert*. Retrieved from http://www.kilvington.schnet.edu.au/construct.htm

Bloom, B. S. (1981). *All our children learning: a primer for parents, teachers, and other educators*. New York, NY: McGraw-Hill.

Brown, J. S., Collins, A., & Duguid, S. (1989). Situated cognition and the culture of learning. *Educational Researcher, 18*(1), 32–42.

Hong Kong Education and Manpower Bureau. (1998). *Information technology for learning in a new era: Five-year strategy 1998-99 to 2002-03*.

Kiesler, J., & McGuire, H. (1987). Aspects of computer-mediated communication. *International Psychologist, 32*(10), 45–67.

Lave, J. (1988). *Cognition in practice: Mind, mathematics, and culture in everyday life*. Cambridge, UK: Cambridge University Press. doi:10.1017/CBO9780511609268

Lave, J., & Wenger, E. (1990). *Situated learning: Legitimate peripheral participation*. Cambridge, UK: Cambridge University Press.

Parker, A. (1997). A distance education how-to manual: Recommendations from the field. *Educational Technology Review, 8*, 7–10.

Parker, A. (1999). Interaction in distance education: The critical conversation. *Educational Technology Review, 12*, 13–17.

KEY TERMS AND DEFINITIONS

21st Century Skills: Communication skills, interpersonal skills, computer skills, etc.

E-Learning: Electronic learning.

Multi-User/Multi-Team: At a time lots of students are access to learn.

No Geographic Constraints: There are no physical boundaries to learn, i.e., the same time national and international student can also log in the site.

Situational Learning: According to the situation/incidents they should learn.

VIL: Virtual and Interactive Learning

Web Architecture: Internet based design.

Web-Based System: Through internet student should learn.

APPENDIX

Case Study 1

Virtual Advisor-Interactive

- **Client Background:** Virtual Advisor is a developer of e-learning content used by the financial, healthcare, and educational industries to educate about various processes, services, and products. Through e-learning, education is more accessible and distributable to a wide audience speaking different languages in different parts of the world.
- **Challenges:** Virtual Advisor had the innovative content and concepts for the interactive features of an e-learning platform, but lacked the technical skill to develop such a platform. With a strong belief in the power of knowledge and the benefits of e-learning, Virtual Advisor sought a partner with a technology solutions background that would be able to develop an interactive Flash teaching tool for a large financial organization. Additionally, the solution would have to be accessible to a global audience.
- **Solutions:** Hearing of AllianceTek's reputation for working closely with clients to discover and develop effective IT solutions, Virtual Advisor sought out the AllianceTek team to help create their e-learning platform. AllianceTek listened closely to what Virtual Advisor wanted to achieve with their platform and how it would be used to educate financial institutions in workshops. AllianceTek's solution manifested as a robust flash-based presentation platform with interactive tutorials for entrepreneurs. The platform was created using Flash, HTML, and XML technologies that included interactive features and multi-user communication systems. Usability was a high priority in the design. For this reason, AllianceTek created an interactive menu bar that allows users to easily navigate to any part of the tutorial, pause a lesson, and manage sound options. Users can upload and download forms and worksheets and access a glossary of terms.
- **Result:** As a result, business lessons were developed for the e-learning platform and were available in three different languages. The e-learning presentations contained many interactive elements but remained easy for the end user to manipulate. The use of multimedia tools, such as images, video, sound, and interactive features, made the platform a highly effective learning tool. Virtual Advisor's clients found the platform very helpful in educating their staff on a variety of important subjects. With the first iteration of the platform a success, Virtual Advisors went on to use AllianceTek's e-learning platform in the healthcare industry.

Source: www.alliancetek.com/cs-virtual-advisor-interactive.html

Case Study 2

NetSpeed Interactive Custom Solutions

Spheris

Remote Workers' Performance Dramatically Improves Through Interactive Online Learning Program

- **Situation:** Since 1993, Spheris has been a leading global provider of clinical documentation and medical transcription technology to more than 500 health systems, hospitals and group practices throughout the US. With a remote workforce of more than 2800 medical transcriptionists performing this tough but critical job, Spheris operation supervisors needed a program-based learning solution that would target specific skill competencies to insure uniformity and ongoing production of high quality material.

- **Solution:** After identifying a set of competencies they wanted to achieve, Spheris looked to NetSpeed Learning Solutions to provide a leadership training program that could be offered in a virtual learning environment to a group of remote workers spread out across the country. They also wanted to provide the training through their own company's web conference platform. The two companies worked together in partnership to convert one of NetSpeed Learning Solutions' classroom programs, NetSpeed Leadership, into a customized, interactive supervisory training experience consisting of seven different leadership courses centered on communication skills competencies. The webinar courses are trainer-led, but provide group learning in virtual breakout rooms, which allows remote participants the ability to actively engage, discuss content and practice their skills. According to Chuck Roberts, Director of Training and Organizational Development, Spheris chose NetSpeed because their leadership skills training content addressed the most critical areas of supervisory skills competency, and the material could be quickly and easily adapted into an online format.

- **Result:** Today Spheris sees evidence of the webinar leadership training program's success in multiple areas across their business. "We've enjoyed considerable cost savings with this program by eliminating travel expenses for training, but there are other benefits as well. The program has made a big impact on our supervisor retention rates, and we can actually see folks putting the skills of being more clear and direct into place. The program has improved overall work performance and helped us provide a better product," says Roberts. The instructional design resources NetSpeed brought to the table helped simplify development of the program, according to Roberts. "Their ability to work with us, lead us through the process, and adjust content so that it maps to our goals has made NetSpeed Learning Solutions a great choice for us."

Source: http://www.netspeedlearning.com/interactive/casestudies/

Case Study 3

Motor Vehicle Sales Authority of British Columbia

Interactive Learning Platform Creates a Successful, Engaging Learning Experience for Students Across a Vast Geographical Area

- **Situation:** The Motor Vehicle Sales Authority of British Columbia (MVSA) is an independent agency created by the Canadian government to ensure that business practices and consumer protection laws are properly adhered to by more than 1,700 motor dealers and more than 7,000 sales professionals throughout British Columbia. As part of their mission, the MVSA provides mandatory certification courses for personnel who directly deal with consumers in retail vehicle sales. When their ability to provide training was hampered by logistics, travel costs, and access to remote, hard-to-reach areas, MVSA turned to NetSpeed Learning Solutions to develop a program that would provide timely, cost-effective and accessible training across a vast geographic area.

- **Solution:** Meet NetSpeed Fast Tracks, NetSpeed Learning Solutions' online, customizable interactive learning platform that leverages emerging technologies in social media such as blogs, videos, interviews, and podcasts - complete with avatars - to help educate, train, and communicate with participants, while fostering a collaborative learning experience. With NetSpeed Fast Tracks, organizations can use a turnkey, state-of-the-art integrated learning platform to deliver their own customized learning content, as well as offer employees a wide variety of already developed customizable content on career development, workplace effectiveness, coaching and communication strategies, and management and leadership practices to help managers, supervisors and individual contributors become more successful in the workplace.

With NetSpeed Learning Solutions' expertise, the MVSA was able to convert their popular, highly successful 2-day classroom certification course into a dynamic, online, blended training program that incorporates preliminary self-study online sessions followed by a series of five 2-hour facilitated webinar "virtual classroom" sessions. "What we really like about NetSpeed Fast Tracks is that we're able to use the built-in administrator tools to go in and see how people are doing. It gives us the chance to reach out and encourage participants to get going and stay involved, which has kept our drop-out rate extremely low. Because this program requires active participation, we feel like our students are getting as much, if not more learning than they had been getting in the face-to-face classroom," says Doug Longhurst, Director of Consumer Services and Professional Development. The program successfully combines the use of traditional and cutting-edge internet 2.0 learning tools to meet all the needs of their multi-generational audience.

First, the MVSA workbook is mailed to students in advance of the start date. Next, the MSVA administrator sends each student an invitation to register and start their self-study sessions on NetSpeed Fast Tracks. After each self-study session is completed, a facilitated webinar solidifies the learning and reviews all the important points. Students document key information in their workbooks, which later serve as a resource for an open book test that is given at the end of training. "With 25% of their grade dedicated to classroom participation, our students are very aware that their participation and attendance is important. It's a different experience than the face-to-face classroom. At first we were skeptical about how well it would be received, but we see a lot of relationship-building as people chat and banter on particular topics. The online environment levels the playing field, too. Shy people are no longer hesitant to participate, and it eliminates the 'blowhard' syndrome. People like it, and they really have fun with it," says Longhurst.

- **Result:** While the MVSA program is only in its second pilot, it has already proved a resounding success. "We had a 100% pass rate on the first group of students tested under this program," says Longhurst. "Not only did our students succeed, but the online learning environment has established a relationship between us and our students that we know will be helpful in the long run. The communication door remains open, it's a natural channel, and it will help us do a better job of performing our public responsibility and serving as a trusted and valuable resource for them in the future." Longhurst also reports that the expense, travel and weather challenges that previously restricted their ability to give classes at remote locations have simply evaporated. "The virtual classroom is a perfect solution for a certain number of our provinces. Working with NetSpeed Learning Solutions made our transition easy," adds Longhurst.

Source: http://www.netspeedlearning.com/interactive/casestudies/

Case Study 4

Florida Virtual School

Connoisseurs of Virtual Learning Find NetSpeed Leadership Webinars a Perfect Fit

- **Situation:** The Florida Virtual School (FLVS) is a publicly funded K-12 online learning school and winner of numerous national and international educational awards. FLVS also trains teachers, administrators, school districts, and states how to deliver a sound, accountable, and successful on-line learning experience. When this industry leader decided to offer a more cohesive, formalized leadership and management program to their 1000+ employees, they wanted a program that could deliver the highest level of excellence and a learning experience that would keep these connoisseurs of online education interested and engaged.
- **Solution:** The Florida Virtual School chose the NetSpeed Learning Solutions Leadership Webinar Series, which offers a broad range of leadership skills training content, with dynamic presentation and a complete follow-up package. Using 90-minute leadership webinars and web-based reinforcement tools, FLVS participants experience maximum learning without the need for face-to-face contact. Online tools provided with the program give FLVS the ability to measure training impact. "NetSpeed Learning Solutions offered us the kind of online leadership training experience we only hoped to find," says Raven McElman, Training and Development Specialist. "They have a deep knowledge of the subject matter, with talented webinar presentations, and truly thoughtful follow-up questions to help with retention. It's an intelligent, creative series that gets people involved, learning and applying their own experience."
- **Result:** According to McElman, it's been a challenge finding an online learning program that will keep her caliber of online experts interested. "My people are always multi-tasking, and they're very savvy. If they're not listening because the content isn't up to par, or it's just a lecture, they're not going to learn. With NetSpeed, I have found an engaging, well-integrated leadership webinar training program with good follow up. The folks at NetSpeed Learning Solutions are instructional design experts when it comes to virtual learning," says McElman.

Source: http://www.netspeedlearning.com/interactive/casestudies/

Chapter 4
Principles of Concurrent E-Learning Design

Knut Arne Strand
Sør-Trøndelag University College, Norway

Arvid Staupe
Norwegian University of Science and Technology, Norway

Tor Atle Hjeltnes
Sør-Trøndelag University College, Norway

ABSTRACT

Instructional design is a process that in many cases requires multidisciplinary collaboration among several stakeholders. Domain experts, pedagogues, technical experts, economists, administrative personnel, customer representatives, instructors, and learners may have very different preferences, and sometimes it is a great challenge to coordinate them all. In this chapter, the authors present the principles of concurrent e-learning design. Concurrent e-learning design is a novel approach to computer supported and cooperative instructional design where several stakeholders actively participate in the design process. The results from a concurrent e-learning design project can typically be a comprehensive design document containing details regarding how higher education e-learning courses should be developed and delivered. The authors have worked to codify this methodological approach for several years and conducted a qualitative analysis of data collected during this period. This analysis has yielded sixteen principles, which are grouped into five categories and presented in this chapter. The chapter describes each principle in detail, discusses whether ERP systems can be of assistance in the instructional design process, and outlines a plan for testing ERP systems in connection with the concurrent e-learning design approach.

DOI: 10.4018/978-1-4666-2193-0.ch004

INTRODUCTION

Educational institutions must increasingly deal with changes, adapt to new competitive situations, and deliver a range of services that together make up complete educational offers for the students. Today, these services are largely based on Information and Communications Technology (ICT), and they are important contributions to the total business of the institutions. E-learning deliveries constitute an important part of this business, since e-learning comprises all forms of ICT supported learning and teaching and varies from e-learning courses for formal higher education to self-paced e-learning systems for informal training.

Corporate institutions create value through activities such as trading, logistics, financial services, or human resource services, and Enterprise Resource Planning (ERP) systems provide important support for these processes, since they are utilized to manage the internal and external resources needed to run the business. Educational institutions also need to design and manage their core resources (e.g. academic courses) so that they satisfy the expectations of students and other stakeholders. The reason for this book is the great potential inherent in educational institutions' use of ERP systems to support design, development, and delivery of academic resource and educational deliveries. The objective is to provide applications, methodologies, and framework suggestions for the use of ERP systems within the education sector. This approach intends to help improve the effectiveness and efficiency of learning and teaching processes and enhance the service level for all stakeholders.

The main aim of this chapter is to present the concurrent e-learning design method (i.e. the sixteen principles of concurrent e-learning design), and to discuss possible links between this method and the use of ERP systems in the education sector. Concurrent e-learning design is as a methodological approach where the objective is to produce holistic designs for e-learning deliveries, i.e. to produce comprehensive descriptions regarding arrangement of ICT-based resources and procedures to promote learning. Such designs must cover aspects such as learning outcomes (what to learn), learning activities (how to learn), technical production and delivery (different learning environments that should be supported), and financial constraints (how to finance the development and delivery). The concurrent e-learning design approach can be used to design various forms of e-learning deliveries which in all cases consist of a complicated design process that involves several stakeholders, requires a multidisciplinary focus, and necessitates information access that can largely be obtained through ERP systems.

The concurrent e-learning design method was initially developed to achieve effective and efficient design and development of e-learning for corporate clients, i.e. to manage and coordinate multidisciplinary requirements so that corporate clients, educational institutions, and other stakeholders could agree upon complex requirements and arrive at mutually agreed solutions. This study is largely based on data from two specific projects where a higher education institution developed formal education for bachelor level students, i.e. instructional design of approved academic courses giving credits. One of these courses was based on an internal initiative and intended for students on campus, while the other was based on initiatives from a corporate client. Consequently, the second e-learning course had to be designed for blended learning (i.e. a mix of different learning environments) and take into account a certain degree of business customization.

In this chapter we present the main principles for successful concurrent e-learning design, which typically can be used when formal e-learning courses are developed at higher education institutions. We believe these principles are useful and should be considered when instructional design activities are to be performed, even if a total concurrent e-learning design approach is not adopted. Involving the client in an interaction with design team experts from different disciplines allows for the design of holistic solutions that take everyone's needs into account. Furthermore, we discuss how the use of ERP systems can help improve the concurrent e-learning design process. To do so, we point out common objectives and discuss how ERP can be used in the concurrent e-learning design process when new academic resources are being developed.

Following this introduction is a background section in which we explain how our research in connection to the concurrent e-learning design method has been conducted and how we have achieved the results presented in this chapter. Next, we present the principles of concurrent e-learning design – this study's main contribution. The next section is a discussion of the usefulness of ERP systems in this context. The chapter closes with a conclusion section summarizing the overall coverage of the chapter and presenting some evaluation-related matters.

BACKGROUND

Design, development and delivery of e-learning can be a huge and complicated practice that undergoes constant change. Several actors with different approaches are working to make improvements in selected parts of this area. Some of the challenges are more general and universal while others are more specific and dependent on the e-learning delivery context. It is typically challenging to define the learning outcomes, identify the relevant subject content, and select appropriate assessment practices in addition to identifying learning activities, methods and teaching strategies that fit the purpose. Furthermore, it might be challenging to select and utilize appropriate technological solutions for development and delivery of the educational environment that also satisfy administrative needs, at the same time limiting spending on the total e-learning delivery within a prudent budget.

These challenges are likely to be strengthened if the e-learning delivery is customized for corporate clients, and this applies independent of whether the client wants formal e-learning courses providing credits or self-paced e-learning systems intended for informal training. In both of these cases the client would like to ensure that the education is in accordance with formal and defined requirements while it also satisfies general and more informal expectations, e.g. suitable technical delivery, sustainable economy, adapted academic content, and a pedagogy that suits the target audience. Satisfied clients are always essential for renewed confidence and the long-term cooperation needed to grow the business and involvement in the design phase is essential to achieve this.

The process that aims to produce new e-learning deliveries is often called instructional design. A number of approaches exist: "It will be a mistake to think that there is a single best model of instructional design. In actuality, there are as many models as there are designers and design situations" (Gagné, Wager, Golas, & Keller, 2005, p. 2). The ADDIE model of instructional design is considered fundamental and generic and the five phases (Analysis, Design, Development, Implementation and Evaluation) deal with topics that we find in several other models.

Challenges in the design of customized e-learning for corporate clients and the methodological approach employed to deal with those challenges have formed the background of the study presented in this chapter. We developed, implemented, and gained some experience in using a new method called concurrent e-learning design. Concurrent e-learning design can be regarded as a situated model (Gagné et al., 2005, p. 39-40) that mainly focuses the first phases of the ADDIE model. It is based on models for instructional design (Kirschner, van Merrienboer, Sloep, & Carr, 2002; Peterson, 2003; Visscher-Voerman & Gustafson, 2004), with a special focus on models where the forthcoming e-learning delivery is represented in distinct models that are developed in parallel (Paquette, 2004; Davidson-Shivers & Rasmussen, 2006). In addition we utilize principles from the field of industrial concurrent design. This means that the design team meets for cooperative sessions in a specially designed facility where appropriate computer tools are utilized and work is conducted by a facilitator. The concept of concurrent design developed as an early phase of the concurrent engineering process; it was originally developed to solve complex and multidisciplinary issues within the space technology institutions (Lonchamp, 2000; Bandecchi, Melton, Gardini, & Ongaro, 2000; Osburg & Mavris, 2005).

The concurrent e-learning design approach includes the client in the design process, so that we are able to fully elicit the client's needs. Furthermore, it is desirable to deal with as many requirements as possible early on in the design phase, in order to avoid major surprises later in the project. This means that stakeholders such as domain experts, pedagogues, technical experts, economists, administrative personnel, customer representatives, instructors and learners should cooperate in the design phase. This multidisciplinary cooperation should contribute to the development of holistic instructional designs that are appealing and cover all relevant requirements. The use of concurrent design should help us do this in a time and cost effective way while simultaneously producing high quality results. This study grew out of an examination of e-learning customized for corporate clients, and we have discovered that many of the challenges faced in this context also are relevant to higher education and educational programs in general. This is because competitive formal education depends on the interplay between factors such as the following:

1. Academic content and learning outcomes;
2. Pedagogy and learning activities;
3. Various technologies that support a range of activities relevant for learning, teaching,

coaching, assessments, administration, and evaluations;
4. Flexibility so that students have the possibility to participate anytime and at any place; and
5. A sustainable business model that contributes to attractiveness for all stakeholders.

We have found that these factors should be considered, although some factors (e.g. technical delivery platform or economic constraints) to some extent are given in advance when higher education institutions design internal courses.

Materials from a Method Engineering Project

The concurrent e-learning design method was developed as a collaborative project between several Norwegian institutions: the Faculty of Informatics and E-Learning at Sør-Trøndelag University College; the Department of Computer and Information Science at Norwegian University of Science and Technology; the research foundation TISIP; and five internationally-operating companies within the telecommunications industry. The project received external funding from the Norway Opening Universities from spring 2009 till spring 2011.

At the moment the method is undergoing further development in an EU-project that belongs to the Leonardo da Vinci Transfer of Innovation program. A part of the Lifelong Learning Programme, the project involves 19 participants from 6 different European countries.

The principles of concurrent e-learning design presented in this chapter constitute a method engineering project: "Method engineering is the engineering discipline to design, construct and adapt methods, techniques and tools for the development of information systems" (Brinkkemper, 1996, p. 276). We consider the concurrent e-learning design method a situational method in which it is essential to adapt the method to the situation of the project at hand. We must consider the goals of the project we are undertaking, and what results we want to produce, each time the method is used for a new project. Furthermore, it is reasonable to note that the result we wish to achieve is usually not an information system in the traditional sense, but rather a design for an e-learning delivery, offering guidelines for learning outcomes, subject content, assessment practices, learning activities, teaching strategies, technological choices for development and delivery, administrative needs, economic constraints, intellectual property right issues, etc.

Reeves, Herrington, & Oliver (2005) offer the concept of design research, a research methodology similar to the one used in the method engineering project we are referring to in this chapter. We claim to employ design research because we have a project that:

1. Develops over several years (the project started three years ago and is still ongoing),
2. Includes cooperation between a number of people (six actors participated in the method engineering project and a dozen were involved in testing and evaluation),
3. Utilizes various research methods (e.g. literature review, design science, action research, and qualitative data analysis) that are suitable to answer the research questions we face as the project progresses,
4. Reveals design principles that can be further developed and used in other contexts (the main focus of this chapter), and
5. Maintains a dissemination agenda.

First, the need for a new method for design of e-learning deliveries was uncovered in a research project where two different e-learning deliveries were studied, i.e. the need for the method was uncovered through qualitative analysis of data from e-learning projects that have been implemented at the higher education institution we belong to (Strand & Hjeltnes, 2009). Then, the concurrent

e-learning design method was developed and documented as part of a project where the design science research method was used (Strand & Staupe, 2010a). Next, the method was tested, evaluated, and improved as part of an action research project in which the method was put into practice (Strand & Staupe, 2010b).

In this chapter we draw on the research data from several projects and use these data to identify and describe the main principles of concurrent e-learning design. We aim to answer the following main research questions:

- **RQ1:** What are the most important principles of concurrent e-learning design?
- **RQ2:** How might designers benefit from these principles?

In order to answer these research questions we have employed a qualitative data analysis and coding of qualitative data in different formats (e.g. video clips, audio recordings, surveys, interview notes, project documents, training materials, design documents, and fully developed courses).

Since we had quite a lot of data in different formats we decided to handle our data using the NVivo 9[1]. Our approach to the coding process was inspired by Bazeley (2007) and Saldaña (2009), in that we carried out iterative coding in three cycles. In the first cycle we used descriptive initial coding to name the ideas in the data and represented them as nodes in NVivo 9. We identified a total of 74 nodes; each node refers to ideas and works to help us aggregate extensive and varied raw data into a brief summary format. In the second cycle we did axial coding to extend the analytic work from the first cycle. During this process all the nodes from the first cycle were categorized in relation to what each node actually concerned. After completing this cycle we had five categories (i.e. adaption to the surroundings, stakeholders, activities, infrastructure, and results) containing their respective nodes. In the third cycle the nodes were reduced to a total of sixteen principles (i.e.

our response to RQ1), and we used data associated with the different nodes to describe each of the sixteen principles (i.e. our response to RQ2).

Figure 1 shows a screen dump from this project where NVivo 9 is used for qualitative data analysis and coding. In this case the node Preparations before the session(s) is selected in the List View, while the Norwegian text in the Detail View below, which is resulting from a survey carried out during the project, states the importance of preparing participants for cooperation sessions (in this context and through this chapter, the term cooperation is used to describe activities that consist of communication, collaboration, and coordination). The principle of training and preparation and the corresponding category (Activities) was later identified based on this node. This example shows that training and preparation is one of several key activities in concurrent e-learning design and it is intended to explain how we worked to answer the main research questions, i.e. how we identified, categorized, and described the principles of concurrent e-learning design.

To summarize this section about research materials and methods, we have conducted a qualitative analysis of data collected over several years in order to identify the principal characteristics of concurrent e-learning design. These principles are grouped into five categories; details of each principle are presented in the next section. Following the enumeration of principles is a discussion of whether ERP systems can be of assistance in the design process – we regard decision support as a crucial potential benefit in this context.

THE PRINCIPLES OF CONCURRENT E-LEARNING DESIGN

This section is regarded as this study's main contribution in which the resulting principles of concurrent e-learning design are presented. In a slightly simplified way we can say that concurrent e-learning design is a method to be used when several stakeholders representing different com-

Figure 1. Use of NVivo 9 for qualitative data analysis and coding

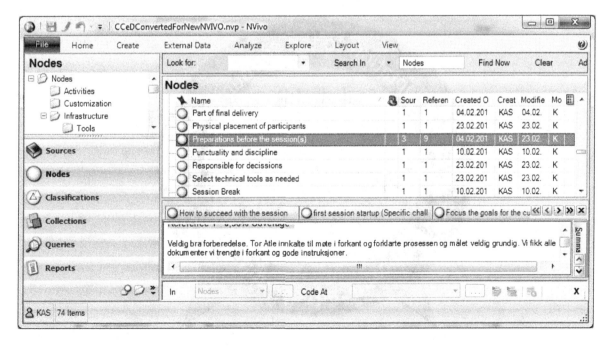

petencies meet to design e-learning courses. This section serves as a guide for the implementation of concurrent e-learning design projects (in this context and through this chapter, the term project includes all the work that must be performed when the method is used to design a specific e-learning course).

We have identified several principles in relation to concurrent e-learning design; in our attempt to present these principles appropriately, we have chosen to categorize them. Figure 2 shows these categories as a wheel. We have placed the principles of adaption to surroundings, which refers to the things that must be considered for every new project, on the outermost level of this wheel. This is where the method meets the environment and where customizations have to be performed. On the next level of the wheel within the external surroundings come stakeholders, activities, and infrastructure, which constitute the framework in concurrent e-learning design. The integration and

interaction of these elements and their adaptation to the external surroundings forms the foundation that will produce the results of the design process. In the center of this wheel we have the results, meaning that results (project deliverables) lie at the core of concurrent e-learning design. Several principles are connected to the results that the projects are meant to produce.

In the remainder of this section, we present sixteen principles of concurrent e-learning design. First, we present separate sections for each category of principles, offering discussion in turn of each principle within the larger category. Finally, all principles are presented in a summarized review.

Adaption to the Surroundings

The process of adapting to surroundings is a method calibration process performed in the initial phase of the project. These activities must occur in

Figure 2. The wheel of principle categories for concurrent e-learning design

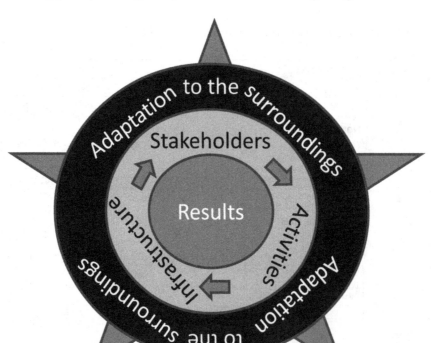

order to adjust the methodological approach to the project in question. In this context it is important to decide what to produce (expected results), who should be involved (relevant stakeholders), how and when things should happen (project activities), and what facilities are needed (infrastructure and tools).

The concurrent e-learning design method can be regarded as a prescriptive framework. We offer concrete examples describing how projects can be implemented. For example, we met with success through the implementation of five cooperation sessions and four defined focus areas. The five different cooperation sessions were:

1. Situation analysis,
2. Possibilities study,
3. Solution selection,
4. Solution design, and
5. Design completion and implementation planning.

The four defined focus areas were:

1. Pedagogical strategies and learning activities, i.e. how to learn,
2. Knowledge and learning outcomes, i.e. what to learn,
3. Technical delivery, i.e. how to conduct distributed communication and dissemination, and
4. Business matters, i.e. which business related needs, economic conditions, and administrative needs must be addressed.

Figure 3 illustrates the default implementation of five cooperation sessions and four defined focus areas. Furthermore, it explains the final result and deliverable (i.e. the design document for the upcoming e-learning course) as an integrated solution that is composed of four different models and developed through five cooperation sessions. Thus, the final deliverable will offer both a holistic perspective and a detailed perspective in relation

to the respective sub-models. We believe this approach can be a good starting point for new projects in which designs for e-learning deliveries are to be developed. At the same time we anticipate the need to make adjustments within each individual project, which allows us to deviate slightly from this approach.

A new project is always something unique that has not been conducted before, a truism that holds for projects that aim to develop new e-learning designs. Projects that are candidates to use the concurrent e-learning design method may be very different, and in size varying from a handful of participants to a dozen or more. Therefore it is important to adapt the method to the current project and surroundings. We present the four different principles connected to the process of adapting to surroundings below.

The Principle of Defining Project Deliverables

The production of project results and deliverables is always very important since these are the very reason the project exist. Results and deliverables are the end products of the design process and they should typically last for a long time after the project is finished. Two kinds of results are produced in concurrent e-learning design: intermediate results, which should typically be available following a cooperation session (different results for different sessions); and final results or actual project deliverables, which will be available at the end of the project. The important thing in this context is to determine the project deliverables and their composition, i.e. to decide what to produce in the particular project we now face. The concurrent e-learning design method provides recommendations in relation to both intermediate results (e.g. a situation analysis document or a study of possibilities document) and final results (e.g. a design document that is composed of an instructional model, a knowledge model, a technical delivery model, and a business model).

Figure 3. Five cooperation sessions and four focus areas to produce a comprehensive design document

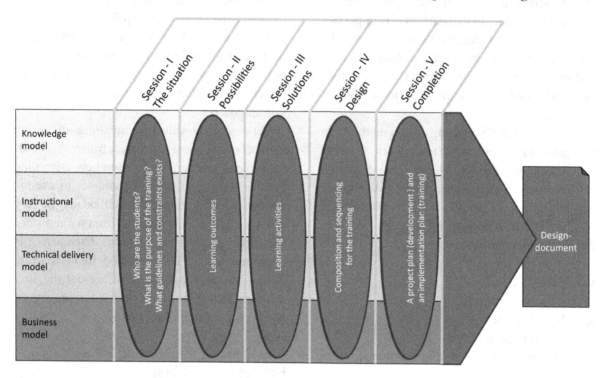

Expected project deliverables can vary significantly between different projects and an initial order that defines the objectives can be very helpful. Our experience shows that it is important to know what the expected project deliverables are, because this creates many constraints in terms of how the project should be organized. More information about project deliverables can be found in the Results section.

The Principle of Defining Participants and Roles

In any project, different participants are needed to fill different roles. Some of these roles contribute most to the articulation work (Schmidt & Simone, 1996), while other roles contribute to the real cooperative work that leads to project deliverables and results. First, we need someone to articulate the work, i.e. a project leader to manage the entire project and a facilitator to facilitate the coopera-

tion sessions. In addition, we need someone to work directly with the project deliverables and results, i.e. a multidisciplinary team where the necessary expertise and decision-making authority are represented, so that stakeholders such as customers, service providers and prospective users can reach comprehensive solutions. It is important to identify what roles are needed and who should fill them as early as possible after the expected project's deliverables and results are described. More information about participants and roles can be found in the Stakeholders section.

The Principle of Defining Activities

The purpose of this principle is to define the expected project process at a general level, i.e. what needs to be done, how this should be performed, and when it will happen. Our recommendation is to produce a plan or outline that would typically list training activities, technical testing requirements related to the equipment to be used, cooperation sessions and focus areas to implement, any activities required between the cooperation sessions, how evaluation will take place, etc.

When working with such a plan, one must also consider how the cooperation between the project participants should take place. Based on the project's final results and deliverables, as well as the themes for the project's cooperation sessions, one should try to put assemble multidisciplinary groups that work together optimally. These groups will typically be responsible for their respective portions of the final deliverables. More information about project activities can be found in the Activities section.

The Principle of Defining the Project Infrastructure

The project infrastructure consists of facilities, technical aids and tools to be used in the project. Concurrent e-learning design projects require, first and foremost, access to a concurrent design facility, i.e. a technically equipped room for cooperation sessions that will serve as a shared workspace and common information space for project resources (Bannon & Bødker, 1997).

As early as possible, one should decide upon the facilities and tools to be used. Once these are in place some customization should be considered in order to appropriately adapt tools to the current project. For example, we have had good experiences with the use of templates that act as guidelines for the design documents to be developed, but these must often be adjusted in relation to the objectives of the current project. This means that the templates for the preparation of the final deliverables should be produced from within the current project.

Once decisions about technical equipment are made and the necessary adjustments are performed, we should test the equipment to be sure it works as intended. In addition, we need

to conduct necessary training for any personnel involved, so they are well prepared when the project work and the cooperation sessions begin. This training is conducted with the objective of describing the kinds of tools available and how they should be used. More information about project infrastructure and tools can be found in the Infrastructure section.

Stakeholders

A primary feature that distinguishes concurrent e-learning design projects from more traditional development projects is the implementation of cooperation sessions where concurrent cooperation (i.e. communication, collaboration, and co-ordination) takes place. It is important to staff the projects so that these sessions can be performed most effectively. These sessions consist of real time multidisciplinary cooperation that requires specific contributions from each participant. Cooperation sessions must be staffed with the necessary stakeholders, e.g. customer representatives, institution staff, service providers, prospective users, different experts and decision makers, in order to ensure comprehensive solutions that are sustainable and viable.

In the remainder of this section concerning project stakeholders, we will first discuss some of the specific roles in more depth. Next, we will discuss the interaction between the different roles that constitute the project team when taken as a whole.

The Principle of Different Roles and Sufficient Authority

A variety of roles are required when we carry out concurrent e-learning design projects; these roles are particularly relevant to the cooperation sessions. In these sessions, we need some roles that contribute to the articulation of the cooperative work, i.e. someone to ensure that the interdependent activities are coordinated, scheduled, aligned, interconnected, integrated, and the like. Furthermore, we need someone who performs the real cooperative work that leads to expected project deliverables. As Schmidt and Simone note, "Cooperative work is constituted by the interdependence of multiple actors who interact through changing the state of a common field of work, whereas articulation work is constituted by the need to restrain the distributed nature of complexly interdependent activities" (1996, p. 158). In the rest of this section, we present some of the most important roles related to concurrent e-learning design:

Project Manager

The project manager is responsible for managing the project from beginning to end; this role resembles traditional project management roles in other project models. It is the project manager's responsibility to implement the project within specified constraints and to perform project planning, management, and monitoring during the project life cycle. The project manager should for instance ensure:

- That an appropriate degree of organization exists,
- That processes are properly followed,
- That cooperation sessions are planned and implemented,
- That a good working environment is maintained, and
- That appropriate aids and tools are available and used properly.
- In order to fulfill these responsibilities, the project manager is granted the authority:
- To manage allocated resources,
- To change the project's organization if needed,
- To organize project meetings and cooperation sessions,
- To negotiate with customer representatives, service providers and other stakeholders, and
- To approve or reject project deliverables.

The project manager is central to the articulation of the cooperative work throughout the project life cycle, but not always particularly active in the cooperation sessions, since the management of these sessions are the facilitator's responsibility.

Facilitator

The facilitator is perhaps the most important role in concurrent e-learning design. This role is responsible for facilitating the cooperation sessions, which normally take place in a concurrent design facility. This means it is a dedicated role that can be compared to a conductor, who ensures that the interactions between the participants are running smoothly. The facilitator helps coordinate cooperation so that the transitions between individual and collective work are natural and appropriate. Facilitators should have expertise in relation to all aspects of the products under development, in the case at hand a design document for an upcoming e-learning course that deals with challenges regarding learning outcomes, learning activities, technical delivery, and business matters. Because of the requirement for multidisciplinary skills in this position, often senior group members occupy this role. Even these individuals may require a lengthy period of practice before they become effective facilitators.

A facilitator must exercise sufficient authority, but should not be too dominant or override the experts. Furthermore, facilitators must be good listeners who sense what is going on, while they also must be very well prepared, so that they understand the tasks and issues they are faced with during the cooperation sessions. The responsibility of the facilitator is:

- To plan, implement and evaluate the cooperation sessions,
- To contribute to relevant information exchange between all session participants so that the objectives of each session are achieved to the greatest extent possible, and
- To contribute to decisions related to multidisciplinary issues that require clarification before the process can proceed.

The facilitator has the authority to organize and lead the cooperation sessions, meaning that the project manager leaves the control of the cooperation sessions to the facilitator.

Session Secretary

The session secretary is an optional role but it can be very useful, especially for the facilitator. This is a person who acts as an assistant to the facilitator in the cooperation sessions. The session secretary may contribute to the technical implementation of the cooperation sessions (e.g. to switch between different screens and workstations so that all participants can see certain aspects of a sub-model under development, and take these into account for other related sub-models). Furthermore, they can perform administrative tasks such as maintaining a decision list of any decisions made during the session or maintaining an action list. A secretary typically accepts responsibility for technical implementation of cooperation session, while also relieving the facilitator of certain administrative tasks faced during the sessions.

Various Experts

Concurrent e-learning design projects must be staffed by various experts who can help to perform the project activities in order to produce the project's deliverables, i.e. to design new e-learning courses or carry out maintenance and updating of existing courses. The purpose of the cooperation sessions is to conduct multidisciplinary cooperation in real time in order to produce comprehensive solutions that take the various experts' needs into account. A variety of experts are required, depending on the requirements that the project deliverables dictate and the areas of expertise that are involved in the production of those deliverables. When we aim to produce comprehensive design documents for new e-learning courses, our default proposal is to use four expert areas, with each responsible for their respective sub-models. These areas have been:

- Instructional designer(s) responsible for pedagogical strategies, learning activities, etc. that will be documented in the Instructional Model,
- Subject matter expert(s) responsible for the development of the Knowledge Model that contains information about competencies to be developed, learning needs, and subject content,
- Technical delivery expert(s) responsible for documenting in the Technical Delivery Model any technical matters such as the selection of technical platforms, infrastructure, solutions, or tools, and

Business expert(s) who are responsible for taking care of business related issues and administrative needs, documenting these in the Business Model (Strand & Staupe, 2010a).

The different experts must exercise sufficient decision authority and take responsibility for decisions within their relevant subjects. Moreover, the different experts must use mutually understandable language. In this context the model elements, which are exchanged between session participants, serve as boundary objects (Carlile, 2002). I.e. these model elements contribute to information exchange between different expert areas and disciplines.

In summary, we conclude that we need a variety of experts, but the particular need varies depending on the requirements of the project deliverables.

Customer Representatives

Customers can participate with several people in the project according to their requirements and needs. A customer representative is in this context one or several persons that will help ensure that the quality of the e-learning products and services are in accordance with customers' requirements. In concurrent e-learning design projects, customers can typically help with the definition of learning outcomes, learning activities, technical deliveries, and business matters. They will typically be responsible for communicating claims on behalf of the customer. Furthermore, they will participate together with the various domain experts and other participants in the decision-making process and help make decisions. In some cases, the project manager can be a customer representative, i.e. the project manager uses multidisciplinary cooperation sessions to bring out new designs for e-learning products and services.

In the bullet list above, we discussed the most important roles for concurrent e-learning design projects. These roles will vary from project to project – the important thing is to get the interplay between them work properly. This is the theme of the next principle.

The Principle of Multidisciplinary Cooperation

Concurrent e-learning design sessions are, as previously mentioned, real time multidisciplinary cooperation between stakeholders such as the facilitator, the session secretary, various domain experts, the project manager, customer representatives, institution staff, service providers, prospective users, and others. The goal is to achieve fruitful and effective cooperation between all these stakeholders, so that they eventually cohere as a high-performing team that produces comprehensive solutions that are sustainable and viable.

Katzenbach & Smith offer the following insight about teams: "A team is a small number of people with complementary skills who are committed to a common purpose, performance goals, and approach for which they hold themselves mutually accountable" (1993, p. 45). In accordance with this insight, implementing the following considerations will achieve superior team effects:

1. A meaningful purpose that is sufficiently challenging and that everyone can identify with,
2. Specific performance goals that clearly indicate what to achieve and how to measure progress along the way,
3. Commitment to a common approach regarding the means of cooperation required to accomplish the team's purpose and goals,
4. A balanced mix of complementary skills (i.e. technical and functional expertise, problem-solving skills, decision-making skills, and a wide range of interpersonal skills), and
5. Mutual accountability in that each participant holds themselves, both as individuals and as a team, responsible for the team's performance.

Effective cooperation in concurrent e-learning design sessions is also affected by the participants' spatial placement. It is for instance appropriate to place the experts that we know will be cooperating closely at joint desks, while those who will interact more sporadically may sit at separate desks. In addition, the facilitator should be placed centrally to maintain physical contact with all participants during the session. Effective multidisciplinary cooperation does not occur on its own, but if we are aware of the matters mentioned in this principle, we believe there is a greater chance of success. Furthermore, the facilitator's performance is very crucial to the success of the undertaking. Effective communication and coordination are the result of effective facilitation; thus the facilitator may be the critical factor responsible for ensuring successful real time multidisciplinary cooperation between all involved stakeholders.

Activities

In any project it is important to decide upon questions such as what should be done, why this should be done, how it should be done, who should be involved, and when it should happened, i.e. to decide upon the activities. In our model for concurrent e-learning design projects, we have defined and used a process that includes some sub-processes and related activities to be performed. Such processes can typically be divided into:

1. A preparation phase where initial and planning activities are carried out,
2. An execution phase where cooperation session activities are performed, and
3. A conclusion phase where final activities such as summative evaluation and reporting is carried out.

Different concurrent e-learning design projects often have different starting points as they specifically adapt to the surrounding environment. As a result, we believe it can be just as appropriate to focus on activities to be performed in the project at hand, rather than describing a general process that usually consists of a sequence of activities that is repeated each time.

In the following text we present some principles that are closely related to the most central activities in concurrent e-learning design projects.

The Principle of Training and Preparation

Some knowledge and experience is beneficial and training can proceed in several ways to achieve this. On the one hand, the participants need to learn about the methodological approach and the basic principles of concurrent e-learning design, and understand what is expected of each participant when cooperation sessions are conducted. Training activities related to the methodological approach, working techniques, equipment, and tools can take place as lecture-based training or more hands-on training sessions where participants can try out methods and technologies in practice. On the other hand, it is very useful to familiarize participants with specific issues and background material directly pertinent to the project at hand. This type of preparation takes place before the project starts, and it can also take place before each cooperation session. It is important to be well prepared before each session; an important part of this preparation is to become familiar with all relevant material, which should be available before the session, e.g. guidelines and requirements in relation to subject content, pedagogy, or technical delivery.

The Principle of Session Plans (i.e. a Plan for the Most Central Activities)

Cooperation sessions are the most central activities in concurrent e-learning design projects and it is necessary to establish a session plan that contains details about all the upcoming sessions. A session plan normally starts with some overall objectives and general information before each session is described in detail. For each session, the plan typically contains information such as:

1. The name of the session (e.g. a study of possibilities),
2. General information (e.g. that we should aim at describing a wide range of possible solutions for the upcoming e-learning course),
3. The date and time when the session will take place,
4. A reference to the infrastructure and the tools to be used during the session,
5. The people who are going to participate and their respective roles,

6. What kind of preparations that are recommended before the session starts and which documents are relevant,
7. The objectives for the session and the deliverables that should be produced, and
8. An overview of how the session will be evaluated.

The facilitator and/or project manager is mainly involved in the session planning work. The final session plan can be regarded as a coordination tool for all project participants, since it offers them the chance to be well prepared for the sessions. The session plan is made early in the project, following the adaption to the surroundings. This means that much is already known about the overall focus areas for the project (e.g. pedagogical strategies and learning activities, knowledge and learning outcomes, technical delivery, and business matters) and the themes for each focus area (i.e. questions related to each focus area that are to be discussed in the respective cooperation sessions). Based on these assumptions and further detailed planning, the details are entered into the session plan.

The Principle of Sessions

The cooperation sessions are, as previously mentioned, the most important activities in concurrent e-learning design. Before the sessions start, we need to know who should participate and what roles they should play (i.e. in compliance with the principle of different roles and sufficient authority). Next, it is important to decide when the project participants should meet for cooperation sessions and what the expectations and goals of each session are. Detailed information concerning each session is summed up and collected in a session plan, which consequently is very important for project coordination.

Participants must have sufficient authority within their respective areas of expertise, and they must attend all sessions throughout the project.

This can be understood as an either-or proposition: managers or others who only want to attend one or a few sessions should be given a role as observers, while participation should be mandatory for those who are responsible within a given field. Mandating attendance is recommended since absences can have strong negative consequences, both for cooperation and progress.

In the cooperation sessions, we want to achieve the benefits of concurrent work, effectively producing comprehensive solutions that satisfy all involved stakeholders and their needs. Here are some pointers for success in cooperation sessions:

*   **Preparation before each session:** Good preparation is important for every session, but especially before the first one. Before the first session, participants are often nervous as they do not know the details of the project. Therefore, participants must be prepared in relation to the method (i.e. how to conduct concurrent e-learning design sessions) and the current project (i.e. what will be produced in both the current session and the entire project, what is expected from each participant, and how they should prepare themselves). Furthermore, it is important to perform technical preparations to ensure that the infrastructure, equipment, and tools are working properly, as well as other preparations such as obtaining coffee and cakes or other suitable food and drinks. Our experience suggests that some food must be available for the participants since the duration is 3 - 4 hours.
*   **The session startup phase:** The first part of a session is always important and the facilitator is central in this context. In this phase, the facilitator should:
    ◦   Ensure that all equipment works in the technical sense,
    ◦   Ensure that all participants become acquainted with each other (i.e. that

they introduce themselves and tell about how they have prepared, or the like),

○ Make a presentation of the project status up to this session,

○ Make a presentation of the objectives and goals of this session and the expected deliverables, and

○ Ensure that the cooperation starts in a satisfactory manner.

• **The session implementation phase:** During the implementation phase, the goal is to achieve effective and efficient cooperation and to produce good results. This is usually achieved through a mix of individual work, cooperative work in small groups, and cooperation between all involved parties. It is the facilitator's responsibility to coordinate the cooperation so that the mix between individual and collective work runs smoothly. The facilitator must provide some breaks to discuss relevant issues and handle cases of common interest in plenum. In this context it is also important to write down all decisions made, as these decisions will guide the future work. Moreover, it is important to register upcoming actions that have to be performed within and between the cooperation sessions. If you have participants without adequate decision-making authority, calling for assistance regarding decisions is a possibility, but this should be worked out in advance.

• **The session termination phase:** The termination phase of a cooperation session is very important, as is the facilitator's role in bringing the session to a close. During this phase it is common to let all participants present what they have achieved in the current session, so that all participants may establish a common view of the project. Furthermore, focus should be main-

tained on decisions made (i.e. to update the decision list) as well as actions to be performed (i.e. to update the action list). As a result, all participants reach a common understanding about these areas and have the opportunity to discuss relevant issues along the way. The work with the decision and action lists is also an important method of determining the work on future tasks and duties that must take place before the next session. Formative evaluation of both the session work (i.e. the process) and the products (i.e. results produced so far) are also common in this phase. Typically, an oral evaluation in which everyone has an opportunity to communicate their views is conducted, follow up with surveys later on.

The sessions are the most important contribution to the upcoming deliverables in concurrent e-learning design, thus it is always important to focus on the objectives and goals for the current session. We should strive for punctuality and discipline as the room, people's time, and the available infrastructure is costly. There are usually no common breaks during a session, but the participants are free to move around the room, eat available refreshments, and engage in discussions with other participants. If required, the participants should also contact the facilitator to discuss issues and assist the facilitator in pointing out important issues and coordinating the participants.

The Principle of Working Activities between the Sessions

The work that occurs between the sessions is of paramount importance in concurrent e-learning design. It is during the sessions that we conduct multidisciplinary cooperation and produce comprehensive solutions, but it is between these sessions that we prepare for this cooperation. Preparation, in which we think through matters that must be considered within the different expert disciplines, is very important to maintain flow and progress through the cooperation sessions.

These preparations help us to strategize how the upcoming session should be carried out, providing insight in relation to how participants should best prepare themselves. Based on the results of these planning activities we could for example send out documents in advance of the next session, so that all participants are properly prepared. In addition to the preparation work for the next session, it is also common to conduct some activities that could be considered a continuation of work from the previous session. During the sessions we can typically determine solutions for issues, but it often requires a little more time to finish the tasks, thus the work must continue after the session. Such activities are normally described in the project's action list so that we know who should do what, what the status is, and what time limits apply.

In conclusion, we emphasize that the activities between the sessions are important for coordinating the project; it is not unusual to place milestones and decision points between the cooperation sessions.

Infrastructure

Infrastructure is in this context realized as the technical and physical circumstances that must be available in order to carry out concurrent e-learning design projects. The infrastructure must support multidisciplinary cooperation, both during the synchronous cooperation sessions when the participants are co-located, and between these sessions when they are distributed and working asynchronously. This means that the participants should be able to communicate, collaborate and coordinate the details of their own activities, while maintaining awareness of activities in the whole environment. In the following section, we examine four principles for infrastructure design.

The Principle of a Concurrent Design Facility

A key infrastructure element for both industrial concurrent design and the concurrent e-learning design method we refer to in this chapter is the concurrent design facility (Bandecchi et al., 2000). This is a room where the team of specialists meets to conduct cooperation sessions. The layout of the room and the location of different equipment are designed to support the design process and facilitate multidisciplinary cooperation between involved experts and other stakeholders. Experts who will cooperate closely will be placed close to one another, while the facilitator and any customer representatives are typically placed in the center of the room. The facility and the software and hardware tools the facility is equipped with constitute the infrastructure for the project. The room is equipped with computer workstations and some large public screens that are used to share design elements among all participants. For the exchange of model elements to function as efficiently as possible we use technological solutions that allow any workstation desktop to be displayed on large screens or video projectors.

Figure 4 shows a representation of the concurrent design facility used in our study. It consist of four desks (desk A-D), each with four workstations and one common large screen that primarily is used to present the desktop from one of the respective workstations. This means that four teams:

- The instructional model team,
- The knowledge model team,
- The technical delivery model team, and
- The business model team is placed on each respective desk.

The management desk is located centrally between the others so that the facilitator can get a good overview and assist the progress of co-

Figure 4. The concurrent design facility realized as a room with the necessary technical equipment

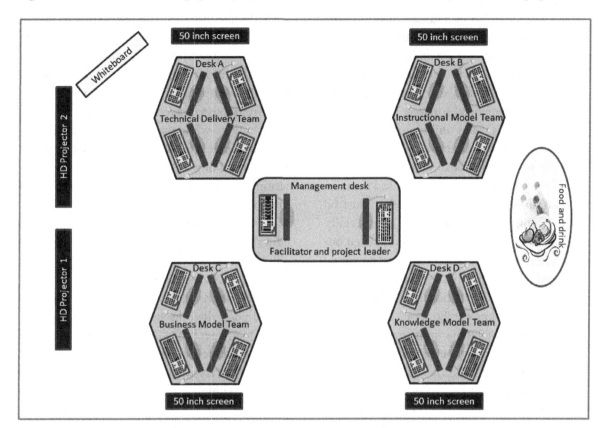

operation. Every workstation is connected to the projectors so that the facilitator or the participants themselves can present content from selected workstations, whenever needed.

Cooperation sessions are intensive and last for approximately 3.5 hours, with no common break. We must therefore consider conditions such as temperature, air quality, and noise, as well as access to food and drink. The participants need the best possible working conditions and they should be able to replenish their energy when needed. In fact, this need is so broad in scope that we could have conducted a separate study related to how the concurrent design facility best should be designed, but this is outside the scope of this chapter. The following principles more specifically discuss the various tools that in many ways become a part of the concurrent design facility.

The Principle of General Tools

General tools are used in many projects, regardless of the involved specialists' areas of expertise or the particular tools the different experts use to solve specific problems within their fields of study.

The facility with technological solutions to display workstation desktops on large screens or video projectors is also one of the general tools. Both hardware-based video splitters as well as software-based solutions are available. Initially, we chose to test out a commercially available software-based solution (i.e. NetSupport School[2]), although we have now developed our own software in order to more effectively meet our specific needs. We also consider the session plan, the action list, and the decision list to be general tools; more in depth description follows.

- The session plan is a tool that is used both for communication and coordination purposes; it helps the participants to prepare themselves. It can be implemented as a document that all project participants may access, but it could also be appropriate to develop specialized software to meet these requirements. More information about this tool can be found above under the "principle of session plans" subheading.

- The action list is a tool that is used to maintain an account of the tasks that must be performed in the project; it is especially vital that tasks that must be completed between the cooperation sessions be registered in the action list. During the cooperation sessions the action list is maintained so that we know who is responsible for what and which time limits exist. Many of these tasks have to be carried out between the cooperation sessions since these tasks often are complementary work from a previous session or preparation for the next.

- The decision list is very important to concurrent e-learning design, as it is used to register significant project decisions. These decisions are made in plenary when cooperation sessions are conducted; they provide guidelines for further work in the project. The decision list is therefore a tool that the participants will refer to throughout the project.

The session plan, the action list and the decision list should ideally be available to all participants, independent of time and place. This demand is discussed below under the subheading "the principle of common information spaces."

The Principle of Expert Tools

Different experts may need specific tools to develop their respective models and solutions, such as subject-specific tools that support design and modeling within a particular subject area. The joint work that the different experts perform as part of the cooperation sessions in concurrent e-learning design are to a great extent conversations between the parties. Participants therefore need tools that allow them to register the most important findings from these conversations and review these contributions, while also editing and expand these contributions. We have had good experiences with the use of modern tools for interactive co-writing; in this context we have tried web-based mind mapping tools to co-edit mind maps (e.g. Mindjet Catalyst[3]), simple web-based document editors (e.g. the open source based Etherpad) and slightly more advanced tools for collaborative writing (e.g. Google Docs[4]).

Furthermore, participants' use of these tools is best controlled through the use of templates. These templates typically contain questions to be answered in each session – we recommend having one template for each area of expertise. Once the template within a given area of expertise is completed, we have a basis to work from in completing the sub-models for the respective fields (i.e. the instructional model, the knowledge model, the technical delivery model, and the business model). These sub-models will together constitute a comprehensive design model for the entire e-learning delivery. As previously mentioned, these templates assist in managing the process, offering an outline of questions and issues the various experts have to deal with during the cooperative sessions. The facilitator plays a key role in leading the participants so that they touch on all relevant aspects of the templates during the sessions and conduct fruitful discussions along the way.

We have discussed some tools that may be suited to concurrent e-learning design, but the different experts should generally be able to select their own tools as needed. An important feature of these expert tools is that they work for synchronous collaborations between several simultaneous users as well as the asynchronous collaboration that typically takes place between the cooperation sessions. Furthermore, communication and integration between the different expert tools is beneficial since the overall model is built up of the sub-models developed using the respective tools. The exchange of product data based on open standards has been studied in connection with industrial concurrent design projects. The standard for exchange of product model data (STEP) is an ISO standard (ISO 10303) that explains how digital product information could be represented and exchanged between different tools. Major computer aided design and computer aided manufacturing systems now contain modules to read and write STEP compliant data, but this is not a typical tool used in instructional design. We therefore recommend using and adapting existing cooperative software, as we have already described.

The Principle of Common Information Spaces

As Schmidt and Bannon note, "Cooperative work is not facilitated simply by the provision of a shared database, but requires the active construction by the participants of a common information space where the meanings of the shared objects are debated and resolved, at least locally and temporarily (1992, p. 27)."

The common information space established in connection with our concurrent e-learning design projects consists of the concurrent design facility (i.e. the room where cooperation sessions are conducted) and the interrelationship between participants, artifacts, information, and the cooperative work taking place within these surroundings. Both the general tools and the special tools that were discussed above are regarded as artifacts in this context. In addition, we regard tools intended to facilitate information sharing to be central artifacts in the common information space. These tools should be easily available to all participants during the whole project so that everyone can take advantage of relevant information and material.

Solutions are available in the form of general tools for enterprise content and document management (e.g. SharePoint[5]) or free web-based office suits that allow collaborative users to create and edit documents online, offering integrated data storage services for these documents (e.g. Google Docs).

We have tested several cloud-based online services that provide secure online workspaces (i.e. Google Docs and Mindjet Catalyst). Project participants have expressed a high degree of comfort working in these cloud-based environments, commenting that it is very beneficial to have easy access to what the other project participants have produced. It is more important to define how services should be used in the current project rather than having endless discussions about what services are best. These services and the information they contain (i.e. session plans, action lists, decision lists, different templates, and models under development) should ideally be available for all participants independent of time and place. Furthermore, these services must support synchronous and asynchronous cooperation among both co-located and distributed participants.

Results

The goal and fundamental reason for performing any project is always the pursuit of results. When we speak of results we include the results we wish to produce along the way as well as the final results that remain when the project is finished.

It is important to know what results you want to achieve early in the project since the results are a primary input for the initial principles regarding adaption to the surroundings. It is common to operate with two categories of results in concurrent e-learning design: the intermediate results, which are to be completed during the project, and the final results, which should be available when the project is finished. The following two principles are related to these particular result categories.

The Principle of Requirements for Intermediate Results

Intermediate results will be available during the project and they are usually prepared in connection with the cooperation sessions (i.e. different results for different sessions). Several benefits accrue when fairly detailed requirements for the intermediate results that should be available after a particular session are described. These detailed requirements are highly effective in the preparation phase, when the session participants make their preparations for the session. They are of great use during the session, since knowing what to do and what the expectations are is essential for the best possible coordination of the cooperative activities. Finally, these intermediate results are of great help later on in the project, when work builds on previous results and decisions.

Typical examples of intermediate results include the following:

- A situation analysis document containing relevant information about the current situation for the upcoming e-learning course,
- A study of possibilities document that describes a wide range of possible solutions in relation to the upcoming e-learning course, or
- A selection of solutions document that contains an evaluation of the possibilities and a selection of solutions that have been chosen to facilitate the project's final e-learning delivery.

A focus on intermediate results has been helpful in relation to the decisions that have to be made along the way. Decisions can be made more quickly and missteps hopefully avoided when decisions are tied to independent intermediate results.

The Principle of Requirements for the Final Results

The final result that should be available after a concurrent e-learning design project varies from project to project. In some projects we want to produce a design document that describes how e-learning products or services should be developed, without beginning the real production of these products or services. In other projects, however, the final deliverables may include a business plan, a marketing plan, a project plan, a concept study, or even a complete and fully developed e-learning course. The determination of the final project results normally occurs as part of the startup activities.

The first principle under the adaption to surroundings category deals with project deliverable definitions, and although these can vary widely, we state that the default deliverable from concurrent e-learning design projects is a design document. The design document is by default composed of the following four sub-models:

- The knowledge model, which covers information about learning outcomes and competencies to be developed,
- The instructional model, which covers learning activities and pedagogical strategies,
- The technical delivery model, which covers technical matters such as technical platforms, technical infrastructure, solutions, and tools, and
- The business model, which covers business related issues and administrative needs.

Furthermore, these sub-models are by default developed through the following five cooperation sessions:

1.   A situation analysis of the current situation in relation to knowledge aspects (Knowledge Model), instructional schemes (Instructional Model), technological aspects (Technical Delivery Model), and financial and administrative issues (Business Model);

2.   A study of possibilities describing a wide range of possible solutions for the e-learning delivery in relation to each of the four sub-models;

3.   Selection of solutions to use in the upcoming e-learning delivery;

4.   Solution design, which is a detailed preparation of the design model that will typically enumerate the order in which instructional activities are to be carried out (Instructional Model), the order in which appropriate learning material will be presented (Knowledge Model), how the different technical solutions should be designed (Technical Delivery Model), and how economic and administrative solutions should be implemented (Business Model); and

5.   Completion of design and implementation planning, where the aim is to complete the design model for the entire e-learning delivery and make plans with respect to development and implementation (Strand & Staupe, 2010a).

Figure 3 that we presented earlier in this section illustrates the default final project result (i.e. the design document for the e-learning delivery) as an integrated solution that is composed of four different models and developed through five cooperation sessions. Thus, the final deliverable offers both a holistic perspective and a detailed perspective in relation to the respective sub-models. Our experience suggests that it is advantageous if a dedicated person is responsible for the final results and the maintenance of this design document. Such a dedicated person will typically be able to ensure that the balance between the holistic perspective and detailed perspective is appropriate. It is also

worth mentioning that we as a higher education institution have experienced several advantages of using this methodological approach and involving external corporate clients, also when the final results are put into production, i.e. when the course implementation takes place. We have for instance experienced increased participation as compared to other courses, which may be due to the fact that external representatives are ambassadors for the new course in their own organization, which in turn has an impact on the employees and results in course participation. Another advantage is the fact that the educational institution establishes a relevant course that is also demanded by other students than those employed in the client's organization.

Summarized Review of the Principles

In this section we have presented sixteen principles related to concurrent e-learning design. These principles are regarded as this chapter's most important contribution; they are repeated in the table that follows. Table 1 acts as a summary of the principles. We have chosen to provide a brief comment regarding each principle in order to emphasize what is covered.

POSSIBLE ERP SUPPORT IN THE DESIGN PROCESS

While this chapter deals mainly with a presentation of the concurrent e-learning design method, this book as a whole concerns challenges related to the design, development, implementation, and management of educational institutions' resources through ERP systems. In this case, there is a lot of overlap in the issues we aim to understand, the solutions we work to realize, and the benefits we want to achieve, as the concurrent e-learning design approach also deals with effectiveness and efficiency related to the design and development of central academic resources, i.e. e-learning courses

Table 1. A summarized presentation of the principles of concurrent e-learning design

Category	Principle	Comment
Adaption to the surroundings	The principle of defining project deliverables.	The project's goals and aims for development must be defined. We want to know as much as possible, as early as possible.
	The principle of defining participants and roles.	Human resource needs must be identified. We want to know what kind of people we need as early as possible.
	The principle of defining activities.	The project work and the activities to be performed must be identified. We want to know what should be done as early as possible.
	The principle of defining the project infrastructure.	Needs related to the facilities, tools, etc., that are to be used in the project must be identified. We need to know what kind of facilities, equipment and tools should be used in the project.
Stakeholders	The principle of different roles and sufficient authority.	Who should participate and what they should be responsible for are both key decisions; i.e. who should cover the respective roles of the project.
	The principle of multidisciplinary cooperation.	The details of multidisciplinary cooperation should be worked out; i.e. identify the participants who will work most closely together (sharing a desk) and those who do not have to work so closely.
Activities	The principle of training and preparation.	We must decide which training activities and other preparations are to be undertaken.
	The principle of session plans.	A session plan should include all necessary information about the sessions that are to be conducted. This plan is very important for both communication and coordination of the project.
	The principle of sessions.	It is important to decide how the sessions should be conducted. This is a crucial activity since this is where the multidisciplinary interaction, which leads to holistic products, takes place.
	The principle of working activities between the sessions.	The work between the sessions is very important and must not be neglected. Between the sessions we make plans for how to conduct the sessions most appropriately, and also perform tasks that require more time.
Infrastructure	The principle of a concurrent design facility.	A concurrent design facility, i.e. a room with the necessary equipment, is needed to conduct concurrent e-learning design. This is perhaps the most important physical installation for concurrent design.
	The principle of general tools.	Typically, we employ some general tools that are reused from project to project. General tools may be of particular assistance in articulation work.
	The principle of expert tools.	The experts who work to develop the project deliverables require some specialized tools.
	The principle of common information spaces.	A common information space is required in order to cooperate on documents and other resources and develop comprehensive solutions that meet everyone's needs.
Results	The principle of requirements for intermediate results.	It is important to be aware of the required intermediate results that are to be produced along the way.
	The principle of requirements for the final results.	It is important to be aware of the requirements associated with the final project results.

and related components that constitute educational deliveries from the institutions. This overlap will be addressed in this section through a discussion of possible ERP support in the design process.

ERP is a major field of study, and there are tens of journals that regularly publish articles on ERP-related themes (Moon, 2007). ERP systems are information systems used to manage organizations' internal and external resources; their value is primarily generated through effective and efficient usage rather than directly from the systems themselves. ERP should help improve business – successful implementations must therefore be directed by business-driven requirements, with the technological choices remaining subordinate. Furthermore, the twofold nature of ERP benefits must be considered: ERP provides a comprehensive perspective of the entire organization, including all departments and functions; it also makes available all details of individual business transactions through ERP databases (Umble, Haft, & Umble, 2003).

ERP systems are used to record, maintain, processes, monitor, and report on financials (e.g. accounts receivable and payable, or standard and period-related costing), human resources (e.g. personnel planning or training, or event management), operations and logistics (e.g. purchasing or project management), and sales and marketing (e.g. sales management or pricing). This data can obviously be helpful in a decision process and it is precisely this use of ERP systems (i.e. as a system to achieve decision support benefits) that we want to highlight in this context.

Decision support is considered important in relation to both ERP (Holsapple & Sena, 2005) and industrial concurrent design (Lonchamp, 2000). Difficulty working with decisions in concurrent e-learning design arises partly as a result of the lack of actionable data to support decision making. In the early project phase, we typically need information about employees' competence and experience when new projects are staffed and decisions regarding appropriate resources are to be made. Later on in the project we will need information about the market and sales figures for previous implementations of specific e-learning products and services within a given market segment, as such data will help us to survey the market space. It may also be appropriate to look at the relevant figures (actual expenses or incomes) from previous years, when making decisions regarding

financial forecasts or financial plans for a project. Many decisions made in the process of developing concurrent e-learning design projects, especially those related to the financial and administrative aspects of new e-learning deliveries, would benefit from the assistance offered by ERP modules for financials, human resources, operations and logistics, and sales and marketing. Data availability and accessibility is crucial to making correct and appropriately-timed decisions throughout a project.

In connection with the project's infrastructure, we chose to focus on two types of tools. These were general tools that are used in multiple projects regardless of the involved experts, and expert tools that are used by various experts when they work to produce their specific parts of the project's deliverables. ERP systems can act both as general tools and as expert tools. On the one hand, project management and selection of participants for the project is something the project manager does in all projects. ERP functions used for these purposes should therefore be regarded as general tools. On the other hand, ERP functions used for decision support should be regarded as expert tools. In concurrent e-learning design we aim to focus on several relevant areas when we develop new e-learning courses, i.e. economic and administrative matters should be addressed in line with learning outcomes, learning activities, and technical deliveries. Relevant data, which can serve as a basis for economic and administrative conditions, are typically available via the institution's ERP system. This could be information such as student course registrations, sales figures for courses, information about employees' competencies, and information about employees' workload. If we are to cover economic and administrative demands in a consistent manner during the design of new e-learning deliveries, it can be very beneficial to have access to this kind of information while participating in cooperation sessions.

Thus far, we have worked to define a concept and a framework for computer supported and cooperative instructional design. This approach has been based on experiences from different subject areas and our findings are summarized with the principles of concurrent e-learning design, presented in this chapter. Since the concept has now been established and actually implemented, it is natural to continue working to improve selected parts of the process.

Improvement of the decision-making process and provision of appropriate tool support are two challenges that arise in the course of the instructional design process. In this section, we have seen that ERP systems are very likely to contribute positively in this context. In the future, it is therefore highly relevant to work on research issues related to the availability of ERP systems. Some questions for further research include:

- Will ERP systems help improve the decision making process?
- If so, how could this possibly be done?
- What kind of support can educational institutions' ERP systems provide?
- What requirements apply to ERP systems intended to support instructional design processes?

Instructional design is a key process available to educational institutions to ensure sustainable and future-oriented educational programs. If the uses of ERP systems can help improve this work it will lead to more effective instructional design processes. Concurrent e-learning design processes would directly benefit from ERP systems, but those pursuing other approaches to instructional design would probably also be able to benefit. We believe the integration of the concurrent e-learning design approach with the use of ERP systems creates a win-win situation. The e-learning design process requires information during the design process that may largely be found in the ERP system, while the resources and information that are created should in turn be plowed back into the ERP system. Instructional design processes need

ERP data, while the ERP systems in turn need data from instructional design processes in order to provide a clear picture of the whole business, since information about educational resources under development might have a value in itself.

CONCLUSION

Our intention in this chapter has been to present the concurrent e-learning design approach, and to contribute a brief discussion regarding the potential of ERP to help improve instructional design processes at educational institutions. Concurrent e-learning design is a novel approach to computer supported cooperative instructional design; the sixteen principles presented in this chapter are intended to explain how this approach works. These principles are the result of several years of method engineering work related to the concurrent e-learning design approach. The results are based on available literature and theories within industrial concurrent design and instructional design, in addition to our own practical experiences applying these theories in relation to the mentioned methodological approach.

The principles presented in this chapter offer a prescriptive framework for concurrent e-learning design. We explain how the principles work and make recommendations about how they should be used, i.e. they consist of high-level guidelines or rules to be followed in the instructional design process. The intention is to provide recommendations that assist instructional designers in using this approach most optimally. There are of course many approaches to instructional design and we have not yet performed enough activities to fully assess the research evidence and the findings from this study. The question remains: how credible are these findings, how well was the data collection and analysis carried out, and how clear are the links between the original data, the interpretations, and the conclusions that are presented as principles in this chapter?

We want to increase the credibility of these findings. This means that we want other practitioners to test the validity-in-practice of these principles and contribute proposals for improvements. We hope this chapter can inspire new attempts to implement real time and multidisciplinary cooperation, which in turn should contribute to comprehensive solutions that satisfy involved stakeholders and their needs. Additionally, we have discussed how the use of ERP systems can help improve instructional design processes when new academic resources are developed. We pointed out common objectives between instructional design and ERP, and discussed how ERP can be used in this context. As an extension of this work, we will specifically study the use of ERP systems for decision support within the concurrent e-learning design processes.

REFERENCES

Bandecchi, M., Melton, B., Gardini, B., & Ongaro, F. (2000). The ESA/ESTEC concurrent design facility. *Proceedings of 2nd European Systems Engineering Conference* (EuSEC 2000).

Bannon, L., & Bødker, S. (1997). Constructing common information spaces. *Proceedings of the Fifth European Conference on Computer-Supported Cooperative Work*.

Bazeley, P. (2007). *Qualitative data analysis with NVivo*. Sage Publications Ltd.

Brinkkemper, S. (1996). Method engineering: Engineering of information systems development methods and tools. *Information and Software Technology*, *38*(4), 275–280. doi:10.1016/0950-5849(95)01059-9

Carlile, P. R. (2002). A pragmatic view of knowledge and boundaries: Boundary objects in new product development. *Organization Science*, *13*(4), 442–455. doi:10.1287/orsc.13.4.442.2953

Davidson-Shivers, A. G. V., & Rasmussen, K. L. (2006). *Web-based learning: Design, implementation, and evaluation*. Upper Saddle River, NJ: Pearson.

Gagné, R. M., Wager, W. W., Golas, K. C., & Keller, J. M. (2005). *Principles of instructional design*. Thomson/Wadsworth.

Holsapple, C. W., & Sena, M. P. (2005). ERP plans and decision-support benefits. *Decision Support Systems*, *38*(4), 575–590. doi:10.1016/j.dss.2003.07.001

Katzenbach, J. R., & Smith, D. K. (1993). *The wisdom of teams*. London, UK: McGraw-Hill.

Kirschner, P., van Merrienboer, J., Sloep, P., & Carr, C. (2002). How expert designers design. *Performance Improvement Quarterly*, *15*(4), 86–104. doi:10.1111/j.1937-8327.2002.tb00267.x

Lonchamp, J. (2000). *A generic computer support for concurrent design*. Advances in Concurrent Engineering: Presented at Seventh ISPE International Conference on Concurrent Engineering: Research and Applications, Lyon Cluade Bernard University, France, July 17-20, 2000. CRC Press.

Moon, Y. B. (2007). Enterprise resource planning (ERP): A review of the literature. *International Journal of Management and Enterprise Development*, *4*(3), 235–264. doi:10.1504/IJMED.2007.012679

Osburg, J., & Mavris, D. (2005). A collaborative design environment to support multidisciplinary conceptual systems design. *SAE Transactions*, *114*, 1508–1516.

Paquette, G. (2004). Instructional engineering for learning objects repositories networks. *Proceedings of International Conference on Computer Aided Learning in Engineering Education* (CALIE 04).

Peterson, C. (2003). Bringing ADDIE to life: Instructional design at its best. *Journal of Educational Multimedia and Hypermedia, 12*(3), 227–242.

Reeves, T. C., Herrington, J., & Oliver, R. (2005). Design research: A socially responsible approach to instructional technology research in higher education. *Journal of Computing in Higher Education, 16*(2), 96–115. doi:10.1007/BF02961476

Saldaña, J. (2009). *The coding manual for qualitative researchers*. Sage.

Schmidt, K., & Bannon, L. (1992). Taking CSCW seriously. *Computer Supported Cooperative Work, 1*(1), 7–40. doi:10.1007/BF00752449

Schmidt, K., & Simone, C. (1996). Coordination mechanisms: Towards a conceptual foundation of CSCW systems design. *Computer Supported Cooperative Work, 5*(2), 155–200. doi:10.1007/BF00133655

Strand, K. A., & Hjeltnes, T. A. (2009). Design of customized corporate e-learning. *International Journal of Media. Technology and Lifelong Learning, 5*(2), 14.

Strand, K. A., & Staupe, A. (2010a). The concurrent e-learning design method. In Abas, Z. (Eds.), *Proceedings of Global Learn Asia Pacific 2010* (pp. 4067–4076).

Strand, K. A., & Staupe, A. (2010b). *Action research based instructional design improvements. NOKOBIT 2010, Norsk konferanse for organisasjoners bruk av informasjonsteknologi* (pp. 25–38). Tapir Akademisk Forlag.

Umble, E. J., Haft, R. R., & Umble, M. M. (2003). Enterprise resource planning: Implementation procedures and critical success factors. *European Journal of Operational Research, 146*(2), 241–257. doi:10.1016/S0377-2217(02)00547-7

Visscher-Voerman, I., & Gustafson, K. (2004). Paradigms in the theory and practice of education and training design. *Educational Technology Research and Development, 52*(2), 69–89. doi:10.1007/BF02504840

KEY TERMS AND DEFINITIONS

Concurrent Design: A methodology developed to effectively solve complex and multidisciplinary issues, through the use of a network of computers, multimedia devices and software tools.

Concurrent Design Facility: This is a room where the team of specialists meets to conduct cooperation sessions. The room is equipped with a network of computers, multimedia devices and software tools. The layout of the room and the location of different equipment are designed to support the design process and facilitate multidisciplinary cooperation between involved experts and other stakeholders.

Concurrent E-Learning Design: A concurrent design approach that is used to design and develop educational deliveries.

Cooperation Sessions: Working sessions that take place in a specially designed room, i.e. a concurrent design facility with a network of computers, multimedia devices and software tools. The word cooperation is used to indicate that session activities consist of communication, collaboration, and coordination.

Facilitator: A person responsible for facilitating the cooperation sessions, which normally take place in a concurrent design facility. This dedicated role can be compared to that of a conductor, who ensures that the interactions between the participants are running smoothly. The facilitator helps coordinate the cooperation so that the transition between individual and collective work is natural and appropriate.

Instructional Design: The practice of designing effective, efficient, and appealing educational deliveries.

Multidisciplinary Cooperation: Concurrent e-learning design sessions facilitate real time multidisciplinary cooperation between stakeholders including the facilitator, the session secretary, various experts, the project manager, customer representatives, service providers, prospective users, and others. The goal of multidisciplinary cooperation is to achieve fruitful and effective cooperation between all these stakeholders so that they cohere as a high-performing team that produces comprehensive solutions that are sustainable and viable.

ENDNOTES

[1] NVivo is a trademark or registered trademark of QSR International Pty Ltd.

[2] NetSupport is a trademark or registered trademark of NetSupport Ltd.

[3] Mindjet Catalyst is a trademark or registered trademark of Mindjet LLC.

[4] Google Docs is a trademark or registered trademark of Google Inc.

[5] SharePoint is a trademark or registered trademark of Microsoft Corporation.

Section 2
Knowledge Management

Chapter 5
Knowledge Management Model for Electronic Textbook Design

Elena Railean
Informational Society Development Institute, Republic of Moldova

ABSTRACT

This chapter aims to describe a new knowledge management (KM) model, which can be considered an enterprise resources planning model proved in Electronic Textbook in Electronic Portfolio technology. The model comprises a dynamic and flexible instructional strategy which allows constructing the personalized digital content through development of core structure of competence. This strategy allows bidirectional transitions from tacit to explicit knowledge and hermeneutic dialogues. The KM model can be described using adjacency matrix and optimized knowledge graphs techniques. The target audience of this chapter is expected to be consisted of educational management students, professionals and researchers working in the field of education including policy makers, consultants, and agencies. Applications and methodologies validate the educational efficiency of KM model for electronic textbook design. The affordance of the KM model for education relies on informational / communicational processes, cognitive processes, and computerized assessment processes.

INTRODUCTION

Learning Management Systems (LMS) is an integrative set of elements or computer programs that accomplish and manage well-defined objective. There are different types of LMS: Information Management Systems (IMS); Learning Content Management Systems (LCMS); Competency (or Competence) Management Systems (CMS); Managed Learning Environment (MLE); Virtual Learning Environment (VLE) etc. Each of

Learning Management Systems can be designed according to instructional objectives or learning objectives. "An instructional objective is a collection of words and/or pictures and diagrams intended to let others know what you intend for your students to achieve" (Mager, p.3). The instructional objectives are measurable and are related to an intended outcome of instruction, rather than the process of instruction and are specific, rather than general, broad, or "fuzzy." The objectives describe the student's performance rather than the instructor's performance. Instead

DOI: 10.4018/978-1-4666-2193-0.ch005

of that, the "learning objectives (often called performance objectives or competencies) are brief, clear, specific statements of what learners will be able to perform at the conclusion of instructional activities. Learning objectives stem from course objectives; course objectives are broad statements reflecting general course goals and outcomes, while learning objectives are targeted statements about expected student performance. Generally, learning objectives are competency-based as they designate exactly what students need to demonstrate mastery of course material" (Mager, 1996). The learning objectives are SMART: Specific, Measurable, Attainable for target audience within scheduled time and specified conditions, Relevant and results-oriented and Targeted to the learner and to the desired level of learning.

There are many pedagogical tools, integrated in LMS, allowing archiving the instructional / learning objectives. One of the main pedagogical tools is electronic textbooks (Полат, Бухаркина, Моисеева, 2004). The electronic textbook is an e-book which contains educational material for teaching and learning methods, which use „the strengths of the computer, such as its ability to organize and reorganize information, its versatility in linking information, its capacity to use various media, its facility in adapting to a particular individual's needs, and its manner of demonstrating new concepts and information" (Frumkes, 1996). The electronic textbook, in its simplest form, must be understood as a computer-readable file, or document, containing an extended narrative and intended as the primary mode for studying course content" (Allison, 2003). Porter (2010) wrote that electronic textbooks are a marriage of a hardcopy book within an electronic environment with software, such as Adobe Acrobat PDF, XML, SGML, HTML files, or hardware, such as a Palm Reader, E-Reader, Sony Reader, and Amazon's Kindle among others. While available in different formats, electronic textbooks must have the following: portability, transferability and search-

ability. The electronic textbooks are available in different formats, which are portable, transferable, and searchable" (Porter, 2010). Usually "digital textbook materials offer quizzes, online journals, the ability to highlight and annotate pages and other interactive options that appeal to students and provide immediate feedback" (Reavy, 2011) and their benefits include interactive learning, easier and faster updating of textbooks and possible significant financial savings.

Stoffa (2007) emphases, that just a linear text in digital form cannot be considered an electronic textbook. In the author point of view an electronic textbook should meet requirements following from general theory and psychology of teaching through encouragement and providing for an active cooperation with educate; providing for a reciprocal feedback; simulation models; exemplary resolved problems; an adequate formulation and expression of thoughts, structure, arrangement and the way of presenting new knowledge and adaptively for an individual style.

Ideally, the instructional design is an enterprise resources planning for didactic processes. But, these processes can rely to scientific management, informational management or knowledge management. The management design models evolve from linear to metasystems. The perspective of the chapter is to describe the metasystems approach for knowledge management model, proved by Electronic Textbook in Electronic Portfolio Technology. The objectives of this chapter are:

1. To note the theoretical –practical issues of knowledge management models.
2. To describe issues, controversies and problems generated by evolution of educational ideal
3. To describe the concept of competence in electronic textbook design
4. To analyse the role of knowledge management in enterprise resources planning models for the education sector

THEORETICAL ISSUES OF KNOWLEDGE MANAGEMENT MODELS

Knowledge management in education is the act of getting learning actors together to accomplish the educational ideal using available strategies, tools and resources. In different period of time educational ideal was achieved through different management models: scientific management, information management or knowledge management. In two of them are widely used Information and Communication Technology (ICT) (Figure 1).

Scientific management, also known as "Piece-Rate System", "Task Management", "Taylorism", "the Taylor System" etc. was proposed in 1890 by Frederic Taylor. Taylor (1911) believes that aim of scientific management is

1. To replace old methods with methods based on a scientific study of the tasks;
2. To select and then train, teach, and develop the workman;
3. To provide detailed instruction and supervision of each worker in the performance of that worker's discrete task and
4. To divide work nearly equally among managers and workers, so that the managers apply scientific management principles to planning the work and the workers actually perform the tasks.

Gilbreth (1921) proves that scientific management is an interdisciplinary science of psychology and management. The role of psychology in management is to obtain the effect of the mind that is directing work upon that work which is directed, and the effect of this undirected and directed work upon the mind of the worker. The principles of psychology to management were applied by Walter Scott and J. Mooney. Nevertheless, the effects of management as added value in enterprise resources planning models for the education were not observed.

After 1960 management used ICT in storing facts, supporting operations and managing people's activities. During time were designed different decision support systems, tutorial systems, expert systems, executive informational system, transaction processing system etc. The focuses of research were directed to Management Information Systems, composed by a system that provides the information necessary to manage an organization effectively. Usually, these systems is designed to enhance communication among employees; to deliver complex material throughout the institution; to provide an objective system for recording and aggregating information; to reduce expenses related to labor-intensive manual activities and support the organization's strategic goals and directions. Nevertheless, according to Wikipedia, towards the end 20 century business management came to consist of six separate branches, namely: human resource management;

Figure 1. The models of management according to ICT trends

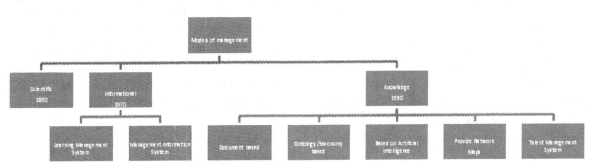

operations management or production management; strategic management; marketing management; financial management and information technology management.

Management Information Systems for educational purposes is named Learning Management System (LMS). LMS is a software application for administration, documentation, tracking, and reporting of training programs, classroom and online events, e-learning programs, and training content. Henninger&Kutter (2010, p. 2) note, that basic functions of LMS are administration of teachers, learners, courses; access to communication tools (both synchronic and asynchronic); presentation of content; tools for building exercises and assessment tools. In case when LMS includes tools to deliver and manage instructor-led synchronous and asynchronous online training based on learning object methodology, is called Learning Management Content Systems (LMCS). These systems manage and track all aspects of didactical processes and traditional classroom training; allow monitoring and tracking the students' performance; deliver measurable content over the Internet and Intranets.

In our Globalisated Age the learning occurs within a social context, which is as formal and nonformal, as real and virtual. Many management systems allow social networking and sharing the data, information and knowledge. Moreover, the content can be developed/personalized by users in order to create an online social environment/community, support messaging system, complete photo albums and video gallery, record and share video files, comment on walls, create blogs, create or maintain a digital portfolio. Examples of open-source software are: ELGG, Mahara, Social Engine, Insoshi and MIXXT.

Management Information Systems is widely applied in online or distance learning, self-instruction or/and self-assessment. Nevertheless, these systems allow using different didactic strategies for the teaching and learning: individual, adaptive, interactive etc. Usually, the individual learning strategies are directed to achievement

the Individual Learning Path (ILP). More widely accepted adaptive models of teaching illustrate the linkages between the knowledge and frame of content. Even the pedagogical theory of adaptive learning is both behaviorist and cognitivist; the practical solutions show the evidence of Intelligent Tutoring Systems and Personalized Adaptive Web Systems.

Other Management Information Systems are developed for knowledge management in schools. These systems evolve from School Administration Tool (SAT) to School Information Management System (SIMS). For example, the system named Capita "can" organize curriculum, provide a complete picture on teachers and learners, track student records, manage the examination process, share student data, send immediate messages, prepare quick letters at home etc. The system EduSwift automates System Administration and Management, Records and Profiles Management, Timetable Generation and Updates, Substitute Management, Fee Management, Attendance Management, Exam Management, Grades Management, Library Management, Web Community Management, Online Content Management and Homework Management. The other similar examples are: Power Vista Roll Call, The Education Edge, Administrators Plus, ampEducation, and SONISWEB.

If Management Information Systems will be analyzed from historical point of view, then Knowledge Management Systems roots can be observed. The main root came from philosofical thinking of, American pragmatists, especially from C. I. Lewis's system of conceptualistic pragmatism, rooted in the thought of Peirce, James and Dewey (Zeleny, 2012). The second root relies to 20th Century efforts to increase effectiveness of knowledge management in the "Knowledge Era" (Morey, Maybury, Thuraisingham, 2002; McInerney, 2002; Wright, 2005; Nonaka&von Krogh, 2009). Both roots arise a scientific problem of how to learn faster and make people work more effective. One of the solutions is how to design a form of specialized technology, based on either a custom database of knowledge, and/or a network of expertise in various relevant areas, in which additional knowledge is created by activities and sharing information through network communities, social media, and internet information access.

The enterprise resource planning models for the education sector are an integral part of the knowledge management system. "Enterprise Resource Planning (ERP) systems are software packages composed of several modules, such as human resources, sales, finance and production, providing cross-organization integration of data through embedded business processes" (Esteves&Pastor, 2001). As was reported by Allen, Kern and Havenhand (2001) new information technologies have brought public sector higher education institutions (HEIs) into increased competition, while their government funding in parallel has been continually eroded. In response to these growing pressures, there has been a call for HEIs to improve operational efficiency and to reduce duplication of resources by implementing advanced information systems that span the institution and improve processes. In response, HEIs have turned their efforts to implementing complex enterprise resource planning (ERP) systems.

Sor (1999) suggests that a better understanding of issues surrounding ERP systems could be achieved by moving the discourse towards management theory and dealing with ERP systems as special cases of theoretical premises that were developed in the 1960's. The evolution of strategies for learning design allows to evidence that knowledge management systems are very different. Theoretically, the focus of learning design is on development the skills, know-how and processes, but in practice these systems include document management; ontology, taxonomy or semantic agents, same Artificial Intelligence techniques, networking and/or social computing. Document based systems allow to create/manage/share documents. Ontology or taxonomy based systems help to create knowledge networks; share

documents with the group, view chat history and found relevant information. The systems, based on Artificial Intelligence Technologies are Decision Making Systems, Expert Systems etc. Talent Management Systems is expected to manage the human capital of organization through processes of recruiting, managing, assessing, developing and maintaining. All these systems can be integrated for knowledge management triggered through electronic textbooks.

The possibility to unite different conceptual designed systems in one knowledge management approach is based on proliferation of new information and radical changes in education systems, environments, and structures, learning content, strategies, methodologies, methods and techniques. There is a shift from closed system to more open system. "There is a change for a new paradigm of learning. The main point is that learning is the core process of the educational system. But, educational system is, first of all, a system that can be real or artificial. The real educational system is open, complex and dynamic, the artificial created system - is a closed pedagogical system (Railean, 2008). As was noted by Wilson (1990) in his book "Quantum Psychology" in the past, information doubled every 10 years, and then it doubles every four years and now in every two hours. Debora Schnitzer (2003) define quantum psychology as a practical approach to becoming mindful of both the relationship between our automatic responses and what triggers them, as well as the mechanism, itself, of those automatic responses.

Quantum psychology, knowledge management, education psychology, cybernetic pedagogic and cybernetic psychologies are main domains that influence enterprise recourse planning for the education sector. This means that knowledge management systems need to be design as enterprise resource planning model in which interdependence between principles will allow observing a synergistic effect.

ISSUES, CONTROVERSIES, AND PROBLEMS GENERATED BY EVOLUTION OF EDUCATION IDEAL

The knowledge management systems for educational purpose rely on the educational ideal. The educational ideal is a kind of excellence, which allows learner to be more adaptive and accommodative at the environment changes. The educational ideal common for Globalization Age is Professionalism, Global Thinking, and Cultural Pluralism. Even the components "Global Thinking" and "Cultural Pluralism" are understudied; the concept of "Professionalism" has been variously defined by sources. So, for Davis (1988) professionalism means putting your client first and acting as an officer of the court; for Leach (2004, p.11) is one of the competencies and for Hagger&McIntyreone (2000, p.13) is a strong practical skills personally understood and justified through an intellectually rigorous process. So, could be considered that professionalism means competence as a state of being well qualified. But, competence forming processes is based on *a priori* knowledge and skills. The competence results from informational, cognitive, assessment processes taking place in real learning environment. If the competence forming processes are directed to Global Thinking, the estimated output is think globally and acts locally. The global problems can turn into actions only by considering ecological, economic, and cultural differences of our local surroundings. Instead of them, issue of cultural pluralism in the curriculum has been raised as a problem for many years now, but fundamental changes have yet to be made. The problem is that lines between Professionalism, Global Thinking and Cultural Pluralism are indistinct and cannot be rigidly defined, first off all because learning in open educational system represent a dynamic self-regulated processes that can be managed through "instructional dynamic and flexible strategy" (Railean, 2010).

Let us identify the solution of this problem in philosophical, psychological, pedagogical, and cybernetic and management roots of competence development principles. Rudic (2011) distinguishes three approaches within rationalist tradition: linear, systemic and metasystemic thinking. Linear thinking, more common to XVI century and 1956, argued the ideas of empiricism, idealism and rationalism in knowledge formation and sharing. In this period the enterprise resource planning models for the education sector focused to reproduce knowledge and develop practical skills. Kant wrote that children are to be educated for the future, in accordance with the ideal of mankind and of its destiny, but for Foucault the knowledge is savoir. The educational system was a pedagogical closed system, in which knowledge retention determines the outcomes of the didactic processes. Between 1956 and 1990 the ideal of education was "re-directed" to systemic thinking. The nature of knowledge became more complex in change. For example French distinguish savoir, savoir-faire and savoir–être components. Bellier (2004) notes that the French approach is generally more comprehensive, considering savoir (compétences théoriques, i.e. knowledge), savoir-faire (compétences pratiques, i.e. functional competences) and savoir-être (compétences sociales et comportementales, i.e. behavioral competencies.

In reality the management of forming/development the savoir structures, as learning design focus, needs more advanced tools to "construct" the core structure of competence. What is the core structure of competence? One of attends to explain this concept was made by Gerard&Rogiers (2009, p. 52). The authors note that structure of competence is a complex construct formed by savoir-reproduire, savoir–faire and savoir–étre, which integrate cognitive, sensory-psycho-motor (known as psychomotor) and socio–emotional domains (known as affective) domains. It was estimated that such construct can be built using textbooks as didactic tool. The recent needs in new tools and, respectively, new enterprise resource planning models for the educational sector is proved by controversies from learning theory to practice and vice versa, from applications to methodologies. Firstly, the psychology of learning is as behaviorist, as cognitivist as well as constructivist. "Cognitive theorists recognize that much learning involves associations established through contiguity and repetition. They acknowledge the importance of reinforcement, although they stress its role in providing feedback about the correctness of responses over its role as a motivator. However, even while accepting such behavioristic concepts, cognitive theorists view learning as involving the acquisition or reorganization of the cognitive structures through which humans process and store information" (Mergel, 2007). Constructivist learning argues that humans generate knowledge and meaning from between their experiences and their ideas.

Secondly, the power of mechanical devices strengthens the pedagogical socio-constructivist approaches for design the knowledge management systems. Before 1990, computer aided instruction and computer aided assessment were widely used methods for individualized learning. "The device makes it possible to present carefully designed material in which one problem can depend upon the answer to preceding and where, therefore, the most efficient progress to an eventually complex repertoire can be made" (Smith&Moore, 2004). In time, the learning processes were based on new and new active methods allowing changes in enterprise resource planning models for the education sectors. Instead of this, Instructional Design and Instructional Systems Design needs "clear instructional objectives; teaching substeps as a way to attain mastery of larger units; allowing students to progress and carefully programmed (or sequenced) instruction" (Criswell, 1989). The effect was new contradictions between how the structure of competence can be and how to manage knowledge between input and output.

After 1990 new paradigm of learning arise a new educational ideal. The savoir- reproduire, savoir- faire and savoir- être structures were needed to become more flexible at the dynamic changes of the learning environment. Moreover, the learning environment had been becoming as real as virtual and savoir - vivre finally consolidated the structure of competence in a dynamic and flexible complex. The philosophy of education explains this trend with "GAE paradigm" (Railean, 2012). The added value was made by theory of bioecological systems and quantum psychology. In order to do this, cybernetics "moved" Information Management to social networking and Knowledge Management. Pedagogy "diversified" the computer based assessment methods from individualized assessment to "self, peer, and group assessment in E-Learning" (Roberts, 2006).

Instead, enterprise resource planning models for the education sectors was re-focused on studding and description of new active methods for competence forming. The controversy appears when competence is defined in "Recommendation of the European Parliament and of the Council on the establishment of the European Qualifications Framework for lifelong learning" as the proven ability to use knowledge, skills and personal, social and/or methodological abilities, in work or study situations and in professional and personal development ... described in terms of responsibility and autonomy. In EQF knowledge means the outcome of the assimilation of information through learning. Knowledge is the body of facts, principles, theories and practices that is related to a field of study or work and can be theoretical (based on recalling) and/or factual (based on direct observation).

One more controversy appears when we try to understand the differences between types of knowledge. Uluoglu (2006) declares that declarative knowledge is defined as the factual information stored in memory and known to be static in nature. Things /events/ processes, their attributes, and the relations between these things/events/ processes and their attributes define the domain of declarative knowledge. Procedural knowledge is the knowledge of how to perform, or how to operate. Professional is skilled in problem solving when he relies on procedural knowledge more than declarative knowledge.

Okada (2005, p. 87) notes that knowledge cannot either be taught or passed on. The knowledge can be both tacit and explicit. Tacit knowledge involved two concepts: know how: technical dimensions that emphases the kind of information, hard-topin-down skills or crafts and "fingertips" feelings; and the "cognitive" dimensions: schemata, mental models, beliefs, and perceptions that reflect our image of reality ("what is") and our vision for the future ("what ought to be"). The interconnections between tacit and explicit knowledge are guaranteed by socialization and externalization. During these phase theory and practice could be woven; tacit and explicit knowledge could be connected, discussed and combined through critical and consensual conclusion. ...the theory and practice combined could be internalized (explicit knowledge became tacit knowledge. Moreover, tacit/explicit knowledge can be modeling using enterprise resource planning models. The advantages for using these models are: to allow simultaneous access to information for planning and control and to facilitate intra-organization collaboration.

The methodology for our investigation is based on qualitative-quantitative research. Qualitative methods allow integrating the knowledge management flow in knowledge graph, which is well represented in adjacency matrix. This means that learning processes are transformative processes, generated by teacher's electronic textbook and incorporated in student's electronic textbook. The knowledge management model allows developing a dynamic and flexible structure of competence. Each cyclical movements results in outputs, in which can be observed the synergistic effect, which can be observed when student passes the

"coefficient of assimilation $K\alpha \geq 0.7$" (Беспалько, 2007). By the synergistic effect we understand the cumulative effect of learning design when output is bigger than sum of components. The components of learning design are knowledge architecture, content, and methods.

THE CONCEPT OF COMPETENCE IN ELECTRONIC TEXTBOOK DESIGN

We use the knowledge management model to design the electronic textbooks. By electronic textbook we mean a computer-readable file, or document, containing an extended narrative and intended as the primary mode for studying course content. In our understanding the electronic textbook design needs to be developed according to new didactical model and new integrated principles for design:

1. The principle of self–regulation is based on the learner' efforts to monitor, manage and improve own learning using different strategies, methods, procedures, and techniques.
2. The principle of personalization is based on engaging the learner in delivering the personal content in a conversational tone using verbal language communication or by pedagogical agents in order to focus learner attention and to increase intrinsic motivation.
3. The principle of clarity is based on strongly interconnected concepts and clarity of task.
4. The principle of dynamicity and flexibility is based on knowledge architecture for own content.
5. The principle of feedback diversity is based on immediate and delayed feedback using Knowledge Management Model as a vehicle to extend the role of feedback in learning.
6. The principle of ergonomics is based on ergonomic interfaces and ergonomic place of work.

The quality of enterprise resource planning models for the education sector depends on modeling the core structure of competence. One of possible techniques is knowledge graph, which represent an optimized oriented graph like an interdependence structure of core concepts. The knowledge graph is formed by nodes and edges. The powerful interconnections among concepts and edges are provided by special design of concepts and its interdependence. Such structures can be "re-constructed" in cognitive structures. This involves different learning methods, but own "learning styles" rely on own architecture of knowledge through personalization the electronic textbook generated content.

The processes of generation of the electronic textbook content are main output of three main processes: information/communication, cognitive activity and computerized assessment. The communication/information processes occur through knowledge transferring over time through a transmitter (for example, the e-Learning platform, instructional system, networked computer, from the source (tutor/mentor, electronic textbook, learner/group of learners, learning environment) to the recipient (the learner' cognitive system). The cognitive activity processes represent the actions of the mental processes redirected to achieve the educational outcome. The assessment processes are self, peer and collaborative actions proved by the diversity of immediate/delayed feedback and feedward.

Let us consider the learning process a discrete process, which occurs in a dynamic system. In such a system each movement from one cognitive state S_0 to other S_n represents a transition from tacit to explicit knowledge. Each transition is caused by one of four phases: "externalization, internalization, intermediation and cognition" (Koulopoulos&Frappaolo, 2000). But, for learning processes the externalization means to capture knowledge in an external repository and to organize it according to taxonomy. In our case, this means to inform the teacher about the students'

characteristics (for example, *a priori* knowledge, learning styles, psychopedagogical particularities etc.) and, then to inform the students about the studied domain (structure, difficulty of concepts, learning methods etc.). That's why we named this phase information.

During internalization the students construct their own understanding of learning subjects. In discrete learning system the strategy can be defined for all cognitive states $S_0, S_1, S_2, ...S_n$. Each cognitive state is characterized by constant: level of knowledge $k_0, k_1, k_2, ...k_n$ and *variable*: time $t_0, t_1, t_2, ...t_n$. The explicit knowledge is extracted from content and then it is filtered and completed by the cognitive structure, which is individual for each of the cognitive systems. As sophistical filters and systems are used, as better is the results. Instead, at the end of internalization the synergy effect can be observed, if the teacher will manage the learning to achieve the coefficient of assimilation $0.3 \geq K\alpha \geq 0.7$. In traditional knowledge management model "internalization helps to communicate a problem or point of interest and map that against the bodies of knowledge already captured through externalization" (Koulopoulos&Frappaolo, 2000). That's why digital text needs to provide metacognition.

The role of metacognition with feedback and feed-ward provide is to provide understanding. As was reported by Catts&Kamhi (2011) the self-management metacognition component for planning and controlling actions is related to reading comprehension in two ways: awareness of when and how to plan is critical for understanding characters' goal-directed behavior in narratives, and ability to evaluate one's comprehension and plan are critical for employing comprehension repair strategies. The role of intermediation is to break tacit knowledge and to transform it in explicit knowledge. Intermediation can be automated using Web 2.0 technologies such as chat, groupware, wiki, and case study. Cognitive skills are developed through co-construction of own electronic textbook content. Problem solving skills are developing over time and authentic tasks.

Not less important role is given to computerized self –assessment. The computerized self –assessment is design especially for motor skills in order to apply main concepts from knowledge graph in learning situations and to receive immediate feedback. The role of immediate feedback is to intensify the automatic processes, which is very important for psychomotor branch of competence. It is not built around a linear cause and effect relationship, but on the interaction between tacit and explicit knowledge. Indeed in some cases, tacit knowledge may lead to explicit knowledge and in others the reverse may be true. Through intermediation the students communicate, make conclusions and construct concept maps at the end of each chapter.

Cognition is the phase of demonstration. The students "integrate" the content in one cognitive structure. The results are evaluated by peers in cooperative or collaborative learning environment. In such environment not teacher, but students are experts. According to Kuolopoulos&Frappaolo the knowledge management solutions are context –sensitive (the student is able to understand the context of the knowledge requirements and tailor the knowledge accordingly); user sensitive (students are able to organize the knowledge in the way most useful for studied domain); flexible (students are able to handle knowledge of any forms); heuristic (students learn about its users and the knowledge it possesses as it is used) and suggestive (students is able to deduce what knowledge needs are, and represent knowledge associations). The knowledge management phases with electronic textbooks are represented in Figure 2.

THE ROLE OF KNOWLEDGE MANAGEMENT IN ENTERPRISE RESOURSES PLANNING MODELS FOR THE EDUCATION SECTOR

Today's enterprise resources planning models of software architecture for the education sector can possibly envelop a broad range of enterprise functions and integrate them into a single unified database repository. Consequently, enterprise resources planning constitute an amalgamation of three most important components:

1. Knowledge Management,
2. Information Technology, and
3. Objectives.

A knowledge management conceptual model provides rules for knowledge creation, knowledge retention, and knowledge transfer and knowledge utilization. All rules are focused on design the knowledge artifacts, including information, meta-data, or/and meta-knowledge. Information Technology "tries" to put knowledge artifacts in teacher –student or/and student – student relationships first, by switching the emphasis from teacher centered philosophy to learner centered philosophy. Learner centered philosophy is done in collaborative learning environment. "In the collaborative learning environment, the learners are challenged both socially and emotionally as they listen to different perspectives, and are required to articulate and defend their ideas. In so doing, the learners begin to create their own unique conceptual frameworks and not rely solely on an expert's or a text's framework. Thus, in a collaborative learning setting, learners have the opportunity to converse with peers, present and defend ideas, exchange diverse beliefs, question other conceptual frameworks, and be actively engaged"(Smith&MacGregor, 1992).

Objectives are designed according to knowledge management phases. The aim to design learning for the information phase is to determine the level of *a priori* knowledge in order to estimate the possibilities to pass cognitive systems from initial state to intermediate. The methodology is based on psychological tests and pretests. For our case, the psychological test represents a tool which measures un-observed constructs through latent variable. Pre-testing is performed to determine students' baseline knowledge for an educational experience or course of study. One of the pos-

Figure 2. The knowledge management phases with electronic textbooks

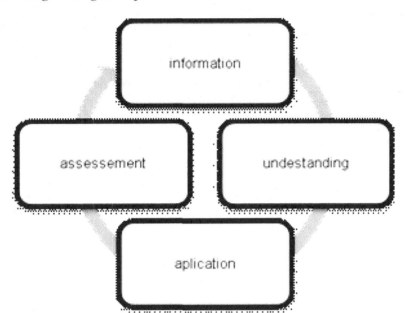

sible methodologies uses methods of gathering information from educational data mining and it's analyzing. For this case the repository of data is gained from education data mining, questionnaires, surveys etc.

Instead, learning designer can organize data according to Bloom (cognitive), Krathwohl (affective) and Simpson (psychomotor) taxonomies. Items, used to get latent variables, are "extracted" from taxonomy verbs. Bloom's taxonomy is a classification of learning objectives related to cognitive domain. The taxonomy provides categories of action verbs arranged in a hierarchy from less to more complexes in six categories: remembering, understanding, applying, analysing, evaluating and creating. Krathwohl taxonomy is the best known of any of the affective taxonomies. It provides five categories of action verbs named receiving, responding, valuing, organization and characterization by a value or value set. Simpson's psychomotor domain allows getting variables which determine the physical or motor skills such as coordination, dexterity, manipulation, grace, strength, speed etc. The action verbs appropriate for this domain can be considered: to choose, to

describe, to detect, to distinguish, to identify, to select, to separate, to construct, to calibrate etc. More actions can be added as result of Information Technology. The difference between Simpson original taxonomy and real needs in action verbs can be proved by Item Response Theory (IRT). According to this theory, the potential of computerized assessment is reflected in a new design of each item, to integrate it in database like battery of items and to present it.

Bloom, Krathwohl and Simpson's taxonomies can be integrated. The idea, proved by concept of "primary and secondary cognitive mechanisms of learning" (Zlate, 1999), is related in Table 1.

It is known that quality of the learning outcomes depends on input. According to knowledge management model understanding is the most important phase and can be described as provide the synergistic effect. The main objective is modeling the hermeneutic dialogue. In order to do this, the knowledge need to be capturing, filtered and stored. The learning management design is an usable form, in which classification and knowledge organization is done in a format that can be much easier to use both for teacher and students. More-

Table 1. Interdependence between Bloom, Krathwohl, and Simpson taxonomies

N	Bloom	Krathwohl	Simpson
1	Remembering: retrieving, recognizing, and recalling relevant knowledge from long-term memory.	Receiving is being aware of or sensitive to the existence of certain ideas, material, or phenomena and being willing to tolerate them. Examples include: to differentiate, to accept, to listen (for), and to respond to.	Perception: chooses, describes, detects, differentiates, distinguishes, identifies, isolates, relates, selects, separates
2	Understanding: constructing meaning from oral, written, and graphic messages through interpreting, exemplifying, classifying, summarizing, inferring, comparing, and explaining.		Set: begins, displays, explains, moves, proceeds, reacts, responds, snows, starts, volunteers.
3	Applying: carrying out or using a procedure through executing, or implementing.	Responding is committed in some small measure to the ideas, materials, or phenomena involved by actively responding to them. Examples are: to comply with, to follow, to commend, to volunteer, to spend leisure time in, to acclaim.	Guided response: assembles, builds, calibrates, constructs, dismantles, displays, dissects, fastens, fixes, grinds, heats, manipulates, measures, mends, mixes, organizes, sketches
4			Mechanism: assembles, builds, calibrates, constructs, dismantles, displays, dissects, fastens, fixes, grinds, heats, manipulates, measures, mends, mixes, organizes and sketches.
5	Analyzing: breaking material into constituent parts, determining how the parts relate to one another and to an overall structure or purpose through differentiating, organizing, and attributing.	Valuing is willing to be perceived by others as valuing certain ideas, materials, or phenomena. Examples: to increase measured proficiency in, to relinquish, to subsidize, to support, to debate.	Complex or overt response: assembles, builds, calibrates, constructs, dismantles, displays, dissects, fastens, fixes, grinds, heats, manipulates, measures, mends, mixes, organizes, sketches.
6	Evaluating: making judgments based on criteria and standards through checking and critiquing.	Organization is to relate the value to those already held and bring it into a harmonious and internally consistent philosophy. Examples are: to discuss, to theorize, to formulate, to balance, and to examine.	Adaptation: adapts, alters changes, rearranges, reorganizes, revises, and varies.
7	Creating: putting elements together to form a coherent or functional whole; reorganizing elements into a new pattern or structure through generating, planning, or producing.	Characterization by value or value set is to act consistently in accordance with the values he or she has internalized. Examples include: to revise, to require, to be rated high in the value, to avoid, to resist, to manage, to resolve.	Origination: arranges, combines, composes, constructs, creates, designs, and originates.

over, the students orally present their own portfolio and receive feedback. The immediate feedback provides the context to develop competence as meta-competence. The meta-competence is concerned with an knowledge in order how to apply skills and knowledge in various task situations, how to monitor and evaluate one's own cognitive processes, how to use effective cognitive aids and tools, how to form higher-order abilities which have to do with being able to learn, adapt,

anticipate and create, rather than with being able to demonstrate that one has the ability to do.

The items are designed according to Bloom, Simpson and Krathwohl taxonomies. At the end of second phase the students took the computerized summative assessment. The number of items differs from 30 to 100, but not less than 30. The test is displayed for 20 minutes, but each item can be viewed less than 2 minute. Each item is elaborated according to psycho- pedagogical requirements. Meaning is created through some forms of representational equivalence between language (symbols) and mental context (environment). When information is subsumed into the learner's cognitive structure it is organized hierarchically. Meaningful learning takes place only if a stable cognitive structure exists.

The application phase aimed elaboration the cognitive schemes through customization / assimilation. These objectives are solved through hierarchy of content and computerized assessment. Application requires knowledge internalization and its dynamic functionality. The internalization provides the connection among knowledge aimed to automate concepts, designed as edge of graph. The assessment strategies integrate the principles into electronic textbook design. In this concept the knowledge competence-building model finally integrates savoir-dire, savoir-faire and savoir-être into functional savoir - vivre structure. The role of assessment is to form a well-defined hierarchy of concepts.

FUTURE RESEARCH DIRECTIONS

In the short term, I intend to extend this work on operational research based on mathematical modeling of learning in open educational system. More work needs to be done to make such models less dependent on educational data mining and more dependent on strategies for learning. As affordance improvements I would like to investigate two techniques: adjacency matrix and knowledge graph.

In the long term, I intend to explore wide-area replication of data into educational data mining. In this context, new algorithms of integrating data mining with pedagogical theory need to be elaborated and tested. It is expected to develop algorithms for new generation of Learning Management System focused on dynamic and flexible structure of competence. Such a structure is probed

by savoir–vivre component of competence, which vitality are based on action verbs characteristics for Bloom, Simpson and Krathwohl taxonomies. The learning objectives result from above mentioned taxonomies.

The emerging trend: metasystems thinking for enterprise resource planning models for the education sector will be future explored. The aim of such research is to explore new algorithms, models and methods which will support learners in understanding and constructing their conceptual and procedural knowledge according to an integrative generalized didactic model. This will allow:

- Using the better integrated learning environment and
- Leading to more coherent learning experiences for students.

The aim focused on generating new knowledge, including electronic textbook in electronic portfolio technology, represent a common source for research the enterprise resource planning models for the educational sector. Currently, state-of-the-art of enterprise resource planning models for the educational sector, with very limited exceptions, cache only static web content and media streams produced by origin servers. My goal here is to overcome limitations of work –related learning environment for learning, including issues such as professional networking, global classrooms, and limits on scholar learning.

While learning can be done at macro and micro level and that learning can be done at different levels: individual, group, organizational and (open innovation) network learning (Lappia, 2011), more research on practical applications of metasystems principles of new didactic model is needed. Future research is based on constructivism learning theory. The metasystems approach of constructivist learning provides the models for thought and presentations the ideas allowing developing metasystems thinking.

CONCLUSION

In this paper the answer to the research question is formulated: How to apply the knowledge management model for electronic textbook design? When learners are engaged in active learning, the information/communication processes, cognitive processes and assessment processes have to be arranged "in order to facilitate students to learn constructively and to progressively recontextualize knowledge, skills and attitudes" (Lappia, 2011, p.586).

We are considering a procedure for metasystems thinking about planning instruction in which the integrated Bloom, Simpson and Krathwohl taxonomies plays a key role. In instructional design the objectives indicate what a learner should be able to do after completing a unit of knowledge. In our case the objectives aimed to develop a core structure of competence. The affordance of structure is based on face–to–face communication, hermeneutic dialogue, self –pacing the content and computerized self-assessment. Each learning activity is related to one of these three patterns.

Work related enterprise resources planning models for the education sector are still rare. The practical experience is obtained from designing the practical applications and its analysing.

REFERENCES

Allen, D., Kern, T., & Havenhand, M. (2001). ERP critical success factors: an exploration of the contextual factors in public sector institutions. In *Proceedings of the 35th Annual Hawaii International Conference on System Sciences, HICSS* (pp. 3062 – 3071).

Allison, K. (2003). *Rhetoric and hypermedia in electronic textbooks*. Ph.D. dissertation, Texas Woman's University.

Bellier, S. (2004). *Le savoir-être dans l'entreprise: Utilité en gestion des ressources humaines*. Paris, France: Vuibert.

Catts, H., & Kamhi, A. (2005). Excerpt from language and reading disabilities. Retrieved from http://www.education.com/reference/article/metacognitive-process-text-comprehension/

Criswell, E. (1989). *The design of computer-based instruction*. New York, NY: Macmillan Publishing Company.

Davis, D. (1988). Professionalism means putting your profession first. *Journal of Legal Ethics*, *2*(1), 341.

Duffy, T., & Jonassen, D. (1992). *Constructivism and the technology of instruction: A conversation*. USA: Lawrence Erlbaum Associated.

Esteves, J., & Pastor, J. (2001). Enterprise resource planning systems research: An annotated bibliography. *Communications of the Association for Information System, 7*(8).

Frumkes, L. (1996). *Design and materials for an electronic textbook for first-year Russian*. Ph.D. dissertation, University of Washington.

Gérard, F., & Roegiers, X. (2009). *Des manuels scolaires pour apprendre: Concevoir, évaluer, utiliser*. Editons De Boeck Universite, Groupe De Boeck.

Gilbreth, L. (1921). *The psychology of management*. The Macmillan Company. Retrieved August 16, 2010, from http://www.gutenberg.org/files/16256/16256-h/16256-h.htm

Henninger, M., & Kutter, A. (2010). Integration of education and technology – A Long-term study about possibilities and adequacy of a learning management system for education. *Journal on Systemics, Cybernetics, and Informatics*, *8*(3).

Koulopoulos, T., & Frappaolo, C. (2000). *Smart things to know about knowledge management.* Cornwall, UK: T. J. International Ltd.

Leach, D. (2004). Professionalism: The formation of physicians. *The American Journal of Bioethics, 4*(2). doi:10.1162/152651604323097619

Mager, R. (1997). *Preparing instructional objectives.* CEP Press.

Mager, R. (2011). *Preparing instructional objectives. A critical tool in the development of effective instruction.* Atlanta, GA: CEP Press, The Center for Effective Performance, Inc.

Mergel, B. (2007). Contemporary learning theories, instructional design and leadership. *Studies in Educational Leadership, 6,* 67–98. doi:10.1007/978-1-4020-6022-9_5

Nonaka, I., & von Krogh, G. (2009). Tacit knowledge and knowledge conversion: Controversy and advancement in organizational knowledge creation theory. *Organization Science, 20*(3), 635–652. doi:10.1287/orsc.1080.0412

Okada, A. (2005). The collective building of knowledge in collaborative learning environments. In Roberts, T. (Ed.), *Computer–supported collaborative learning in higher education.* Hershey, PA: Idea Group Publishing. doi:10.4018/978-1-59140-408-8.ch004

Porter, P. (2010). *Effectiveness of electronic textbooks with embedded activities on student learning.* Ph.D. dissertation, Capella University.

Railean, E. (2006). Concept mapping in instructional design of educational software. *Proceedings of 8th International Conference on Development and Application Systems.*

Railean E. (2008) Aspects of teaching and learning processes in the closed and open didactical systems. *Learning Technology Newsletter, 10*(4).

Railean, E. (2010). *A new didactical model for elaboration the electronic textbooks.* ICVL 2010.

Railean, E. (2010). Metasystems approach to research the globalised pedagogical processes. *Annals of Spiru Haret University Mathematics – Informatics Series, Special Issue New Results on E - Learning Methodologies, 31* – 50.

Railean, E. (2012). Issues and challenges associated with the design of electronic textbook. In Khan, B. H. (Ed.), *User interface design for virtual environments: Challenges and advances* (pp. 238–256). Hershey, PA: IGI Global. doi:10.4018/978-1-61350-516-8.ch015

Reavy, A. (2011). *Schools looking forward to future with electronic textbooks.* Retrieved from http://www.sj-r.com/top-stories/x767223962/Schools-looking-forward-to-future-with-electronic-textbooks.

Roberts, T. (2006). *Self, peer, and group assessment in e-learning.* Hershey, PA: Idea Group Publishing. doi:10.4018/978-1-59140-965-6

Rudic, G. (2011). *Center for Modern Pedagogy blog.* Retrieved from http://www.pedagogiemoderne.com/blog

Schnitzer, D. (2003). *What is quantum psychology?* Retrieved from http://users.skynet.be/sky52523/en/peronal_development/quantum_psychology.htm

Schütt, P. (2003). The post-Nonaka knowledge management. *Journal of Universal Computer Science, 9*(6), 451–462.

Smith, B., & MacGregor, J. (1992). What is collaborative learning? In Goodsell, A. S., Maher, M. R., & Tinto, V. (Eds.), *Collaborative learning: A sourcebook for higher education. National Center on Postsecondary Teaching, Learning, & Assessment.* Syracuse University.

Smith, W., & Moore, J. (2004). *Programmed learning: Theory and research. An enduring problem in psychology*. Princeton, NJ: D. Van Nostrand company, Inc.

Stoffa, V. (2007). *Modelling, simulation, animation in e-learning courses*. Retrieved from http://www.ittk.hu/netis/doc/textbook/stoffa_animation_eng.pdf

Taylor, F. (1911). *The principles of scientific management*, (pp. 5 – 29). New York, NY: Harper Bros. Retrieved August 16, 2010, from http://www.fordham.edu/halsall/mod/1911taylor.html

Thamisgith. (2011). *Electronic textbooks - Better for students, better for the environment*. Retrieved from http://thamisgith.hubpages.com/hub/Electronic-Textbooks---Better-For-Students--Better-For-The-Environment

Uluoglu, B. (2006). *Declarative / procedural knowledge*. Retrieved from http://www.designophy.com/designpedia/design-term-1000000001-declarative-.-procedural-knowledge.htm

Уилсон Р. Квантовая психология. Киев: Янус. (1998). 304 с.

Zeleny, M. (2012). *Knowledge-information circulation through the enterprise: Forward to the roots of knowledge management*. Retrieved from http://www.bnet.fordham.edu/zeleny/pdf/kn_infor_cir.pdf

Zlate, M. (1999). *Psihologia mecanismelor cognitive* (The psychology of cognitive mechanisms).

Iasi, Romania: Polirom. Беспалько, В. (2007). Параметры и критерии диагностической цели (The parameters and criterions for diagnostic aim). В: Образовательные технологии. 1. Полат, Е.,

Бухаркина, М., & Моисеева М. (2004). *Теория и практика дистанционного обучения* (Theory and practice of distance learning). Москва: Академия.

ADDITIONAL READING

Lappia, J. (2011). Towards design guidelines for work related learning arrangements. *Journal of European Industrial Training, 35*(6). doi:10.1108/03090591111150103

McInerney, C. (2002). Knowledge Management and the dynamic nature of knowledge. *Journal of the American Society for Information Science and Technology, 53*(12), 1009–1018. doi:10.1002/asi.10109

Morey, D., Maybury, M., & Thuraisingham, B. (2002). *Knowledge management: Classic and contemporary works*. Cambridge, MA: MIT Press.

Wright, K. (2005). Personal knowledge management: supporting individual knowledge worker performance. *Knowledge Management Research and Practice, 3*(3), 156–165. doi:10.1057/palgrave.kmrp.8500061

Chapter 6

Institutional Knowledge Repositories:
Enterprise Content Management in Academics

Gayatri Doctor
CEPT University, India

ABSTRACT

An Institutional Knowledge Repository (IKR) is "a digital archive of intellectual product created by the faculty, research staff, and students of an institution and accessible to end users both within and outside of the institution, with few if any barriers to access." This chapter discusses the growing trend in Open Access Repositories, Institutional Repositories worldwide. It throws light on the concepts of enterprise resource planning and enterprise content management and then explores academic institutions in India who have already initiated the use of Institutional Knowledge Repositories, as an enterprise content management system for knowledge sharing & management with regard to content, access, and other factors.

INTRODUCTION

The development of the internet and application of information technologies on academic campuses has led to significant changes in scholarly communication among both faculty and students. Technology is opening up avenues for innovation in design and delivery of courses, sharing of expertise and content among faculty and students. Educational material is now being created in digital formats. This digital educational material is used for teaching and for enhancing the traditional method of imparting education. The traditional model of imparting education is being transformed to a new model of imparting education. This new model or the modern profile of education is characterized by the digital nature of information & knowledge that is involved between the academic institutes, the teachers, students and the educational resources (Mahadevan & Rahman, 2002).

Nonaka's dynamic theory of organizational knowledge creation holds that organizational knowledge is created through a continuous dialogue between tacit knowledge (derived from personal experience and reflects individual be-

DOI: 10.4018/978-1-4666-2193-0.ch006

liefs) and explicit knowledge (formal codified knowledge that can be communicated to others) via four patterns of interactions - socialization, combination, internalization and externalization (Nonaka, 1997). Once knowledge is explicit, it can be transferred as explicit knowledge through a process Nonaka calls "combination" (Nonaka, A dynamic theory of organizational knowledge creation, 1994). This is where information technology is most helpful, for information can be digitized, stored and shared.

Academic institutions grow and revitalize themselves through the knowledge they create, their processes for passing that knowledge on to others and the exchanges and relationships they foster among people. Knowledge management in academics can be thought of as a framework or an approach that enables people within the institute to develop a set of practices to collect information and share what they know, leading to action that improves services and outcomes. A Knowledge management system in its initial stages can be broken into several subcomponents like repositories, collaborative platforms, networks, culture (Tiwana, 1997).

In simplest terms, a Digital Repository is where digital content, assets, are stored and can be searched and retrieved for later use. A repository supports mechanisms to import, export, identify, store and retrieve digital assets. A Digital Repository can hold a wide range of materials for a variety of purposes and users. It can support research, learning, and administrative processes. Digital Repositories in Academic Institutions may include research outputs and journal articles, theses, e-learning objects and teaching materials or research data. A repository in an academic institution is a type of content management system that both holds the core intellectual assets of the institution (a university or college), and enables them to be used to support a variety of business processes as defined in the institution's information strategy (Hayes, 2005). The creation of repositories is becoming a growing requirement in academic

institutions for capturing and managing intellectual assets, information and knowledge sharing.

Open Access (OA) [1] means free and online access to scholarly literature that can be freely disseminated further with proper author attribution. It brings down barriers to the scientific communication by using Internet (Suber, 2007). Open Access accelerates research, enriches education, and shares learning across rich and poor nations (David, 2005). Open-access (OA) literature is digital, online, free of charge, and free of most copyright and licensing restrictions. The Budapest (February 2002), Bethesda (June 2003), and Berlin (October 2003) definitions of "open access" are the most central and influential for the Open Access movement. When authors make their articles freely available in digital form on the Internet, they are said to be "self-archiving" (Bailey, 2006).

There are two primary vehicles for delivering Open Access to research articles, namely OA Journals and OA Archives. OA Journals or Publishing is like conventional scholarly publishing involving peer reviewing of submitted articles by authors. The difference being that published content is freely accessible over Internet. Various business models sustain such open access publishing. The Directory of Open Access Journals (DOAJ) [2] covers free, full text, quality controlled scientific and scholarly journals. OA archives or repositories refer to uploading published or pre published documents in publicly accessible digital repositories. These repositories provide easy access to there collection and allow other systems to harvest their metadata associated with documents. The exchange of such metadata is in accordance to now well-established "Open Archives Initiative–Protocol for Metadata Harvesting (OAI-PMH) [3]" protocol. OA archives are of two types – institutional and subject oriented. Institutional Repositories hold documents authored by its staff members and students. Subject repositories hold documents pertaining to a particular subject area.

Open-Source [4] software is computer software whose source code is available under a copyright license that permits users to study, change, and improve the software, and to redistribute it in modified or unmodified form. OA repository software needs to be Open Source, such that institutions and organizations even with minimal resources could run it. There are many systems of open-source software to build and maintain OA archives (Crow, 2004).

INSTITUTIONAL REPOSITORY (IR)

Institutional repositories hold documents of scholarly materials that may provide first hand information on research findings of researchers of the host institutions. They also increase access to scholarly materials, as these are freely available to the scholars and peer groups. An institutional repository may include full-text contents of journal articles, conference papers, book chapters, monographs, research reports, project reports, theses, dissertations, patents, presentations, computer programs, tutorials, convocation addresses, audio materials, video materials, multimedia materials, handbooks, data books, technical manuals, beside many others types of documents. Institutional repositories have capability to build up collections for different users' categories and incorporate different forms of documents (Das, Sen, & Dutta, 2005).

An Institutional Repository (IR) is "a digital archive of intellectual product created by the faculty, research staff, and students of an institution and accessible to end users both within and outside of the institution, with few if any barriers to access" (Rajshekhar, 2003).

For an Academic Institution, this would include materials such as research journal articles, before (pre prints) and after (post prints) undergoing peer review, and digital versions of theses and dissertations, but it might also include other digital assets generated by normal academic life, such as administrative documents, course notes, or learning objects.

An Institutional Repository is defined by Clifford Lynch as "A university-based institutional repository is a set of services that a university offers to the members of its community for the management and dissemination of digital materials created by the institution and its community members" (Lynch, 2003).

Institutional Repositories help in establishing priority to your research findings, long-term preservation of research papers, improved research knowledge management, integrated view of your institutional research which is otherwise distributed over a large number of external sources. It is advantageous for Academic Institutions to have an Institutional Repository to provide seamless access to the digital intellectual product of the Institution and promote knowledge sharing. Hence they are also referred to as Institutional Knowledge Repositories (IKR).

The structure of an Institutional Repository can be seen in Figure 1.

The Open Society Institute (OSI)[10] helps organizations with an important facet of their repository planning: selecting the software system that best satisfies their institution's needs. These software should be:

- With an Open Source license—that is, they are available for free and can be freely modified, upgraded, and redistributed;
- Comply with the latest version of the Open Archives Initiative metadata harvesting protocols to ensure that each implementation can participate in a global network of interoperable research repositories.

The Open Society Institute's Guide to Institutional Repository Software discusses different Institutional Software like DSpace, Eprints, Archimede, CDSware, Fedora, iTor, OPUS etc. These software's allow an institution to implement a complete framework for an OAI compliant repository without resorting to in-house technical development (Crow, 2004).

Figure 1. The structure of an institutional repository

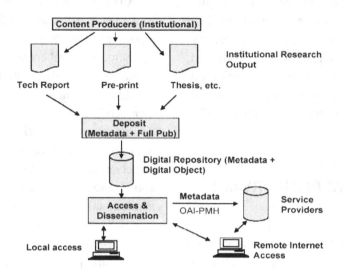

There is a growing trend worldwide in the creation of Open Access digital repositories. As can be seen from Figure 2, the Directory of Open Access Repositories (Open DOAR)[6] lists a total of 2116 Open Access Repositories in the world. Of these, it lists 406 Open Access Repositories in United States of America, 200 Open Access Repositories in United Kingdom, 147 Open Access Repositories in Germany and 52 Open Access Repositories in India. The Registry of Open Access Repositories (Open ROAR)[5] lists a total of 1900 Open Access Repositories in the world. Of these, it lists 395 Open Access Repositories in United States of America, 214 Open Access Repositories in United Kingdom, 134 Open Access Repositories in Germany and 75 Open Access Repositories in India. This indicates that the development of Open Access Repositories in India is still in nascent stages as compared to other countries.

From Figure 3 it is seen that the Directory of Open Access Repositories (Open DOAR) lists a total of 2116 Open Access Repositories of which 1900 are Institutional Repositories and The Registry of Open Access Repositories (ROAR) lists a total of 1900 Open Access Repositories of which 1550 are Institutional Repositories. This indicates that the development of Institutional Repositories

form a major component of the Open Access Repositories in the World.

From Figure 4, it is observed that Open DOAR lists 286 Institutional Repositories in United States of America, 146 Institutional Repositories in United Kingdom, 131 Institutional Repositories in Germany and 47 Institutional Repositories in India while ROAR lists 232 Institutional Repositories in United States of America, 132 Institutional Repositories in United Kingdom, 81 Institutional Repositories in Germany and 50 Institutional Repositories in India.

A few Institutional Repositories available at Academic Institutions are DSpace@MIT (Massachusetts Institute of Technology) e-Prints SOTON (University of Southampton) while subject based Open Archives are RePEc (Research Papers in Economics), SSRN (Social Science Research Network).

In the Indian context, Premier academic institutions, like Indian Institute of Science; Indian Institute of Management, Kozhikode; Indian Statistical Institute, Bangalore; Indian Institute of Technology, Delhi etc. have established open access institutional knowledge repositories (IKR's) that disseminate research outputs of the respective institution. Subject specific Reposi-

Figure 2. Number of open access repositories

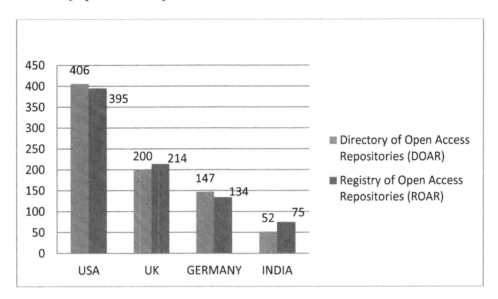

tories like Librarian's Digital Library (LDL) of Documentation Research and Training Centre (DRTC), Bangalore for library and information professionals and OpenMed@NIC, maintained by National Informatics Centre, for Medical and Allied Sciences are also in existence. There is a growing trend in the creation of Institutional Knowledge Repositories in India.

ENTERPRISE RESOURCE PLANNING (ERP)

Enterprise Resource Planning (ERP) is a concept for planning and managing resource organization, so it can be used optimally to produce more values for all parts and for all those having concern with the organization (Hardioni, 2009). ERP consists

Figure 3. Institutional and open access repositories

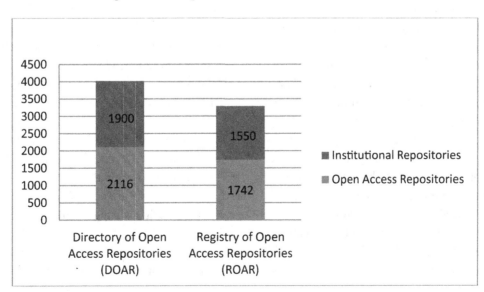

Figure 4. Number of institutional repositories

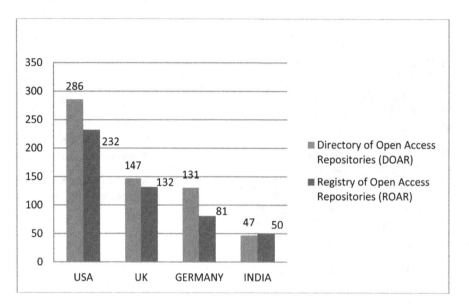

of three words, i.e. enterprise, resource, and planning. Enterprise is a company or an organization which describes a business situation in common, in one corporate entity, in many measurements/size, starting from a small business like café and up to a large business like telecommunications' company. Resource can be a company's asset consisting of finances, human resources, consumers, suppliers, orders, technology and strategy as well. Planning is a strategy or plan that will be applied by the companies to reach out their targets (Rao, 2000). The advantages that they can get by using ERP's system because ERP offers integrated system in a company, enables management to manage operation, helps to carry on the implementation of supplier management with their multiple capability.

ERP's system consists of a group of modules which support many functions and processes in a company (See Figure 5). ERP's modules are built to support this process by integrating data in every stage of process. Besides, ERP's system, ideally, must be able to fulfill the support of main business process and their supporter's business. ERP has seven main modules, i.e. finances, sale and distribution, production, human resources,

maintenance of production's tool, purchase, quality of management, and material management (Scott, 2004).

Enterprise Resource Planning (ERP) in Academics

Even in Academics, ERP is playing a tactical role in designing and managing academic resources (See Figure 7). Academic institutions and universities all over the world are facing challenges in designing robust Enterprise Resource Planning applications and methodologies to align themselves with the expectations of students and other stakeholders (Enterprise Content Management-ERP & ECM).

ERP in academics can be defined as follows:

- Enterprise = Academic Institution
- Resources = Academic Institutional Assets, Intellectual Capital
- Planning = Strategy, Knowledge Sharing, Knowledge Management

Intellectual Capital is the sum of its human capital (talent- skills and knowledge of the people), structural capital (intellectual property, methodologies, software, documents and other knowledge artifacts) and customer capital (client relationships) (Stewart, 1997).

An Academic Institution's Intellectual Capital is the sum of its human capital (talent- skills and knowledge of the people- faculty & students), structural capital (intellectual property – the published scholarly material of its faculty, methodologies, software, documents – technical reports, question banks and other knowledge objects) and customer capital (client relationships- students, corporate).

If an academic institution focuses on improving learning outcomes, making a tangible difference to the teaching and learning processes, it must use a range of comprehensive technologies, content and services seamlessly integrated to create a sustainable, robust, learning infrastructure and deliver learning and ensure knowledge assurance (See Figure 6). The key technologies being Campus ERP, Learning Management Systems, Content Authoring and Management, Virtual Classroom, Online testing and assessment.

From first contact with a prospective student through graduation and alumni relations, aca-

demic ERP software for colleges and universities should efficiently manage the full student lifecycle by combining into one solution Admissions/CRM, Registration, Financial Aid, Fiscal Management, Document Management, Student Services, Portals, Built-in Course Management/LMS, Development, Alumni Relations.

Enterprise Content Management (ECM)

Enterprise Content Management (ECM) is the strategies, methods and tools used to capture, manage, store, preserve, and deliver content and documents related to organizational processes (See Figure 8). ECM covers the management of information within the entire scope of an enterprise whether that information is in the form of a paper document, an electronic file, a database print stream, or even an email ("What is Enterprise Content Management (ECM)?", 2010).

Enterprise Content Management (ECM) is an umbrella of tools and strategies that allow an organization to create, manage, deliver, store and dispose content and documents related to organization's business needs. ECM tools and strategies

Figure 5. ERP modules

Figure 6. Integrated learning solution

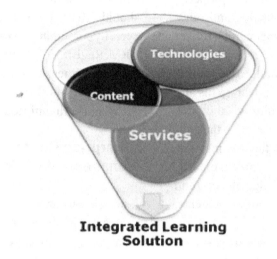

allow the management of an organization's unstructured information, wherever that information exists.

Enterprise Content Management (ECM), as a form of content management combines the capture, search and networking of documents with digital archiving, document management and workflow. It specifically includes the special challenges involved in using and preserving a company's internal, often unstructured information, in all of its forms. Therefore, most ECM solutions focus on Business-to-Employee (B2E) systems.[7]

Enterprise Resource Planning (ERP) seeks to combine all the traditional business applications, making them exchange information among themselves. This can help not only to reduce data entry but also facilitate lean operations leading to more significant cost advantages. And lower costs translate into a competitive advantage for a business. Enterprise Content Management (ECM) seeks to

Figure 7. Academic ERP modules

Figure 8. Enterprise content management

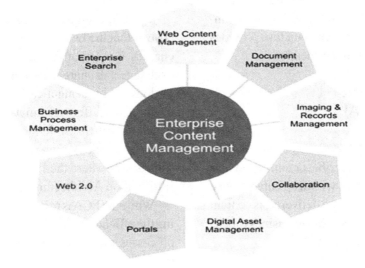

go further, seeking to create a knowledgebase of the enterprise's business experience and content resources. Enterprise Content Planning (ECP) typically features a common content repository that accommodates all kinds of content and permits online Web access from anywhere in the world.

ECM accepts both structured and unstructured content in its data repository that has a uniform structure. The ECM content repository is separate from transactional databases and is optimized differently. The repository is optimized for

query and analysis rather than transaction speed. Under ECM systems, users can extract business knowledge by querying the content repository. All kinds of queries are facilitated through the use of metadata attached to the documents that constitute the repository's content.

Enterprise Content Management is used as a uniform repository for all types of information. ECM is used as a content warehouse (both data warehouse and document warehouse) that combines company information in a repository with

Figure 9. Enterprise content architecture

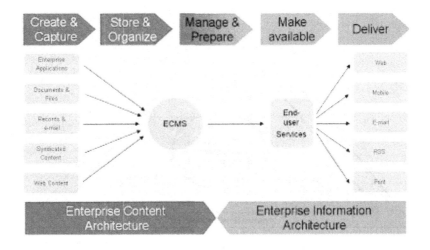

a uniform structure. Expensive redundancies and associated problems with information consistency are eliminated. All applications deliver their content to a single repository, which in turn provides needed information to all applications.

Enterprise Content Architecture (ECA)

The role of an Enterprise Content Architecture (ECA) is to structure, describe, organize and harmonize content resources within an enterprise so that they can be managed and delivered as content products to end users according to business needs and requirements (See Figure 9).

One of the main drivers for establishing an ECA is to reduce the costs for producing and managing content. Simply put, an ECA will bring valuable content resources to the surface so that they can be accessed and found. The reverse scenario is that you don't find the content resources you are looking for and need to re-produce them. Furthermore, if a content product needs to be delivered in different ways – such as via different channels that require different format and structure for the content product - the ECA makes

sure that the content resources from which the content product is built can be reused.

What is even more important than reducing costs is that the ECA provides the foundation that enables users (humans aswell as machines) to exchange and share information and knowledge. Is does so by semantically integrating content resources of different formats, structure and types which are otherwise living on their own islands (or kept in silos) somewhere in the enterprise. This is also where the ECA meets the Enterprise Information Architecture (EIA).

While the ECA is primarily focused on supporting the effiency of enterprise content management processes, the EIA is primarily focused on supporting the information needs within the enterprise - to provide the right information at the right time to the right user. Is does so by defining, organizing and describing content products in ways that it supports how different users in different usage contexts look for information and how they want / need the information delivered to them. It goes without saying that need to have both an ECA and an EIA and that they need to harmonize while still being allowed to be different.

An Enterprise Content Architecture semantically organizes content resources that may be of

Figure 10. Institutional repository architecture

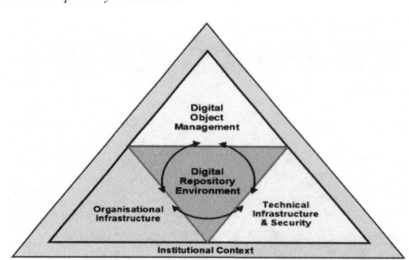

Table 1. Institutional repositories in India registered at DOAR

Repository name	Num. Recs.	Pubs	Confs	Theses	Unpub	Other	Base URL	Software
CMFRI Digital Repository	3633	+	+	+	+	+		EPrints
Delhi College of Engineering Repository	326				+	+		DSpace
Dhananjayarao Gadigil Library	1539	+			+	+		DSpace
Digital Knowledge Repository of Central Drug Research Institute	135				+		OAI	DSpace
Digital Library at Indian Statistical Institute, Bangalore	191							DSpace
Digital repository of Cochin University of Science & Technology	995			+		+	OAI	DSpace
DRS at National Institute Of Oceanography	3763		+	+			OAI	DSpace
DSpace @ GGSIPU	133			+		+	OAI	DSpace
dspace @ sdmcet	67	+		+	+	+		DSpace
DSpace at CUSAT	3199	+	+	+		+		DSpace
DSpace at IBS Ahmedabad	171	+	+		+	+	OAI	DSpace
DSpace at Indian Institute of Management Kozhikode	290		+	+	+		OAI	DSpace
DSpace at National Chemical Laboratory	407			+	+	+	OAI	DSpace
DSpace at NCRA	84			+	+	+		DSpace
DSpace at Vidyanidhi	5480			+			OAI	DSpace
DSpace@IITB	1657		+				OAI	DSpace
DSpace@INFLIBNET	1144		+			+	OAI	DSpace
Dspace@NITR	653	+	+	+			OAI	DSpace
DSpace@PDPU	64				+		OAI	DSpace
DSpace@TU	938		+	+				DSpace
DU Eprint Archive	170	+	+	+		+	OAI	EPrints
eGyankosh	6190					+		DSpace
Electronic Theses and Dissertations at Indian Institute of Science	206			+			OAI	DSpace
Eprint@NML	1419	+	+	+		+		EPrints
Eprints@IARI	82		+	+	+			EPrints
EPrints@IITD	2141			+			OAI	DSpace
ePrints@NII	10				+		OAI	EPrints
Eprints@SBT MKU	21						OAI	EPrints
ICRISAT Open Access Repository	3399		+			+		DSpace
IIT Roorkee Repository	823		+			+		DSpace
IMSc Eprint Archive	41		+			+	OAI	EPrints
Indian Academy of Sciences: Publications of Fellows	39024						OAI	EPrints
Indian Institute of Astrophysics Repository	4211			+		+	OAI	DSpace
Indian Institute of Management Kozhikode Digital Library		+				+		[Unknown]

continued on following page

Table 1. Continued

Repository name	Num. Recs.	Pubs	Confs	Theses	Unpub	Other	Base URL	Software
Indian Institute of Petroleum Institutional Repository	439							DSpace
Institutional Repository of Intectual Contributions of Delhi Technological University	841			+		+	OAI	DSpace
Kautilya Digital Repository at IGIDR	193		+	+	+		OAI	DSpace
Knowledge Repository of Indian Institute of Horticultural Research	160				+	+		DSpace
Mahatma Gandhi University Theses Online	913			+				Nitya
Management Development Institute - Open Access Repository	325	+	+			+	OAI	DSpace
National Aerospace Laboratories Institutional Repository	1320		+	+	+	+	OAI	EPrints
National Science Digital Library	504	+						DSpace
NISCAIR Online Periodical Repository	2020					+		DSpace
Open Access Repository of IISc Research Publications	18949	+	+		+	+	OAI	EPrints
Raman Research Institute Digital Repository	3568				+	+	OAI	DSpace
Sardar Vallabhbai National Institute of Technology EPrints	14		+				OAI	EPrints
Vidya Prasarak Mandal - Thane	411		+			+		DSpace

Source: http://www.opendoar.org

different granularity and be more or less structured. The architecture – relationships between content following certain rules – is created with the use of metadata, such as taxonomies. The ECA also addresses how to structure, describe and store content resources for optimal production, management and delivery of content products to content workers and end users in the business.

IKR as ECM in Academics

The Institutional Repository Architecture like the Enterprise Content Architecture (ECA) is to structure, describe, organize content resources within the repository so that they can be managed and delivered to end users. The Institutional Knowledge Repository architecture is shown in Figure 10. They can be either open or closed. An open architecture can be contributed to by a group of persons not necessarily the platform develop-

ers. Open Source IR usually posses this type of architecture. The open architecture of most IR platforms can be further sub-divided into three-tier architecture and plug –in architecture. Most IR possess the three tier architecture except for EPrints that has a flexible plug-in architecture for developing extensions (Adewumi & Ikhu-Omoregbe, 2011).

Faculty and research staff in Academic Institutions is into publishing scholarly material consisting of articles, journal papers, conference papers, case studies, books compiled etc. These scholarly publications and teaching material represent the structural intellectual capital of individuals and the institution. They are knowledge intensive and need to be captured to facilitate knowledge sharing, bring visibility to research and be useful to other faculty and the institution.

Institutional Repositories are emerging technologies for capturing structural intellectual capital, knowledge sharing and management in academic and research institutions, especially in developing countries like India.

Institutional Knowledge Repositories are Enterprise Content Management Systems which need to be developed for sharing and preserving academic content like intellectual capital, teaching material of faculties, students of an Academic Institution.

Institutional Knowledge Repositories in Indian Academic Institutions

Academic Institutions in India have already initiated the use of Institutional Knowledge Repositories, as an enterprise content management system for knowledge sharing & management with regard to Content - the types of content and the amount of content they have made available, Access - whether the repository is available only on the institutional intranet or open for access on the internet, the Repository Software being used and other factors. The Repositories could be in different stages of development, pilot testing or currently hosted only on the Institute Intranet.

The Directory of Open Access Repositories (DOAR) lists 47 Institutional Repositories in India while the Registry of Open Access Repositories (ROAR) lists 50 Institutional Repositories as on 18[th d] Oct, 2011. Table 1 lists the 47 Institutional Repositories available in India, which have been registered in DOAR. It can be observed that the table indicates the repository name, the software used, the number of records available in the repository, the base URL (whether OAI enabled or not) and the type of content – Publications, Conference Papers, Theses, Unpublished information, Others.

The DSpace Website, has a link "Whos using Dspace"[8]. This site indicates that there are 81 users of DSpace in India and of them 27 users are Institutional Repositories. Of these Institutions like Narmada College of Science & Commerce, Federal Institute of Scienec and Technology (FISAT), IES Management and Research Centre have

their repositories on the Institute Intranet, not open to the public.

There exists a DSpace Users Club[9] where Institutions like Bharatesh Education Trust's Global Business School, Belgaum, M N Dastur & Company (P) Ltd, Kolkata, Deccan College of Medical Sciences, Hyderabad, Trident Institute of Management Sciences, Belgaum, Indian Statistical Institute, Kolkata, R. K. College of Engineering & Technology, Rajkot, Pandit Deendayal Petroleum Univesity, Gandhinagar are registered. This indicates that these Institutions have installed or are in process of installation of a Institutional Repository.

A lot of other Institutions like IIM Ahmedabad, Nirma University, Calorex Foundation are using DSpace for their Institutional Knowledge Collection on their Institutional intranet whereas some Institutions like CEPT University is in the implementation stage on their intranet.

CONCLUSION

Knowledge Management and Information Management, often used synonymously, are concepts that are needed to be used in the future (if not already doing so). Information Professionals and Librarians will have to envisage new ways of working, new organisational relationships, new services, and new professional roles, requiring the letting go of some much-loved 'traditional' frameworks. The future will include a blend of centralised services, such as enterprise content management systems and institutional repositories, customer relationship management systems, and enterprise-level federated search engines. The concepts of the library catalogue, authority control, classification and standards will be challenged by the rapidly expanding use of social networking tools, such as blogs and wikis (Mcknight, 2007).

There will be an increasing prevalence of different content management systems within organisations. The library online catalogue and digital repositories of research publications, licensed image collections, digital copies of past examination papers, digital reading list resources and the like will be increasingly complemented by web content management systems, searchable repositories of digital learning objects and curriculum resources, in-house manuals, and other institutional intellectual property in content management systems (Mcknight, 2007).

REFERENCES

AAIM. (2010). *What is enterprise content management (ECM)?* Retrieved September 20, 2010, from http://www.aiim.org/What-is-ECM-Enterprise-Content-Management.aspx.

Adewumi, A., & Ikhu-Omoregbe, N. (2011). Institutional repositories: Features, architecture, design and implementation technologies. *Journal of Computing, 2*(8).

Bailey, C. (2006). *What is open access.* Retrieved from http://www.digital-scholarship.com/cwb/WhatIsOA.pdf

Crow, R. (2004, August). *A guide to institutional repository software.* Open Society Institute. Retrieved from http://www.soros.org/openaccess/pdf/OSI_Guide_to_IR_Software_v3.pdf.

Das, A. K., Sen, B. K., & Dutta, C. (2005). *Digitization of scholarly materials in India.* ICDE Conference 2005, Tokyo.

David, P. (2005). *Fulfilling the promise of scholarly publishing: Can open access deliver?* IFLA 2005 Satellite Meeting No 17, Oslo, Norway. Retrieved from http://www.ub.uio.no/konferanser/ifla/IFLA_open_access/programme_abstracts.htm.

Enterprise Content Management-ERP & ECM. (n.d.). Retrieved June 14, 2011, from http://www.ademero.com/resources/learning-center/enterprise-content-management/erp-and-ecm.php

Hamilton, S. (2004). *Justification of ERP investments part 4: Replacing or re-implementing an ERP system.* Retrieved February 1, 2012, from http://www.technologyevaluation.com/Research/ResearchHighlights/Erp/2004/02/research_notes/TU_ER_XSH_02_13_04_1.asp

Hardiono, A. D. R., & Tintri, D. (2009). ERP analysis and implementation module of sale & distribution by tiny ERP. *Proceedings PESAT (Psikologi, Ekonomi, Sastra, Arsitektur & Sipil)* Universitas Gunadarma – Depok. ISSN 1858-2559

Hayes, H. (2005, August). *Digital repositories helping universities and colleges.* JISC Briefing Paper - High Education Sector. Retrieved from http://ww.jisc.ac.uk/uploaded_documents/HE_repositories_briefing_paper_2005.pdf

Lynch, C. (2003). *Institutional repositories - Essential infrastructure for scholarship in the digital age.* ARL Bimonthly report 226. Retrieved from http://www.arl.org/newsltr/226/ir.html

Mahadevan, S., & Rahman, S. (2002). *Modern profile of a digital library and the associated learning object model for posting, meta-tagging and integrating content into digital libraries.* 32nd ASEE/IEEE Frontiers in Education Conference, November 6-9, 2002, Boston, MA.

Mcknight, S. (2007). *A futuristic view of knowledge and information management.* Retrieved October 18, 2011, from http://www.ub.edu/bid/19mcknig.htm

Nonaka, I. (1994). A dynamic theory of organizational knowledge creation. *Organization Science, 5*(1), 14–37. doi:10.1287/orsc.5.1.14

Nonaka, I. (1997). *Organizational knowledge creation.* Knowledge Advantage Conference.

Rajshekhar, T. B. (2003). *Improving the visibility of indian research - An institutional open access model.* Indo-US Workshop on Open Digital Libraries and Interoperability.

Rao, S. S. (2000). Enterprise resource planning: Business needs and technologies. *Industrial Management & Data Systems*, *100*(2), 81–88. doi:10.1108/02635570010286078

Stewart, T. (1997). *Intellectual capital*. Double-Day Business.

Suber, P. (2007, June). *Open access overview*. Retrieved from http://www.earlham.edu/~peters/fos/overview.htm

Tiwana, A. (1997). *The knowledge management toolkit - Practical techniques for building a KM system*. Pearson Education.

Wikipedia. (n.d.). *Open access*. Retrieved June 1, 2011, from http://en.wikipedia.org/wiki/Open_access

ENDNOTES

[1]   Wikipedia definition of Open Access http://en.wikipedia.org/wiki/Open_access

[2]   Directory of Open Access Journals (DOAJ) http://www.doaj.org/

[3]   Open Archives Initiative – Protocol for Metadata Harvesting (OAI-PMH) http://www.openarchives.org/

[4]   Wikipedia definition of Open Source Software http://en.wikipedia.org/wiki/Open_source_software

[5]   Directory of Open Access Repositories (Open DOAR) http://www.opendoar.org/

[6]   Registry of Open Access Repositories (ROAR) http://roar.eprints.org/

[7]   Wikipedia http://en.wikipedia.org/wiki/Enterprise_content_management

[8]   Whos using DSpace http://www.dspace.org/index.php?option=com_customproperties&view=show&task=show&Itemid=151&bind_to_section=33&cp_text_search=&cp_country=india&cp_institution_type=&cp_production_version=&cp_database=&cp_operating_system_platform=&cp_public_not_public=

[9]   DSpace Users Club http://dspaceclub.blogspot.com/

[10]   Open Society Institute (OSI) http://en.wikipedia.org/wiki/Open_Society_Institute

Chapter 7

Learn to Learn to Integrate ERP–Systems and Content Knowledge Using Problem Based Learning and Cases:
A Swedish Business School's Experiences

Annika Andersson
USBE, Umea School of Business and Economics, Sweden

ABSTRACT

Research in the integration of technology and content knowledge using problem-based learning (PBL) is a challenge. Thus, the aim of this chapter is to describe experiences and lessons learned from integrating ERP-systems (enterprise resource planning systems) into economic topics course using PBL and cases created for the integration of technology and content knowledge in a business school setting. The mission was to develop the economic students' analyzing abilities using a ERP-system as a pedagogical tool. A summary table describes how problem-based learning and cases were developed and used within collaboration among universities, colleagues, businesses, and students to accomplish integration of both technology and content knowledge. The experience was that students developed abilities to analyze technology from both theory and a deeper understanding of theory by analyzing technology. The lessons learned were that integration of technology and content knowledge using problem based learning and cases is a never-ending cooperative and learning process.

INTRODUCTION

Research on integrating technology and content knowledge using problem-based learning (PBL) has been described as a challenge (Fishman and Davis, 2006; Hyo-Jeong and Bosung, 2009). One explanation is that insufficient repertoires are available for integrating technology and subject fields using problem-based learning (Hyo-Jeong and Bosung, 2009). I agree with these authors that insufficient repertoires are a challenge. Nevertheless, use of technology to enhance students under-

DOI: 10.4018/978-1-4666-2193-0.ch007

standing has been studied by Barak et al. (2005) - but in chemistry. The results were that theories and chemical concepts were better understood.

According to Ferdig (2001), innovations need to contain authentic, real-world problems because they are interesting and are engaging the students. One technology that businesses use frequently is ERP-systems, but the leaders' buyer competence has been found to be limited. Future leaders also need to use the ERP-system as a tool for decision-making. Thus, they need to learn how to use and integrate business processes with the information in the system (Davenport, 1998; Dechow and Mouritsen, 2005). The problem is that learning takes time and learning within projects can exceed the time and budget frames. One way to solve this problem is to learn about business processes before participating in an ERP-project (Andersson and Linderoth, 2008) or before becoming a participant in business that need to use ERP-systems as tools in their daily routines.

Therefore, we need to share experiences from integrating ERP-systems, methods, subject fields and pedagogy that have been both successful and failures. Together we can learn how to create exercises that are a challenge, and Ferdig (2006) argues that the exercises should not be too hard or too easy to engage the students. Ferdig (2006) discussed this dilemma and referred to Vygotsky (1978) and his definition of the "Zone of Proximal Development". However, individuals that are engaged in a learning situation and the "Zone of Proximal Development" probably differ among students. To satisfy individuals and keep them interested and not frustrated, as claimed by Ferdig (2006), perhaps is the challenge. Our business school has implemented "ERP-systems as a pedagogical tool" with a learning perspective and shown that we learn more together by participating in the development of methods and applications. The system is used to understand business processes and to learn how to analyze and make decisions built on theory learned, for example, from organizational learning, change, marketing, finance and accounting.

In this chapter methodologies and applications used in the project "ERP-system as a pedagogical tool" will be described within a business school in Scandinavia. The education projects' history, start-up considerations and changes required concerning the methods and applications are also discussed. The methods developed and used are described, and this projects collaboration among colleagues, IT-personnel, students and other universities are discussed. This project was indeed dependent on those actors. The chapter describes methods and implementation concerns that have been tried. Accounts also come from student evaluations of their ability to use a ERP-system for exercises and analysis to acquire a deeper knowledge in for instance, marketing, finance and entrepreneurship. Further, evaluations and advice from teachers that had a connection to the project were taken into consideration every time before lessons were created. Finally, evaluations from students and colleaugues were used to develop the educational methods.

In this chapter the experiences as a project leader and a driving force within the project are described. A complete member and actor in a study could be related to Gold (1958), who describes levels of participation with the respondents in the project. At the same time that I am the author who has participated in this project as a coordinator, tutor and examinor. It is a self response, i.e., because the author was a complete member, it was not possible to observe myself in action. Another problem could be self-bias, i.e., an individual responsible for the project could be rather positive. On the other hand, information of thoughts and experiences since 2007 are described, and examples of structures and methods that did not work out or had to be changed are also discussed. I try to describe both methods that worked out successfully as well as bad experiences. The intention is to give a broad picture of the project.

The aim is not to evaluate myself as a teacher or coordinator but instead to share my experiences with those interested in ERP education and pedagogical methods.

The net effect is that there are several pedagogical methods that can be used to train students' creativity, ability to use reports, understand the system, how to use an ERP-system and their critical abilities. PBL- Problem Based Learning and Cases are two pedagogical methods that probably can be used to train those abilities. The intention is that readers should understand how we implemented and used ERP-systems as a pedagogical tool in our business school. The aim is to describe experiences and lessons learned from integrating ERP-systems (enterprise resource planning systems), economic topics, cases and PBL. Thus, this chapter describes how PBL was used together with cases that were created for integration of technology, pedagogy and content knowledge (TCPK) in a business school. I anticipate that readers can create and develop methods that we can share and use in the future. It is hoped that the mistakes and problems that were observed within this project can be avoided in other projects.

BACKGROUND

Project Management, ERP-System Implementation, and Learning

A project as an organizational form is often used for learning, for example, when routines are to be changed. That is, the aim with a project or a temporary organization is often to create learning in a new area within time and budget frames (Ekstedt et al, 1999; Lundin and Söderholm, 2003). One example of a project where mutual learning is important is an ERP-project. The buyer needs to describe the companies' business processes and routines in detail for a supplier. This buyer competence is needed to be able to change or structure

the organization to implement a system that supports the processes and integrates information. Moreover, the information has to be integrated in a way that makes reports useful for analysis (Davenport, 1998).

The managers and the project participants can probably find a couple of different solutions on how to structure the organization and which processes the system should support (Davenport, 1998). Therefore, the future mangers and participants in ERP-projects in business that have trained and are prepared for problem solving and decision-making are probably more employable. The terms used within informatics are important for business students to understand. When they become future managers in business, they are probably expected to have the competence to discuss with expertise from a data consultancy within a project or before making decisions concerning ERP-projects.

In research, it is found that the competences to buy and participate in ERP-projects among leaders in business are limited. According to this, investments in ERP-systems often fail or exceed time- and budget frames (Standish-Group, 2006). The budget frames for these projects are at least 250.000€ and for buyer companies a great investment that needs consideration because of the effect the system can have on the business processes for a long time (Scott and Vessey, 2000; Wood and Caldas, 2001). Those projects therefore need leaders with competence in ERP, for example concerning, functions, terms, process knowledge of their own organization and ability to model those processes before a supplier is contracted (Dechow and Mouritsen, 2005). Probably students can learn before they are employed by a company. However, learning is viewed as a problem within ERP-projects and participants have to learn before or after the project (Linderoth and Lundqvist, 2004).

Nevertheless, most economic students who are going into business need to have competencies on how ERP-systems can be used in practice and how the system could support business administrative processes. That is, business schools' students who are going to be leaders in business need to train in ERP-systems to get an understanding of business processes, theories and the technology. On the other hand, according to Rienzo and Han (2011), previous research has focused on the software itself, i.e., how to integrate and how to teach ERP with focus on the software. Rienzo and Han (2011) argue that it is expected that graduate business students truly understand business processes. In their study that included the "hands-on experience" from sales and purchase cycle, they found that hands-on, step-by-step assignments did not produce a comprehensive understanding of business processes.

However, Rienzo and Han (2011) suggest that assessment tools for exercises might include the complexity of business processes to be able to incorporate Klahr and Simon's (1999) five learning components: time, active engagement, mental representations, self-explanations and externalizing thoughts. In trying to integrate these five learning components, interaction among students and teachers are probably useful. According to Vygotsky, the "zone of proximal development", the competence levels of students are increased through both the level of the assignment and interaction among teachers and peers (Rienzo and Han, 2011). From previous research, they suggested that it is important to include interaction among students when writing assignments that use "ERP-systems as a pedagogical tool". Rienzo and Han (2011) argue that earlier education and research had a focus on the software (ERP) and this focus is not useful if we want business students to learn about and understand business processes.

When lecturing on using ERP-systems, the methods used are undoubtedly important in developing an understanding of business processes, students' creativity and their ability to learn. Put another way, the students can acquire the competence to analyze reports and to apply theories learned, using a real-world situation. Roth and van Eijck (2010) argue that thoughts are made in the past and it is important to prepare the students for problematic situations in the future to develop their creativity and ability to learn. It is surmised that one way to teach business students can be to evaluate reports. In that case they have to use and develop their analyzing abilities. If they can find and analyze reports from the system they are probably better prepared to find opportunities and threats and to make decisions. To accomplish this, students need to get the time (Klahr and Simon, 1999) for reflection and analysis when they still are students. They also need a sense of ownership and opportunities for active participation, collaboration and social interaction (Ferdig, 2006). Problem-based learning can perhaps fulfill the need for students to be prepared for decision-making and real-world problems.

Problem-Based Learning (PBL)

Problem based learning is a pedagogical method where the students are involved in a real world problem that needs analysis and reflection. Ferdig (2006) argues that this pedagogy engages the students and keeps them interested and motivated. When using problem-based learning there are no right solutions, but it is required that students build their decisions on theory. With this method, the students also are trained to cooperate in groups and to support their opinions, both in oral and in written form. The thoughts behind using this method are to support the students' creativity and ability to work in teams that develop solutions. By learning together and discussing solutions built on information and theories, the students are perhaps well prepared for a professional future. The aim is that students in their solution should demonstrate their competences and abilities to make decisions. The students are expected to show their critical ability by explaining both the positive and negative consequences if their solution are to be implemented.

Cases

Cases are often used as a pedagogical method, because it challenges the students analyzing ability when they need to make a decision on a real life case. The cases could be from half a page up to a couple of pages. Teachers using cases often present them both in written and oral form. The teacher's task is to challenge the students' thoughts and to ask questions concerning the consequences related to the students' decisons. When the mission is to learn about both theories and practical things like technology, cases could be used. Researchers in the education field recommend the use of cases (Newman, et. al, 1995; Ferdig, 2006) in education because they have found them interesting and meaningful to the students. For example the students can get information about a technological project and information concerning some challenges the project team experienced, but not with any recommendations or solutions. Then the students are supposed to make decisions concerning the project teams' challenges within the project. There could be real world cases when the managers are invited to explain their choices and thoughts concerning the problem. However, according to discussions in the media, the buyers' competences within ERP-project are low and there is a need to learn more about the use of technology. One way to prepare for challenges within business is to educate students in both organizational theory and technology, for example the processes in ERP-systems. These abilities are valuable in ERP-projects that require both organizational and technological competence.

Technology, Pedagogy, Content Knowledge, Integrated (TPCK)

In learning situations, where the students are expected to use technology, research has found that integration of technology and content knowledge is a challenge. The problem according to Hyo-Jeong and Bosung (2009) is that teachers are expected to know how to use technology even if they are not educated in system use. Researchers in the field of educational studies have found different explanations for this problem. In one research project, Hyo-Jeong and Bosung (2009) studied teachers' ability to integrate technology, pedagogy and the theoretical field. The authors used a questionnaire and the students were respondents. The results showed that the teachers did not have the technological competence that was required to use technology in education. The researchers (Hyo-Jeong and Bosung, 2009) then followed up with interviews with the teachers. One of the teachers said that the computers are usually something that is standing in a corner of the lecture hall or in the computer hall. Another teacher explained that the teachers' education was focused on pedagogy and content knowledge, but there were no integration concerning the technology that was implemented in the school. Ferdig (2006) argues that pedagogy is an innovation building block and that teachers need to be trained in technology to be able to integrate (TPCK). The author also argues that active participation, collaboration and social interaction are important, and this integration relates to findings from the project described in this chapter.

Integration of the theoretical field and problem-based learning with technology, however, is now becoming a challenge in education (Hyo-Jeong and Bosung, 2009). According to these authors, the teachers have learned pedagogy and content knowledge but they need to have technological knowledge and competence to be able to teach students. Additionally, the teachers' challenge is to integrate pedagogy, technology and content knowledge in their lectures. The challenge is to use technology as a learning tool that will increase the students understanding of theory. Researchers have also found that usually computers are available but not integrated naturally in education. In case technology, where pedagogy and content knowledge are integrated, it is called (TPCK) and is discussed by Ferdig (2006) as well as Hyo-Jeong and Bosung (2009). The latter authors have found that it is a problem to understand how teachers with limited competence in technology could integrate this tool as a natural and supporting part of education.

Moreover, in informatics ERP-system are often integrated with content knowledge and pedagogy. In economics, methods to learn business processes, supporting analysis abilities, increased theorethical knowledge and to apply those in reality need to be developed - from my point of view, in a never ending learning process. Anyway, the students in business administration are expected to use ERP-system in their future career as employees or managers (Rienzo and Han, 2011). In business a practical, generic competence, can increase their employability. However, it is probably more important that the business students have the ability to apply theories learned in a problematic decision-making situation.

Bachelor of Science in Business and Economics

Theoretical fields included in the programme Bachelor of Science in Business and Economics are, for example, marketing, leadership, organization, accounting, finance, and entrepreneurship. There are, of course, challenges for universities and higher education to create exercises that support the students learning concerning the ability to understand business processes and increase the competence to analyze the reports from ERP-system. In Figure 1, the three (TPCK) technology, content knowledge and pedagogy that are to be integrated are illustrated. Our point of view is that integration is a continous process and the arrows are therefore pointing in both directions depending on the need to make (TPCK) mesh when developing for instance the exercises. Technological competences for economic students are, for instance, competence to laborate and model the processes that can support business processes. These competencies are found important for managers in

business (Somers and Nelson, 2003). Many business schools have adopted ERP software with an attempt to integrate their curricula (Corbitt and Mensching, 2000). Researchers have suggested studies focusing on the use of pedagogy, training and learning of ERP software. Moreover, the need to understand and have the ability to apply content knowledge in practical problem areas, analyzing situations and making decisions are a challenge.

We must take into consideration that content knowledge differs in levels among courses within a programme. To mesh the theories and the system, there is a need for interaction among teachers. Interaction for learning and development are found important on each level and course where the education in ERP is to be implemented. Moreover, the pedagogical model used in the university and the methods of applying it are to be discussed with colleagues and leaders in the university. Another thing to reflect on is that the students coming to universities have more experience with computers and software than years ago. Young people grow up with computers. Thus, they have competencies in software, creating blogs, homepages, playing interactive games without any problem with instructions. The students therefore are found to be well prepared for doing exercises within the ERP-systems, but the teachers do not often have the same experience.

To increase the competence, employability, and the opportunity to be creative and productive within business, universities can collaborate to develop methods for ERP learning. This action could be important in gaining quality in educational methods as well as satisfying some of the competence required in business. The challenge is to create both pedagogical methods and business system applications that are useful in education. My hope is that we can share experiences within this book and in an international network in the future. The case presented below describes experiences from implementation of "ERP-systems as a pedagogical tool" in a business school.

Figure 1. Integration of ERP-systems, hardware, economic topics, PBL, and cases

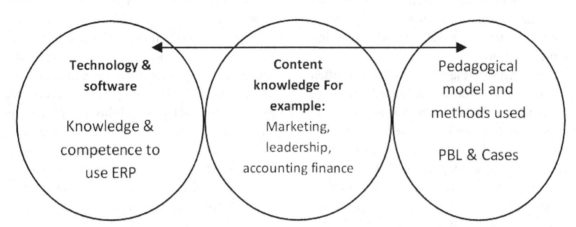

ERP-SYSTEMS AS A PEDAGOGICAL TOOL: A LEARNING PROCESS

An educational project conducted in a business school is presented here. In the description experiences from integration of technology, pedagogy and content knowledge are discussed. The author as a project leader did acquire a combination of a control and a learning perspective. The control part was for instance to keep the time and budget frames for the project and the deadlines for each of the courses. The project leader did also need to have control of the examination of the students. To acquire more knowledge about the students learning, an oral and a written anonymous evaluation was conducted at the same time as the training. The intention with this was that the project leader and the teachers should learn in a long-term perspective. It was found that continuous development was required depending on the systems development on the market and the students' knowledge base when they attended. Every year the students' knowledge base was higher and the requirements for advanced exercises increased. Continuous sharing of experiences within and between universities, with colleagues, students, and consultants was thus found necessary.

History and Implementation

When participating in a research conference including both the field of informatics and business administration a network with a steering committee was built with other researchers interested in ERP-system. There was another business school that had an infra structure with a couple of business systems available that perhaps could be hired by other universities and schools. Then I participated in a conference with the network SANTE– Scandinavian Association Network for Teaching Enterprise systems and discussed the problem of getting resources to implement a business system in education for students at a business school. In informatics, there are many schools that have experiences concerning, for example, building ERP-systems but not in business administration.

One idea was to share resources to be able to implement business systems in education for economic students. A couple of internal and external meetings were accomplished with colleagues, professors and students, who had ideas and asked about the pedagogical methods that could be used and how to integrate content knowledge. I agree with Ferdig (2006) who argues that if the students are in control of their learning this can entail ownership of a project. In fact, students are represented within the board at the business school and that made them involved in the decision concerning implementation of business systems. However, the board then needed an investigation of the market and a calculation concerning the resources needed before they decided to start up a pilot project.

To implement a couple of ERP-systems with support, licences and support from IT personnel was calculated to be 500.000 € for investment, and addtional costs for support every year. All investments in that class can have impact on resources for education. Therefore, alternative solutions were of interest. In December 2006 the board made a strategic decision to implement business systems in education. Collaboration concerning resources such as infrastructure between universities was the solution that was decided upon. The intention was to create opportunities to collaborate in creating cases and to share experiences. Nevertheless, creating cases together did not work out in the beginning, but we do not know what might be happening in the future.

A couple of meetings were accomplished between the university that owned the infrastructure of ERP-systems and our business school. The local IT supporters and the supporters from the other university did meet to share knowledge, opportunities and threats. I found it important to plan the education together with the local IT department concerning technology, for instance, required computers and implementations of virtual pc's, which made it easier to access the system. Investments in computers that had the resources needed were prepared with icons for easy access to the ERP-systems that were used in education. If the computers were not prepared, it should have taken two hours for the students to access the program. When the computer labs were rebuilt, the IT supporters worked both day and night to be able to prepare the lecture halls and computers in time.

Moreover, I found that it was necessary to check the aviability of the computer labs for about six months before each session. Even if the lecture halls were booked, there were sometimes re- buildings that made it necessary to have spontaneous lectures in another room waiting for the computers to be moved. I then learned to check the availability a couple of times before the sessions and that flexibility and a good relationship with the IT-manager's is needed when you use technique in your lectures. I planned to be at least half an hour before the student's to prepare the lecture hall because the student's were early, interested and needed answers to questions before the session or lecture.

Planning in Detail

A problem discussed by Hyo-Jeong and Bosung (2009) was that lecturers did not have the competence in technology. In this case competence required to educate students with an ERP-systems as a tool in order to learn business processes and analyzing reports. That was a challenge in this case because it was important to mesh theory, terms and models used in the theoretical education with exercises in the systems' processes. Therefore, negotiations concerning collaboration with consultancy firms were conducted, and one of them was engaged. A contract and the agreements were signed by both parties and checked with the university lawyer. The engagement of consultants made a solution to the teachers' limited competence in technology and we learned a lot through our collaboration with experts from business. The collaboration with the computer consultancy made us able to educate both students with limited technological knowledge and those with experiences from ERP-systems.

Moreover, continuous discussions with the consultancy and meetings with colleagues were accomplished before every course so that the theories, pedagogical methods and the examination could be meshed. After a while, it was found that the colleagues needed information about when the ERP-education was planned so they could make their schedules mesh also. A plan for each semester was therefore created that included information about for example, time, place, number of students, which groups and in what courses the education was planned. That document did indeed save time and resources and should have been made at the first semester.

Pilot Project

At first, a pilot project started up where the education "ERP-systems as a pedagogical tool" was implemented at two programs, Retail and Supply Chain Management and the Entrepreneurship programs. The education was organized for a three-year period at different courses in business administration. Every session started up with a lecture that discussed ERP-systems, research in the area and processes that should be obtained during the session.

Development and Evaluation

The coordination and the collaboration among the course leaders in the program, responsible teachers and the consultants did work out well. Nevertheless, it was found that the teachers needed an education in ERP-systems that included research in the area, how ERP-systems support business processes, and how systems could be used for analysis. A teacher education then was scheduled where the lecturers participated.

Subsequenly, every group of students was introduced to the system's processes and this method was used to make an initial understanding of a company's processes. Thereafter the exercises in the system begun and they were related to the theories and terms used in the other lectures. The coordination between theory and practice in the system are hard to develop if the lecturers were not interested or participated in the meetings. The coordination between theory and exercises was

also dependent on the consultants understanding of economic subjects. The consultants that were engaged were educated at a business school and perhaps therefore they understood that the theories and the exercises must mesh. A challenge was that the system did include terms in two languages but the students instead saw an opportunity to learn the terms in another language before international carriers.

To increase the quality of the education we have discussed the methodologies used both before and after each session. A continuous learning is needed because we have been quite alone in developing ERP education that is integrated with the programs and the courses included, at least in Scandinavia. Therefore, the discussions among students and colleagues have been used to learn how the students understood the exercises and if the terms used in the theories became clearer. Another experience was some exercises were too easy and some of them too difficult to understand. We also found that the students did not learn enough theories or terms used in business in the first semester. Therefore, we had to change the exercises and begin the education at the third semester for all programmes.

We also found that the students learn more if they participated in guest lecturers with leaders from companies that have implemented ERP-systems. In some instances, the students got a description of the problem that the manager wanted them to consider. The students are, when cases from business are used, expected to come up with a solution, present it orally and written, and reflect upon the consequences with their decisions.

Retail and Supply Chain Management Programme

In the end of the programme the exercises and analyses that the students have accomplished over a three-year period, are grounds for great role-playing. In the role-playing they were expected to be familiar with all the processes in the system and the reports that were analyzed. The students present suggestions for organizational development that are consistent with the figures in the data base in the ERP-system. A business game has been developed that include exercises and analysis in all the processes within an ERP-system. The aim with the business game is to create understanding and competence by doing exercises in a database that includes a company's all business processes, for example the sales process and how it affects other processes and how this process can be integrated with the stock. Another aim is that the students as future managers should learn to use the ERP-system as a tool for decision-making. They should be able to be critical buyers making requirements for the system and be clear about how the systems processes and information should be designed and integrated. Analyzing of reports concerning for example liquidity, sales, stock inventory, campaigns, logistic are examined. The business game included for example, team and time management, individual exercises, written reports, role-playing and presentations.

In the last examination, after three years of the pilot project, it was obvious that the students could apply theories learned in earlier courses within the programme. The students also could make decisions from analyzes of data in the system and then make sales, organizational changes and a new marketing plan.

However, motivation is needed and probably more exercises are required between the lectures in ERP-systems. The students' motivation and interest in ERP-system and applying theories in the exercises used has been great. The students can write in their CV (Currilum Vitae) that they have experiences from business systems because the education is obligatory and examined at every session. The thoughts are that the experiences from ERP-system should make the students more employable.

The students did evaluate the project "ERP-system" as a pedagogical method as important in the education in business and economics and

request more sessions and lectures. They argue that they depend on this education and did understand how to apply the theories learned by analyzing and laborate within the system.

Entrepreneurship Programme

In higher levels of the program, the students solved a problem together with leaders from business. The students were supposed to have a dialogue with a company. They at first learn in lectures how to model companies' business processes in detail. Then the students in pairs observe the companies processes and they have to find and analyze time thieves or insufficient routines in one or two processes. The examination within the entrepreneurship programme was developed to be a student project. In the projects, the students did model the business processes within a company that they already collaborated with from the beginning of the program.

In the initial lectures, they learned how to model the processes and then their mission was to suggest organizational change and/or system support for the business processes. Thereafter the students sought information concerning solutions that can be used in their company. A report was created of the students' groups that were presented for the companies' managers, professors, course leaders and the consultants on a "board meeting". The aim with the examination was that the students should gain competence and knowledge concerning how to model a company's processes to be able to create changes for efficiency. The students learned how to search for information and decide on solutions making the companies more effective. In the presentation, there must be a calculation concerning their suggestions and the ROI-return of investment. They also have to reflect upon the consequences both in the negative and positive sense. Moreover, the students' suggestions for organizational change and system support have been taken into consideration in the companies. Actually, most of the students' suggestions that they presented for their examined companies has been implemented or created changes within the companies.

From Project to Institution

After the pilot project, we found out that we needed do develop and make changes in the education for all programmes. We found that the education was forgotten if the students only trained one day and then had to wait for the next session for a couple of months. The education was then accomplished in two or three days a couple of times over the programme. The students explained in written evaluations that they needed time to reflect and to focus on the reports in the system.

The learning process is still evolving but the budget limits for learning about how to educate and develop exercises and exams are regularly exceeded. It is quite difficult to calculate the time needed for development and learning within a project. It was found useful to utilize the education through collaboration between technological expertise from business, course leaders in the programmes, managers and the project leader. The use of consultants with technological expertise was found to be a solution for the limited technological competence in ERP-systems that lecturers in business schools often have. That is, it is important that the project coordinator can act as an intermediary who can explain terms used from different expertise areas. Important aims for the intermediary are to explain both terms used in the computer consultancy and the theoretical models used in different courses in a programme. Moreover, the project leader has to plan for multiple meetings that can be platforms for development of the courses

After three years of experiencies and evaluations, again a decision was made by the board at the business school that "ERP-systems as a pedagogical tool" should be implemented in all programs and inscribed in the course plans. In the pilot project, there were about 80 students

a year. After the boards decision we have over 400 students that are examined and educated in "ERP-systems as a pedagogical tool" each year. Organizing 400 students required planning of about half a year before the lectures and exercises in the system. Planning lectures, lecture halls, exercises, technique control integration with course leaders in the program, hiring and integrate consultants, calculate time frames, research lectures and internal information were a challenge. It was a challenge that required huge of resources and planning because the students needed access to tutors for instance, in the exercises, explaining documents. The, exams needed to be integrated with the course and the teachers needed enough time for individual examination of students.

One problem was that we did not calculate for time to manage the students that did not attend or pass in the sessions. It was necessary to manage them in to groups and give them individual information to be able to exam them. This was found to be necessary because the generic competences were inscribed in the course plans.

The course leaders and other colleagues were given the opportunity to attenda couple of lectures and exercises in ERP-systems. There were 12 teachers attending to the lectures and exercises with the aim that they should be able to act as tutors within the sessions, but they could not attend if they had too much to do in other courses. A recommendation is therefore to motivate and give time for the teachers that are interested in becoming tutors because they can support the consultants and the project leader during the sessions. Actually, the management group was interested to have teachers available for tutoring. Anyway, the responsibility for the lectures was the project leader, and this resulted in that this person had to attend at all lectures, develop the exercises, fill in the student lists, user names, schedules, hire technique, consultants, lecture halls and being responsible for the exams.

The students were enthuastic and did not take any time for coffee breaks, but some of them needed more exercises and had questions on a higher level. Those students had already worked in some ERP-system. That was no problem because we had access to the consultants that knew all the processes in the system. The consultants attended and were acting as tutors at every lecture to sequre quality and support the students advanced questions.

The intention of the lectures was that the students at the business programm's should gain for instance, ability to apply theories in a practical setting, competence in decision-making, learn be critical buyers, able to suggest changes, make presentations and understand how to integrate the information for optimal decision-making.

Solutions and Recommendations

There are reasons to evaluate the "ERP-systems as a pedagogical tool after each session and lecture to learn how to further develop the methods used. Recommendations are that time for development of exercises, implementation of the systems and management of students that do not pass in the regular sessions must be considered. It was found that there was not time enough for development, and the budget and time frames were exceeded. This observation relates to earlier studies that have found that learning takes time, and the project therefore should be evaluated and redesigned depending on its goals.

However, is the learning process or keeping the budget and time frames most important in education projects? Our resources are limited and therefore the question has to be answered before implementing ERP-systems in education. Of course there must be both learning and control in education projects. In this project there was a need for multiple meetings, discussions and information even before it was decided that the education using ERP as a tool should be implemented. Actually, we did not calculate the time needed for discussions between lectures or for internal information. If keeping of time and budget

frames are most important, this project should be seen as a failure, but if the project had a learning perspective, it was a success. For example, time to develop the exercises continuously and examine the students that missed or did not pass the session took time to administer and were not included in the initial time frames.

On the other hand, when or how can we learn that a project that requires learning does not often keep the time frames even if they are well planned? Experiences from the project are that it takes time to learn and to reflect, which relates to Klahr and Simon (1999). It took more time than calculated to coordinate people and to translate terms from different expertise areas. Flexibility in the lectures and additional exercises were found important to have in the event that an individual needed challenges, for example, if the students already have worked in some ERP-system. Every student must be treated as an individual; in other words listening and communicate with individuals in the sessions and lectures were important and fruitful to understand in what level they were concerning ERP-systems and technology.

Another experience was that the hardware and software did not communicate in the same way in every campus involved. Configurations were needed and we learned that nothing can be taken for granted even though it worked in one town. Learning took time and a couple of lessons were learned. In the Table 1 are listed important things to consider before implementation of ERP-system in a business school. The intention with Table 1 is to give an understanding of the role that technology, pedagogical model, content knowledge, different participants and research played in the pedagogical project described. Learning was a process among the business school, universities, Scandinavian Association Network for Teaching Enterprise systems, business, lecturers and of course the students.

It was a challenge but possible to use the ERP-system as a pedagogical tool. The students were involved in problem-based learning and cases

Table 1. Parties involved in integrating (TPCK) using ERP-systems as a pedagogical tool

INTEGRATION	Technology and ERP-system	Pedagogical model (PBL) & Development of pedagogical exercises and methods	Theory/Content knowledge
Research & researchers	Understanding terms, the problem area & learning needed in ERP-projects	The need to share methods & experiences from integrating technology, pedagogy and content knowledge	Theories in the courses, project and learning theories were used to develop exercises and exams
Collaboration universities (SANTE)	Infrastructure is shared between universities - contract needed	Exercises and models used are communicated, discussed in conferences. Important in the learning process to argue about our solutions. To create and develop quality.	Informatics' departments have often education of students. Integrated education in business schools need to be developed can be enriched through collaboration.
Lecturers, course leaders in the program, colleagues	Lecturers need education in the ERP-systems function. Important before discussions concerning, mesh among, theories, learning outcomes and exercises in ERP.	Lecturers are experts concerning pedagogical models and theoretical fields. Project leader as an intermediary translate terms and learning outcomes, collaborate, develop exercises acc to pedagogical models.	Lecturers describe the field, theoretical models books, and articles. Course leaders explain the structure of the course. Learning outcomes in each course are discussed
Management & The board business school	The board makes decisions; budget frames and contract. Communicate decisions among the employees. Explain expectations and make resources available.	Communicate strategies, educational planes, and delegate. The departments discuss pedagogical models and development of courses.	Decisions concerning the theoretical fields and courses that will be involved in ERP-education, responsible for laws; board of govenors.
Business and commerce	Consultants with expertise in ERP-systems collaborated in sessions and lectures - Contract needed		
Students	Exercises, laborate and analysis. The students findings in the database and their questions was a part of the development of exercises	Learned to analyze reports, how to solve problems and make decisions, Evaluations before, within and after the lectures developed the education.	The theories they have learned, a ground for the analysis, decision-making and to understand the consequences. Multiple solutions were presented and discussed.
IT-managers	Important, configure the system and the hardware; implement software, solutions to technological issues. Frequent communication needed.	Not involved	Not involved

where they trained to analyze organizational processes, reports and to make decisions concerning organizational change or system support. With the methods used and the continuous learning process it was possible to incorporate more of Klahr and Simon's (1999) five learning components: time, active engagement, mental representations, self-explanations and externalizing thoughts. It was also possible to integrate (TPCK) using problem-based learning and cases depending on the expertise with different competences that were involved in the process (see Table 1).

FUTURE RESEARCH DIRECTIONS

Future emerging trends in Europe (cf. the Bologna process) are that the students should be employable and thus have competencies that business requires for instance experiences and ability to use ERP-systems for analyzing. These generic competencies have to be inscribed in course plans. Generic competencies are the ability or the aptitude to do something that business needs. Here in Scandinavia we are quite alone using ERP as a pedagogical tool to educate economic students, and future leaders in analysis. This chapter described a project that has going on for four years in Scandinavia, but there is really a need for sharing experiences among universities all over the world to develop the education in ERP-systems. In the economic area, universities and business schools need to collaborate and share ideas and not develop the wheel repeatedly. From my point of view, we need experiences and stories from different subject fields and apply them in other fields. In the future, the book can be used in universities that engage in learning concerning competencies that make the students employable. Future research can be concerned in collecting cases with teacher instructions to be used in education. Important could be to evaluate the students' carrier and thoughts after they have finished their education in ERP in business schools.

CONCLUSION

This chapter describes experiences from implementation of "ERP as a pedagogical tool". The case describes how a business school at a university has integrated technology, pedagogy and content knowledge (TPCK) using pilot projects, problem-based learning (PBL) and cases. In this chapter, problems, required changes and things that did not turn out so well are described. However, research showed collaboration between universities, teachers, businesses, IT-managers and students, technology, pedagogy and content knowledge could be integrated. The experiences are only from one business school but together with the other chapters included in this book there are probably great experiences. The vision is that we can find partners to with whom to collaborate, share experiences, competence and knowledge. Universities and schools that engage in ERP-education need to cooperate to acquire as much quality as possible in this kind of education. It is important that future managers have knowledge

and competences to analyze the business before decision making and ERP-systems can be useful in understanding business processes.

REFERENCES

Andersson, A., & Linderoth, H. (2008). An explorative study of ERP-projects learn not to learn – A way of keeping budgets and deadlines in ERP-projects? *Journal of Enterprise Information Systems*, *2*(1), 77–95. doi:10.1080/17517570701793830

Barak, M., & Yehudit, J. D. (2004). *Enhancing undergraduate students' chemistry understanding through project-based learning in an IT environment*, (pp. 118-139). Wiley InterScience. Retrieved June 31, 2011, from www.interscience.wiley.com

Davenport, T. H. (1998). Putting the enterprise into the enterprise system. *Harvard Business Review*, (July-August): 121–131.

Dechow, N., & Mouritsen, J. (2005). Enterprise resource planning systems, management control and the quest for integration. *Accounting, Organizations and Society*, *30*, 691–733. doi:10.1016/j.aos.2004.11.004

Ekstedt, E., Lundin, R. A., Söderholm, A., & Wirdenius, H. (1999). *Neo-industrial organizing*. New York, NY: Routledge.

Ferdig, R. E. (2006). Assessing technologies for teaching and learning: Understanding the importance of technological pedagogical content knowledge. *British Journal of Educational Technology*, *37*(5), 749–760. doi:10.1111/j.1467-8535.2006.00559.x

Fishman, B., & Davis, E. (2006). Teacher learning research and the learning sciences. In Sawyer, R. K. (Ed.), *Cambridge handbook of the learning sciences* (pp. 535–550). Cambridge, UK: Cambridge University Press. doi:10.1017/CBO9780511816833.033

Gold, R. L. (1958). Roles in sociological fieldwork. *Social Forces, 36*, 217–223. doi:10.2307/2573808

Hyo-Jeong, S., & Bosung, K. (2009). Learning about problem based learning: Student teachers integrating technology, pedagogy and content knowledge. *Australasian Journal of Educational Technology, 25*(1), 101–116.

Klahr, D., & Simon, H. A. (1999). Studies of scientific discovery: Complementary approaches and convergent findings. *Psychological Bulletin, 125*(5), 524–543. doi:10.1037/0033-2909.125.5.524

Linderoth, H., & Lundqvist, A. (2004). Learn not to learn: Paradoxical knowledge creation and learning in ERP-projects. In *Proceedings IRNOP VI, 2004*, (pp. 409-422). Turku, Finland: Academy University Press.

Lundin, R. A., & Söderholm, A. (1995). A theory of the temporary organization. *Scandinavian Journal of Management, 11*(4), 437–455. doi:10.1016/0956-5221(95)00036-U

Rienzo, T., & Han, B. (2011). Does ERP hands-on experience help students learning business process concepts? *Decision Sciences Journal of Innovative Education, 9*(2), 177–207. doi:10.1111/j.1540-4609.2011.00300.x

Roth, W.-M., & Van Eijck, M. (2010). *Fullness of life as minimal unit: Science, technology, engineering and mathematics (STEM) learning across the life span* (pp. 1027–1048). Siley Periodicals, Inc., Science Education. doi:10.1002/sce.20401

Scott, J. E., & Vessey, I. (2000). Implementing enterprise resource planning systems: The role of learning from failure. *Information Systems Frontiers*, (August): 213–232. doi:10.1023/A:1026504325010

Somers, T. M., & Nelson, K. G. (2003). The impact of strategy and integration mechanisms on enterprise system value: Empirical evidence from manufacturing firms. *European Journal of Operational Research, 146*, 315–338. doi:10.1016/S0377-2217(02)00552-0

Standish Group. (2006). *Chaos report 2006*. Retrieved from http://www.standishgroup.com/chaos/beacon_243.php-2006-11-07-14.59

Wood, T., & Caldas, M. P. (2001). Reductionism and complex thinking during ERP implementations. *Business Process Management Journal, 7*(5), 387–393. doi:10.1108/14637150110406777

Chapter 8
Towards an Ontology–Based Educational Information System

Erika Nyitrai
Eötvös Loránd University, Hungary

Balázs Varga
Eötvös Loránd University, Hungary

Adam Tarcsi
Eötvös Loránd University, Hungary

ABSTRACT

Nowadays in higher education, we create lots of documents and datasets for every activity. We have to maintain course, program, and syllabus information, and also the connections between the course themes. We can download some documentation for this information, but there are many questions difficult to answer. Also we can find some HR related or organizational issues. The authors are working for an ontology which is able to picture the connections between the actors of a higher education system. Their ontology is built with integrating some existing one, for example AIISO (Academic Institution Internal Structure Ontology), FOAF (Friend of a Friend) and DC (Dublin Core). The ontology has four connected parts. These can describe an organization with its internal structure, the program and courses of a University, the people connected with the organizations, the courses or some documents. The authors can also characterize course materials, such as documents, books, or multimedia contents and can connect the knowledge base with ERP systems also.

INTRODUCTION

At education, mainly at higher education all of the participants (executives, funders, students, teachers and researchers) need a lot of information. In the meanwhile the information system should cover all the processes of the institution.

The sharpening competition in the education, the lifelong learning and the spreading of e-learning based education require an adaptation and a new way of administration – first of all – from the universities. The information needed to the more effective operation and decisions requires up to date ERP system and an integrated educational

DOI: 10.4018/978-1-4666-2193-0.ch008

system as well as the more efficient operation and management decision require faster, up-to-date, accurate information. In the near future not only for higher education but all educational institutions are concerned.

In today's educational environment, large amount of data are generated each day, which management is more and more a serious challenge for the education. In order to the effective operation the further utilization, of the stored data is required. In a typical educational institute the structured access to the information can increase the efficiency of data processing.

In such an integrated system there are some issues that can answer by using a training-related otology-based component.

For example, some common situations:

1. Skills management issues
    a. What are the competencies and skills that the student is able to learn by graduating on a course or training?
    b. How the knowledge elements are grouped (the precognitions are enough for the course, the new knowledge elements are corresponds to the official expectations, etc.)?
2. HR system related questions
    a. What does industry needs of the training (the abovementioned skills and knowledge requirements are enough for a certain job, or a task)?
3. Organizational issues
    a. What kind of resources are available in the educational institution?
        i. Is there enough adequate knowledge of the instructors for teaching a course?
        ii. Which areas of teacher capacities are defective or where are some oversupplies?
    b. Is there enough efficiency?
        i. What is the ratio of the overlapping knowledge?
        ii. Where we can find shortage?
        iii. Where overlaps are shown, are obligate or not?
        iv. The deficit is corrigible by keeping the training capacity; does the university need some new colleagues?
        v. Is there any task, which would be suitable by using the existing resources?
        vi. Which industry or educational institutes are linked with the university? These connections are accessible in the training (there are fellowship agreements, traineeship in the industry, industry-education projects are available, etc.).
4. Course management issues
    a. What kind of resources are available for a student for learning (classes, books and notes, available samples, demo solutions, trial software etc.)?

For answering the questions we need to create a multiple knowledge base which may be useful for human-resource or other decision support.

Such a knowledge base can be divided into several parts. First of all, the terms and the concepts of field of science have an important role to formalize the basis of the - industrial - requirements. These linked with the special filed of a knowledge help characterize the individual institutions and the trainings they provide. The structure of the institutions, the provided trainings, the contents of the courses can be described in a uniform structure. The materials used for the courses, the literature referenced can be connected to the system. The knowledge base may relate to the persons (teachers, students, employee of any project) took part in the life of the university. These relationships may be useful on making various human resource management decisions, designing educational strategies or creating different statements.

Based on the breakdown mentioned above the knowledge base can be divided into major components. The components are interrelated, not fully isolated, but the relationships between the components are much looser than the contexts within the components. Building up a machine-readable knowledge base, also known as ontology system a number of reusable building blocks can be integrated, like thesauruses and ontologies.

What is a Semantic Web and What is Ontology?

The term Semantic Web was coined by Tim Berners-Lee, the inviter of the Word Wide Web Consortium (W3C) and it is a web of data that will enable machines to understand the data. The information available on World Wide Web is exclusively understandable for humans. The goal of Semantic Web is to transform the mainly unstructured enterprise information into Knowledge resources. In the Semantic Web approach information has a well defined meaning and this will enable computers to know how to process the information, formalize and manage know-how and other kinds of knowledge.

The information model is represented as a graph with nodes representing the resources using unique identifiers called Uniform Resource Identifier (URI), and the edges representing the relationship between them with the description of properties for a specific domain. Resource can be anything such as a person (like students, teachers), a document, a product, etc. which is described at the specified address pointed by the URI. The representation between the nodes and the edges is formally specified in a machine processable way. The formal information representation is defined in form of Subject-Predicate-Object triples using XML syntax of Resource Description Framework (RDF), can be accessed by the software agents. The knowledge base can be supplemented with inference rules with the help of RDF Semantics (RDFS) and can be sharable by using Web On-

tology Language (OWL). Thus the information is represented as ontology as a set of shared vocabulary and the definition of axioms specify the relationships between them, so the explicit logic describes consequences. In other words an ontology is a data model that consists of a representational vocabulary with precise definitions of the meanings of the terms of this vocabulary extended with a set of formal axioms. Ontology is a specific organization of conceptual knowledge in a given area based on the idea of class, or concept, and relying on a generally taxonomic organization of classes.

In a learning/teaching environment may be considered a portion of the web where ontologies are an adequate technological approach to include semantic information on the contents taught and on the connection between knowledge and persons (students and professors) which helps communicate. Ontological technologies can help building an education information system. In e-learning domain, though standard schemas like Dublin Core (see below) have been applied to describe learning objects. A simple structure cannot help students learn complex knowledge and relationships among topics. From the student point of view, to complete a learning task not only requires a comprehensive understanding of what the learning materials talk about, but also needs to know semantic connections/relations between these materials. In such situation, ontologies can be applied as a new approach to integrate the content, context and structure of the learning materials.

Additionally in the Educational Information System the semantic technologies are usable for data processing and for queries as well. The data processing phase we can use annotation technologies and the processing of documents with the same structure can be effective. The functionality of the inference systems may be used for querying of the knowledge repository.

The fast, accurate supplying of data is expected by the supervisory authorities (e.g. Ministry of Education), the management of institution, but also by the students, teachers as well. Effective management requires a holistic record of the revenues, expenditures, human resources and other facilities. An education based knowledge-base and information system assist managers in decision making, improve predictability, helping to meet the future competition. Education needs special information based on the student registration system - which is mainly not part of an ERP system – to assist in education planning, local and central data processing and other information needs of the administration.

Educational Information System

An ERP system supports manufacturing, service and merchant activities; integrated with financial, accounting, sales, procurement, human capital management information and business processes. The range functionality of the core ERP systems are extended with marketing, supply chain management, supplier relationship management and customer relationship management, e-commerce functions to operate more efficiently while collaborating with government agencies, and other business partners.

The main advantage of an ERP system is to record, store and access information in order to facilitate the management decisions and to improve efficiency.

Although higher education organizations differs from other organizations as they operates in different environment, but they are also part of a country's economical environment as educational service companies. To correspond with academic purposes university ERPs adapt student information management functions to support administrative and academic business activities. These ERP systems have a special expectation as these institutions are governmental and do business mainly for non-profit purposes.

The core of an academic ERP system usually supports student administration (enrolment procedures and student enrolment, financial support for students, student data), human resource management (monitoring of employees) and finance (accounting, payments, investments, budget). It is possible to include some other programme add-ons, e.g. assets management (contracts, subsidies, grants, etc.) or for monitoring student and developmental services of institutions.

An academic ERP should support all organizational processes, like campus management for student and academic services as an educational administration system, management of scholarships and fees, student life-cycle management, financials including grants management, human resource management, procurement, analytics, research, and asset management as well adapted into the local higher education environment.

Although there are ERP systems, modules for higher education institutions, such as the SAP Higher Education and Research industry solution, the complete introduction of these is often not feasible, as on one hand it require a large-scale modification of the university structure. On the other side the customization of the ERP system corresponding to local regulations needs development project. The cost of these projects in smaller countries such as Hungary is not profitable. An additional barrier of the usage of such an industry solution in smaller countries is the lack of the experts for an introduction of a particular module. In such cases the integration of the ERP system and an educational administration system – which corresponds the local regulations - is required in order to transfer student's and staff's information to the financial and human resource management modules of the ERP system (Tarcsi A., 2005), (Bíró & Tomcsányi, 2006).

Building a suitable knowledge base is required in all cases; the methods are the same in both cases. In this chapter the knowledge base built on the educational information system of the Eötvös Loránd University (ELTE) is presented.

The Educational Information System of the ELTE is shown in Figure 1.

Figure 1. Architecture of an ontology-based educational information system

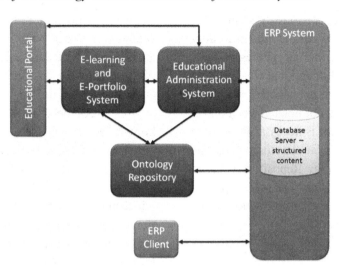

An Educational Information System is an IT system based on a common database integrating the following points and business processes:

- **Enterprise Resource Planning (ERP):** ERP is a business management system that integrates all of the financial, material, and human resource business processes of the institution. ELTE uses SAP ERP system.
- **Educational Administration System:** This system supports the aspects of student life and the teaching process, including admissions, enrollment, registrations, course management, student accounting, academic program management, used for educational administration as: managing student and teacher records and the education management, administration of curricula, time-tables, administration of courses and examinations. ELTE uses the ETR Education System, one of the Educational Administration System used in the Hungarian higher education.
- **E-learning and E-Portfolio System, aka. Learning Management System:** An integrated E-learning System supports collaborative learning by various means of communication – forums, chat, collective discussion, group calendar, documents and application sharing, prompt message sending, curriculum author environment, distance learning supporting environment, examination system etc - in both synchronous and asynchronous manners. The system also contains a multi-authored material editor - which uses reusable elements -, a research support system and an E-portfolio System. The e-portfolio is a professional competence presentation and storing tool for professional materials, a reference repository or library of their works and interests to collect the most successful work and researches of the students and the teachers and also a tool to outline the future goals and to support the job searching process. ELTE uses an integration of Moodle LMS and Mahara ePortfolio system.
- **Ontology Repository:** Using Educational Information Systems the description of the educational process and of the educators, students, and also of the courses is stored and processed in the Educational Administration System. The communication platform for the education and the

library of the training materials is the E-learning and E-portfolio System. At a common enterprise data is hidden in documents, e-mails, human processes, etc. in contrast an Educational Information System the contents are mainly structured, but the meaning is not notated as an ontology, which means it is necessary to extract more information from the stored data. The Educational Ontology Repository is based on these obtained data. The second part of this chapter presents the production of the ontology repository.

BACKGROUND

In an enterprise environment complex IT systems store large data sets in relational databases. These relational systems are ideally suited to store, process, manage, and maintain the structured data in a well-known data structure, with high efficiency and to serve to answer the required queries according to the business processes, so to the business requirements. In general, an Enterprise Resource System (ERP) uses relational database systems as well to implement business processes and to record information to business.

In our days information management's another possible approach is to generate and use of semantic data. The vision of the Semantic Web is defined by Tim Berners-Lee in a book published in 1999. (Berners-Lee, 1999), thus computers may be able to interpret information from different sources and combine it with meaning in order to solve a problem or answer a question. It is not necessary the semantic data to manage in an online environment, it is possible to build systems offline or mixed (online and offline) as well, here the web means only the fundamental technologies behind the term of the semantic data processing, although to XML-based data processing and to define and identify resources (like documents, persons, etc.) with the style of

URI-s (Unified Resource Identification) the web or Internet is not required. The components of the semantic web can be produced with a usage of a high number of standards and tools. The usage of these allows us to add information (meanings and other properties for data processing) from any resources, persons, in order to obtain further knowledge elements.

The simplest semantic data description language is the XML-based RDF (Resource Description Framework) (RDF Working Group, 2004), which allows us to formulate and publish information of any object (denoted by URI). Each such a statement consists of three components, subject, property and an object. The subject is the object we would like to characterize, the property is an attribute to specify and the object is the value of the property. With usage of such a triples we can easily create graphs to describe knowledge and the relationships. In order to formulate the structure of the knowledge, it is necessary to add more opportunities to the language, like the RDFS (RDF Schema) (Brickley & Guha, 2004) language or the OWL (Web Ontology Language) (OWL Working Group, 2007), which provide even more tools to describe the structure and background information in contrast to the RDFS.

With the above-mentioned languages and semantic technologies we can produce knowledge bases and ontologies of a particular industry or field of science to model and describe the concepts, knowledge and the relations between them. The structure and the content of an ontology can be extensible, reusable describing and characterizing different areas. A well-designed ontology is also used to obtain additional information from the knowledge storage in order to explore directly non accessible links and possible deficiencies. Nowadays a number of inference algorithms and software packages can be use.

Advanced database management systems are now able to efficiently manage semantic data and implement logical conclusions on. Most ERP systems are extensible with modules that are also capable of semantic data management, as well as large enterprises are also making big efforts to benefits semantic technologies (Amin Anjomshoaa, 2006).

The Semantic Technology adoption in an Enterprise has three major reasons or appearance (Cirrus Shakeri, 2011):

- Document, unstructured document processing: The large volumes of data can be turned into machine-processable semantics, while related data is linked together and enriched with metadata.
- Delivering more intelligent and adaptable business solutions with semantic processing of data via machine reasoning, natural language processing.
- Better decision support with in-memory / online computing and data processing an enterprise can make semantic processing of high volume of linked data feasible for enterprise applications.

The most obvious application of Semantic Web in business field is changing the web to a processable resource for machines. The information which is available on Web today is mostly produced to be human-understandable. The process of changing this information to Knowledge is time and budget consuming. On the other hand the policy makers need to have access to the last updated information and usually the human-based method of information processing is not economical.

Semantic ERP is a blend of Semantic technology with Enterprise's legacy applications, ERP system to help users get a view of Enterprise Knowledge for search, query, reports and application purposes, enabling natural language dialogue while bridging the structured and unstructured content.

The approach starts from information sources where semantic content (i.e., meaning) is extracted.

Information sources can come from within the enterprise such as ERP, CRM, or BW systems, the public Web, social networks, enterprise data repositories, documents, or from the company's business network of customers, vendors, or partners. A part of the meaning in an ERP system can be extracted from the data dictionary where properties and relationships between various business objects are stored, the other meaning can be extracted from other sources such as documents or directly from the experts.

Several articles deal with semantic development methods, like (Hamid Nach, 2008) and (Dau). The different methodologies may be built by linear, cyclic, incremental methods. In general, it is needed to have a detailed knowledge and a structural overview of the selected areas. It is also important to know those ontologies that are already available in the selected target area; some of them can be used when developing a new semantic system. The next step is the categorization of objects available, creation of class hierarchy and the classification of the entities. The methodology of the course ontology of Sinead and Boyce is is similar to the outlined above (Boyce & Pahl, 2007), like the ORM framework (Tserng, Yin, Dzeng, Woud, Tsai, & Chen, 2009) as well. In our research the cognition of the target area and the mapping of the available ontologies are in parallel.

THE BASIC ELEMENTS OF AN ONTOLOGY-BASED EDUCATIONAL ERP SYSTEM

For an Educational System a high number of information sources are required. The abovementioned system parts can be built from the available documents of the universities, including:

1. Accreditation documents, training networks, proposed subject recruitment sequence;
2. Course content websites, bibliographic references, curriculum resources;

3. Class schedules and other course pages to connect courses and teachers;
4. Personal data collections (FOAF files) and other personal information from the Educational Administration System;
5. Publication lists, thesis;
6. Project Schedules, project documentations;
7. Tender, competition results;
8. Thesis;
9. Documentations of the industrial relations;
10. Documentation of events (conferences, workshops, etc.)
11. Department's information, university websites.

An Educational Information System can build up based on the main components detailed below.

Components of Describing the Structure of Institute, Fields of Specialization, Trainings, and Courses

The base of knowledge can be built up by processing the chosen training. The primary process of training is possible with the collection of subject knowledge, out of which subject knowledge-based ontology can be reared. The main elements are courses, characteristics of subjects and their relations. For customized description of data, a definition of new ontological system is needed. The description is possible with the usage of RDF and OWL.

Formerly, several projects were dealing with researches that describe the system and the structures of universities, their trainings, courses and colleagues in semantically viewpoints also.

In 2000 during SHOE project, researchers of University of Maryland publicized an ontology that is able to describe a university system. In this ontology, the description of people, institutions, publications and workgroups split on the highest level. Among people lecturers, researchers, un-

dergraduates and graduates and other colleagues are characterized. Institutional description refers to universities and their parts, including departments, faculties and main research groups too. Register of publications contains publications of universities and rating them into different types of groups. The last section describes temporary workgroups, where participants of current courses and participants of temporary research groups and conferences are sorted (Heflin, és mtsai., 2000).

As a researcher of University of Mary Washington, Dr. Partick Murray-John was also dealing with editing educational ontology (Murray-John, 2008). People, courses, documentation and places are also a part of this ontology as well. With the help of it, timetable of a current group can be pictured too.

Academic Institution Internal Structure Ontology (AIISO) was also published in 2008 (Styles & Shabir, 2008). The two main components of this ontology are the description of universities and the structure of obtainable knowledge. System of universities can be described on more levels by their departments and relations, while units of knowledge are divided on the base of topics, courses, modules and fields of study. The correlation between different units of knowledge is less elaborate; structure of institutions gets more emphasis.

Description of courses' content is strongly connected to the next part too, which contains necessary knowledge to find a place on a special field. Content of courses can be depicted in two ways. The first solution presupposes that the effect of training is defined – such as training experts happens because of an order of a firm. In the other case, traditional contents of courses are pictured by different parameters. S. Sosnovsky and T. Gavrilova's article (Sosnovsky & Tatiana, 2005) is an example to the latest one, where he detailed an ontology for teaching programming language C. This ontology does not contain the curriculum of only one course, but they formed the basic knowledge-based ontology of programming language with the help of their experience in education. Thanks to the flexibility of the system, this ontology can be used for educational methods of different subjects.

The other mode of ontological description of course content is the construction based on literature (Boyce & Pahl, 2007). The ontology in Boyce & Pahl's article was made on the base of a professional book by using its definitions and connections. In this article, role of „ls-a" relation is highlighted, which is usually appropriate to describe definitions but in some cases characterization of a more special relation is needed.

Ontology of educational content was prepared by employees of Corvinus University of Budapest, Department of Information System. In their project on ontology-development in higher education, connection between educational elements were also examined and used. Main groups in describing course content are fundamental concepts, statements, rules of sentence construction and conclusion (Borbásné Szabó, 2006).

Component of Describing Special Knowledge and Fields of Science

To processing the structured knowledge is useful to create an ontology, which consist the possible knowledge of the chosen scholarship. This knowledge of the concepts, theorems, proofs, methods, skills, equipment usage patterns, etc. The subset of this knowledge can be covered by a course, and major subset can be the expected output of the training system. The description of the existing special field of knowledge ontologies can be used.

Characterization of workforce market is accomplished in different ways by former researches. Employees of Corvinus University of Budapest, Department of Information Systems are in charge of dealing with the output of education. In 2007 more models were made that are able to correlate elements of education with expectations of workforce market (Vas, 2007). In this model,

competences appearing in output were examined and summarized by a working group by using ontology. Expectations on workforce market were divided into groups of tasks and tasks. These were connected by competences solving tasks. Materials – which are necessary to gain competences – are also mentioned in the ontology (Borbásné Szabó, 2006). Later, instead of materials, fields of knowledge start to attach to competences and materials also remain in the system but connecting in another way.

Another approach have been used by the researchers of the University of Piteşti, Faculty of Economic Sciences. When classifying of the possible job positions they used existing classification systems. In their research, they used the HR-XML schema, and a categorization system used by number of national statistical office: German Classification of the Industry Sector (WZ2003) and the North American Industry Classification System (NAICS), and for the classification of the professions: the Romanian Classification of Occupations (COR), the German Occupation Code (BKZ) and the Standard Occupational Classification (SOC) System (Popescu & Popescu, 2010). The Hungarian equivalent of these systems are the Products and Services Classification System (Termékek és Szolgáltatások Osztályozási Rendszere, TEÁOR) and the Uniform Classification System of Occupations (Foglalkozások Egységes Osztályozási Rendszere, FEOR). The TEÁOR is the Hungarian translation of the NACE Rev.2, as it is compulsory at the European Union, each Member State have a similar in their own language. The NACE classification of activities designed to integrate well into our system (Statistical Classification of Economic Activities in the European Community, Rev. 2, 2008).

Component of Describing Aids, Publications, and Literature Elements

We can connect for each course a collection of objects, which summarizes the materials used. That could mean notes, programs, pictures and other multimedia elements. These can be described by the known formats, such as DC (Dublin Core) or MOWL (Multimedia Web Ontology Language).

Both Dublin Core and MOWL are adequate to make a semantic description for training materials. The set of usable groups is different in the two ontologies, so when creating an own ontology, we have to decide which one of the modes we choose. MOWL is a multimedia extension of OWL. It is mainly used to characterize multimedia content. But the number of those classes that can help in characterizing training materials is low, so if we choose this way of description, we have to crate classes that describe training materials.

Developers of MOWL are researchers of Indian Institute of Technology. They deal with construction and proving the efficiency of MOWL in more of their articles. In their article (Gaurav Harit, 2006) and (Karthik Thatipamula, 2005) presented what kind of groups and characteristics should be created as an OWL extension to handle multimedia materials – especially videos. They argue on the possible ontological educational methods to annotate videos automatically in their article (Anupama Mallik, 2008).

The development of Dublin Core has been started about a decade ago. They had only some elements at the beginning, which became the base of later versions. Now 15 main terms helps to describe content semantically. The description of correlation between groups can be accomplished by many characteristics. Description of Dublin Core can be found on site (Dublin Core Ontology).

With the help of the basic elements of Dublin Core, characteristics of digitally stored articles can described, as researchers of University of Barcelona introduce it in their article (Assumpció Estivill, 2005). Based on stored characteristics, materials connected to a given characteristic – topic, author, system, format etc. – can be easily found by a semantic search. Other features of these materials can be seen on the base semantic description, so search can be continued this way. By using the basic idea and expanding the field of stored material, technique can be applied to reach not only articles but optional digitally stored training materials. The authors of the article only use the theory of DC 15 to characterize the stored material.

The other example of Dublin Core's usage is the system Mind@UW developed by University of Wisconsin. They also used DC-based semantic description to represent materials. Via (MINDS@ UW HOME) web interface we can search among stored digital materials, mostly on the base of DC elements' content. It can be found in (Kirstin Dougan, 2007) documentation that what kind of value DC elements should be filled with to achieve the wished material with later searches.

Two conclusions can be derived from the examples above. On the one hand, we have the possibility with the help of DC elements to describe features of digitally stored materials by defining in semantic relationships that helps in further searches. So DC elements can be used efficiently to characterize any training material semantically in the description developed by us. On the other hand, the elements of Dublin Core – similarly to rules of other ontologies - offer freedom for ontology-makers. It is good and problematic at the same time. It is good, as we can store the data used quite arbitrary to characterize entities, so our hands are not tied. Although, it effect is that ontologies based on DC are not totally compatibles with each other as some of the elements believed to be standard ontology-makers use differently. This way different – even on similar fields – descriptive ontologies cannot be matched without problems; it is hard to do searches that require more DC-based ontology. While constructing our ontology, our footing was Dublin Core to characterize training materials, but we also added many other classes and properties that fit to our aims. These classes serve as a tool to describe those characteristics of materials that Dublin Core does not allow. It is needed from more aspects. On the one hand, more sophisticated questions can be carried out by using new classes and properties. On the other hand, attachment to other parts of our ontology – structural construction, human relations – can be solved more easily.

Component of Personal and Relationship Networks

The students, teachers, researchers, so the participants of education and they relationships also can be linked to objects or other knowledge elements as well. The description of the relations between teachers may come into play. The personal information can be described by FOAF (Friends Of A Friend) format (FOAF Project). The publication-management ontology also can be achieved. For managing internal working groups this information is very helpful. In this part also can be manage the results of a course or a project. When attaining information handling, elements of LOD cloud can also be integrated, such as IEEE Papers ontology. Mapping and handling internal relations can also get a role that may mean great help when managing working groups. It can be used to know who stands in a teacher-student/ group mate/project partner etc. relationship with whom, and if they had common results.

The Friend-of-a-Friend (FOAF) defines a vocabulary for describing people and the relationships between them, as well as the things that they create and do. It enables people to create machine-readable web pages for people, groups, organisations and other related concepts. The main classes and properties in the FOAF vocabulary include the commonly-used classes are foaf:Person - describing people, foaf:Document - for the documents that people create; some of the properties are foaf:mbox_sha1sum - used as an identifier for a

person, and foaf:knows - to create a link to a friend. In our case with foaf:knows we can describe the connection between persons (students, teachers, and researchers) in the Educational Information System, like Bob taught Alice, while Alice were a classmate of Charles and Bob has a research project with Daniel.

As an ontology FOAF is extensible. One of the useful extensions is the Resume ontology by (Bojars). A resume or Curriculum Vitae (CV) is a written record of person's education and employment, which contains a record of a university/ college teacher's education and employment, also including a list of books and articles that they have published and courses that they have taught, used when they are applying for a job (Tarcsi, 2005).

Integration of Accomplished Ontologies

In the planned ontology-system there are many construction units that had been used in other projects formerly. Among these there are ones that can be found in Linked Object Data cloud (Cyganiak, 2011). If enough data is stored in the system defined by us, an ending point can be named as a part of the cloud.

THE PROCESS OF THE ONTOLOGY CONSTRUCTION

Constructing an ontology system is the base of our work. The content of the prototype is made of a base that was well observed before. The prototype became Eötvös Lóránd University – its Faculty of Informatics – which is our workplace, so we can see its structure. As a base of scientific model, we chose a course called Algorithms and Data structure – we have years of experience in this field. These former experiences make it less difficult to construct ontology system and fill it with content.

Since 2006 we use the SAP ERP system in our University, but the SAP NetWeaver Business Warehouse (SAP BW) component has not yet been introduced, although with its data warehouse it is possible to efficiently store and search information from a variety of sources. So it was not possible to use and to try the SAP BW data modeling and semantic search capabilities.

The integration of the SAP ERP and the ETR Educational Administration System was developed by the ELTE in Hungary, as our University was the first higher education institute, where a professional ERP system was introduced. Through the integration the data transfer is loaded automatically. The next step of the integration is the course based linking of the Moodle e-learning system and the ETR Educational Administration System, the information of the individual courses, instructors and the students synchronized from the ETR to the Moodle, where the teachers are able to create, upload materials and communicate with students and create test. In our case the data collection for the ontology system was performed manually. In long-term we created the method and the development plan for the daily data synchronization. As the three main components use real other technologies, the development is a bit complex. SAP ERP needs ABAP development; the data synchronization is possible with Web Service calls. As the PHP based Moodle e-learning system is well documented and open source it is needs the simplest development. The bottleneck is the ETR system, - which uses ASP.NET technology – as it is an incompletely documented, closed system, used only in Hungary, but as we have some development experience from the SAP-ETR integration, we decided to collect data directly from the ETR database.

We use Protege system for the ontology development during our research. It is a open source ontology-maker that was developed by Stanford University. Due to the flexibility and effectiveness of the tool, it is used in several projects in development. Program has online documentation and a wiki is connected to it too (Protege Home

Page) Thanks to its customizable plug-in system, a variety of plug-ins and applications can be downloaded or made.

Classes and relations of ontology have been made by reuse of existing thesauruses and ontologies. In the followings, we list them.

Used Ontologies and Metadata

AIISO: Academic Institution Internal Structure Ontology (AIISO RDF, 2008)

In this ontology – as mentioned in the introduction – it is possible to describe the internal structure of universities. The ontology is specially designed for this purpose, the structure deals with the description of higher education institutes. The elements of the FOAF are customized into the ontology. In our current research the Organisation and the KnowledgeGrouping classes were used. The classes are broken into parts, but not all of them are integrated into our system, and also the relationships. With the used object it is possible to describe the departments of the institutions and the properties of the educational entities.

DCTerms: Dublin Core Metadata Initiative Metadata Terms

DCTerms is used to describe a number of electronically or paper-based publications, like documents, books and websites. The description methods is used in many large institutions, numerous documentary records are based on it. The current version of the DCTerms was published in 2010. The elements of DCTerms are integrated into our system.

FOAF: Friend of a Friend

The FOAF ontology is used to describe personal and contact information. Each person is assigned to a FOAF description that characterizes him or her at the related persons. The current FOAF version was published in 2010. Some basic classes were integrated into our system, such as the Organisation – used through the AIISO -, the Person and the Document classes. In addition of the classes the properties were also used in ontology creation.

NACE: Statistical Classification of Economic Activities in the European Community

In the EU the NACE system is generally accepted for grouping and describing activities. The NACE classes are built on each other hierarchically and explain an industrial activity. These categories can be used to specify if a job candidate has an appropriate knowledge, or to define for a position what knowledge sets, skills are needed. The current version of NACE was published in 2008. The class hierarchy is downloadable.

Mode of Usage

Integrating ontologies is possible in more ways during development. One of the possible solutions is that if the existing expression hierarchies and ontologies are fully adapted in the new ontology. The advantage of this import is that classes and relations worked out are on hand. The disadvantage is that is some cases it causes the duplication of classes. In these situations it is possible to match classes, but a more divided hierarchy appears, which is harder to visualize it in Protege.

The other way is to retain only some parts of existing ontologies. In this case, import takes more time in a technical point of view but Protege system is more understandable and easier to deal with. In this last case, we must not forget that if we would like to attach further elements of inbuilt ontologies to the system and visualize it in Protege, it becomes a manual task again. We decided to choose the second option during developing in

order to be able to depict it graphically and be understandable.

If we have to deal with a greater operating ontology, not a prototype and visuality gets less emphasis, it is more advisable to use the first option.

Processed Data Sources and Documents

During the development, we observed many document-structure of educational organization, such as a description of subject, a timetable, a structure of a training. Parts of the documents are included in the ontology as individuals.

In our work we used well-known information and information achievable on online sites of ELTE. Structure, subject information and data on teachers can be found on portal of ELTE IK.

THE ESTABLISHED ONTOLOGY SYSTEM

The outlined Ontology System (See Table 1) can be classified into several major categories. One of the main classes is for a description of the institution, with its departments. Another group will be divided into classes, which describe the structure of the individual courses. The details of the training contents explained in the third group, where the knowledge components, course materials, course notes, thus the building blocks of an educational curriculum and how the units connected to industrial activities are also described. The last group will be divided into classes, which has been described the elements and their connections to colleagues.

Table 1. The classes of the ontology

Name	Description, the role in the developed system	Origin / Source of information
foaf:Organization	Class for describing the institution. Any institution or group can be assigned to the elements of the class. The hierarchy between institutions can be built using different groups of properties.	ERP System
aiiso:Department	The class containing the departments of the higher educational institutions.	ERP System
aiiso:Faculty	The class containing the faculties of the higher educational institutions.	ERP System
aiiso:School	The class containing the institutes of the higher educational institutions.	ERP System
aiiso:KnowledgeGrouping	The entities of this class summarize knowledge elements in administrative or logical aspects. For example an administrative point of view is a summary of a course topics while a logical aspect is a list of the concepts of a filled of science.	
aiiso:Course	Administrative unit of knowledge describes course content and characteristics. The entities of the class can be related to each other with multiple associations (e.g. precondition, equivalence, etc).	Educational Administration System
CompletedCourse	The elements of the class can help to describe the courses completed. The class creates a link between peoples and their completed courses.	Educational Administration System
aiiso:Module	Another administrative unit of knowledge, to describe modules. A module is a set of courses, which form an academic program or specialization. Several modules and other special items build an academic specialization Modules are also related to each other.	Educational Administration System
aiiso:Programme	The degree courses, academic programs are listed in this class.	Educational Administration System
Example	The description of the trainings is linked tightly to educational contents and related literatures, publications. For this purpose we've implemented the Example class. The description of the class is based on the Dublin Core which can be later integrated with other ontologies.	Partially from E-Learning System
Format	The class contains the possible formats of the examples.	
Language	The class contains the possible languages of the examples.	
EducationalLevel	The individual elements of knowledge and the training levels can be described with the help of this class.	Educational Administration System
Topic	Topic is an elemental unit of knowledge to use for characterization of subjects and course materials, like thesis, algorithms, etc.	Partially from E-Learning System
Discipline	This class is used to combine a group of Topics. The classes can also be connected to each other to determine the part-whole relationships.	Partially from E-Learning System
nace:Section, nace:Activity, nace:Division, nace:Group	In these classes can be found the NACE classifications and properties. All the NACE classes are imported to the ontology.	
nace:Class	The lowest level of NACE classification to describe the professions. NACE does not offer more detailed resolution.	
foaf:Person	This section describes the persons like students, teachers and researchers. As there is a lot of type of relationship between them, we used a wide spectrum of properties.	ERP System
foaf:Document	Class of the documents related to persons, like a personal web site, etc.	Educational Administration System
foaf:Image	A special class of the documents to define images related to persons.	Educational Administration System

Figure 2. Description of institution-structure

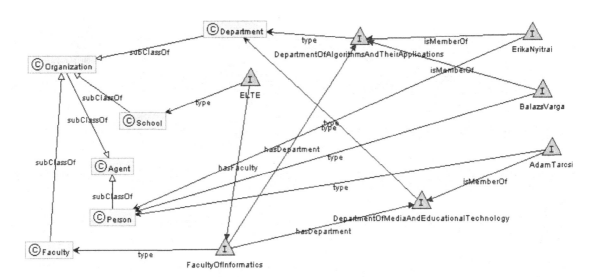

Description of Institution-Structure

Characterizing structures of institutions and their relationships is possible with using classes and properties of AIISO. This part of ontology can be seen in Figure 2.

Besides giving usual data on institutions (name, web address, etc.) relations of institutions also get a role. AIISO constructs hierarchy in institutions by part of and organization property connections. Our developed ontology divides the two ways to more characteristics to make the relationships more clear. Meanwhile we have the possibility to tell about an institution that which institution it is connected to or what kind of subunits it has without knowing its place in hierarchy.

Description of Training Structure

In this situation we observed the structures in ELTE, although its structure complies the structure defined in AIISO. This part of ontology can be seen in Figure 3.

In the characterization of the individual courses we used the classes defined in AIISO.

Description of Trainings' Professional Content and Usage on Workforce Market

Content description of training consists of more factors. On the one hand, content of courses, characteristics of used training materials and classification of activities on workforce market appear. The last one happens with adopting NACE hierarchy. The draft of knowledge-elements' description was shaped during research with its characteristics. This part of ontology can be seen in Figure 4.

Description of Individuals Connected

Formerly introduced modules can be connected to individuals in more points. Their data and relations can also be characterized. It can be done by using a part of the characteristics mainly of FOAF classes, but several properties defined by us can appear (Figure 5).

Figure 3. Description of training structure

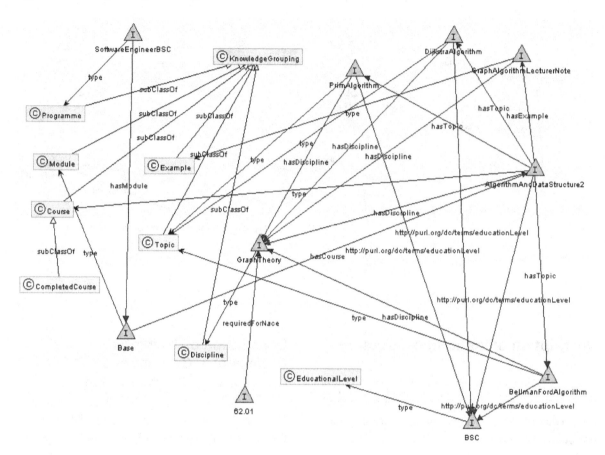

POSSIBILITIES OF USAGE

Usage of the framed ontology is possible in more fields. On the one hand, it can be used as a simple data collector and information searcher system although a well-filled system is adequate to do more complex tasks.

After processing training, more efficiency consideration can be done regarding the structure of training. One of the most easily analysable fields is to discover overlapping knowledge. These are topics that are equally introduced on courses. In a well-organised educational process there is no need of perfect overlaps. A topic can be part of educational process based on different points of view or in different depths, but straining super-

fluous duplications off gives an opportunity to negotiate about useful experiences in free time.

Examination of the order of taking up subjects increases efficiency. It can be prescribed in the case of a course that what kind of former knowledge the student should possess to accomplish it. Usually assumptive subjects are prescribed. These lists of assumption can be formed into lists of knowledge units. More usage is possible. On the one hand, it is observable if the composition of assumptions is right in content. On the other hand, a teacher can get a more accurate picture about the grounding of the students. It can also be observed whether the grounding is sufficient or the content of the course should be expanded with introducing further coherences and relations.

Figure 4. Description of institution-structure

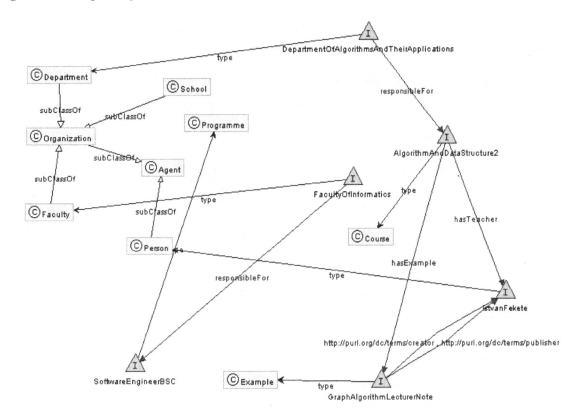

The not really well grounded fields can also be found more easily it may offer help in constructing course materials or course plan.

The developed system can also be used to discover weak points. It is possible that an enterprise searches for young candidates experienced in special fields. If an institution wants to satisfy this need, it has to guarantee that students who graduated there have a proper knowledge of the field. Structure of training can be observed and it can be strained off that what kind of topics need strengthening to guarantee sufficient knowledge at the end.

With this module – lucidity of student's knowledge – the content of degrees also becomes clear. It can be increased by the acceptance of training in the branch and content of training at different universities can be compared more easily.

Several administrative processes are simplified by the usage of the introduced knowledge-base. Among administrative processes at universities reorganisations of fields of studies occur. With introducing European Credit Transfer System and Bologna System, more institutions also reorganised its field of studies not only the other structures. New and old fields have been present in more institutions. As a result, many of the students had to take up courses that were not proper for the training. In these cases, equivalence of contents has to be monitored. It is not a complex matter if an expert does it. But it is quite difficult to make such a task by only administrative tools.

Figure 5. Description of institution-structure

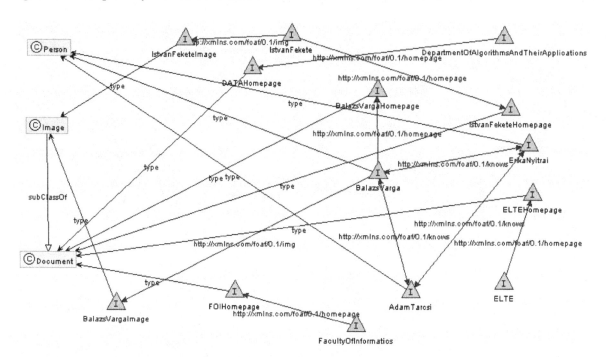

The ontology helps us to reduce the time of these processes and they can be automatized.

A similar situation occurs when a student accomplishes courses in another institution or even a part of the training. The acceptance of the knowledge can be simplified with a system that provides information on the correlation of topics.

The question can be, in the case of every graduates, that if he/she was successful in accomplishing the necessary educational tasks before getting a degree. To check this, an educational ontology system may also help as requirements, some of equivalencies; opportunities in decision can be followed in this system. The automatizing supporting interface can make shorter a part of the tasks of administrators that also may increase efficiency in the operation of institutions.

Query of personal experiences and relations may be useful too. The module is special in a sense that it needs consideration to decide which data should be revealed. In every case we would like to reach data, we must take data protection into consideration and if someone does not want to share his/her data, we must respect it.

But even in the case of small amount of data, we can meet many possibilities of usage. Firstly, we have information that characterizes skills and qualification of a person. We can get to know the groups he/she was in connection with, what projects he/she participated in, what kind of publications he/she wrote. With the help of these, it is easier to organize a research group, regarding former works based on different topics or common experiences of colleagues. If a working group operates already, but we need an expert, the system can also help in choosing the right person.

The ontology or the developed system may also be used to find the appropriate person, with a certain expertise for a working group. From the ERP point of view the ontology system mainly solves the demands for the human resource management decision making processes, like starting a new training course, evaluate professors. From the student point of view the ontology is usable to when a student is looking for a job, or a university partner enterprise searching qualified students or researchers based on the NACE classification code system.

Example Queries

Information for Job Search

Situation: A job seeker intends to find a job as a programmer. He/she knows the profession's NACE classification.

Question for Ontology System: What are the requirements knows for the "62.01 - Computer programming activities" position?

The query:

```
Topic that has Discipline some
(inverse(requiredForNace) value nace_
r2:62.01)
```

Querying Executive Information

Situation: A potential student would like to find an appropriate training. He/she knows that the topic of graph theory can benefit from future work. He/she is looking for institutions with related education. He/she would like to personally inquire about the training

and therefore he/she decided to find the executives of the responsible departments.

Question: *"Who are the executives of the institutions that deal with graph theory education?"*

The DLQuery of the question:

```
isDirectorOf some (
aiiso:responsibleFor some (
aiiso:Course or aiiso:Module or
aiiso:Programme that
(hasModule some (hasCourse some (has-
Discipline some {GraphTheory}))
or hasCourse some (hasDiscipline some
{GraphTheory})
or hasDiscipline some {GraphTheory}))
or
inverse(aiiso:part_of) some (
aiiso:responsibleFor some (
aiiso:Course or aiiso:Module or
aiiso:Programme that
(hasModule some (hasCourse some (has-
Discipline some {GraphTheory}))
or hasCourse some (hasDiscipline some
{GraphTheory})
or hasDiscipline some {GraphTheo-
ry})))
)
```

Figure 6. The question and the response of the prototype systems is the following, using the Protege DL Query query interface

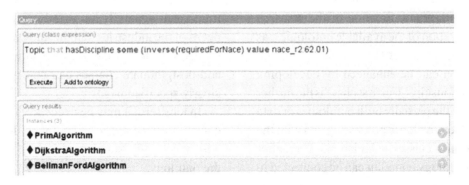

Figure 7. The question and the answer in Protégé

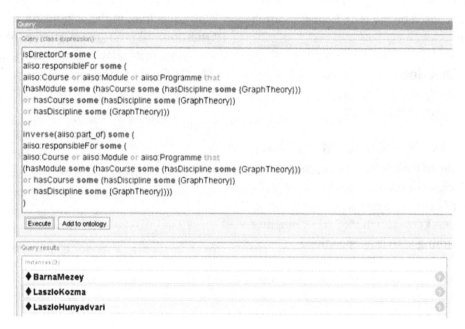

FUTURE RESEARCH DIRECTIONS

Currently the prototype of the ontology is ready. A number of recorded entities are low; therefore the system can be used only in a limited range.

The future task can be divided into several groups. Our first goal is to record additional information of the Eötvös Loránd University, Faculty of Informatics. For this a number of information is available online on the training courses and on the structure of the faculty. In longer term the institution and the training structure and also the content knowledge of the courses are need to be examined in Hungarian and foreign (European and overseas) higher education institutes.

Another important direction of the research was the integration of the available ontologies, as previously mentioned at the following research the integration can be enhanced by developing stronger relationships. The first phase is the further integration of the partially built ontologies or data sources with equivalence processing and with the customization of classes and relations. Thereafter additional ontology endpoint can be connected to the system, like publication databases, or special

field ontologies. Later on with sufficient amount of data, the system can appear as a new endpoint in the LOD cloud.

Furthermore additional modules can be prepared to compare and analyze trainings or courses revealing the shortcomings or unnecessary parallels helping the objective evaluation and comparison of the institution. The institutions' internal efficiency can be increased through the elimination of unnecessary duplications or the exploration of the knowledge shortage.

The developed ontology system can be useful in improving the industrial relations as the industrial needs can be linked to the trainings offered by the universities. Although The basic concept of trainings is generally not strictly serve the actual needs of the industries, but the knowledge base of specialized modules, vocational trainings, further and postgraduate courses can be complied with clearly specified needs.

In long term it may be necessary for a specific query interface and / or language development which naturally supports the data querying of the ontology.

CONCLUSION

In this chapter we presented a vision to describe and link the available information of higher education institutions. The outlined knowledge base can be used to solve several problems, questions and can provide a basis for developing a variety of applications as well. Already existing ontologies and knowledge bases can be integrated into our model. In addition the system can be expanded, with sufficiently large data content the ontology endpoint can appear in the LOD cloud. With the integration of the ERP system, the designed knowledge base may support the effective decision-making.

REFERENCES

AIISO RDF. (2008). Retrieved from http://vocab. org/aiiso/schema-20080925.rdf

Amin Anjomshoaa, S. K. (2006). Exploitation of Semantic Web technology in ERP systems. *IFIP TC8 International Conference on Research and Practical Issues of Enterprise Information Systems* (pp. 417-427). Vienna, Austria: IFIP International Federation for Information Processing.

Anupama Mallik, P. P. (2008). *Multimedia ontology learning for automatic annotation and video browsing*. ACM International Conference on Multimedia Information Retrieval.

Assumpció Estivill, E. A. (2005). Use of Dublin Core metadata for describing and retrieving digital journals. *Proceedings of the 2005 International Conference on Dublin Core and Metadata Applications*.

Berners-Lee, T. (1999). *Weaving the Web: The original design and ultimate destiny of the World Wide Web by its inventor*. San Francisco, CA: Harper.

Bíró, A., & Tomcsányi, R. (2006). *SAP bevezetés az ELTE-n informatikus szemmel*. Networkshop 2006.

Bojars, U. (2001). *Extending FOAF with Resume Information*. Retrieved from http://www. w3.org/2001/sw/Europe/events/foaf-galway/ papers/pp/extending_foaf_with_resume/

Borbásné Szabó, I. (2006). *Educational ontology for transparency and student mobility between universities*. 28th International Conference on Information Technology Interfaces; ITI 2006, Cavtat, Croatia.

Boyce, S., & Pahl, C. (2007). Developing domain ontologies for course content. *Journal of Educational Technology & Society, 10*(3), 275–288.

Brickley, D., & Guha, R. (2004. 02 10). *RDF vocabulary description language 1.0: RDF schema*. Retrieved from http://www.w3.org/TR/ rdf-schema/

Cirrus Shakeri, D. F. (2011). *Semantic technologies at SAP – A strategic perspective*. Semantic Technology Conference, San Francisco.

Cyganiak, R. (2011). *The linking open data cloud diagram*. Retrieved from http://richard.cyganiak. de/2007/10/lod/

Dau, F. (n.d.). *SAP community network*. Semantic Technologies for Enterprises. Retrieved from http://www.sdn.sap.com/irj/scn/go/portal/prtroot/ docs/library/uuid/10e372a0-7258-2e10-2a85-c8 94c6340b61?QuickLink=index&overridelayou t=true

Dublin Core Ontology. (n.d.). Retrieved from http://dublincore.org

European Communities. (2008). *Statistical Classification of Economic Activities in the European Community, Rev. 2*. Retrieved from from: Eurostat's Metadata Server: http://ec.europa.eu/eurostat/ramon/nomenclatures/index.cfm?TargetUrl=LST_NOM_DTL&StrNom=NACE_REV2&StrLanguageCode=EN&IntPcKey=&StrLayoutCode=HIERARCHIC

FOAF Project. (n.d.). Retrieved from http://www.foaf-project.org/

Gaurav Harit, S. C. (2006). Using multimedia ontology for generating conceptual annotations and hyperlinks in video collections. *Proceedings of the 2006 IEEE/WIC/ACM International Conference on Web Intelligence.*

Hamid Nach, A. L. (2008). *Implementing ERP in SMEs: Towards an ontology supporting managerial decisions*. International MCETECH Conference on e-Technologies.

Heflin, J., Hendler, J., Luke, S., Gasarch, C., Zhendong, Q., Spector, L., et al. (2000. 04). *University ontology*. Retrieved from http://www.cs.umd.edu/projects/plus/SHOE/onts/univ1.0.html

Karthik Thatipamula, S. C. (2005). Specifying spatio temporal relations for multimedia ontologies. *PReMI 2005. Lecture Notes in Computer Science, 3776*, 527–532. doi:10.1007/11590316_83

Kirstin Dougan, T. D. (2007). *Bibliographic/multimedia database model documentation*. University of Wisconsin. *MINDS@UW HOME*. (n.d.). Retrieved from http://minds.wisconsin.edu

Murray-John, D. P. (2008). *Keyword domainizer review*. Retrieved from http://www.patrickgmj.net/project/university-ontology

OWL Working Group. (2007). *Web Ontology Language (OWL)*. Retrieved from http://www.w3.org/2004/OWL/

Popescu, M., & Popescu, E. (2010). *A human resource ontology for recruitment* (pp. 896–900). Annals Economic Science Series.

Protege Home Page. (n.d.). Retrieved from http://protege.stanford.edu/

RDF Working Group. (2004. 02 10). *Resource description framework (RDF)*. Retrieved from http://www.w3.org/RDF/

Sosnovsky, S., & Tatiana, G. (2005). *Development of educational ontology for C-programming*. 11th International Conference Knowledge-Dialogue-Solution, Varna, Bulgaria.

Styles, R., & Shabir, N. (2008). *Academic institution internal structure ontology (AIISO)*. Retrieved from http://vocab.org/aiiso/schema

Tarcsi, A. (2005a). *Oktatási információs rendszerek Magyarországon* [in Hungarian]. 3th International Conference on Management, Enterprise and Benchmarking, Budapest.

Tarcsi, A. (2005b). *Learner's data description in Educational Information System*. 5th International Conference of PhD Students, Miskolc.

Tserng, H. P., Yin, S. Y., Dzeng, R., Woud, B., Tsai, M., & Chen, W. (2009). A study of ontology-based risk management framework of construction projects. *Automation in Construction, 18*(7), 994–1008. doi:10.1016/j.autcon.2009.05.005

Vas, R. (2007). *Tudásfelmérést támogató oktatási ontológia szerepe és alkalmazási lehetőségei* [in Hungarian]. Doctoral dissertation, Corvinus University, Budapest.

Section 3
ERP Adoption and Implementation

Chapter 9
ERP Adoption:
Is it Worth the Investment?

Jorge A. Romero
Towson University, USA

ABSTRACT

Enterprise Resource Planning (ERP) has been a major investment for most companies since the early nineties. ERP is a type of investment that has an integrated approach, and has been widely adopted, but there is little empirical evidence about how ERP implementation affects company performance. This chapter begins with the discussion of ERP investment and its role as a commodity or as a strategic investment. Then follows a discussion of an industry in which companies have invested enormous amounts of money on ERP. Finally, in spite of the growing dominance of ERP systems, there is still little empirical evidence on the type of benefits that companies get from an ERP implementation. Therefore, it is important to understand the effects of ERP in cross-functional systems.

INTRODUCTION

The decision to implement an ERP system is treated as a strategic decision because ERP implementation involves comprehensive redesign of business processes and information technology infrastructure within the company (Grabski, Leech, and Schmidt, 2011). In the late 1980s, companies started to change their way of operating

with the introduction of Material Requirements Planning Systems. In addition to that, the business environment started to evolve and companies faced outdated, complex software programs that made it difficult to assimilate and synchronize the fragmented activities that existed in the different departments of the company. This business environment forced companies to look for an alternative software system that could collect data, synchronize processes, and generate information more effectively and in real time.

DOI: 10.4018/978-1-4666-2193-0.ch009

Companies started to implement ERP systems in the early 1990s. Some of them were trying to replace their legacy systems, and some other ones decided to implement a new ERP system because their systems were still using a two-digit year that will generate a problem after December 31, 1999. In many cases, patching an old legacy system was a long ordeal and implied a bigger investment than getting a new ERP system. The widespread use of ERP systems will require that schools teach business process integration in order that students learn and understand to take decisions in an integrated environment. There are several Universities that are already using SAP as part of the SAP University Alliance, but there are also open source alternatives with no annual fee such as Open Bravo that can be used as an alternative (Huynh and Chu, 2011). Some Universities have already started to use open source ERP packages as a cheaper alternative to SAP offered through the SAP University Alliance. Wilson and Lindoo (2011) describe the successes and failures of SAP in online education, and the implementation of SAP in one university and the lessons that they learned during the implementation of SAP.

IS ERP A COMMODITY?

ERP is a type of information technology (IT). So, understanding this type of information technology and its effects on business performance is essential to evaluate investments on ERP and the short term and long term implications. Carr (2003) argued that IT is essential for the survival of a business but that its ability to provide strategic advantage has diminished to the point at which IT is a commodity. Proponents of this view of IT as a commodity believe that ERP-driven improvements in company performance relative to competitor performance are short-lived and small.

In contrast, Clemons and Row (1991) suggested that benefits resulting from an innovative application of IT can be more readily defended

if the system utilizes unique resources of the innovating company so that competitors cannot fully benefit from imitation.

ACCELERATED IMPLEMENTATION VERSUS TRADITIONAL IMPLEMENTATION

It is well-known that as implementation of ERP begins, managers anticipate the organizational changes necessary to successfully implement and use the ERP, and they begin making these changes. Thus, some types of organizational benefits of the implementation surface early. It is necessary to understand the different types of organizational benefits to know which organizational benefits might surface during ERP implementation and which are likely to surface later. Further, some types of benefits, such as low cost of operations, are largely internal to the organization, i.e., do not depend on the actions of competing organizations. Other types of benefits, such as profitability, depend on the actions of competing organizations. For example, is the competitor also installing a superior enterprise system so that profits, if any, that the enterprise system bestows have to be shared? Such a view of organizational benefits from ERP first implies that the implementation of an ERP by one organization must not be viewed in isolation, but the implementation of similar ERP by other companies must be considered as well. It also implies that the typology of organizational benefits must be coherent in an accounting sense so that the true pattern of rise, fall and trade-off between benefits are visible in the analysis.

Technology changes faster than ever (Smith and Reinertsen, 1992), and if a company takes too much time to introduce a new product, competitors may observe this situation and introduce the new product earlier than the first company. Therefore, the more time the company takes to introduce the new product, the higher the expected return of competitors' reactions may be (Payne, Bettman, and Luce, 1996). Companies that make faster decisions can take advantage of opportunities, such as the implementation of new technological capabilities in order to be one step ahead of the competitors (Stevenson and Gumpert, 1985), and a quick use of these opportunities may provide companies a first-move advantage (Makadok, 1998; Smith, Grimm, Gannon, and Chen, 1991).

Decision speed is very important in new projects, and especially in dynamic environments (Chen and Hambrick, 1995). Many dynamic markets are caused by new technologies (Dodge, Fullerton, and Robbins, 1994). Taking extended periods of time may mean too much deliberation in decisions, and this may be counterproductive. In the case of an ERP implementation, if a company takes a long time to implement ERP, other companies may start the implementation before the first company sees benefits from its implementation, and the second company may see benefits earlier because it is using the accelerated implementation. Time is very valuable and the importance of it can be seen for example in investment decisions (Kocher and Sutter, 2006), and the way companies manage time as a source of competitive advantage (Stalk, 1988). Also, from a strategic point of view, time is as important as money, productivity, and innovation (Stalk, 1988). Past research has shown that the speed with which decisions are made can affect performance (Baum and Wally, 2003; Eisenhardt, 1989; Forbes, 2005; Judge and Miller, 1991; Mintzberg, Raisinghani, and Theoret, 1976). Because of these factors such as dynamic environments and speed of decisions, there may be a gap between the ERP needs of companies and the practical ERP training that students receive at universities (Edwards and Hepner 2010).

The higher costs of accelerating an implementation appear almost immediately in accounting and financial reports, but the key benefits may remain unacknowledged for years. A balance sheet will show a fast implementation as a liability and not as an asset, therefore misleading us and valu-

ing monetary profit more than time (Reinertsen and Smith, 1991). While time is a core business performance variable, management seldom tracks it as precisely as costs (Stalk, 1988).

Little attention has been paid to the effects of length of implementation and decision speed, and their effect on performance (Forbes, 2005), and results are not conclusive if decision speed improves company performance. Previous studies based on speed of decisions and implementations have found contradictory results related to their effects on performance. Eisenhardt (1989) looked at eight microcomputer companies in fast-moving environments and found a positive correlation between faster decision making and improvements in profitability. Judge and Miller (1991) looked at 36 organizations in three industries and found a positive correlation in dynamic environments, but a negative correlation in low-velocity environments (hospitals and textiles). They did not find a significant relationship across industries, and they concluded that this type of effect should be studied at the industry level. Wally and Baum (1994) based on a survey from 151 CEOs analyzed the interactions of speed and performance, and they found that they were positively correlated. Perlow, Okhuysen, and Reppening (2002) based on a case study of an internet company, concluded that speed may be initially a source of competitive advantage, but in the long term it might actually generate a self-destructive and increasing need for speed.

Fast strategic decisions may have a positive impact on competitive performance leading to the early adoption of new business models that can provide competitive advantages (Jones, Lanctot, and Teegen, 2001). Fast strategic decisions may also lead to the early adoption of efficiency-gaining process technologies even in established industries where almost all the opportunities have already been studied (Baum, 2000). Therefore, the above observations lead to the following research question: is speed related to performance in industry settings where competitors are implementing the same type of ERP?

Romero, Menon, Banker, and Anderson (2010) focused on a specific industry where there was a high concentration of companies that installed the same type of ERP. Using an industry of those characteristics let them control for other factors that may have affected that industry, and let them isolate the ERP effect. They looked at four strategic performance measures: profitability ratio (PROF), productivity ratio (PROD), capacity utilization ratio (CAPA), product mix ratio (MIX), and price recovery (PRICE) ratio (Banker, Chang, and Majumdar, 1996). The profitability ratio is obtained multiplying the four ratios in the following way (Banker et al., 1996):

$$PROF^t = PROD^t * CAPA^t * MIX^t * PRICE^t$$

They found that the sources of competitive advantage were coming from productivity and capacity utilization.

FUTURE RESEARCH DIRECTIONS

A review of the research on ERP reveals that a majority of research has focused on post-implementation impacts of ERP (Bendoly and Cotteleer, 2008; Gattiker and Goodhue, 2005). The possibility that there might be differences in the impact of ERP during implementation is still an area of interest. According to Stratman (2007), there are still mixed evidence on the installation of ERP that cannot promise positive returns from ERP investments, and Reck (2004) states that previous studies provide conflicting results on firm performance after an ERP implementation (e.g. Poston and Grabski 2001 and Hunton, Lippincott, and Reck, 2003). The published ERP literature provides a good starting point, but I note that further research is needed in the Figure 1.

This chapter provides a blueprint to conduct future research and understand the implications of investments on ERP. Anderson, Banker, Menon, and Romero (2011) examines the ERP impact on performance based on the duration of the implementation. They used the performance of companies that did not implement ERP as a benchmark, and they looked at three different periods as follows: pre-implementation, during implementation, and post-implementation period. Anderson et al. (2011) followed Penman (2003) to analyze the components of return on assets using the Dupont Model, and for each component of the Dupont Model, they used the following model.

$$KPI = \sum (\alpha D + \beta D AvgKPI)$$
$$+ (\gamma_1 D^p + \gamma_2 E^p + mF^p + {}_1G^q + \eta_2 H^q + \eta I^q) AvgKPI$$

where KPI represents each component of return on assets in the Dupont Model for a company that implemented ERP, and AvgKPI is the average of the same component of return on assets in the Dupont Model, but for the companies that did not implemented ERP in the same quarter. They found that companies that installed ERP using an accelerated implementation outperformed companies that installed ERP using a traditional implementation in different dimensions.

Anderson et al. (2011) proposed that the implementation period is a period of change, and management has to take many strategic decisions during that period of time. They concluded that companies that used the accelerated implementation spent less time on taking decisions because they realized that no advantage can be obtained deliberating for a long time.

In traditional longer implementations, the validity of the value added of the ERP system is in question, because by the time the system goes live the pre-implementation business conditions may have changed. Therefore, installing the accelerated SAP, companies can reduce the level of risk. Their results confirm that a shorter implementation predicts subsequent higher performance.

Figure 1. ERP strategic dimensions and its impact on performance based on the duration of the implementation

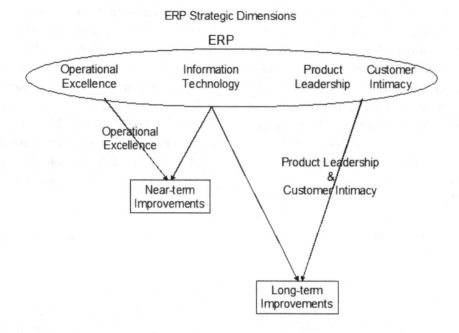

The results and the model proposed by Anderson et al. (2011) to measure performance effects and timing of improvements can be generalized and applied to other industries and other types of information technology applications.

CONCLUSION

This chapter contributes to the ERPliterature discussing previous research onERP and how much we know about the effects of ERP investments. In a period of increasing global markets and shortened product life cycles, previous research has not given much attention to the speed of ERP implementations.It is also important to note that an ERP system consist of different modules and that it is possible that some modules are fully operational before the whole implementation is declared complete. Therefore, companies may start to see benefits early from those modules that are fully operational.

Students in a traditional curriculum learn about different aspects of a company taking a series of courses in an independent way, but it is important to teach them that as technology evolves with the use of ERP, all business processes are integrated, and students need to understand how an ERP systems work, the performance implications of using ERP systems, and the benefits or limitations of ERP systems (Cronan, Douglas, Alnuaimi, and Schmidt, 2011; Huynh and Chu, 2011). Also, as technology and current business environments evolve, the ERP curriculum needs to be relevant and current in order that ERP is integrated into the curricula of Universities.

REFERENCES

Anderson, M., Banker, R. D., Menon, N. M., & Romero, J. A. (2011). Implementing enterprise resource planning systems: Organizational performance and the duration of the implementation. *Information Technology Management, 12*(3), 197–212. doi:10.1007/s10799-011-0102-9

Banker, R. D., Chang, H., & Majumdar, S. K. (1996). A framework for analyzing changes in strategic performance. *Strategic Management Journal, 17*, 693–712. doi:10.1002/(SICI)1097-0266(199611)17:9<693::AID-SMJ847>3.0.CO;2-W

Baum, J. R. (2000). A longitudinal study of the causes of technology adoption and its effects upon new venture growth. *Frontiers of Entrepreneurship Research,* 1-12.

Baum, J. R., & Wally, S. (2003). Strategic decision speed and firm performance. *Strategic Management Journal, 24*(11), 1107–1129. doi:10.1002/smj.343

Bendoly, E., & Cotteleer, M. (2008). Understanding Behavioral sources of process variation following enterprise system deployment. *Journal of Operations Management, 26*(1), 23–44. doi:10.1016/j.jom.2007.03.002

Carr, N. (2003). IT doesn't matter. *Harvard Business Review, 81*(5), 41–49.

Chen, M., & Hambrick, D. (1995). Speed, stealth and selective attack: How small firms differ. *Academy of Management Journal, 38*, 453–483. doi:10.2307/256688

Clemons, E., & Row, M. (1991). Sustaining IT advantage: The role of structural differences. *Management Information Systems Quarterly, 15*(3), 275–292. doi:10.2307/249639

Cronan, T., Douglas, D., Alnuaimi, O., & Schmidt, P. (2011). Decision making in an integrated business process context: Learning using an ERP simulation game. *Decision Sciences Journal of Innovative Education, 9*(2), 227–234. doi:10.1111/j.1540-4609.2011.00303.x

Dodge, H. R., Fullerton, S., & Robbins, J. E. (1994). Stage of the organizational life-cycle and competition as mediators of problem perception for small businesses. *Strategic Management Journal, 15*(2), 121–134. doi:10.1002/smj.4250150204

Edwards, S., & Hepner, M. (2010). Providing ERP resources for the classroom. *Proceedings of the Association of Business Information Systems,* Dallas, Texas.

Eisenhardt, K. M. (1989). Making fast strategic decisions in high-velocity environments. *Academy of Management Journal, 27*, 299–343.

Forbes, D. (2005). Managerial determinants of decision speed in new ventures. *Strategic Management Journal, 26*, 355–366. doi:10.1002/smj.451

Gattiker, T., & Goodhue, D. (2005). What happens after ERP implementation: Understanding the impact of inter-dependence and differentiation on plant-level outcomes. *Management Information Systems Quarterly, 29*(3), 559–585.

Grabski, S., Leech, S., & Schmidt, P. (2011). A review of ERP research: A Future agenda for accounting information systems. *Journal of Information Systems, 25*(1), 37–78. doi:10.2308/jis.2011.25.1.37

Hunton, J., Lippincott, B., & Reck, J. (2003). Enterprise resource planning systems: Comparing firm performance of adopters and non-adopters. *International Journal of Accounting Information Systems, 4*, 165–184. doi:10.1016/S1467-0895(03)00008-3

Huynh, M., & Chu, H. (2011). Open-source ERP: Is it ripe for use in teaching supply chain management? *Journal of Information Technology Education, 10*, 181–194.

Jones, G. K., Lanctot, A., & Teegen, H. J. (2001). Determinants and performance impacts of external technology acquisition. *Journal of Business Venturing, 16*, 255–283. doi:10.1016/S0883-9026(99)00048-8

Judge, W. Q., & Miller, A. (1991). Antecedents and outcomes of decision speed in different environmental contexts. *Academy of Management Journal, 34*, 449–463. doi:10.2307/256451

Kocher, M., & Sutter, M. (2006). Time is money-Time pressure, incentives, and the quality of decision-making. *Journal of Economic Behavior & Organization, 61*, 375–392. doi:10.1016/j.jebo.2004.11.013

Makadok, R. (1998). Can first-mover and early-mover advantages be sustained in an industry with low barriers to entry/imitation? *Strategic Management Journal, 19*(7), 683–696. doi:10.1002/(SICI)1097-0266(199807)19:7<683::AID-SMJ965>3.0.CO;2-T

Mintzberg, H., Raisinghani, D., & Theoret, A. (1976). The structure of 'unstructured' decision processes. *Administrative Science Quarterly, 21*, 246–275. doi:10.2307/2392045

Payne, J. W., Bettman, J. R., & Luce, M. F. (1996). When time is money: Decision behavior under opportunity-cost time pressure. *Organizational Behavior and Human Decision Processes, 66*, 131–152. doi:10.1006/obhd.1996.0044

Penman, S. (2003). *Financial statement analysis and security valuation* (2nd ed.). McGraw-Hill/Irwin.

Perlow, L., Okhuysen, G., & Reppening, N. (2002). The speed trap: Exploring the relationship between decision making and temporal context. *Academy of Management Journal, 45*, 931–955. doi:10.2307/3069323

Poston, R., & Grabski, S. (2001). Financial impacts of enterprise resource planning implementations. *International Journal of Accounting Information Systems, 2*, 271–294. doi:10.1016/S1467-0895(01)00024-0

Reck, J. (2004). Discussion of firm performance effects in relation to the implementation and use of enterprise resource planning systems. *Journal of Information Systems, 18*(2), 107–110. doi:10.2308/jis.2004.18.2.107

Reinertsen, D., & Smith, P. (1991). The strategist's role in shortening product development cycles. *The Journal of Business Strategy, 12*(4), 18–22. doi:10.1108/eb039425

Romero, J. A., Menon, N., Banker, R. D., & Anderson, M. (2010). ERP: Drilling for profit in the oil and gas industry. *Communications of the ACM, 53*(7), 118–121. doi:10.1145/1785414.1785448

Smith, K. G., Grimm, C. M., Gannon, M. J., & Chen, M. (1991). Organization information processing, competitive responses, and performance in the US domestic airline industry. *Academy of Management Journal, 34*, 60–85. doi:10.2307/256302

Smith, P., & Reinertsen, D. (1992). *Shortening the product development cycle. Research Technology Management*. May-June.

Stalk, G. (1988). Time – The next source of competitive advantage. *Harvard Business Review, 66*(4), 41–51.

Stevenson, H., & Gumpert, D. (1985). The heart of entrepreneurship. *Harvard Business Review, 63*(2), 85–94.

Stratman, J. (2007). Realizing benefits from enterprise resource planning: does strategic focus matter? *Production and Operations Management, 16*(2), 203–216. doi:10.1111/j.1937-5956.2007. tb00176.x

Wally, S., & Baum, J. R. (1994). Personal and structural determinants of the pace of strategic decision making. *Academy of Management Journal, 37*, 932–956. doi:10.2307/256605

Wilson, J., & Lindoo, E. (2011). Using SAP ERP software in online distance education. *Journal of Computing Sciences in Colleges, 26*(5), 218–222.

ADDITIONAL READING

Abdinnour-Helm, S., Lengnick-Hall, M., & Lengnick-Hall, C. (2003). Pre-implementation attitudes and organizational readiness for implementing an enterprise resource planning system. *European Journal of Operational Research, 146*(2), 258–273. doi:10.1016/S0377-2217(02)00548-9

Aral, S., Brynjolfsson, E., & Wu, D. J. (2006). Which came first, IT or productivity? The virtuous cycle of investment and use in enterprise systems. Proceedings of the Twenty Seventh International Conference on Information Systems, Milwaukee.

Bajwa, D., Garcia, J., & Mooney, T. (2004). An integrative framework for the assimilation of enterprise resource planning systems: Phases, antecedents, and outcomes. *Journal of Computer Information Systems, 44*(3), 81–90.

Bendoly, E., & Cotteleer, M. (2008). Understanding behavioral sources of process variation following enterprise system deployment. *Journal of Operations Management, 26*(1), 23–44. doi:10.1016/j.jom.2007.03.002

Gattiker, T., & Goodhue, D. (2005). What happens after ERP implementation: Understanding the impact of inter-dependence and differentiation on plant-level outcomes. *Management Information Systems Quarterly, 29*(3), 559–585.

Gulledge, T., & Simon, G. (2005). The evolution of SAP implementation environments: A case study from a complex public sector project. *Industrial Management & Data Systems, 105*(6), 714–736. doi:10.1108/02635570510606969

Hendricks, K., Singhal, V., & Stratman, J. (2007). The impact of enterprise systems on corporate performance: A study of ERP, SCM, and CRM system implementations. *Journal of Operations Management, 25*(1), 65–82. doi:10.1016/j. jom.2006.02.002

Jacobson, S., Sheperd, J., D'Aquila, M., & Carter, K. (2007). *The ERP market sizing report 2006-2011*. AMR Research.

Karimi, J., Somers, T. M., & Bhattacherjee, A. (2007). The role of information systems resource in ERP capability building and business outcomes. *Journal of Management Information Systems, 24*(2), 221–260. doi:10.2753/MIS0742-1222240209

Liang, H., Saraf, N., Hu, Q., & Xue, Y. (2007). Assimilation of enterprise systems: The effect of institutional pressures and the mediating role of top management. *Management Information Systems Quarterly, 31*(1), 59–87.

Lieberman, M., & Asaba, S. (2006). Why do firms imitate each other? *Academy of Management Review, 31*(2), 366–385. doi:10.5465/ AMR.2006.20208686

Mabert, V. A., Soni, A., & Venkataramanan, M. A. (2003). Enterprise resource planning: Managing the implementation process. *European Journal of Operational Research, 146*(2), 302–314. doi:10.1016/S0377-2217(02)00551-9

Melville, N., Kraemer, K., & Gurbaxani, V. (2004). Review: Information Technology and organizational performance: An integrative model of IS business value. *Management Information Systems Quarterly, 28*(2), 283–322.

Mitchell, R. (2006). Exxon Mobil: Focus on flexibility. *Computerworld, 40*(44).

Olhager, J., & Selldin, E. (2003). Enterprise resource planning survey of Swedish manufacturing firms. *European Journal of Operational Research, 146*(2), 365–373. doi:10.1016/S0377-2217(02)00555-6

Olson, D. (2004). *Managerial issues of enterprise resource planning systems.* McGraw-Hill/Irwin.

Ranganathan, C., & Brown, C. V. (2006). ERP investments and the market value of firms: Toward an understanding of influential ERP project variables. *Information Systems Research, 17*(2), 145–161. doi:10.1287/isre.1060.0084

SAP. (2010). SAP annual report.

Umble, E. J., Haft, R. R., & Umble, M. M. (2003). Enterprise resource planning: Implementation procedures and critical success factors. *European Journal of Operational Research, 146*(2), 241–257. doi:10.1016/S0377-2217(02)00547-7

Weidong, L. (2005). Complexity of information systems development projects: Conceptualization and measurement development. *Journal of Management Information Systems, 22*(1), 45–83.

Yu, C. S. (2005). Causes influencing the effectiveness of the post-implementation ERP system. *Industrial Management & Data Systems, 105*(1), 115–132. doi:10.1108/02635570510575225

KEY TERMS AND DEFINITIONS

Accelerated Implementation: It is an ERP implementation done in a short period of time. It could be few months.

Accelerated SAP: It is a SAP enterprise resource planning systems that can be installed in a short period of time and faster than the regular implementation.

Enterprise Resource Planning: System that integrates and synchronizes all the activities of a company.

ERP Implementation: It is period of time when a company is implementing an ERP system.

ERP: Enterprise Resource Planning.

Firm Performance: A measure of performance of a company.

IT Implementation: The implementation of an information technology application such as an ERP system.

SAP: It is a German software company of enterprise resource planning systems.

Chapter 10
Business Process Simulation in Academia

Y. Callero
University of La Laguna, Spain

R. M. Aguilar
University of La Laguna, Spain

V. Muñoz
University of La Laguna, Spain

ABSTRACT

In light of the proliferation of information technology in every area of society/business, its adoption by academia seems like a natural extension of this trend. What the authors find, however, is that few examples exist of the use of Business Process Management to improve processes in academia. This chapter presents simulations as a necessary mechanism for understanding and overseeing organizations as they undergo a continuous process of change. Enterprises, their organization, business processes, and supporting information technology must be understood as socio-technical systems that consist of people (human actors) and technical subsystems and their complicated relationships. In designing, redesigning, and improving such systems, modeling and simulation methods are not only relevant, but essential.

INTRODUCTION

Service organizations are typically structured according to the work division principle, by means of which groups of specialized workers are created, along with managers to supervise them. Nowadays, however, processes are increasingly complicated, with a greater number of tasks to be performed resulting in more complex manage-ment. This, along with the changes taking place in corporate settings (more demanding clients, the need for increased competitiveness and market innovation) means that a rigid organizational structure is not the best option for today's companies, which must be organized around their processes. Reengineering is the process for effecting these changes.

One of the disciplines that has emerged to address this problem is Business Process Reen-

DOI: 10.4018/978-1-4666-2193-0.ch010

gineering (BPR). Muthu, Whitman and Cheraghi (2006) expose that "reengineering is the fundamental rethinking and radical redesign of business processes to achieve dramatic improvements in critical, contemporary measures of performance such as cost, quality, service and speed" (pp. 8). A decisive element in this process of change is the creative use of information technology.

The use of information technology should be extended to Academia. There are several online applications that allow students to resolve many bureaucratic issues without having to waste time waiting in line. Furthermore, there are several applications, like Moodle, which increase professors' capacities to work with their classes. In contrast, it is hard to find examples of the use of BPM to improve processes in Academia. The use of BPM in private and public companies shows that it is a powerful tool to aid in tactical decisions in an organization. As such, Academia should also take advantage of this tool.

This chapter presents simulations as a necessary mechanism for understanding and overseeing organizations as they undergo a continuous process of change. Business Process Simulation (BPS) is an important tool within BPR. Business process simulation is a powerful tool for process analysis and improvement. Enterprises, their organization, business processes, and supporting ICT must be understood as socio-technical systems that consist of people (human actors) and technical subsystems and their complicated relationships. In designing, redesigning, and improving such systems, modeling and simulation methods are not only relevant, but essential (Barjis, 2010).

BUSINESS PROCESS SIMULATION

One of the main challenges is to create simulation models that accurately reflect the real-world process of interest. Moreover, we do not want to use simulation only to address strategic questions, but also for tactical and even operational deci-

sion making. Simulations can be used to predict performance under various circumstances, e.g., different business process reengineering alternatives can be compared with the current situation. The value of such predictions stands or falls with the quality of the simulation model.

Business process simulation involves developing an accurate simulation model which reflects the behavior of a process, including the data and resource perspectives, and then performing simulation experiments to better understand the effects of running that process. There are several steps involved in simulating a business processes. First, the business process is mapped onto a process model, possibly supplemented with process documentation facilities. Then, the sub processes and activities are identified. The control flow definition is created by identifying the entities that flow through the system and describing the connectors that link the different parts of the process. Lastly, the resources are identified and assigned to those activities where they are needed. The process model should be verified to ensure that the model does not contain errors. Before a business process can be simulated, the performance characteristics, such as throughput time and resource utilization, need to be considered. For statistically valid simulation results, a simulation run should consist of multiple sub runs, and each of these sub runs should have a sufficient run time. During the simulation, the simulation clock advances. The simulation tool may show an animated picture of the process flow or real-time fluctuations in the key performance measures. When the simulation is finished, the simulation results can be analyzed. To draw useful and correct conclusions from these results, statistical input and output data analysis is performed (Wynn, Dumas, & Fidge, 2007).

Business process simulation is regarded as an invaluable tool for process modeling due to its ability to perform quantitative modeling (e.g., cost-benefit analysis and feasibility of alternative designs) as well as stochastic modeling (e.g., external factors and sensitivity analysis). Simulation has been used to analyze and design systems in different application areas, as a "decision support tool" for business process reengineering, and to improve the orchestration of supply chain business processes.

Business Process Simulation Tools

Alternatives exist for choosing a BPS tool. Several studies present techniques for evaluating these kinds of tools.

Bradley, Browne, Jackson and Jagdev (1995) defined seven different categories for evaluating business process re-engineering software tools. The seven categories are as follows:

1. Tool capabilities, including a rough indication of modeling, simulation and analysis capabilities.
2. Tool hardware and software, including, e.g., the type of platform, languages, external links and system performance.
3. Tool documentation, covering the availability of several guides, online-help and information on the learning curve of the tool.
4. User features: amongst others user friendliness, level of expertise required, and existence of a graphical user interface.
5. Modeling capabilities, such as identification of different roles, model integrity analysis, model flexibility and level of detail.
6. Simulation capabilities, summarizing the nature of the simulation (discrete vs. continuous), handling of time and cost aspects and statistical distributions.
7. Output analysis capabilities such as output analysis and BPR expertise.

With respect to modeling capabilities, pattern research is used to evaluate the possibility of modeling various control flow patterns, data patterns and resource patterns (Aalst, Hofstede, B. Kiepuszewski, & Barros, 2003). Pattern research is used to evaluate the modeling capabilities of a

tool in terms of its complexity. The complexity of modern business processes is increasing. In order to manage this complexity, Becker, Kugeler and Roseman (2003) have formulated six main quality criteria for business process models. These criteria are:

1. **Correctness:** The model needs to be syntactically and semantically correct.
2. **Relevance:** The model should not contain irrelevant details.
3. **Economic efficiency:** The model should serve a particular purpose that outweighs the cost of modeling.
4. **Clarity:** The model should be (intuitively) understandable by the reader.
5. **Comparability:** The models should be based on the same modeling conventions within and between models.
6. **Systematic design:** The model should have well-defined interfaces to other types of models such as organizational charts and data models.

Law and Kelton (1991) describe desirable software features for the selection of general purpose simulation software. They identify the following groups of features:

1. General capabilities, including modeling flexibility and ease of use.
2. Hardware and software considerations.
3. Animation, including default animation, library of standard icons, controllable speed of animation, and zoom in and out.
4. Statistical capabilities, including random number generator, probability distributions, independent runs (or replications), determination of warm-up period, and specification of performance measures.
5. Customer support and documentation.
6. Output reports and plots, including standard reports for the estimated performance measures, customization of reports, presentation

of average, minimum and maximum values and standard deviation, storage and export of the results, and a variety of (static) graphs like histograms, time plots, and pie charts.

Each selection is fixed by a particular scope so the above classification is more a guideline than a rule. BPS tools can be useful and practical. An introduction to these tools follows, with supportive material from Jansen-Vullers and Netjes (2006).

Business Process Modeling Tools

Business Process Modeling tools are developed to describe and analyze business processes. The analysis part may provide data that is useful for managing these processes. The tool supports the process to establish the control flow of business processes, the resource roles involved, documents being used and it also documents instructions for the execution of steps in the business process. As a result, reports can be generated for process documentation, manuals, instructions, functional specifications, etc.

Protos

Protos is a modeling and analysis tool developed by Pallas Athena, and is mainly utilized to specify in-house business processes. The main use of Protos is to define models of business processes as a step toward either the implementation of quality management systems, the redesign of a business process, communication enhancement between process stake holders, or the implementation of workflow management systems. A process can be analyzed with respect to data, user and control logic perspective, and by making use of simulation.

ARIS

ARIS Simulation is a professional tool for the dynamic analysis of business processes. It is an integral part of the ARIS Toolset; processes re-corded in the ARIS Toolset are used as the data basis for business process simulation.

Enterprise modeling is supported by a number of different views (process, function, data, organization and product) and the modeling approach called ARIS House.

The process modeling part supports the definition of business processes represented in Event-driven Process Chains (EPCs). Other modeling techniques supported in the ARIS House are, e.g., value chains (also for modeling the control flow), organization charts (for modeling relationships between resources), EPCs, and function allocation diagrams (for supplementary information such as data and systems).

Business Process Management Tools

Business process management (BPM) systems can be seen as successors of Workflow Management (WFM) systems. The core functionality of a WFM system is automating the "flow of work." With the introduction of BPM, the functionality is broadened to support the whole process life-cycle. BPM is defined as: Supporting business processes using methods, techniques, and software to design, enact, control, and analyze operational processes involving humans, organizations, applications, documents, and other sources of information. Some BPM tools offer a simulation tool to support the design phase.

FLOWer

FLOWer is a flexible, case-based BPM system. When handling cases the system only prevents those actions that are specifically not allowed. This results in a flexible process where activities for a case can be executed, skipped or redone.

The FLOWer systems consists of a FLOWer Studio, FLOWer Case Guide, FLOWer CFM (Configuration Management), FLOWer Integration Facility, and FLOWer Management Information and Case History Logging. The graphical design environment, Studio, is used to define processes, activities, presidencies, data objects and forms. Work queues are used to provide work to users (defined with CFM) and to find cases satisfying specified search criteria. Case Guide is the client application that is used to handle individual cases. However, FLOWer does not provide explicit simulation or output analysis functionality.

FileNet

FileNet is considered one of the leading commercial BPM systems. The FileNet system includes a FileNet Process Designer, a FileNet Process Simulator, a FileNet Process Engine, a FileNet Process Administrator and a FileNet Analysis Engine.

First, a process structure is modeled graphically with the Process Designer and tasks are assigned to work queues. These work queues and the associated users are created outside the Process Designer. Then, the process definition is fed to the Process Engine to start the execution of the workflow. The execution data for individual cases is logged by the Process Engine and can be accessed with the Process Administrator. Further, execution data is aggregated and parsed to the Analysis Engine. Reporting and analysis of the aggregated data is facilitated by twenty out-of-the-box reports, each graphically presenting the data related to one performance indicator. The Process Simulator in FileNet can be used to evaluate the performance of a created design. The Process Simulator is a separate tool, which can partly import the process definition created. After simulation, an animation and a summary of the simulation results are provided. Simulation data can also be presented in Excel reports.

General Purpose Simulation Tools

Simulation tools may be tailored toward a specific domain, such as logistics (e.g., Enterprise Dynam-

ics) or SPEEDES in the military domain. In this section, simulation tools not tailored toward a particular domain are considered.

Arena

Arena is a general purpose simulation tool developed by Rockwell Automation. The Arena product family consists of a Basic Edition for uncomplicated processes and a Professional Edition for more complex, large-scale projects in manufacturing, distribution, processes, logistics, etc. The Professional Edition also provides (and allows definition of) templates for complex repetitive logic, e.g., for packaging and contact centers. When the tool is opened, a number of process panels are available, e.g., for basic and advanced processes and for reporting.

The model can be created by dragging and dropping from the process panel to the model window. By double-clicking on the icons, options for the different building blocks can be set such as delay types, time units and the possibility to report statistics. Many more building blocks are available and can be attached when necessary. When a model has been created and is completely specified (from the Arena viewpoint) and it is syntactically correct, it can be simulated.

Warm-up and cool-down periods can be specified, as well as run length and confidence intervals. Several statistics are provided by default, but the larger part needs to be added manually by adding record building blocks where necessary.

CPN Tools

CPN Tools was developed by the computing science group of Aarhus University in Denmark. CPN Tools is a tool for editing, simulating and analyzing Colored Petri Nets. The tool is interesting because of its user interface, which was designed in cooperation with leading HCI experts, and includes a number of novel interaction mechanisms such as the use of two-handed input by means of a mouse and a trackball. When editing a net (a process model), feedback facilities provide contextual error messages and indicate dependency relationships between net elements. The tool features incremental syntax checking and code generation, which take place while a net is being constructed. A fast simulator efficiently handles both untimed and timed nets. Untimed nets are generally not applicable for modeling and simulating (realistic) business processes, but several earlier projects already showed that timed CP-nets can model business processes. The correctness of the model developed can be tested using existing Petri Net techniques, such as the generation of state spaces and the analysis of boundedness and liveness properties, which are all implemented in CPN Tools.

SIGHOS

SIMULL, the Simulation Group from the Departmento de Ingeniería de Sistemas y Automática at the University of La Laguna, has been working on BPS for many years. Originally, their efforts were focused on the simulation of hospitals. Thus, a specific tool, SIGHOS, was designed. SIGHOS stands for SImulación para la Gestión HOSpitalaria, that is, Hospital Management Simulation. Soon, it became clear that the main ideas applied to simulate a hospital could be generalized and extended to deal with other organizations, such as call centers.

SIGHOS' main modeling structures were introduced in Aguilar, Castilla and Muñoz (2009), together with the initial efforts to parallelize the tool. Some of these structures have been superseded due to the use of workflow patterns as a generic modeling component. The rest of this section will revisit the main features and modeling capabilities of SIGHOS, and will update, modify or add new definitions, so to underscore the importance of workflows in the new generic modeling framework.

With SIGHOS, one can model a business process, simulate the future performance of a system, visualize an operation and analyze how a system will perform in its "as-is" configuration. Firstly, one has to define the BP model, which in PSIGHOS is called Simulation. Activities, resources, time tables … and all the properties of a model are included in a Simulation. Once the process model is defined, it is possible to simulate it by defining an Experiment. An Experiment defines the properties associated with a simulation execution, such as the number of CPU threads that PSIGHOS is allowed to manage in the execution and the number of simulations to execute. The data obtained by a simulation can be visualized dynamically and in real time by the use of a View. A View collects specific pieces of simulation information for processing. For example, with a View one can define graphical structures to visualize the simulation data or save the data to an external file to analyze them using data mining tools.

EXAMPLE OF A POSSIBLE USE OF BPS IN ACADEMIA WITH SIGHOS

In this section, an example of the use of BPS in Academia will be discussed. Firstly, the academic process will be presented. Secondly, the way that this process is modeled by SIGHOS will be explained. This explanation focuses on modeling concepts more than on technological developments. For a deeper understanding of that aspect, check the SIGHOS user's guide (http://sourceforge.net/projects/sighos). Finally, an example of the results that can be obtained with a BPS tool and its utility in the decision-support process will be shown.

The process example that is used in this section is a basic description of a student's enrollment process, consisting of three basic phases. Firstly, the availability checking phase, in which a student applies for a place in a specific course and the system checks this request. Secondly, the place reservation phase, in which a place is reserved until the student's confirmation is received. Finally, the place assignment phase, in which the system allocates the place to the student. Between each phase, the process must check several conditions in order to continue its execution. For example, between the first and the second phase it is necessary to check if there is a place available for the student request. If not, the systems inform the student of this fact, so that the student can apply for another place. The complete process is illustrated in Figure 1. That is the structure that will be modeled with SIGHOS.

The first and most important modeling component of SIGHOS is Simulation. In SIGHOS, a Simulation is a container for the rest of the modeling components, as well as the framework for performing the simulation itself. A Simulation has an associated □nalization timestamp and comprises a set of Resources, Resource Types, Activities, Workflows and Element Generators.

Though adaptable to user needs, SIGHOS encourages a methodological approach to develop a computational model. Hence, the construction of a model can be accomplished by adhering to a set of ordered steps:

1. Creating the different ElementTypes that appear in the system
2. Declaring ResourceTypes
3. Creating individual Resources and defining timetables by associating resource scheduling with roles
4. Defining typical Workgroups required to perform tasks in the system
5. Creating Activities
6. Associating Workgroups and durations with each Activity
7. Defining the Flows executed by the Elements in the system
8. Associating ElementTypes with Flows and with creation patterns by means of ElementCreators and ElementGenerators.

Typically, the simulation model is declared inside the Experiment. An Experiment can be used to handle multiple replications of the same simulation experiment.

Create the ElementTypes

Elements represent the main actors of the simulation, that is, the entities that actively interact with the system by carrying out Activities. Patients in a hospital, calls in a call center, documents in a document management system - they can all be considered the Elements of a simulation.

Elements are classified into several Element-Types. The reason is twofold: on the one hand, ElementTypes can be useful for statistical purposes when collecting the simulation results, and simply obey the logical structure of the system being modeled; on the other hand, different priorities can be associated with each Element Type. Priorities serve to create urgent Elements, such as patients with a more serious illness, or incidents that should be handled promptly.

In the example, the Element is the student who tries to enroll in a course, so only one general ElementType is defined, called "student."

Declare ResourceTypes

SIGHOS uses Resources to represent any human or material assets needed to carry out a task. Simulation tools do not, in general, treat resources as individual entities of the model. For example, any level-one operator in a call center can answer a call. SIGHOS de□nes roles or Resource Types

Figure 1. Course enrollment process

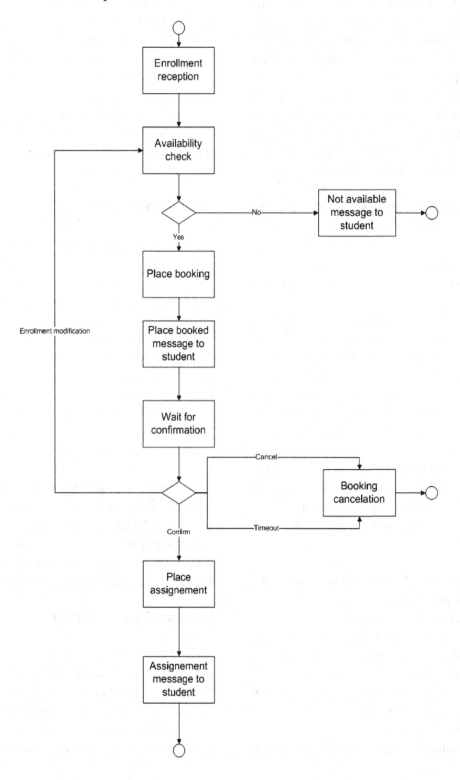

associated with each individual Resource by the use of the ResourceType object.

In the example, one actor exists who can carry out all the activities, so only one ResourceType is needed. Define a ResourceType as university-Worker.

Create Individual Resources

Resources are defined by a description and a TimeTableEntry. A TimeTableEntry {c, ta, rt} indicates that Resource r will be available during time period ta $\geq$ 0 for the role rt, following the time pattern indicated by c.

C is normally defined as a cyclic time pattern. One Cycle defines a sequence of events that starts at a given instant and is repeated at intervals defined by a probability function. The number of repetitions of the Cycle can be determined using a pre-established value of iterations or by indicating a limit timestamp. One must focus on the SimulationWeeklyPeriodicCycle for our example. The SimulationWeeklyPeriodicCycle is a kind of Cycle defined to model events during a week. With a SimulationWeeklyPeriodicCycle it is possible to define the human university worker timetable starting the cycle event at minute 480 (8 AM) and define infinite iterations of the cycle. Then, 25 Resources for human workers are defined. This definition represents one full-time worker on each faculty secretary's office at the University of La Laguna.

Define Workgroups

Since any Activity usually requires more than one Resource to be carried out, these resources are grouped into Workgroups. A Workgroup is a set of pairs (rt, k) where rt is a ResourceType and k is the number of Resources of that type. The use of different Workgroups in an Activity allows, for example, for the "operation" Activity to be carried

out with a Workgroup consisting of a surgeon, two assistant surgeons and two nurses and to last one hour. The same Activity could be performed by one surgeon and two nurses and last two hours.

In our example, only one human worker carries out each process activity, so it is only necessary to define one workgroup for each activity.

Create Activities

An Activity is considered an atomic piece of work or logical step of the process, and generally requires human and/or machine resources. An Activity is a task that can be solved in time t if the associated Workgroup is available.

In this case, each box in Figure 1 represents an activity, so they are defined in a model.

Associating Workgroups and Durations with Each Activity

Each activity needs resources to carry out its purpose, so it is necessary to associate these resources to each activity using Workflow objects. This association is defined by a time period which indicates the length of time employed by the role or the ResourceType in carrying out the activity.

The human worker workgroup defined above is associated with each activity of a particular duration. To keep the model description simple, only those activities lasting between five and twenty-five minutes are shown, depending on their complexity.

Defining the Flows Executed by the Elements

SIGHOS utilizes Synchronizing Workflow Models (Bartosz Kiepuszewski, 2003) to define a complex hierarchy of classes and interfaces that represents different behaviors from the workflow patterns.

Before defining the workflow associated with the barrel shipping process model, it is necessary to introduce the concepts of Variable, Condition and hooks in SIGHOS. For the course enrollment process model, it is necessary to take into account some variable values that change dynamically during the process. The current availability of free places in a course, a Boolean variable in this case, is one example of these values. Variables can be defined in each of the simulation objects. For this example, the best way to define the variables that are needed is to define them in relation to the Element object, in this case the student. The process is quite simple and the Variables can be fixed in the Elements creation. Usually, the Variables' value is defined probabilistically in an effort to cover all of the process's possible paths so as to simulate the behavior of every different process. For example, this model has to define one Variable which indicates if the student has modified, confirmed, canceled, or ignored (timeout) the

request before the place is reserved, as seen in Figure 1. The likelihood of each possible behavior occurring is not the same, so that has to be taken into account when a model is defined.

In a more complex model, it is possible to modify the Variables dynamically during the simulation. This is made possible by using hooks, which will be described below.

Variables are used in the definition of Conditions and hooks. Focusing on Conditions, this structure is used to define points in the model where it is necessary to make a decision depending on the state of the process. In this case, an example of this kind of decision point occurs when the systems wait until a student responds after the place is reserved. A Condition object is defined by a logic expression, in Java code, whose values can be defined by Java code or by an expression to access the simulation system of environment variables

Figure 2. Results of the initial simulation

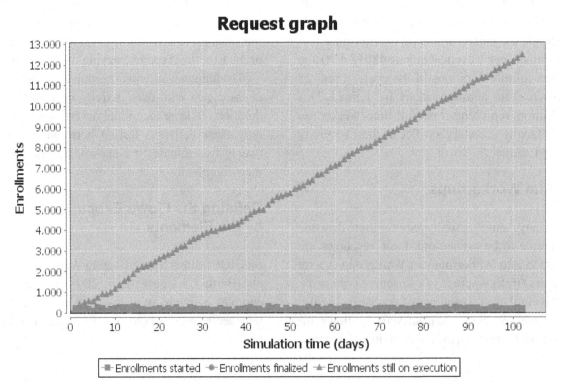

Finally, SIGHOS Flow objects provide hooks where users can define actions to modify the system of environment variables. Simulation-UserCode objects are designed to do that. These objects are defined by a hook identifier and the user Java code, which represents an action to do in the simulation instant represented by the hook. Examples of hooks defined in the Flow objects are:

- **BEFORE_CREATE_ELEMENTS:** This event is used to define actions before the Elements creation.
- **BEFORE_ROLE_ON:** This event is used to define actions before a Resource becomes available for a specific role.
- **BEFORE_REQUEST:** This event is used to define actions before an Activity is requested.

- **AFTER_START:** This event is used to define actions after an Activity starts its execution.
- **IN_QUEUE:** This event is used to define actions before an Activity is requested for which insufficient Resources exist to execute it.

In this example, one possible hook can be defined when a student modifies a request. As seen before, if a student modifies a request, it is because there is a Variable in which an initial value, chosen probabilistically, exhibits that behavior. When a student modifies a request, the probability of a new modification is lower than before, which makes it a good option to define a hook that changes the value of this Variable using another probability.

Figure 3. Results of simulating one additional worker

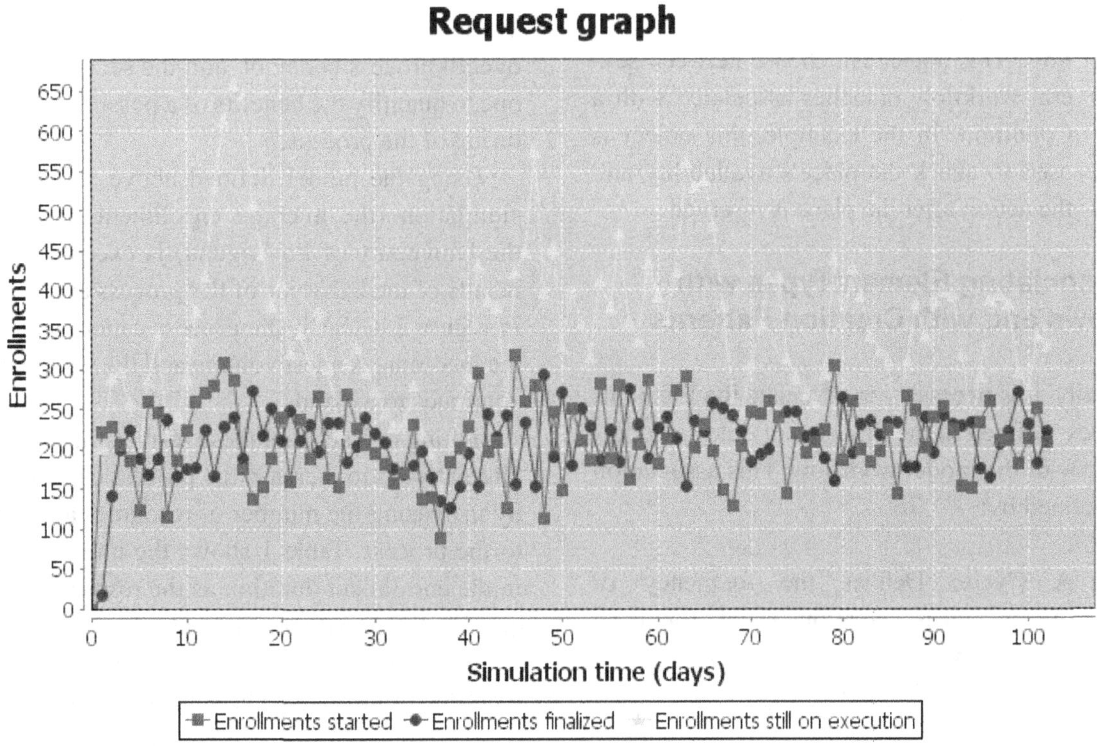

Request graph

Table 1. Benefits of incorporating more workers into each faculty secretary's office

1 worker	2 workers	3 workers	4 workers
92.6%	93.9%	94%	94.08%

A workflow is a sequence of steps that defines the tasks to be done in a process. In SIGHOS, a workflow is defined by a set of Flow objects linked to another Flow object. SIGHOS defines a set of Flow structures to simulate the workflow control-flow patterns, as discussed at the beginning of this section. For the enrollment example workflow definition, two types of Flow objects are used:

- **SingleFlow:** This object is used to define the task of a process. Each SingleFlow is defined by a descriptor, the user methods associated with it and the Activity representing the task to be executed. For this model, eight SingleFlows are defined.
- **ExclusiveChoiceFlow:** This Flow is used to represent the decision point of the workflow. This object can choose between several workflow branches associated with a Condition. In the example, this object is used to check the place's availability and the action after the place is reserved.

Associating ElementTypes with Flows and with Creation Patterns

Finally, it is necessary to associate the Element-Types, defined in the first step of our methodology, with the model workflow. This association is defined by:

- **A Cycle:** Defines the frequency of the instances' creation event for each ElementType.

- **An ElementCreator:** Defines the amount of instances to create in each creation event and associates each instance with its start point in the workflow. In this case, the amount of incoming requests were defined using historical data for the University of La Laguna.
- **A TimeDrivenGenerator:** Associates the Cycle with the ElementCreator.

Simulation Tests and Results

SIGHOS defines several structures for capturing the information output by a simulation. The structure that manages the simulation information captured is the InfoReceiver. Associating Views to the InfoReceiver, a user can capture pieces of simulation information and manage them as desired.

For the enrollment example, two Views are defined. One graphical View which shows the enrollments requested, finalized and still being executed each day; and another View which calculates the average duration of the enrollments. With the first one, it is possible to understand the overall process behavior, and the second allows one to quantify the benefits of a possible restructuring of the process.

Using the model defined above, a 100-day simulation (the average enrollment period at the University of La Laguna) is executed. The results of the behavior of the process are shown in Figure 2. Clearly, the process cannot manage the incoming request volume and the wait queue continues to expand.

Taking into account these results, the obvious alternative is to increase the process capabilities by increasing the number of resources allocated to the process. Table 1 shows the improvement in the enrollment duration as the resources allocated to the process are increased.

The results show that the incorporation of one worker is quite beneficial, as seen in Figure 3, but incorporating more than one worker may not be the best strategy.

But what if no workers are available for the secretary's offices? The strategy is impossible to implement if this is the case. Another option may exist

There is a value that indicates the probability of a request modification by a student. Imagine that is it possible to decrease this value by creating student tutorials, training your workers to provide better service and answer questions more efficiently. Imagine that decrease from an initial value of 40% to 20% of the students. With that reduction, simulations indicate that the initial case increases its operating capacity by 8% without increasing its resources. Moreover, if one decides to incorporate one worker in each secretary's office in the reduction case, the operating capacity increases by 94.17%. That result is better than the increment obtained in the initial case incorporating four workers in each secretary's office.

That is a simple example of what can be obtained by using a BPS tool specific to Academia. There are more complex models, tools and methodologies that can be used to gain a deeper understanding of an academic process, but these, in general, follow the same steps discussed in this section.

CONCLUSION

Business Process Simulation is an important tool within Business Process Reengineering. BPS is used in a wide range of areas to aid in the decision support system of many companies. It is time to incorporate this technique within Academia to increase the functionality of the organizational and academic processes in universities.

Many commercial and research tools are used to implement BPM via BPS. It is hard to define an absolute rule to classify each tool and to single one out as being clearly better than the rest. That is why different perspectives for classifying BPS tools must be presented and considered. This is a good starting point for those readers not familiar with this field.

The reader must understand and visualize the many benefits of BPS. This chapter discusses what this system can accomplish for Academia.

REFERENCES

Aalst, W. M. P. V. D., Hofstede, A. H. M. T., Kiepuszewski, B., & Barros, A. P. (2003). Workflow patterns. *Distributed and Parallel Databases*, *14*(1).

Aguilar, R., Castilla, I., & Muñoz, R. (2009). Hospital resource management. In Merkuryev, Y., Merkuryeva, G., Piera, M. A., & Petit, A. G. (Eds.), *Simulation-based case studies in logistics: Education and applied research* (pp. 84–65). Heidelberg, Germany: Springer. doi:10.1007/978-1-84882-187-3_5

Barjis, J. (2010). The relevance of modeling and simulation in enterprise and organizational study and organizational modeling and simulation. *Lecture Notes in Business Information Processing*, *63*, 15–26. doi:10.1007/978-3-642-15723-3_2

Becker, J., Kugeler, M., & Roseman, M. (2003). *Process management: A guide for the design of business processes*. Heidelberg, Germany: Springer.

Bradley, P., Browne, J., Jackson, S., & Jagdev, H. (1995). Business process re-engineering (BPR) - A study of the software tools currently available. *Computers in Industry, 25*, 309–330. doi:10.1016/0166-3615(94)00044-Q

Jansen-Vullers, M. H., & Netjes, M. (2006). Business process simulation - A tool survey. In K. Jensen (Ed.), *Seventh Workshop and Tutorial on the Practical Use of Coloured Petri Nets and the CPN Tools (pp. 77-96)*. Aarhus, Denmark: University of Aarhus Press.

Kiepuszewski, B. (2003). *Expressiveness and suitability of languages for control flow modelling in workflows*. PhD thesis, Queensland University of Technology, Brisbane, Australia.

Law, A. M., & Kelton, W. D. (1991). *Simulation modeling and analysis* (3rd ed.). New York, NY: McGraw-Hill.

Muthu, S., Whitman, L., & Cheraghi, S. H. (2006). *Business process reengineering: A consolidated methodology*. Paper presented at the 4th Annual International Conference on Industrial Engineering Theory, Applications and Practice. San Antonio, Texas.

Wynn, M., Dumas, M., & Fidge, C. (2007). Business process simulation for operational decision support. *Lecture Notes in Computer Science, 4928*, 66–77. doi:10.1007/978-3-540-78238-4_8

ADDITIONAL READING

Aalst, W. M. P. V. D. (2003). *Patterns and XPDL: A critical evaluation of the XML process definition language*. Brisbane, Australia: Transition.

Bahill, A. T., & Szidarovszky, F. (2009). Comparison of dynamic system modeling methods. *Systems Engineering, 12*(3), 183–200. doi:10.1002/sys.20118

Callero, Y., & Aguilar, R. (2009). Use of simulation in e-government process development: A case study using the simulation tool Sighos. In R. Aguilar, A. G. Bruzzone, & M. A. Piera (Eds.), *21st European Modeling Simulation Symposium proceedings* (pp. 72-79). Tenerife, Spain: University of La Laguna.

Castilla, I., & Aguilar, R. (2009). Java for parallel discrete event simulation: A survey. In R. Aguilar, A. G. Bruzzone, & M. A. Piera (Eds.), *21st European Modeling Simulation Symposium proceedings* (pp. 72-79). Tenerife, Spain: University of La Laguna.

Hinz, S., Schmidt, K., & Stahl, C. (2005). Business process management. *Lecture Notes in Computer Science, 3649*, 220–235. doi:10.1007/11538394_15

Hlupic, V., & Robinson, S. (1998). Business process modelling and analysis using discrete-event simulation. In D. J. Medeiros, E. F. Watson, J. S. Carson, & M. Manivannan (Eds.), *WSC '98 Proceedings of the 30th Conference on Winter Simulation* (pp. 534-548). Los Alamitos, CA: IEEE Computer Society Press.

Kiepuszewski, B., ter Hofstede, A. H. M., & van der Aalst, W. M. P. (2003). Fundamentals of control flow in workflows. *Acta Informatica, 39*(3), 143–209. doi:10.1007/s00236-002-0105-4

Moreno, L., Aguilar, R. M., Martin, C. A., Pineiro, J. D., Estevez, J. I., Sigut, J. F., & Sanchez, J. L. (2000). Patient-centered simulation to aid decision-making in hospital management. *Simulation, 74*(5), 290–304. doi:10.1177/003754970007400504

Russell, N., Hofstede, A. H. M. T., & Mulyar, N. (2006). *Workflow ControlFlow patterns: A revised view*. BPM Center Report BPM-06-22. Retrieved from http://www.workflowpatterns.com/documentation/documents/BPM-06-22.pdf

Workflow Management Coalition. (1999). *Terminology & glossary*. Retrieved from http://www.wfmc.org/standards/docs/TC-1011_term_glossary_v3.pdf

KEY TERMS AND DEFINITIONS

Business Process: A set of one or more linked procedures or activities which collectively realize a business objective or policy goal, normally within the context of an organizational structure defining functional roles and relationships.

Business Process Reengineering (BPR): The study of organizational processes in order to improve them.

Business Process Simulation (BPS): The use of simulation for BPR.

Process: A formalized view of a business process, represented as a coordinated (parallel and/or serial) set of process activities that are connected in order to achieve a common goal.

Workflow: A sequence of steps which defines the tasks done in a process.

Workflow Engine: A software service or "engine" that provides the run time execution environment for a process instance.

Workflow Management System: A system that defines, creates and manages the execution of workflows through the use of software, running on one or more workflow engines.

Section 4
Customer Relationship Management

Chapter 11
CRM for Academic Institution and Universities

Viral Nagori
GLS Institute of Computer Technology, India

ABSTRACT

"Keep your customers happy and satisfied to create value in the long run for the firm." The statement is the motto of all business organisations to become a successful enterprise. Customer relationship management is mainly used to identify the buying habits of the customers, analyse trends and patterns, and market the product to the targeted customers. Academic institutions and universities are considered as a service industry, so the scope and role of CRM would be drastically different compared to manufacturing industries. In the Indian context, the main customers of the institutions or universities are parents of the students who spend significant amount on their children's education. The companies that recruit graduate students are also considered as the customer for academic institutions and universities. The chapter discusses the fundamentals of CRM, its uses and application in academic environment, and technology supporting CRM. The major emphasis of the chapter is on how to automate communication among the students, parents, and faculties. The chapter also focuses on streamlining and providing the details of the performance of students for the campus interview and final placements to the companies. The chapter also throws light on the role of technology in CRM implementation in academic institutions and universities. Advantages offered by CRM in academic environment are also discussed. The chapter provides guidelines for successful implementations of CRM in academic environment. To narrow down the scope of the study, it is confined to CRM for academic institutions universities offering higher education (graduate/post graduate courses) in Indian environment.

INTRODUCTION

The target audience of the chapter are software companies which implement CRM module in ERP package. The chapter is also useful to management and trusties of universities and institutions for deciding to implement CRM in their educa-tion setup as well as for faculties, and staff of the institutions using CRM. The companies who recruit fresh college graduates are also indirect beneficiary.

In the month of Oct, 2011, while searching through an e-database of reputable journals at Indian Institute of Management, Ahmedabad

DOI: 10.4018/978-1-4666-2193-0.ch011

(IIM –A), I looked at more than 600 articles, research papers, and edited chapters on Customer Relationship Management(CRM). More than 400 articles out of those 600 have been published in the last decade. Though the term CRM is not a new concept, it seems that people started researching on it rather recently. The origin of CRM lies in the relationship marketing (Berry, 1983) during the period of late 1980s and early 1990s. CRM is defined as an approach enabling organisation to identify, attract and retain the most profitable customer by building relationship with them (Hobby, 1999). In order to enhance this relationship, an application of IT integrated with ERP suit is commonly used, which is known as CRM (Hugh Wilson, Feb, 2010).

CRM is the combination of people, process and technology (Chen, 2003). CRM is for the people (Customers), CRM improves and reengineer the process and IT is the technology which enables CRM benefits to the company and to the customers. CRM is also defined as a philosophy and a business strategy supported by a system and technology designed to improve human interaction in a business environment with goal to improve customer value (Greenberg, 2010). The enterprise which focuses on customer values will have better chances of survival in the long run(Roger M, Feb, 2010). The better customer relationship will lead to better profitability for the firm (Winer, 2001). Many companies are moving from product centric culture to a customer centric culture, so that they can sense and meet customer demands for changes in features of the product and services, distribution channels and pricing structure (Wang Mei-Ling, Nov,2010).

Earlier it was belief that CRM is only for manufacturing organisations, but CRM is also applicable for service industry. CRM is extensively used for all kinds of industries ranging from manufacturing to information (Sawhney, 2004). The use of CRM for academic institutions and academic is something relatively new concept. While search-ing electronic database at IIM-A in the month of Oct, 2011, I came across 3 articles which are extensively dealing with CRM in academic.

CRM Perspective for Academics

CRM perspective for academic would be different from manufacturing industry and service industry. Education industry doesn't have any tangible product like manufacturing industry. At the same time, it doesn't state any pre decided stated return on the service provided. Students when joining institution or university, they are like raw material. As a process the knowledge is imparted on them and as an output, they are ready to be consumed by the corporate or might opt for higher studies.

CRM has been part of curriculum for management and computer science student. The effects of CRM in the curriculum have been acknowledged by many researchers (Hennig-Thurau, 2011). But very few researchers have thrown light on use of CRM in higher education.

Education institutions and universities are undergoing through radical changes in how they operate and interact with their student, parents, alumni, donors, faculty members and staff members (Lavanya, Mar. 2011). The concept of CRM is applicable in higher education because the services offered by education institution are comparable to the term services used within economic context (Wang Mei-Ling, Nov,2010). Education institutions have intensive and continued relationship with their students, who will become alumni, and in turn they might become donor or might join as a faculty in the same institution. Further, due to increased competition in the market of education institutions, students and parents are increasingly able to acquire excellent service delivery (Wang Mei-Ling, Nov,2010).

CRM collaborated with web based environment provides an excellent platform for an institute, university, students, parents, alumni, and companies to interact with each other.

Need for CRM in Academia

The main customer for any academic or educational institute is student. But in Indian context, it has to be parents. In India, numbers of self financed colleges are increasing compared to granted colleges. Parents are spending high fees on the education of their children. They expect better communication and information on their children's progress as well academic news and events in return of the high fees. Parents play a significant role in education process (Plevyak, 2001). Research has proven that children whose parents are engaged in school events have fewer behaviour problems and greater academic success (Aronson, 1996). In an Indian education system parents are decision maker, while children are service receiver.

The new generation students, who have grown up with electronic gadgets and are much techno savvy compared to the previous generation students. They can easily learn and update to the use of new technologies. Another drastic change, observed is that they want to control the environment in which they study. They are more aware about the values of their opinions, their performance and their future prospects after study.

The administrators wanted lifetime interactions with the alumni, because the same alumni will be the donors of the future for the academic institutions and universities. In addition, some of the alumni might become entrepreneur and will be campus recruiter for the next batches of students. Faculty and staff members can provide immediate referral about the campus news and events to the students as well as to the campus recruiters. Campus recruiters are interested in having a constant watch on the performance of the students throughout the year for final placement and internship projects. Last but not the least, institution will benefit largely when a instant communication established among all the above stakeholders.

CRM ARCHITECTURE FOR ACADEMIA

Figure 1 shows the interaction of different stakeholders with the CRM module.

The following could be the sub modules of CRM system based on stakeholders interacting with the system:

- Student module
- Faculty module
- Alumni module
- Campus recruiter module
- Parent module
- Administrator's module

Now we will discuss the functionality of each of the sub modules.

Student Module

Students demand technology resources to be an integral part of their learning environment (Lavanya, Mar. 2011). They expect virtual access of 24*7*365 with their faculty members. Students expect that learning resources have to be available online, which they can access from their dorms or home. Students also want real time access to the information regarding exam schedule. They expect that the moment examination schedule is prepared; they should be informed by SMS alert facility. In addition, they want email on campus news and events. New arrival in library resources could also be informed to the students by email or SMS facility. Students expect that their assignments, term work, projects and presentation should be available to them in advance, so that they have enough time on hand to complete it. Students can also be informed about the change in classes schedule and upcoming holidays, so that they can plan their trip back to home.

Student can also be provided internal blog facility where they can share knowledge with

Figure 1. CRM architecture for academic

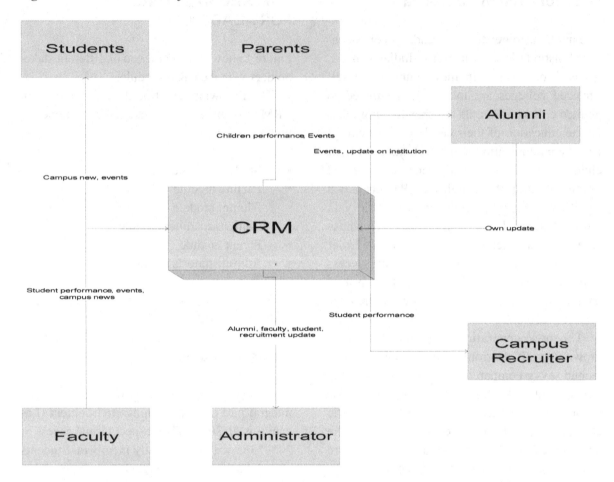

each other as well as with faculty members and alumni. Online chat facility with faculty members and alumni will also ease out their difficulties in academic matter. The past records on campus recruitment, opinion of alumni on different campus recruiter could also be provided as an additional functionality.

Most important, students should be aware about the performance evaluation criteria and continuous feedback on their performance, so that they can reach to the desired level of performance satisfaction.

Faculty Module

The functionality of faculties and students modules are closely linked. They are sharing resources and developing strategies to excel in learning.

Faculty will be providing input on student performance based on the evaluation criteria. They also update campus news and major campus events. Suppose Infosys is coming for the placement, then they will update it on campus events, so that students, parents and alumni can receive the information. If past records about the students are available to the faculties, then they can prepare separate learning program for the needy students to improve his academic performance. Faculties can also share additional knowledge and resources with students and alumni. They can act as mediator for student interaction with industry and final placement. Faculty can update their profile also through web base interface.

Alumni Module

Past students become alumni, and alumni are one of the best sources for future donations and employment. Alumni wanted to know that what the latest update are about their institute, on what projects the institute is working, what kind of activities are carried out in the institution, and what are the events and news on the campus. They are also interested to know about the current batch performance, so they can help them with the placement activities. Alumni module can provide all of the above facilities. There is very special soft corner in the heart for their past institution.

At the same time, alumni can update their current company, their current designation and the city in which they are living. They can add additional qualification, if they obtained after graduating from the institution.

Campus Recruiter Module/ Industry Partner Module

Companies who provide internship projects as well as final placement are interested in updating themselves continuously about the performance of the student in the academic curriculum. The module can provide information about the performance of student in class test, term work, assignment, projects, and presentations. Companies are also interested to know about the extracurricular activities like sports, cultural festivals, and other competitions going on in the campus for the personality development of the student, because this will help them to recruit the best employee for the company in the future.

Parent Module

Parents are expecting that their children will get best of education from the best of the school and excel in academic career with flying colours as a return of the fees they paid. Today's parents are taking keen interest in the educational activities of their children. Institute related information can influence parent's attitude and behaviour towards the institution (Tatar, 1998). Institute can build a positive relationship with parents by providing them institute related information inclusive class schedule, policy for student advancement, and facilities provided by the institute. Parent's module can also include functionality of SMS alert about the performance of student in test and their attendance, so they also can monitor the progress of the student and make them aware about their children's absence on particular day. The day student has not attended session, immediate SMS alert can be sent to the parent and response can be verified.

Administrator's Module

Institute directors, trusties and management are considered as an administrator. They were looking for the overall reports about every single activity carried out in the institute or university including student's performance, drop out ratio, faculty advancement, alumni activities and campus news. They can also generate donor's contribution for various events and activities of the institution and identify and target the donors for the future contribution. A report on how many students are opting for higher education after passing from the institute will also be very helpful in designing future course and curriculum. In addition to that the grants obtained by institution for various projects can also be scrutinised and monitor for its effective use.

ADVANTAGES OF CRM FOR ACADEMIC INSTITUTION AND UNIVERSITIES

The CRM module once implemented fully will offer following advantages to academic institutions and universities:

- CRM will automate communication among faculty members, students, parents, and alumni.
- With help of CRM module, parents can track their children's academic performance records and attendance and if required can take timely action.
- Student is well informed about the campus news and major campus events.
- Students can be informed in time about change in exam schedule or lecture schedule.
- Institute can analyse about placement records and how many students are going for higher education.
- Institute can also have an analysis on donation pattern as well as grant obtained for various projects.
- Corporate can track students' performance records through out the years for final placement.
- Current students can have a better interaction with alumni.
- Overall better interaction between industry and institute for placement management activities.

Classification of Proposed CRM Architecture

CRM are classified into four categories: Strategic, operational, analytical and collaborative. CRM for academic will be combines of strategic and analytical both. It is strategic because, use of CRM in academic will create customer centric environment and implementation will enhance value of

services for customers. IT is of analytical nature, because customer, i.e. student related data could be analysed for strategic and tactical purposes and in turn better policy could be set up which will increase customer's satisfaction.

Guidelines for Successful Implementation of CRM in Academia

The following guidelines will help academic institutions and universities in implementing CRM successfully:

- Remember that CRM is not just technology, its combination of process, people and technology.
- CRM is philosophy and strategy to increase the value of the customers rather than the software.
- Requirement analysis for the functionality of CRM has to be carried out before the design and development of it.
- The stakeholders and beneficiaries of CRM should be consulted before implementation of CRM.
- Training to the staff should also be provided on use of CRM.
- Web enabled CRM will serve better purpose compared to stand alone CRM software.
- CRM should not become hindrance in operational task of institutions and universities.

FURTHER SCOPE OF STUDY

The scope of the studies here is confined to only institutions and universities which offer higher education (degree and post gradation). The similar kind of study could be carried out for applicability of CRM in high school, primary school, and pre-primary school with respect to Indian scenario. Also the issues pertaining to implementation of CRM in academics could be explored further.

REFERENCES

Aronson, J. Z. (1996). How schools can recruit hard-to-reach parents. *Educational Leadership, 53*(7), 58–60.

Berry, L. L. (1983). Relationship marketing. In Berry, L., Shostack, G., & Upah, G. (Eds.), *Emerging perspectives on services marketing* (pp. 25–28). Chicago, IL: American Marketing Association.

Chen, I. A. (2003). Understanding customer relationship management (CRM): People, process and technology. *Business Process Management Journal, 9*(5), 672–688. doi:10.1108/14637150310496758

Greenberg, P. (2010). *CRM at spped of light* (4th ed.). Mcgraw Hill.

Hennig-Thurau, L. M. (2011). Modeling and managing student loyalty: An approach based on the concept of relationship quality. *Journal of Service Research, 3*(4), 331–344. doi:10.1177/109467050134006

Hobby, J. (1999). Looking after the one who matters. *Accountancy Age, 28*, 28–30.

Lavanya. (Mar. 2011). Customer relationship management and higher education: A vision. *Advances in Management, 4*(3), 18-22.

Martin, R. (2010). The age of customer capitalism. *Havard Business Review,* January.

Moshe, T. (1998). Primary and secondary school teachers' perceptions and actions regarding their pupils' emotional lives. *School Psychology International, 19*, 151–168. doi:10.1177/0143034398192004

Plevyak, H. (2001). Communication triangle for parents, school administration and teachers: A workshop model. *Education, 121*(4), 768–773.

Sawhney, M. S. (2004, January 15). Creating growth with services. *MIT Sloan Management Review,* 45.

Wang, M.-L., & Yang, F. F. (2010). How does CRM create better customer outcomes for small deucational institutions? *African Journal of Business Management, 4*(16), 3541–3549.

Wilson, H. (2010). Factors for success in CRM systems. *Journal of Marketing Management, 18*, 193–219. doi:10.1362/0267257022775918

Winer, R. (2001). A framework for customer relationship management. *California Management Review, 43*(4), 89–105.

KEY TERMS AND DEFINITIONS

Academics: It refers to set up of education institute and universities which have admits students on full time basis and lectures are scheduled in campus.

CRM: Customer relationship management is an approach which increased the value of services provided to the customer and in turn increases the customer's satisfaction.

CRM Architecture: It is the proposed framework or a structure by which different stake holders interact with the CRM module.

Service Industry: It is the classification of industry where there is no production of tangible products. They are into selling of idea, concepts and other facilities.

Stakeholders: Stake holders are the people who either going to use the facilities provided by the CRM or indirect beneficiaries of it.

Chapter 12
ERP Modules for Industry–Institute Interaction, Training and Placement, and Alumni Management

P. A. Khatwani
Sarvajanik College of Engineering Technology, India

K. S. Desai
Sarvajanik College of Engineering Technology, India

ABSTRACT

Industry-institute interaction, training, and placement are very important aspects to be considered while designing any system to improve the methodologies for the education sector. This chapter deals with the different modules related to industry institute management, training and placement, alumni database, and management to be covered while designing an erp system for improving these most important areas for any academic institution. Some of the modules to be covered in industry-institute management are as follows: database of industries, industrial visits for enhancing knowledge of students as well as faculty, regular lectures from speakers from industry, providing technical training to staff from industry by means of workshop/seminar/small term courses, and providing technical/consultancy services to industry. Some of the modules to be covered in training and placement management are as follows: database of industries, vocational training to students for enhancing their knowledge, database of students and their academic performance, arrangement of programmes for soft skill development, guidance to students for written exam, group discussions, and personal interviews. Some of the modules to be covered in alumni management are as follows: database of alumni, networking of alumni, interaction with alumni for different issues like industrial visits, placement, guest lectures, institutional developments, et cetera.

DOI: 10.4018/978-1-4666-2193-0.ch012

INTRODUCTION

In recent years education has been strongly influenced by global trends, especially as a result of the call by governments for universities worldwide to improve their performance and efficiency. Rising expectations from Industry, quality and performance requirements, and competitive education environments demands the education sector to adopt new strategies in order to improve their performance. Establishing technology as a strategic resource for faculty, staff and students is imperative for education institutions to succeed in the 21st century. The implementation of the Enterprise Resource Planning (ERP) systems in the education sector hopes of helping them to cope with the changing environment.

The performance of any institution would be enhanced by the good placement of their students and therefore Industry Institute Interaction, Training and placement are the important aspects to be considered while designing any system to improve the methodologies for the education sector. Enterprise Resource Planning of Student, Institute and Industry Information Systems and Management (ERPSIIM) would give opportunities to improve efficiency and effectiveness in the area of Institute Industry Interaction and Training and Placement.

The different modules related to Industry Institute Interaction management, Training and Placement, Alumni database and management to be covered while designing an erpSIIM system for improving teaching methodologies in education are discussed in this chapter.

The main objective of the paper is to help the institution to enhance its name and fame in this competitive market, which is very well met on implementation of ERPSIIM by way of making the students more knowledge oriented resulting into more placements. Now-a-days, all the institutes are ranked on the basis of % of students placed per year and the salary packages offered to them. More placements and higher packages are mainly depending on the level of knowledge acquired by the students during the course of their studies. This

will definitely be achieved by the institutions on development and implementation of ERP covering the contents highlighted in this chapter.

The inclusions of contents like placement, training and industry interaction in ERPSIIM also results into overall academic development of any institutions. Because if any institution will follow these 3 areas, then automatically the academic level of students will improve as follows:

- **Industry Interaction:** Students will interact with the technocrats from industry through visits.
- **Training:** Students will get the chance to work in industry to be familiar with the latest technology available in the industries.
- **Placement:** Encourages the students to keep themselves updated with the latest technological changes taken place in the industries.

The impacts and hence effects of the said ERP system can be best explained by the following flow chart (Figure 1).

BACKGROUND

Before going through the main modules of the Industry Interaction management, we would like to discuss the important aspects of ERP, planning in education and implementation of ERP in education and key to its success. To meet higher education challenges demanding huge amount of internal and external reporting and requires monitoring of day-to-day operations which consume lot of time leaving little time for policy making. Various modules and portals in ERP enable one to manage all functions of the enterprise (Gururao, n.d.).

Strategic Planning in Education (Chang, 2008)

A strategic plan in the education sector is the physical product of the strategic planning process

Figure 1. ERP for education sector and ERPSIIM flow chart

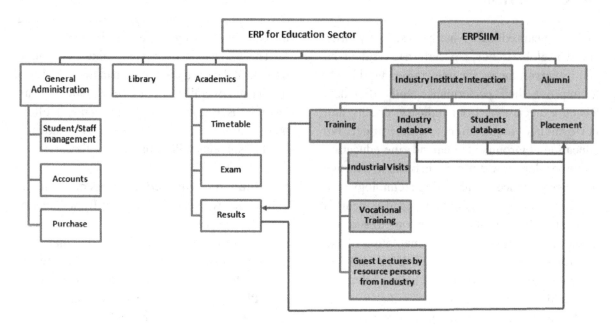

and embodies the guiding orientations on how to manage an education system within a larger national development perspective, which is evolving by nature and often involves constraints.

Any management involves four basic stages: Analysis, planning, implementation and evaluation. In the education sector, the management operations related to planning work consist of:

- **System analysis:** It is a review of how the system functions (internal dynamics) to meet people's needs and economic demand. It also examines various driving forces behind the education system and external conditions.
- **Policy formulation:** A policy is a set of the goal and purposes (specific objectives). Education policies are defined along the following threefold dimension:
  - Access (access, participation, including gender and equity issues)
  - Quality (quality, internal efficiency, relevance and external effectiveness)
  - Management (governance, decentralization, resource management)

- **Action planning:** The policy formed may be established as the framework, which requires implementation by giving the main goals and priorities, as well as the strategies to achieve them. It should be credible: that human and financial resources are available for carrying out the policy. Action planning is the preparation for implementation.

Enterprise Resource Planning (ERP) System in Education: Implications

There are many issues which lead to critical questions about the success and the benefit of ERPs after implementation in education sector. The core part of these issues centralizes on whether or not the system improves user performance, and also whether ERP systems meet staff requirements in education environments. Studying the impacts of ERP systems on user performance is a significant way to assess the utility of these applications in higher education institutions and how they contribute to performance efficiency and effectiveness.

Studies (Abugabah & Sanzogni, 2010) show the benefit and impacts of ERPs which is becoming unavoidable from both academic and practical perspectives, due to the effect on individual performance, the high costs of these applications and the effects on educational services and outcomes. ERP evaluations are broadening from technical aspects to include human, organizational and technological aspects. Studies (Abugabah & Sanzogni, 2010) show the importance of ERPs and their effects on user performance will be realized, and thus the extent to which ERPs fulfill their role for target organizations will be recognized.

Success factor for ERP implementation is an important aspect to be studied. Some ERP skills (Mohamed & McLaren, 2009) to be emphasized for development of ERP are discussed below:

- **ERP Technical Knowledge:** ERP administration, networks, OS, System Analysis, Programming language, data management, etc.
- **Technology management Knowledge:** Knowledge of ERP concepts, ability to learn new technologies and understand technological trends
- **Business Functional Knowledge:** Ability to understand and interpret problems
- **Interpersonal Skills:** Ability to learn, proactive, deliver effectively, to teach others
- **Team Skills:** Ability to work cooperatively in a team environment, plan projects, etc.

The success factor (Mohamed & McLaren, 2009) may be judged by the satisfaction criteria of the user. The same may be divided into two categories User Knowledge and Involvement (knowledge and involvement of employees) and ERP Project Team and Service (end-user relationship with internal project team). Failing to fulfill these criteria may lead to failure of ERP implementation. The problems accounting for the same may technical as well as non-technical ones. Thus the developers and the users have to work in accordance for success of ERP implementation.

INDUSTRY INSTITUTE INTERACATION MANAGEMENT

The preparation of the students, ready for getting established in the industry is the prime requirement for any education institute. Thus the interaction between the Industry and Institute should be highly encouraged. The modules and parameters to be considered under this section are discussed below.

Industry Database

This module deals with the details of the local, small scale and large scale industries, situated at national/inter-national level. Regular industrial visits for the students may be arranged according to their respective branch during the course to be studied. These industries may also be approached for placement of the students after the completion of the course:

- **Branch wise industries:** Sorting of industries according to engineering branch
- **Regional industries:** Grouping of regional industries
- **State level industries:** Grouping of industries in the state
- **National level industries:** Grouping of industries in the country
- **International level industries:** Grouping of industries outside the country

Listing of details such as name and contact details of the proprietor/group, HR person, Nature and scope of business, salary structure with cadre may be done for the above categories. Also a survey of the job placements by the company during the previous years may be done and the listing of the same may be done.

Identification and listing of eminent technical persons should be done which would allow the students to take the benefit of their technical knowledge by means of any kind of interaction with them which is discussed in the training modules.

Preparation of Students' Database

This module involves collection of details of students. The data can be sorted mainly in two ways:

- Year/Batch wise
- Branch wise

Personal details such as name, age and address of the students may be listed. Other details such as academic performance, participation in co-circular and extra circular activities may also be added. Also, include the details of industries visited by the students during the tenure of their courses as well as the project work carried out by the students at the industries. The sorting according to the same may be useful for the placement process.

The other area involving the students is the alumni. Data dealing with the pass out students and their placements is always useful for a good interaction with the industry.

- **Alumni:** Sorting may be done according to their present status
  - Further studies
  - Own business
  - Serving in industry
  - Serving in academic institution/research organisation

Training Modules

Visits to Industry

The students should be made familiar with the industry environment and therefore frequent industrial visits should be planned in each semester of the course. The database of the industries as discussed earlier may be approached for the planning of the same.

Vocational Training

Vocational training acts as a vital tool in preparing the students with the environment and the needs of the industry. The training may be compulsory or voluntary as per the policy of the institute/university.

Arranging Guest Lectures by Resource Persons from Industry

The problems faced in the industry and the actual working environment or the day to day issues of industries may be made familiar to the students by arranging guest lectures by the eminent persons from the Industry. The database of the resource persons as discussed earlier may be approached for the planning of the same.

A common database or plan of action may be made for the above training modules. Listing of the following details may be done as the plan of action:

- Preparation of Institute level terms and conditions for students to undergo training/visits
- Request letters to industries for permission before the commencement of academic year
- Branch wise sorting of industries and students
- Student details-name, contact, result/academic performance
- Orientation about the industries should be given to the students
- Preference of Industries by student
- Allocation of industries to student on the basis of merit / any other parameters
- Submission of training reports in e form, which can be referred as when required.
- Arrangement of guest lectures.

Placement

The policies and plan of action for the placement of the students is discussed here. The database of the industries and the students serves half the purpose for the placement activity. The policies should be made in advance so as to allow every student an equal chance of getting placed. The sorting of the students as discussed earlier would help for the same.

The important things to be considered are discussed below:

- Preparation of institute level terms and conditions for students
- Letters of invitation to industries for placement before the commencement of academic year.
- Availability of past records of branch wise placements
- Orientation about the industries should be given to the students
- Recording and display of the shortlist and selection of students

Once the policies are decided and the framework developed as discussed in the chapter may serve for the development of effective ERP in Industry Institute Interaction management. Consideration and working on the technical and non technical problems during the implementation would lead to the success of the ERP.

CONCLUSION

In this era of competition, the performance of any academic institute is judged mainly on the basis of % of students placed in the reputed national/inter-national level industries/organizations during the year. This will mainly depend not only on the academic performance of the students but also on the practical exposure gained by the students during the course of their studies. The implementa-tion of ERP modules by the academic institutions will really help them in enhancing the speed of work required to be carried out in these important areas as discussed in this chapter. On successful implementation of all the said modules of ERP by any academic institution, the students will get the benefit of achieving excellence in academic performance through practical exposures by visiting the industries or working on any project with the industries. Generation of man-power ready to be used by the industries/organizations is the need of the present day.

REFERENCES

Abugabah, A., & Sanzogni, L. (2010). Enterprise resource planning (ERP) system in higher education: A literature review and implications. *International Journal of Human and Social Sciences, 5*, 395–399.

Chang, G.-C. (2008). *Strategic planning in education: Some concepts and methods, directions in educational planning*. Symposium to Honour the Work of Francoise Caillods, 3-4 July, 2008.

Gururao, K. (n.d.). *ERP 4 educational institutes*. Retrieved from www.advisor2u.com

Mohamed, S., & McLaren, T. S. (2009). Probing the gaps between ERP education and ERP implementation success factors. *AIS Transactions on Enterprise Systems, 1*, 8-14. Retrieved from http://enterprise-systems.net

KEY TERMS AND DEFINITIONS

Database: Collection of data on any one area of interest.

ERP: Enterprise Resource Planning.

Guest Lectures: Arrangement of lectures of eminent personalities from industries/institutions for the benefits of students.

Industry Institute Interaction: Communications between the industries and institutions for the benefit of students.

Module: Sub-division or chapter of ERP related to any one area of action.

Placement: Placing the students on job at industries by the institutions.

Vocational Training: Students deputed to industries for project work.

Section 5
Course and Curriculum Development

Chapter 13
Design, Development, and Implementation of an ERP Security Course

Theodosios Tsiakis
Alexandrian Technological Educational Institute of Thessaloniki, Greece

Theodoros Kargidis
Alexandrian Technological Educational Institute of Thessaloniki, Greece

ABSTRACT

Contemporary organizations rely on ERP systems to implement their business processes. Moreover, there is a high demand from companies for ERP systems because it is an effective management system that optimizes productivity. It is important for next generation managers to understand what ERP systems are as well as the impacts for an organisation to implement an ERP system. This reliance on ERP indicates the importance of studying security issues and requirements in an ERP Environment. Information Security is both a theoretical and practical discipline and can vary from a technical aspect to the management aspect. Educational institutions must educate students to concepts, strategies, and tools that promote security of ERP systems so that after studying the certain course students understand technical, technological, management, and human security problems, identify and respond to information security challenges in ERP systems, evaluate and implement security solutions and tools to protect ERP systems against risks, and finally design information security policies, and evaluate and apply organizational security objectives. This chapter examines how universities and educational institutions are responding to current educational needs by integrating an enterprise resource planning (ERP) security course to current curriculum programs and propose a course framework.

DOI: 10.4018/978-1-4666-2193-0.ch013

INTRODUCTION

Companies all over the world use ERP (the abbreviation of Enterprise Resource Planning) systems to effectively manage business processes across organizational departments and information among global subsidiaries. ERP is a software-driven business management system that integrates all facets of the business (including planning, manufacturing, sales, finance, accounting, human resources and marketing) and is been used to support the core organisational activities of manage operational business information for corporate resource planning (Chou *et al.*, 2005) (Romsdal *et al.*, 2007). It can be seen more as a method than single software. ERP becomes the core application software in the information management of enterprises (Deng *et al.*, 2010).

According to Marnewick and Labuschagne, (2005) definition were ERP is "A packaged business software system that lets an organisation automate and integrate the majority of its business processes, share common data and practices across the enterprise and produce and access information in a real-time environment" emerge that ERP system is something more than simple software and illustrates the four conceptual components that make up an ERP system (alike as the 4ps in marketing model that stand for people, product, promotion and price): people, product, process and performance. This reliance on enterprise resource planning (ERP) systems to implement business processes and integrate financial data across their value chains increases and evidence the importance of security in ERP system (Hendrawirawan et al., 2007).

ERP systems vary from other IT systems, due to the fact that ERP implementation includes technological, operational, managerial, strategic, and organizational related components (Ifinedo, 2007). Gupta and Kohli, (2006) report, that the most important reasons, for companies to implement ERP systems, are for the improvement

of the level of systems integration and for the improvement and standardization of processes. Implementation is successful only if it planed and executed carefully because ERP systems are huge and complex systems (Huang et al., 2004). Dimensions of ERP systems success are similar with the six categories that used to indicate Information systems (IS) success (Kerimoglu et al., 2008): System quality, information quality, use, user satisfaction, individual impact and organizational impact. Different strategies for implementing ERP successfully are (Aladwani, 2001):

- **Organizational strategies:** Include change in strategy development and deployment, management techniques, organizational structure and resources, managerial style and ideology, communication and coordination, and IS function characteristics
- **Technical strategies:** Include technical aspects of ERP installation, ERP complexity, adequacy of in-house technical expertise, and time and cost of implementation
- **People strategies:** Include staff and management attitudes, involvement and training

Successful implementation of ERP is considered to be depending on three distinct groups (Wu and Wang, 2006):

1. ERP package developers
2. Developers using an ERP system
3. ERP system users.

Young (2007) states that ERP implementation project is the single biggest project that an organisation has ever launched but from the moment the company successfully implements the ERP, the attention is headed forward to the most efficient use of the system. Still, the phase of ERP implementation is a complex task and a large number of adopters have encountered problems, in a form of failure, in different phases either caused by cancellations or cost/time overruns (Ngai, et al., 2008). Academics as Basoglu et al. (2007) report, started to be interested in ERP systems, especially in their failure factors, especially at users important role in the organizational adoption and success of ERP projects as it happens in other IS projects. Successful implementation of ERP systems by Dey and Cheffi (2010), can result from effective management of the generic risks of ERP system. The common problems of ERP (such as inadequate user involvement & training, lack of controls, poor implementation of systems & task-technology fit etc.) can be transformed into risks. ERP project risks are often seen and reported as critical success factors (CSFs) (Ojala et al., 2006). Exposures to security risks are heightened by the increased use of telecommuting, VoIP, wireless laptops, PDAs, and other mobile devices (Russell, 2006). ERP risk can be defined according to Peng and Nunes (2009) as "the occurrence of any event that has consequences or impacts on the use, maintenance and enhancement of the implemented ERP system". Risks in an ERP system, can be classified into four categories (Hsu et al., 2006):

1. **Business risks:** Risks that may prevent or encumber enterprise to achieving its business goals or objectives
2. **Control risks:** Risks that affect the enterprise's policies or procedures
3. **System risks:** Risks that the ERP system does not function as designed and
4. **Security risks:** Risks associated with unauthorized access to the information systems.

Security constitutes the main control risk for ERP systems. Managers should be capable to define, determine and set the security policies to ERP system. For the majority of enterprises, ERP security starts with user-based controls where authorized users log in with a secure username and password (Van Holsbeck and Jeffrey, 2004). Many companies firms are still not prepared to

tackle the need for a rigorous ERP security audit. The following factors contribute to this (Hendrawirawan et al., 2007):

- Complex structure of ERP kills security and leads to security vulnerabilities
- A shortage of staff members trained in ERP security
- Inadequate attention towards security implementation
- Lack of ERP Tools for security
- Customization of ERP Systems to firms inhibits the development of standardized security solutions

The majority of IT/IS security managers focus on technical issues and solutions and do not give the right attention end users' lack of IS security awareness. IT managers particularly need to raise the concern of information security awareness and train company employees to protect both themselves and corporate. Information security awareness is described as a state where users in an organization are aware of their security mission and distinguished in two categories: framework and content (Rezgui and Marks, 2008). There is a large variation of security awareness from organisation to organisation and from department to department (May, 2008).

All that motivates to create a course that studies ERP from the perspective of implementing ERP by the information systems security management that set ERP system possible. The course will provide students with a basic understanding of the principles of information security and management that are applied in a business environment thus in medium to large organisations.

SECURITY CONSIDERATION

Information Security in the integrated enterprise resource planning (ERP) environment demand a new way of thinking. Security has to stop from being and remain an afterthought. Consider the paradox, that although Enterprise Resource Planning (ERP) systems are essentially the single most expensive software system, concerns about investing on securing the most valuable asset are on the end of the implementation process. Security concerns according to Hughes and Beer (2007) fell into one of the two areas:

- It is rather difficult for enterprises to understand how to securely configure an ERP system
- The management of access and authorization roles—for both the ERP and third-party software integrated with the ERP—is huge

It is fundamental in security that complexity kills is. Unfortunately, ERP systems have (inherently) a complex structure spanning many functional areas and processes along a firm's value chain (Hendrawirawan et al., 2007). Administrators are the ones that determine and define the security requirements centrally. They are tasked with the creation and generation of roles and profiles in order to group user/individual transactions and so to grant and monitor user access and facilitate approvals by data owners (Vance, 2008), (von Solms and Hertenberger, 2004).

The debate about the inclusion of IT into the curriculum for business students has a long story (Magnusson et al., 2009). The concept of Information Technology Security (ITS) consist a major current issue as the threats to information systems from a multitude of factors (such as hackers) are increasing dramatically. Dependence on Information Security is at all levels of personal, community/state and corporate life. At the academic field, the necessity of information security is twofold. Academic institutions (universities) need instructors/educators who can communicate the underlying theory of Information Security (IS) to students in order to have them prepared to apply principles of security to enterprise processes and enterprises need qualified staff to support protection of their assets (tangible and not). Parker (1992) indicates that "the generally accepted role of information security is to address the symptoms of unethical behavior rather than to attempt to change that behaviour".

Developing a specific/applied/general thematic of Information Systems Security curriculum involves many challenges and the gravity of the process of creating and designing both a practical and managerial curriculum from the curriculum designers, should be given into the employers' needs (Ralevich and Martinovic, 2010). The determination of the right mix of content is also challenging and firstly depends on the background of the students and secondly on what other topics the course covers (Walden, 2008).

Ideal for the course content is to incorporate both technical and management perspectives to ensure its relevance to practice. And due to the nature of both of the subjects balancing theory and practice is fundamental in the area of management (Abawajy, 2009).

The basic driver for a every security program was information security triad of confidentiality, integrity, and availability (also referred as CIA) (Peltier, 2005). A security course focuses on the concepts, principles, and techniques for system security (Du et al., 2006).

The truth is that the concept of Information Security is quite broad and cannot be adequately covered in its totality by a single course but a security related course teaches students how to:

1. Design,
2. Implement,
3. Analyze,
4. Test, and
5. Operate

a system with the goal of making it secure (achieve security) (Sharma and Sefchek, 2007). Du et al. (2006) further mentions raising everyone's understanding of the information security requirements of the business serves as a common baseline. It is practical at this point to mention the myths about security in ERP (Polyakov and Medvedovskiy, 2010):

- **Myth 1:** Business applications are only available internally # But there are workstations connected to the internet
- **Myth 2:** ERP security is a vendor's problem # Vendor is responsible for problems in program and architecture. Clients are responsible for implementation architecture errors, Defaults/Misconfigurations, Human factor, Policies/ processes/etc
- **Myth 3:** Business application internals are very specific and are not known for hackers # But products especially popular are on the attack by hackers
- **Myth 4:** ERP security is all about Segregation of Duties (SoD) # It is like spending all money on video surveillance systems, biometric access control and leaving the back door open for housekeepers.

ERP COURSE FUNDAMENTALS

Students (graduates) from economics and business programmes may be confronted with ERP systems in their role as users of these systems and in their managerial role as they will have to manage the impact of ERP systems on business processes (Vluggen and Bollen, 2005). Educational institutes have incorporated ERP systems into their business curriculum in order to provide students with a better understanding of business process theory and information management concepts. Both the demand and need by the markets for well trained enterprise resource planning profession-

als, strengthen by industry-wide acceptance of ERP, engender universities to create ERP-related courses and particularly to join alliances with ERP software vendors (Young, 2007), (Becerra-Fernandez et al., 2000) (Yang and Jiang, 2009). In the international level, SAP, Oracle, PeopleSoft, Microsoft consist the major players at offering ERP software for educational purposes (Pollack, 2002), (Guthrie and Guthrie, 2000). At local level there are smaller vendors as for example in Greece, Altec is the most recognisable.

ERP vendors dispense their software products to educational institutions on one of the following methods:

- Full version of the product at low, discounted and attractive price.
- Full version of the product for free (evaluation), with limited chronically period of use of time (one year licence).
- Demonstration (Demo) version of the product with limited options and features.

The integration of ERP face the following challenges (Hayes and McGilsky, 2007):

- Selecting and implementing an appropriate ERP software package
- Selecting and training appropriate faculty
- Developing the curriculum and
- Administering the ERP initiative

The integration of ERP into universities curriculum has been driven by a number of factors such as (Shakleton et al., 2001), (Ravesteyn and Köhler, 2009):

- Students realise the market need and job opportunity;
- Industries are searching for graduates with analogous ERP skills and

- Academics are trying to go with the flow of current issues in the information technology industry

Introducing and setting ERP in education sector is a major investment both in time and money (Joseph and George, 2002). The adoption and implementation of an ERP in academic environment, involves high costs and efforts, mainly because of the huge initial investments in time and resources needed for the acquirement of skills to setup, configure, operate and maintain the ERP software and hereupon to develop a new curriculum. ERP curriculum needs 1) to evolve 2) to reflect and 3) to support the strategic usage of companies ERP system (Hawking et al., 2005). Deng et al. (2010) detect two certain problems in ERP curriculum. First the ellipsis of management concepts and second the incomplete teaching content. Moreover Fan et al. (2011) analyse the problems in the teaching of ERP due to:

- Failure to connect ERP with other relative courses
- Too much emphasis on theories and methods and omission of application
- Lack of setting a combination of cases with software
- Shortage of teachers with continuously updated knowledge and extensive practical management experience

The introduction of ERP software for educational purposes can cause the following problems that should be solved (Vluggen, and Bollen, 2005):

- Surmount the resistance of using software and changing the existing curriculum.
- Finding the needed financial resources for using ERP software.
- Creating a multidisciplinary team of faculty members.

- Implementing and maintaining a technical infrastructure for ERP usage.

Developing an ERP curriculum can fall in one of the following approaches (Ravesteyn and Köhler, 2009):

- **ERP training:** Teaching a particular ERP system of a developer/supplier
- **ERP via business processes:** Presentation of business processes and related concepts with the use of ERP system
- **Information systems approach:** Instruction of information systems concepts
- **ERP concepts:** Teaching ERP related skills (ex. selection and implementation of ERP software)

As Peltier (2005) refers, learning is a process that consists of three key elements:

1. **Awareness:** Stimulation, motivation and remembrance of the students of what is expected from them.
2. **Training:** Teaching a skill or using of a required tool.
3. **Education:** An in-depth, specific tuition process.

Moreover, in order for the teaching process to be effective the teaching/learning context should be configured in that way so that students are encouraged to react with the level of cognitive engagement that course objectives require (Davidson and Näckros, 2007). Higher or third level educations (such as universities, colleges, academies, technological institutes) face the challenge and need in pedagogy to enable students understand, retain and apply ERP appropriately and to improve the students' practical ability (Joseph and George, 2002), (Deng et al., 2009). They need to enable a much deeper understanding of business operations and a cleaner vision of interlinked aspects of business activity (Rienzo and Han, 2011).

CREATION OF A SPECIFIC ERP SECURITY COURSE

It is proper before developing the approach, to define that ERP security curriculum will be a full ERP course, offering both theoretical lectures and practical exercises and will form of course of 6 ECTS (European Credit Transfer System) credits. That means 6 ECTS are equivalent to 160

hours of study, including class, assignments, etc for a full-time student. The delivery method of the course will be the classical in person lectures provided by the lecturer, guest lectures in contemporary issues by industry and academia experts, assigns, projects, exercises and content support through blackboard learning system (e-class) that provides student oriented collaborative learning environment.

Course Description

This course will address ERP systems security. The primary goal of the course (course objective)

Table 1.

Week	Thematic Topic	Description
1.	ERP and Business/Process Drivers and Implementation Methods	Introduction to business functions and process. Implemented by ERP
2.	Information Security Principles, Concepts and Definitions	This covers the definitions of confidentiality, integrity, availability, asset, vulnerability, authentication, etc
3.	Network security fundamentals	information security principles associated with the underlying networks and communications systems
4.	Introduction to Cryptography	The role of cryptography in protecting systems, assets and practices
5.	Risk Assessment and Management	Understanding, Identifying and categorizing risks, assets at risk, threats and vulnerabilities of a system
6.	Security management	How the management process should be implemented in enterprise. The importance of policies, standards and procedures
7.	Security in ERP system	Defining security requirements in an ERP system
8.	Authentication and User setting in a particular ERP Software - part I	Setting the goals of system security, user types, roles, profiles, authentication polices, passwords and more.
9.	Part II continued	
10.	Auditing ERP System	Define audit requirements, tasks, monitoring of end user access and activity, database changing etc
11.	Part II continued	
12.	Business Continuity Management - Planning	Instant response to a security incident, and assurance that enterprise can continue functioning after a security incident
13.	Legal, Ethical, and Social implications of security	Identify and distinguish the needs of the different parties having a stake in the security of an ERP system
14.	Course Overview	

is to develop analytical and critical thinking skills for securing ERP systems so that enterprise can optimize its performance. The focus is more on giving (exposing) students an overview of key areas in information security rather than an in-depth analysis of a particular area. The course will present to students a systemic and management overview of information security, what security forms, what drives the needs for information security, what are the requirements to implement it and how to integrate it into the systems design process.

Course Topics

Our approach for the course will be to cover selected topics from a very broad area like security and ERP with the goal to prepare student to think and act as mentioned above, with analytical and critical thinking about security. Topics may include:

*   Introduction to Information Security Concepts
*   System Threats and Risks
*   Metrics for Information Security
*   Protecting Systems
*   Network Vulnerabilities, Attacks and Protection
*   Access Control Fundamentals
*   Authentication
*   Performing Vulnerability Assessments
*   Conducting Security Audits
*   Basic Cryptography and appliances of Cryptography
*   Business Continuity Planning and Procedures
*   Human Factors
*   Legal, Ethical, and Social Implications

Course Structure

The week by week course structure of at least 13 weeks has as seen in Table 1.

Course Learning Outcomes:

Students upon completion of the training course will have both a comprehensive overview of information security concepts and an in-depth understanding of applying security to ERP system. Furthermore, students will be able to:

*   Provide an understanding of principal concepts, major issues and basic approaches in information security (confidentiality, integrity, availability, vulnerability, threats, risks, countermeasures, etc)
*   Have knowledge and understanding of concepts, issues and approaches in information security relating to information security management
*   Understand the current business environments in which they have to operate information security management
*   Evaluate vulnerability of an information system and establish a plan for risk management
*   Demonstrate how to secure an ERP system by detecting and reducing threats
*   Evaluate enterprise security policies and procedures

CONCLUSION

Securing an ERP system consist a complex task and requires good managerial and technical skills as communication and especially awareness. Awareness that translated into that user(s) is aware of security risks and has the ability to set policies and apply procedures. And for a security related ERP course the result should be that students gain awareness into specific knowledge about how information security affects the ERP business ecosystem and understand the risk that exists around enterprise information.

REFERENCES

Abawajy, J. (2009). Design and delivery of undergraduate IT security management course. In The *Proceedings of the Third International Conference and Workshops, ISA 2009*, Seoul, Korea, June 25-27, 2009, (pp. 402-411).

Aladwani, A. (2001). Change management strategies for successful ERP implementation. *Business Process Management Journal*, 7(3), 266–275. doi:10.1108/14637150110392764

Basoglu, N., Daim, T., & Kerimoglu, O. (2007). Organizational adoption of enterprise resource planning systems: A conceptual framework. *The Journal of High Technology Management Research*, 18(1), 73–97. doi:10.1016/j. hitech.2007.03.005

Becerra-Fernandez, I., Murphy, K., & Simon, S. (2000). Enterprise resource planning: Integrating ERP in the business school curriculum. *Communications of the ACM*, 43(4), 39–41. doi:10.1145/332051.332066

Chou, D., Tripuramallu, H., & Chou, A. (2005). BI and ERP integration. *Information Management & Computer Security*, 13(5), 340–349. doi:10.1108/09685220510627241

Davidson, A., & Näckros, K. (2007). Practical assignments in IT security for contemporary higher education. In the *Proceedings of World Conference on Information Security Education 2007*, (pp. 25-32).

Deng, Q., Jin, X., Yin, A., & Tu, B. (2010). Design of teaching system of compound ERP talents. In The *Proceedings of the International Conference on Computer Application and System Modeling (ICCASM 2010)*, (pp. 340-343).

Deng, Q., Yin, A., & Tu, B. (2009). Design and application of practical teaching framework of ERP course. In The *Proceedings of the 4th International Conference on Computer Science & Education, ICCSE '09*, 25-28 July 2009, (pp. 1346-1348).

Dey, P. K., & Cheffi, W. (in press). Risk management in enterprise resource planning projects: Case study of an UK-based organization. [in press]. *International Journal of Production Economics*.

Du, W., Shang, M., & Xu, H. (2006). A novel approach for computer security education using Minix instructional operating system. *Computers & Security*, 25(3), 190–200. doi:10.1016/j. cose.2005.09.011

Fan, C., Zhang, P., Liu, Q., Yang, J., & Xi, W. (2011). Research on ERP teaching model reform for application-oriented talents education. *International Education Studies*, 4(2), 25–30. doi:10.5539/ies.v4n2p25

Gupta, M., & Kohli, A. (2006). Enterprise resource planning systems and its implications for operations function. *Technovation*, 26(5-6), 687–696. doi:10.1016/j.technovation.2004.10.005

Guthrie, R., & Guthrie, R. (2000). Integration of enterprise system software in the undergraduate curriculum. In The *Proceedings of the Information Systems Education Conference 2000*, Vol. 17.

Hawking, P., McCarthy, B., & Stein, A. (2005) Integrating ERP's second wave into higher education curriculum. In The *Proceedings of the PACIS 2005*, (pp. 1001-1008).

Hayes, G., & McGilsky, D. (2007). Integrating ERP into BSBA curriculum of Central Michigan University. *International Journal of Quality and Productivity Management, 7*(1), 12–27.

Hendrawirawan, D., Tanriverdi, H., Zetterlund, C., Hakam, H., Kim, H., Paik, H., & Yoon, Y. (2007). ERP security and segregation of duties audit: A framework for building an automated solution. *Information Systems Control Journal, 2*, 1–4.

Hsu, K., Sylvestre, J., & Sayed, E. (2006). Avoiding ERP pitfalls. *Journal of Corporate Accounting & Finance,* (May/June): 67–74. doi:10.1002/jcaf.20217

Huang, S., Chang, I., Li, S., & Lin, M. (2004). Assessing risk in ERP projects: Identify and prioritize the factors. *Industrial Management & Data Systems, 104*(8), 681–688. doi:10.1108/02635570410561672

Hughes, J., & Beer, R. (2007). A security checklist for ERP Implementations. *EDUCAUSE Quarterly, 30*(4), 7–10.

Ifinedo, P. (2007). An empirical study of ERP success evaluations by business and IT managers. *Information Management & Computer Security, 15*(4), 270–282. doi:10.1108/09685220710817798

Joseph, G., & George, A. (2002). ERP, learning communities, and curriculum integration. *Journal of Information Systems Education, 13*(1), 51–58.

Kerimoglu, O., Basoglu, N., & Daim, T. (2008). Organizational adoption of information technologies: Case of enterprise resource planning systems. *The Journal of High Technology Management Research, 19*, 21–35. doi:10.1016/j.hitech.2008.06.002

Magnusson, J., Oskarsson, B., Gidlund, A., & Wetterberg, A. (2009). Process methodology in ERP-related education: A case from Swedish higher education. In The *Proceedings of the BIS 2009 Workshop, LNBIP 37,* (pp. 214–219).

Marnewick, C., & Labuschagne, L. (2005). A conceptual model for enterprise resource planning (ERP). *Information Management & Computer Security, 13*(2), 144–155. doi:10.1108/09685220510589325

May, C. (2008). Approaches to user education. *Network Security,* (9): 15–17. doi:10.1016/S1353-4858(08)70109-0

Ngai, E. W. T., Law, C. C. H., & Wat, F. K. T. (2008). Examining the critical success factors in the adoption of enterprise resource planning. *Computers in Industry, 59*(6), 548–564. doi:10.1016/j.compind.2007.12.001

Ojala, M., Vilpola, I., & Kouri, I. (2006). Risks in ERP project – Case study of IS/ICT management capability maturity level and risk assessment. In The *Proceedings of the Frontiers of eBusiness Research.*

Ottar, B., Anita, R., & Erlend, A. (2007). Holistic ERP selection methodology. In *Proceedings of the 14th International EurOMA Conference: Managing Operations in an Expanding Europe,* Ankara, Turkey.

Parker, D. (1992). Teaching the ethical use of information assets. *Information Security Journal: A Global Perspective, 1*(1), 13-16.

Peltier, T. (2005). Implementing an information security awareness program. *Information Security Journal: A Global Perspective, 14*(2), 37-49.

Peng, G., & Nunes, M. (2009). Identification and assessment of risks associated with ERP post-implementation in China. *Journal of Enterprise Information Management, 22*(5), 587–614. doi:10.1108/17410390910993554

Pollack, T. (2002). Educational opportunities in enterprise resource planning (ERP). In *Proceedings of the 2002 ASCUE Conference,* June 9 – 13, 2002, Myrtle Beach, South Carolina, (pp. 191-197).

Polyakov, A., & Medvedovskiy, I. (2010). ERP security. Myths, problems, solutions. Source Barcelona 2010. Retrieved October 1, 2011, from http://dsecrg.com/files/pub/pdf/ERP%20Security.%20Myths,%20Problems,%20Solutions.pdf

Ralevich, V., & Martinovic, D. (2010). Designing and implementing an undergraduate program in information systems security. *Education and Information Technologies, 15*(4). doi:10.1007/s10639-010-9123-y

Ravesteyn, P., & Köhler, A. (2009). Industry participation in educating ERP. *Communications of the IIMA, 9*(2), 45–56.

Rezgui, Y., & Marks, A. (2008). Information security awareness in higher education: An exploratory study. *Computers & Security, 27*(7-8), 241–253. doi:10.1016/j.cose.2008.07.008

Rienzo, T., & Han, B. (2011). Does ERP hands-on experience help students learning business process concepts? *Decision Sciences Journal of Innovative Education, 9*(2), 177–207. doi:10.1111/j.1540-4609.2011.00300.x

Russell, R. (2006). A framework for analyzing ERP security threats. *In Proceedings of the Euro-Atlantic Symposium on Critical Information Infrastructure Assurance*, March 23-34 2006, Switzerland

Shakleton, P., Ramp, A., & Hawking, P. (2001). IS '97 model curriculum: Where do enterprise resource planning systems fit. *Business Process Management Journal, 7*(3), 225–233. doi:10.1108/14637150110392700

Sharma, S., & Sefchek, J. (2007). Teaching information systems security courses: A hands-on approach. *Computers & Security, 26*(4), 290–299. doi:10.1016/j.cose.2006.11.005

Van Holsbeck, M., & Jeffrey, Z. (2004). *Security in an ERP world*. IT Toolbox Security. Retrieved December 12, 2004, from http://hosteddocs.it-toolbox.com/MH043004.pdf

Vance, A. (2008). ERP security tools: Data mining and analysis software can help auditors test access controls for key enterprise resource planning systems. *Internal Auditor, 65*(1), 25–27.

Vluggen, M., & Bollen, L. (2005). Teaching enterprise resource planning in a business curriculum. *International Journal of Information and Operations Management Education, 1*(1), 44–57. doi:10.1504/IJIOME.2005.007447

von Solms, H., & Hertenberger, M. (2004). A case for information ownership in ERP systems, security and protection. In *Proceedings of the Information Processing Systems, IFIP 18th World Computer Congress TC11 19th International Information Security Conference* 22–27 August 2004 Toulouse, France.

Walden, J. (2008). Integrating web application security into the IT curriculum. In the *Proceedings of the 9th ACM SIGITE conference on Information technology education (SIGITE '08)*. ACM.

Wu, J., & Wang, Y. (2006). Measuring ERP success: The ultimate users' view. *International Journal of Operations & Production Management, 26*(8), 882–903. doi:10.1108/01443570610678657

Yang, J., & Jiang, H. (2009). Research of ERP practice teaching system of the economics and management majors of independent institutes. In the *Proceedings of the Second International Conference on Education Technology and Training*, (pp. 56-59).

Young, M. (2007). Enterprise resource planning (ERP): A review of the literature. *International Journal Management and Enterprise Development, 4*(3), 235–264. doi:10.1504/IJMED.2007.012679

Chapter 14
University of Ottawa Department of Family Medicine Faculty Development Curriculum Framework

Colla J. MacDonald
University of Ottawa, Canada

Martha McKeen
University of Ottawa, Canada

Donna Leith-Gudbranson
University of Ottawa, Canada

Madeleine Montpetit
University of Ottawa, Canada

Douglas Archibald
University of Ottawa, Canada

Christine Rivet
University of Ottawa, Canada

Rebecca J. Hogue
University of Ottawa, Canada

Mike Hirsh
University of Ottawa, Canada

ABSTRACT

In response to the challenges faced by rapid expansion and curriculum reform, the Department of Family Medicine (DFM) at the University of Ottawa (U of O) developed a Faculty Development Conceptual Framework (FDCF) and companion plan as a first step toward meeting the challenges of providing quality opportunities for the continuing professional development of preceptors in Family Medicine. The FDCF outlines the processes, opportunities and support structures needed to improve preceptors' teaching skills and effectively deliver a newly revised "Triple C" competency-based curriculum. The FDCF acts as a quality standard to guide the design, delivery, and evaluation of a vibrant Faculty Development (FD) Program. It further provides a structure for implementing Enterprise Resource Planning (ERP) web applications to facilitate the flow of information between seven teaching sites, provide consistency among programs, and play a tactical role in the sharing of academic resources. This chapter introduces the DFM's FDCF so other medical departments may benefit from the authors' experiences and adapt or adopt the framework applications and methodologies to improve the effectiveness and efficiency of FD products and processes. Modifications to the framework are expected as this program continues to evolve.

DOI: 10.4018/978-1-4666-2193-0.ch014

INTRODUCTION

Effective faculty development (FD) within the context of a department of family medicine (DFM) should provide the support structures and opportunities to motivate preceptors (physicians who teach medical students and residents in clinical settings) to improve their teaching skills so they may effectively train postgraduate (PG) and undergraduate (UG) learners. Cultivating a skilled cadre of preceptors requires stable mechanisms of support, development of new and varied teaching and learning strategies, and preceptor recognition. To ensure the desired outcomes are achieved and that knowledge acquired by preceptors is transferred into the workplace, effective evaluation strategies must also be implemented.

The DFM at the U of O has developed a Faculty Development Curriculum Framework (FDCF) to serve as a roadmap for a comprehensive three-year companion FD plan. The FDCF acts as a quality standard to guide the design, delivery and evaluation of a vibrant FD program. The FDCF provides the support structures and opportunities preceptors need to improve their teaching skills and effectively deliver a quality newly revised 'Triple C' competency-based curriculum. 'Triple C' is a competency-based curriculum that is focused on the continuity of education and patient care, is centred in family medicine and, is comprehensive. The 'Triple C' Curriculum ensures that all Family Medicine (FM) learners are competent and prepared to provide comprehensive care in an evolving society (College of Family Physicians of Canada, 2011). The FDCF provides a structure for implementing Enterprise Resource Planning (ERP) web applications to facilitate the flow of information between the seven teaching sites, provide consistency among programs, and play a tactical role in the sharing of academic resources.

The objective of this chapter is to share our FDCF so that other medical departments may benefit from our experiences and adapt or adopt the framework applications and methodologies to improve the effectiveness and efficiency of FD Programs.

BACKGROUND

The DFM at the U of O includes approximately 30 geographic full-time faculty members (GFTs) and over 260 voluntary part-time preceptors (VPTs). The VPTs include physicians from both urban and rural settings, with a wide range of experience and teaching skills. The DFM learners range from first to fourth year medical students to first and second year FM residents comprising Canadian trained as well as International Medical Graduates. Faculty members and learners are supported by allied health professionals and specialists in areas such as behavioural medicine, palliative care, obstetrics and pharmacology.

In the past five years, the DFM has grown at both the postgraduate and undergraduate levels, necessitating an increase in recruitment of preceptors. During this time, the DFM did not have a fully developed FD program to offer the newly recruited preceptors. The rapid expansion and popularity of family medicine as a discipline has dictated a growing need for an effective FD program to assist preceptors as they develop their teaching skills (Frisch & Talbot, 1984).

There has been a worldwide shift in the delivery of medical education programs, from a focus on clinical rotations to a competency-based curriculum (American Institute of Medicine, 2001; College of Family Physicians of Canada, 1989; Frank, et al., 2005; General Medical Council, 2001; Tannenbaum et al., 2009; 2011). Transitioning to a competency-based curriculum is a massive conceptual, cultural and logistical shift for residency programs and involves the creation of an integrated curriculum that places emphasis on experiential learning versus learning that takes place after a designated amount of time (typically four weeks) in a rotation. Thus, future FM residents will need to repeatedly demonstrate competency in all areas of their learning before they graduate at the end of their two-year program. A complete change in the structure and operation of residency programs is required to provide learners an opportunity to demonstrate these competencies. Furthermore, FD is required to support preceptors with implementing the new curriculum.

In response to the challenges faced by rapid expansion and curriculum reform, the DFM has invested considerable resources and energy into its FD program by recruiting a Director of Faculty Development. The Director is supported by a Physician Lead and an advisory group of physicians representing both the PG and UG programs. The development of a FDCF with a supporting FD plan was seen as a necessary prerequisite to provide direction to meet the challenges the DFM faces in providing quality opportunities for the continuing professional development of its teachers.

In order to foster the continued development of experienced preceptors, the DFM at the U of O has focused on developing a robust and stable FD Program. The College of Family Physicians of Canada (CFPC) stipulates that each family physician is to acquire 250 credits every five years to maintain their professional practice license. The DFM FD plan offers continuing medical education credits for proposed FD activities to support preceptors in meeting this requirement.

THE FACULTY DEVELOPMENT CURRICULUM FRAMEWORK

The FDCF (Figure 1) provides a visual representation of the supports and resources necessary to sustain a robust FD program. Embedded in the conceptual framework is a wide array of teaching and learning opportunities for preceptors to nurture medical education excellence and scholarly pursuits regardless of their teaching experience or

the training level of their learners (first year medical student to second year resident). The FDCF incorporates strategies to recognize preceptors for their involvement and time in FD activities and provides necessary support structures in order to assist them in their efforts to become effective preceptors, nurture and maintain effective relationships with learners, and promote interest and participation in scholarly activities. Through the process of participating in the teaching and learning opportunities provided by the FD program, and in particular through formal support and recognition from the DFM, a thriving learning community will emerge that upholds the ideals of lifelong learning. The FDCF based ERP applications will facilitate the flow of information between the seven teaching sites and increase consistency in the teaching strategies and content as well as increase access to teaching resources.

Furthermore, through involvement in and support from the FD program, preceptors remain grounded in the attitudes and behaviours consistent with the values and principles outlined in the 'Triple C' competency-based curriculum. An understanding of all the elements of the framework is achieved through a comprehensive orientation, as well as structured self-reflection activities, and ongoing assessment and evaluation. Through effective FD, the skills acquired are translated to the workplace in a meaningful way, benefiting all stakeholders including learners, patients and their families.

Support

The DFM FD program is grounded in several support structures:

• **Director of Faculty Development:** The Director of FD is an educator with specialized experience in the area of curriculum design and program evaluation. With the support of a Physician Lead, an advisory

Figure 1. The faculty development conceptual framework

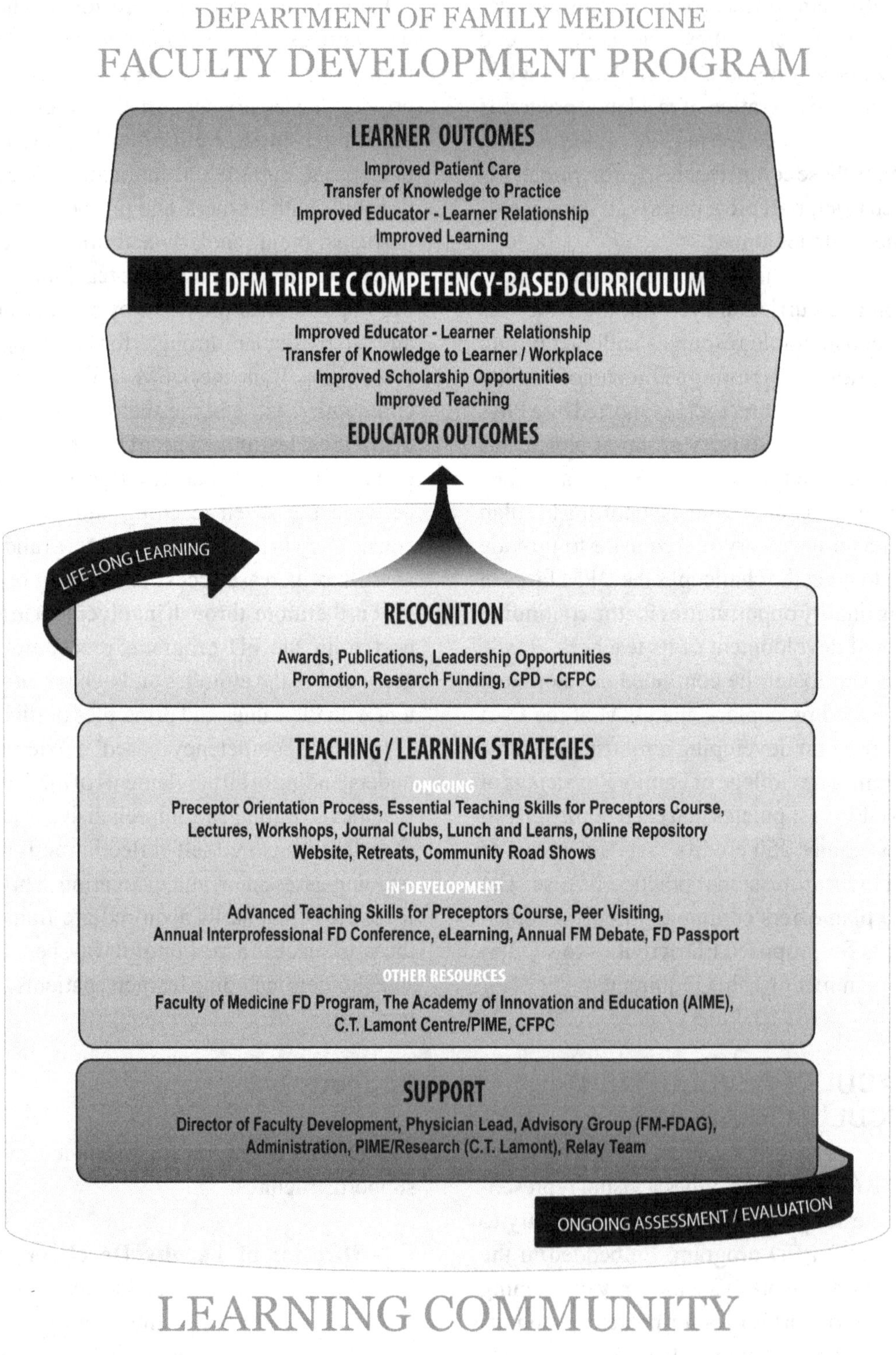

DEPARTMENT OF FAMILY MEDICINE
FACULTY DEVELOPMENT PROGRAM

LEARNER OUTCOMES

Improved Patient Care
Transfer of Knowledge to Practice
Improved Educator - Learner Relationship
Improved Learning

THE DFM TRIPLE C COMPETENCY-BASED CURRICULUM

Improved Educator - Learner Relationship
Transfer of Knowledge to Learner / Workplace
Improved Scholarship Opportunities
Improved Teaching

EDUCATOR OUTCOMES

LIFE-LONG LEARNING

RECOGNITION

Awards, Publications, Leadership Opportunities
Promotion, Research Funding, CPD – CFPC

TEACHING / LEARNING STRATEGIES

ONGOING
Preceptor Orientation Process, Essential Teaching Skills for Preceptors Course,
Lectures, Workshops, Journal Clubs, Lunch and Learns, Online Repository
Website, Retreats, Community Road Shows

IN-DEVELOPMENT
Advanced Teaching Skills for Preceptors Course, Peer Visiting,
Annual Interprofessional FD Conference, eLearning, Annual FM Debate, FD Passport

OTHER RESOURCES
Faculty of Medicine FD Program, The Academy of Innovation and Education (AIME),
C.T. Lamont Centre/PIME, CFPC

SUPPORT

Director of Faculty Development, Physician Lead, Advisory Group (FM-FDAG),
Administration, PIME/Research (C.T. Lamont), Relay Team

ONGOING ASSESSMENT / EVALUATION

LEARNING COMMUNITY

group and administration, the Director supports family medicine educators by

- ◦ Organizing FD sessions and events
- ◦ Developing and delivering relevant curriculum resources
- ◦ Supporting teaching practices through FD sessions and workshops on Essential Teaching Skills for Preceptors
- ◦ Evaluating all FD sessions so that continued improvement can take place
- **Physician Lead:** The Physician Lead collaborates closely with the Director of FD to ensure that the FD program is relevant and responsive to family medicine preceptors' needs. The Physician Lead is also available to provide support to the FM educators as needed. Finally, the Physician Lead serves as a liaison between the DFM and the preceptors in the teaching environments.
- **Advisory Group (FM-FDAG):** The Family Medicine FD Advisory group is made up of family physicians, some of whom have academic administrative responsibilities for teaching (i.e. Unit Program Directors, Academic Day Coordinator, Community Practice Directors, UG Director, etc.). Their role is to work with the Director and Physician Lead to ensure that the FD Program provides educators with practical and innovative opportunities for professional development. (PD)
- **Administration:** Family medicine preceptors are supported by the DFM administration. In particular, the Manager and the Coordinator of Special Projects and Faculty Support serve as points of contact for any teacher looking to engage in PD.
- **PIME/Research (C.T. Lamont Centre for Research in Primary Care):** The

C.T. Lamont Centre is the research arm of the DFM. The Program for Innovation in Medical Education (PIME) is a DFM research venture headed by a PhD educational researcher who advises, supports and funds members of the DFM faculty who are interested in pursuing scholarly activities in medical education.

- **Relay Team:** The DFM created and sustains the "Relay Team" - a devoted group of DFM preceptors trained to teach learners in difficulty and assist fellow preceptors in challenging learning situations. The role of relay team members is to provide skilled support:
  - ◦ In the areas of direct observation and evaluation of residents who require additional academic support. Relay team members provide one-on-one supervision of learners in difficulty.
  - ◦ To assist fellow preceptors with creating and implementing a learning plan with appropriate objectives, learning strategies and resources to address the needs of residents under their tutelage struggling to meet the requirements of the residency program.

TEACHING AND LEARNING STRATEGIES

The FD program offers a wide variety of teaching and learning strategies to support continued PD of family medicine preceptors throughout their teaching careers. These strategies will be rolled out in a multi-tiered approach allowing preceptors teaching all academic levels (first year medical student to second year resident) and with varying skill levels or teaching experience to take part in programs that match their needs. The FD program focuses specifically on strategies to make preceptors better teachers. Clinical skills are addressed in continuing medical education (CME). The DFM FD program builds on the current teaching and learning delivery mechanisms, creates innovative solutions to medical education problems, and introduces leading-edge teaching strategies.

'Ongoing' FD Activities and Resources

Essential Teaching Skills for Preceptors Course

An Essential Teaching Skills for Preceptors course has been developed taking advantage of content already in existence at the DFM, the U of O Faculty of Medicine, and at other universities. Essential Teaching Skills for Preceptors consists of a four-hour workshop followed by four 30-minute online sessions that cover relevant, authentic and convenient "just for you" teaching of medical education theory and skills (See Appendix A for an agenda of the workshop). Preceptors receive four Mainpro-C and four Mainpro-M1 credits for completing this course. Mainpro credits are granted by the CFCP upon meeting certain requirements. The learning outcomes of the Essential Teaching Skills for Preceptors course are:

- Describe the revised DFM 'Triple C' competency-based curriculum;
- Perform direct observation of a resident;
- Provide constructive feedback to a resident;
- Use a variety of assessment tools to evaluate a resident.

Upon completion of the workshop, preceptors are expected to complete four 30-minute independent study online modules. Preceptors are given 30 days from the workshop to complete three of the online modules (Being an Effective Preceptor, Learning Plans, and Learners in Difficulty). Three months after the completion of the third module, participants complete the fourth module: a reflection on practice.

Preceptor Orientation Process

The DFM offers a comprehensive orientation process for new preceptors to ensure a smooth transition from clinician to preceptor. A preceptor orientation manual (available online and in hardcopy) provides information on DFM administration policies and procedures, the faculty career matrix, the essentials of PG education (including the goals, learning objectives, teaching strategies) and the roles and responsibilities of faculty members. An interactive orientation workshop to support the orientation process is offered prior to each new academic year. A similar Clerkship Preceptor handbook exists for the UG preceptors. An orientation for new physicians teaching first year medical students is offered in conjunction with the Faculty of Medicine.

Initial Essential Teaching Skills 'Train-the-Trainer' Session

This was offered to a small group of preceptors from each of the seven DFM clinical teaching units and from the community teaching practices to support preceptors interested in facilitating future sessions of Essential Teaching Skills for Preceptors. The Train-the-Trainer session provided an opportunity to reflect upon learners' experiences during the initial course offering. In an informal FD needs analysis conducted in the summer of 2011, preceptors also reported they wanted more in-house faculty development. By training an instructor from all sites, we were able to increase consistency in teaching content and strategies across sites and conveniently offer the essential teaching skills course in-house at each teaching site. Minor modifications and improvements were made to the original course based upon the information gathered from the train-the-trainer session along with the course evaluations. The course was then translated into French to accommodate the U of O francophone preceptors and residents.

Lectures

Lecture sessions focus on providing educators with the quintessential knowledge and skills necessary to teach learners. Topics are varied and introduce innovations in medical education and direction on how to share this new information with learners. These Mainpro accredited lectures are webcast live and archived on the DFM's website for future referral by our preceptors.

Workshops

Workshops are small group, interactive, Mainpro-C accredited programs and focus on hands-on teaching skills. They may be repeated several times over a three-year period and are customized to meet the needs of participants.

Journal Clubs

In each of the DFM's teaching sites, the Community physicians and residents organize their own Journal Clubs. Support from administration is available, as needed, to coordinate journal club scheduling, house a library of relevant articles and facilitate the acquisition and distribution of relevant materials. Support from the University's library services is also available to help identify and retrieve relevant articles.

Lunch and Learns

These sessions are held on a regular basis at each of the DFM teaching units where faculty review and discuss teaching issues over lunch. The Manager and Coordinator of Special Projects and Faculty Support work closely with the Unit coordinators to provide support where needed, in particular in the promotion and documentation of Lunch and Learn sessions. Unit Lunch and Learns are made accessible to affiliated community and rural preceptors either live or via webcast or videoconferencing.

Online Repository

'Faculty Favourites' is an online repository that offers FM preceptors a convenient, up-to-date, relevant and accessible list of resources to enhance their teaching skills. Faculty members are encouraged to share links to websites or resources that they find useful, allowing Faculty Favourites to continually develop and grow over time. Eligible resources must be related to improving clinical teaching. To maintain quality of Faculty Favourites, users are asked to anonymously rate the resources. Faculty Favourites will be continually updated in response to suggested websites and resources and raters' feedback. The online repository is one of the FDCF based ERP applications that facilitates the sharing of academic resources between and among teaching sites.

Website

The DFM maintains a recently redesigned website. The new Faculty Development page (http://www.familymedicine.uottawa.ca/eng/index.html) is richly populated with relevant content. Conferences, important dates, sessions and meetings are accurately logged and kept up-to-date to ensure reliability and timeliness. Archived webcasts, slides from FD presentations, and other interactive eLearning materials are also housed on the FD page. The website is a key component of the ERP, which makes information readily available to all preceptors associated with the DFM regardless of their location.

Retreats

A number of retreats each year provide faculty the opportunity to develop their teaching skills in a collegial milieu. The DFM Annual Faculty Retreat focuses on a variety of educational opportunities, including continuing medical education as well as Mainpro accredited FD. These sessions range from interactive lectures to hands on experiential workshops and may involve in-house experts as well as invited guest speakers. The annual faculty retreat also provides faculty with opportunities to network with their colleagues and allows for significant time to share, problem solve and collaborate. The DFM undergraduate program holds two retreats each year catering to the needs of clerkship; one on examination question writing, the other on clerkship specific teaching issues. In addition to the annual retreat for all preceptors, the DFM also organizes retreats and meetings throughout the year to specifically accommodate and address the individual cultural, language and availability needs of community preceptors and its francophone unit (Montfort).

Community Road Shows

The DFM collaborates with the U of O's Distributed Medical Education program and DFM's FD program to organize quarterly events that bring FD opportunities to the DFM's rural educators. These Mainpro accredited sessions are open to FM physicians willing to teach both PG and UG learners.

In-Development Faculty Development Activities and Resources

Advanced Teaching Skills for Preceptors Course

The Advanced Teaching Skills for Preceptors Course will be offered to preceptors who have completed the Essential Teaching Skills for Preceptors course and would like to continue to improve their knowledge and skills with regard to teaching. The course will be a convenient package of more advanced skills deemed necessary to be an effective teacher. With a similar format to the Essential Teaching Skills for Preceptors course, the Advanced Teaching Skills course will

consist of a four-hour workshop followed by four 30-minute online sessions that will cover relevant, authentic and convenient "just for you" teaching of medical education theory and skills specifically for preceptors of FM residents. Preceptors receive four Mainpro-C credits and four Mainpro 1 for completing this course.

Peer Visiting

A renewed activity within the DFM, peer visiting is a strategy to facilitate learning and educator-learner relationships. Peer visiting is a process wherein preceptors and their residents consult with their peers about problems and challenges related to teaching and learning. The peer visit is an informal, self-initiated, needs-based visit by one preceptor-resident dyad visiting another preceptor-resident dyad at their place of work for the purpose of exploring areas such as interpersonal relationships, communication, teaching and learning styles and feedback. The visit is an educational exercise, a formative assessment of learning and teaching focussing on the relationship between teacher and learner. Peer visiting is voluntary and focuses on joint problem solving rather than evaluation. Peer visiting provides a unique opportunity to visit another practice and discuss problems that confront all family medicine physicians.

Annual Interprofessional FD Conference (Coming in 2013)

An event geared toward all family medicine educators (physicians, residents, medical students, allied health professionals, etc.) the Annual Interprofessional FD Conference promotes interprofessional education and development. The Faculty Development Conference will be a one-day event held on the same day each year (e.g. first Friday in February). The purpose of the conference will be to provide a forum where:

- Preceptors, non-preceptor faculty physicians, non-physician educators, residents, medical students, and allied health professionals participate in lectures/workshops, network, collaborate and socialize;
- The most relevant topics of importance to the primary care team, both physicians and allied healthcare professionals are addressed in a collaborative manner;
- An interdisciplinary audience and approach to faculty development is focused upon;
- Keynote speakers stimulate and motivate innovation, scholarship and professionalism;
- Hands-on workshops provide opportunities to learn new concepts, skills and practices that can be transferred to practice;
- Residents-preceptors communicate and enhance working relationships.

eLearning Link on FD Webpage

New modules, applications, and programs will continually be developed and added to the website to allow easy access to interactive learning materials that promote professional development. Resources have been set aside in 2012 to develop:

- A library of Ethics scenarios
- A bank of videos of clinical assessments to hone feedback, direct observation and SOO examination skills

Annual FM Debate

The FM-FD team will host an Annual FM Debate to feature in house experts and invited guests deliberating over relevant issues. This event will be followed by an informal reception to allow further discussion, networking and nurturing of the medical education community. Topics will be chosen with the hope of attracting family physicians as

well as other specialty colleagues and allied health educators. This will serve as the closing event for the Annual Interprofessional FM Conference.

FD Passport

As involvement in faculty development is a clear expectation for all active faculty members, the DFM hopes to encourage sustained participation with the implementation of a five-year FD passport system. Each FD event within the DFM and Faculty of Medicine for the U of O will be awarded with a point value similar to the CFPC Mainpro system. Faculty members will be encouraged to obtain a set number of points of medical education professional development based on their level of teaching involvement within the DFM. Some offerings will be mandatory for certain teaching roles to facilitate teaching skills and consistency among programs. Other sessions will be optional based on needs and interests. In recognition of participation, whether as a participant or facilitator, the DFM will help facilitate documentation to help determine candidates for the Faculty of Medicine Teaching Skills Attainment Award. Membership in the program will be recognized at the Annual DFM Faculty Retreat.

Other Resources

The DFM encourages its preceptors to seek out other FD opportunities outside of the Department. When developing its annual FD program and schedule, the FD Advisory Group endeavoured to ensure the DFM FD program offerings are specific to FM and do not duplicate options offered elsewhere. While the list below is far from being exhaustive, it provides a snapshot of the resources available locally to preceptors:

- **Faculty of Medicine FD Program:** The Faculty of Medicine offers its own program for PD to all of its clinical departments. The DFM FD program strives to complement this program by offering topics that focus on family medicine.

- **The Academy of Innovation and Education (AIME):** AIME is an organization associated with the U of O that supports innovation, research and education as well as FD. The DFM encourages preceptors to participate in relevant AIME workshops and their annual conference.
- **Program for Innovation in Medical Education/PIME:** PIME supports the DFM clinical teachers who wish to pursue scholarly activities through funding and allocation of research resources (see previous Support section for more detail).
- **CFPC:** The College of Family Physicians of Canada is a national organization that houses its own resources for Continuing Professional Development of Family Physicians.
- **Academic Support Process (ASP):** In response to a needs assessment conducted by the DFM, three physicians, with the support of an eLearning consultant, developed "The Academic Support Process (ASP)" website. The ASP website provides online resources, including an interactive web-based tool that supports preceptors in developing learning plans for their residents. A number of workshops with the DFM's preceptors have been conducted to introduce preceptors to the use of the ASP tool and how it can help them improve their teaching skills when working with residents https://uottawa.academicsupportplan.com/
- **ACES:** A number of the DFM's physicians have been trained in teaching the ACES (Acute Critical Events Simulation) course. ACES is an acclaimed, intensive two-day program focusing on the basics of resuscitation of the critically ill pre-arrest patient. Modules on stabilization of the airway,

breathing and circulation are included, and learning methods include hands-on task training and high-fidelity simulation.

- **RaTS:** The Residents as Teachers (RaTS) program is now compulsory for all residents. This course offers residents education on how to be effective teachers and also how to provide useful feedback.

EVALUATIONS

Session Evaluations

All FD sessions are evaluated immediately following the event. A summary of the feedback is provided to the presenters within 10 business days of the session. These summaries are provided to the FM-FDAG to review in order to validate effectiveness of these sessions. This will allow us to continually improve our programs every year based on participants' feedback and suggestions. The evaluation forms are common for all formal teaching sessions in the DFM. The forms ensure that faculty development sessions incorporate the CanMEDS-FM competencies where applicable. Furthermore, these forms provide opportunity for participants to comment on all aspects of a presentation including content, structure, and learning outcomes. See Appendix B.

Recognition

Educators are recognized and rewarded for their involvement in PD through a variety of mechanisms including the dissemination of FD Awards, recognition (verbal and through publications) of excellent participation in FD events, and promotions. For example, The Teaching Skills Attainment Award at the Faculty of Medicine acknowledges faculty members' commitment to professional development in medical education by rewarding participation in programs designed to enhance teaching skills. All preceptors in the

DFM are eligible to apply for the Teaching Skills Attainment Award. See Teaching Skills Attainment Award link:

http://www.medicine.uottawa.ca/facdev/eng/teaching_skills_attainment_award.html

The goal is to foster self-motivation among educators to improve their teaching and learning skills. Educator development will also be subject to self-assessment, assessment by their learners, and assessment by the Department, which will foster continual feedback and improvement.

Effective Dissemination Strategies: An Exercise in Culture Change

An effective Faculty Development Plan requires deliberate dissemination strategies to promote awareness of and participation in the continuous medical education opportunities available in the DFM. Various tactics have been implemented to advertise and support FD opportunities at both undergraduate and graduate levels, for various clinical teaching environments (GFT, Rural, and Community) and for both Anglophone and Francophone faculty members.

Using the FDCF as a guide, FD offerings are communicated through the FD administrative team directly to all DFM faculty using an updated database of teaching Faculty members (lecturers, assistant, associate, and full professors as well as allied health care teachers). Faculty members are affiliated with either a Teaching Unit or the Director of Community Practice and Rural Practice. Unit Program Directors and Postgraduate Coordinators at each of the DFM's seven teaching units and the Community Co-Directors are the point of contact for communication and promotion of events both locally (in the unit or community) and centrally at the DFM. To facilitate and support a learning community and active engagement in FD events, the Coordinators and Unit Program Directors also actively promote the scheduling and dissemination of in-house events via teleconferencing, webcasting and archiving of local FD offerings. To facili-

tate department wide participation, registration to central and off site events (e.g. lunch and learns) is the responsibility of the FD Administration staff.

The DFM central FD administrative staff, with the help of the Unit Postgraduate Coordinators, continually updates the FD calendar and brochure, organize webcasts, create the newsletter, and maintain the FD website. Evaluations for both local and central events are distributed and collated by the FD administration team through the Postgrad Coordinators and are then shared with the FM-FDAG.

The FDCF based ERP applications will facilitate the flow of information between all seven teaching sites and increase consistency in the teaching strategies and content as well as increase access to teaching resources. Outreach Communication strategies include the following:

- University of Ottawa: DFM-Faculty Development webpage
- Pulse: E-Letter distributed every two weeks to communicate information on upcoming FD
- DFM Newsletter: Communicates information about FD events over the coming year.
- Faculty Development Calendar: Promotes events on the DFM website and is updated weekly
- Faculty Development Rural Road Shows
- Annual FD Site Visits
- Annual Faculty Development Brochure with Calendar available at all FD events and on the website, also distributed to Preceptors on Site Visits.
- Annual Retreats: FD booths at the DFM Community Retreat, Montfort Retreat/FD Day, Rio Day
- Community Physician Dinners: Community Co-Directors highlight upcoming FD offerings and include these in the minutes of the dinner
- GFT Monthly Meetings
- Unit Postgraduate meetings

- Orientation: Annual event
- Monthly Postgraduate Program Committee meeting: Time devoted to FD to communicate upcoming offerings.

It is the expectation of the FD team that, through proactive and sustained communication with the DFM faculty membership via multiple champions from all levels and domains within the department, our timely and relevant Faculty Development program will support a learning community of effective medical educators (Figure 2).

FUTURE RESEARCH DIRECTIONS

The implementation of the FDCF will take place over the next three years in the DFM. Each activity

Figure 2. Dissemination chart for faculty development - an exercise in culture change

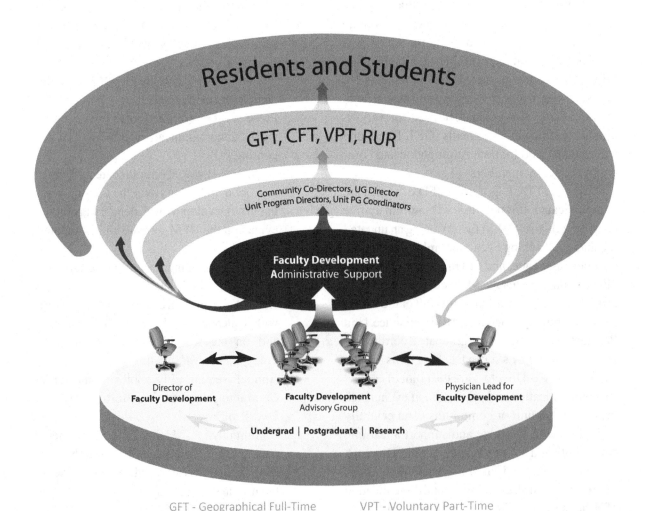

Dissemination Chart for Faculty Development:
an exercise in culture change

will be evaluated in order to continually improve the program. Modifications to the framework are expected as the framework continues to evolve based on research findings.

CONCLUSION

The FDCF and companion program plan serve as a dynamic roadmap for FD at the DFM. The Development of a robust FD Program will further the strategic priorities of the DFM and facilitate leadership in the area of FD education. Most importantly, the DFM's guiding principle of making FD meaningful, relevant and accessible to all faculty promotes a culture of equality. If all the DFM's diverse educators feel their voices are being heard and their FD needs satisfied, a learning community is expected to result with faculty working toward common goals. This learning community will undoubtedly raise the profile of the DFM at the U of O and in Canada. The success of the FD program will rely on the continued support of the DFM's administration and the engagement of its preceptors who, as adult learners, will help shape and guide the direction of the FD program in the future.

ACKNOWLEDGMENT

The authors would like to acknowledge Nicholas Papiccio who programmed the conceptual framework and dissemination diagram.

REFERENCES

American Institute of Medicine. (2001). *Crossing the quality chasm: A new health system for the 21st century. Washington, DC: National Academy Press College of Family Physicians of Canada, Section of Teacher's of Family Medicine. (1989). Report of the task force on curriculum.* Willowdale, ON: Author.

College of Family Physicians of Canada. Section of Teachers of Family Medicine. (2011). *'Triple C'+ CanMeds-FM.* Retrieved from http://www.cfpc.ca/triple_C/

Frank, J. R. (Ed.). (2005). *The CanMEDS physician competency framework. Better standards. Better physicians. Better care.* Ottawa, Canada: The Royal College of Physicians and Surgeons of Canada. Retrieved from http://rcpsc.medical.org/canmeds/index.php

Frisch, S. R., & Talbot, Y. (1984). Faculty development in family medicine: A survey of needs and resources. *Journal of Medical Education, 59*(10), 831–833.

General Medical Council. (2001). *Good medical practice.* London, UK: General Medical council.

Tannenbaum, D., et al. (2009). *CanMEDS-FM.* Working Group on Curriculum Review. Retrieved from http://www.cfpc.ca/uploadedFiles/Education/CanMeds%20FM%20Eng.pdf

Tannenbaum, D., Konkin, J., Parsons, E., Saucier, D., Shaw, L., & Walsh, A. (2011). *Triple C competency-based curriculum: Report of the working group on postgraduate curriculum review – Part 1*. Mississauga, Canada: College of Family Physicians of Canada.

ADDITIONAL READING

Casimiro, L., & MacDonald, C. J., L., Thompson, T-L, & Stodel, E. J. (2009). Grounding theories of W(e)Learn: A framework for online interprofessional education. *Journal of Interprofessional Care, 23*(3), 1–11.

Chambers, L. W., Conklin, J., Dalziel, W. B., MacDonald, C. J., & Stodel, E. J. (2008). ELearning education to promote interprofessional education with physicians, pharmacists, nurses, and nurse practitioners in long-term care facilities: Promising potential solutions. *International Journal of Biomedical Engineering and Technology, 1*(3), 233–249. doi:10.1504/IJBET.2008.016958

Halabisky, B. L., Humbert, J., Stodel, E. J., MacDonald, C. J., Chambers, L. W., & Doucette, S. (2010). E-learning, knowledge brokering, and nursing: Strengthening collaborative practice in long-term care. *Computers, Informatics, Nursing, 28*(5), 264–273. doi:10.1097/NCN.0b013e3181ec28b9

MacDonald, C. J., Archibald, D., Kellam, H., Sun, R., Stodel, E. J., & Puddester, D. (2011). Evaluation of online health and wellness resources for healthcare professionals. *International Journal of Advanced Corporate Learning, 2*(4), 18–23.

MacDonald, C. J., Archibald, D., Puddester, D., & Bajnok, I. (2011). Renewal through team development: Experiencing an emerging program design in interprofessional education for healthcare practitioners. *Evaluation and Program Planning Journal,* Spring, 1-18.

MacDonald, C. J., Archibald, D., Puddester, D., & Whiting, S. (2011). Managing disruptive physician behaviour: First steps for designing an effective online resource. *Knowledge Management & E-Learning: An International Journal, 3*(1), 98–115.

MacDonald, C. J., Archibald, D., Trumpower, D., Casimiro, L., Cragg, B., & Jelley, W. (2010). Quality standards for interprofessional healthcare education: Designing a toolkit of bilingual assessment instruments. *The Journal of Research in Interprofessional Practice and Education, 1*(3), 1–13.

MacDonald, C. J., Archibald, D. B., Stodel, E. J., Chambers, L. W., & Hall, P. (2008). Knowledge translation of interprofessional collaborative patient-centred practice. *McGill Journal of Education, 43*(3), 283–308. doi:10.7202/029700ar

MacDonald, C. J., Breithaupt, K., Stodel, E. J., Farres, L. G., & Gabriel, M. A. (2002). Evaluation of web-based educational programs via the demand-driven learning model: A measure of web-based learning. *International Journal of Testing, 2*(1), 35–61. doi:10.1207/S15327574IJT0201_3

MacDonald, C. J., Stodel, E. J., & Casimiro, L. (2005, September). Online training for healthcare workers. *eLearn Magazine*. Retrieved from http://elearnmag.org/subpage.cfm?section=case_studies&article=33-1

MacDonald, C. J., Stodel, E. J., & Casimiro, L. (2006). Online dementia care training for healthcare teams in continuing and long-term care homes: A viable solution for improving quality of care and quality of life for residents. *International Journal on E-Learning, 5*(3), 373–399. Retrieved from http://www.irrodl.org/index.php/irrodl/article/view/325/744

MacDonald, C. J., Stodel, E. J., Casimiro, L., & Weaver, L. (2006). Using community-based participatory research for an online dementia care program. *The Canadian Journal of Program Evaluation, 21*(2), 81–104.

MacDonald, C. J., Stodel, E. J., & Chambers, L. W. (2008). An online interprofessional learning resource for physicians, pharmacists, nurse practitioners, and nurses in long-term care: Benefits, barriers, and lessons learned. *Informatics for Health & Social Care, 33*(1), 21–38. doi:10.1080/14639230801886824

MacDonald, C. J., Stodel, E. J., & Coulson, I. (2004). Planning an eLearning dementia care program for healthcare teams in long-term care facilities: The learners' perspectives. *Educational Gerontology: An International Journal, 30*(10), 1–20.

MacDonald, C. J., Stodel, E. J., Farres, L. G., Breithaupt, K., & Gabriel, M. A. (2001). The demand-driven learning model: A framework for web-based learning. *The Internet and Higher Education, 4*(1), 9–30. doi:10.1016/S1096-7516(01)00045-8

MacDonald, C. J., Stodel, E. J., Hall, P., & Weaver, L. (2009). The impact of an online learning resource designed to enhance interprofessional collaborative practice in palliative care: Findings from the caring together pilot project. *Journal of Research in Interprofessional Practice and Education, 1*(1), 42–66.

MacDonald, C. J., Stodel, E. J., Thompson, T.-L., & Casimiro, L. (2009). W(e)Learn: A framework for interprofessional education. *International Journal of Electronic Healthcare, 5*(1), 33–47. doi:10.1504/IJEH.2009.026271

MacDonald, C. J., & Walton, R. (2007). E-learning education solutions for caregivers in long-term care (LTC) facilities: New possibilities. *Education for Health, 20*(3), 1–9. Retrieved from http://www.educationforhealth.net/articles/showarticlenew.asp?ArticleID=85

Puddester, D., MacDonald, C. J., Archibald, D., Sun, R., & Stodel, E. J. (2010). Caring for physicians and other healthcare professionals: Needs assessments for eCurricula on physician and workplace health. *International Journal on Advances in Life Sciences, 2*(1&2), 63–72.

Redwood-Campbell, L., Pakes, B., Rouleau, K., MacDonald, C., Abdullahel, H., & Pottie, K. (2011). Developing a curriculum framework for global health in family medicine: Emerging principles, competencies, and educational approaches. *BMC Medical Education, 11*(46). Retrieved from http://www.biomedcentral.com/1472-6920/11/46

Steinert, Y., Mann, K., Centeno, A., Dolmans, D., Spencer, J., Gelula, M., & Prideaux, D. (2006). A systematic review of faculty development initiatives designed to improve teaching effectiveness in medical education. *Medical Teacher, 28*(6), 497–526. doi:10.1080/01421590600902976

KEY TERMS AND DEFINITIONS

'Triple C' Curriculum: Is comprehensive, focused on continuity, and centred in family medicine. The College of Family Physicians of Canada (CFPC) recommends that all family medicine postgraduate training program in Canada adopt this competency-based curriculum (http://www.cfpc.ca/triple_C/).

CanMEDS-FM Roles: Family Medicine Expert, Communicator, Collaborator, Manager, Health Advocate, Scholar and Professional which identify the knowledge, skills and attitudes necessary to become a well-rounded, competent family physicians who can provide effective primary healthcare to patients (http://www.cfpc.ca/uploadedFiles/Education/CanMeds%20FM%20Eng.pdf).

Curriculum Domains: The University of Ottawa FM program content is organized around four human life cycle topics (Maternity/Newborn Care; Care of Children/Adolescents; Care of Adults and Care of the Elderly) and an additional four healthcare related topics (Procedural Skills; Behavioural Medicine and Mental Health; End-of-Life Care and Care of Special Populations).

Curriculum Framework: An organized plan or roadmap that identifies processes, content, supports and expected outcomes in a curriculum.

Faculty Development: Faculty Development is a process within a department that provides opportunities to individual faculty members for growth as a teacher, as a scholar and professional and as a person (http://www.podnetwork.org/faculty_development/definitions.htm).

Family Medicine Competency-Based Curriculum: A curriculum designed to emphasize the development of competencies in the four principles of family medicine and the CanMEDS-FM Roles as defined by the College of Family Physicians of Canada.

MAINPRO® (Maintenance of Proficiency): Is the College of Family Physicians of Canada (CFPC) program designed to support and promote the continuous professional development for family physicians (http://www.cfpc.ca/MAINPRO/).

Preceptor: A clinician teacher who has a faculty appointment in the DFM and who is responsible for supervising the learning of one or more assigned postgraduate learners for the duration of their training.

Principles of Family Medicine: The Family Physician is (1) a skilled clinician and (2) a resource to a defined practice population; (3) FM is a community-based discipline and (4) the patient/physician relationship is central to the role of the Family Physician (http://www.cfpc.ca/Principles/).

Resident: An individual who has received a medical degree and is registered in a recognized postgraduate training program. In family medicine, this training program is usually two years in length.

APPENDIX A: AGENDA FOR ESSENTIAL TEACHING SKILLS FOR PRECEPTORS IN FAMILY MEDICINE

Session	Structure	Learning Objectives
Developing Essential Preceptor Skills	Face-to-Face Half-Day Workshop 8:30-12:30 (Coffee and muffins; and light lunch provided)	After completing this workshop, learners will be able to: • Describe the revised DFM Triple C Competency Based Curriculum • Conduct an effective direct observation of a resident • Provide constructive feedback to a resident • Use a variety of assessment tools to evaluate a resident
Tips and Tricks for Being a Good Preceptor	Online Module 1 Anytime and place you have Internet access To be completed within 10-days of the workshop	After completing this module, learners will be able to: • Prepare for the resident • Describe adult learning principles • Ask effective questions
Learning Plans	Online Module 2 Anytime and place you have Internet access To be completed within 20-days of the workshop	After completing this module, learners will be able to: • Describe what a learning plan is and its benefits • List the components of a learning plan • Create a learning plan • Use a resident's learning plan as a tracking and assessment tool
Learners in Difficulty	Online Module 3 Anytime and place you have Internet access To be completed within 30-days of the workshop	After completing this module, learners will be able to: • Recognize the signs of a resident in difficulty • Describe the necessary steps to take when a resident is in difficulty • Describe the resources available to access when a resident is in difficulty
Reflection on Practice	Online Module 4 Anytime and place you have Internet access Beginning three months after the completion of module 3, to be completed within 10-days	After completing this module, learners will have reflected upon: • What they personally learned in the course • How the course affected their clinical teaching • How the course changed their clinical practice

APPENDIX B: TEACHING SESSION EVALUATION FORM

All responses will be pooled and will remain anonymous

This section is completed by the administrator
Name of session: _____ **Presenter:** _____ **Date:** _____ **Curriculum Domains:** __Behavioural Medicine __Adults __Children/ Adolescents __End-of-Life Care __Elderly __Maternity/ Newborn __Procedural Skills __Special Population __Other **Session Objectives:** __Behavioural Medicine __Adults __Children/ Adolescents __End-of-Life Care __Elderly __Maternity/ Newborn __Procedural Skills __Special Population __Other **Teaching Format:** __Seminar/ Workshop __Problem/ Case Based Learning __Team Based Learning __Small Study Group __Individual Readings __One on One Case Discussion __Simulation/ Virtual __eLearning __Other

O - I did not attend this session

Teaching Session

Please indicate if you agree with each of the following statements regarding the teaching session.

	Strongly Disagree*	Disagree*	Agree	Strongly Agree	Not applicable
The objectives of the session were met	O	O	O	O	O
The teaching strategies used were appropriate	O	O	O	O	O
Relevant resources and references were provided	O	O	O	O	O
I am likely to employ the skills/knowledge taught					
The presenter was engaging	O	O	O	O	O
The presenter encouraged questions and/or interaction during this session	O	O	O	O	O

*If you indicated "Disagree," please provide comments in the spaces below.

1. What was the most valuable aspect of the teaching session?
2. How could the teaching session be improved and/or what should be added (consider length, balance of theory and clinical knowledge, teaching strategies, etc)?

Compilation of References

AAIM. (2010). *What is enterprise content management (ECM)?* Retrieved September 20, 2010, from http://www.aiim.org/What-is-ECM-Enterprise-Content-Management.aspx.

Aalst, W. M. P. V. D., Hofstede, A. H. M. T., Kiepuszewski, B., & Barros, A. P. (2003). Workflow patterns. *Distributed and Parallel Databases, 14*(1).

Abawajy, J. (2009). Design and delivery of undergraduate IT security management course. In The *Proceedings of the Third International Conference and Workshops, ISA 2009,* Seoul, Korea, June 25-27, 2009, (pp. 402-411).

Abugabah, A., & Sanzogni, L. (2010). Enterprise resource planning (ERP) system in higher education: A literature review and implications. *International Journal of Human and Social Sciences, 5,* 395–399.

Adewumi, A., & Ikhu-Omoregbe, N. (2011). Institutional repositories: Features, architecture, design and implementation technologies. *Journal of Computing, 2*(8).

Aguilar, R., Castilla, I., & Muñoz, R. (2009). Hospital resource management. In Merkuryev, Y., Merkuryeva, G., Piera, M. A., & Petit, A. G. (Eds.), *Simulation-based case studies in logistics: Education and applied research* (pp. 84–65). Heidelberg, Germany: Springer. doi:10.1007/978-1-84882-187-3_5

AIISO RDF. (2008). Retrieved from http://vocab.org/aiiso/schema-20080925.rdf

Akyalcin, J. (1997). *Constructivism: An epistemological journey from Piaget to Papert.* Retrieved from http://www.kilvington.schnet.edu.au/construct.htm

Aladwani, A. (2001). Change management strategies for successful ERP implementation. *Business Process Management Journal, 7*(3), 266–275. doi:10.1108/14637150110392764

Allen, D., Kern, T., & Havenhand, M. (2001). ERP critical success factors: an exploration of the contextual factors in public sector institutions. In *Proceedings of the 35th Annual Hawaii International Conference on System Sciences, HICSS* (pp. 3062 – 3071).

Allison, K. (2003). *Rhetoric and hypermedia in electronic textbooks.* Ph.D. dissertation, Texas Woman's University.

American Institute of Medicine. (2001). *Crossing the quality chasm: A new health system for the 21st century. Washington, DC: National Academy Press College of Family Physicians of Canada, Section of Teachers of Family Medicine. (1989). Report of the task force on curriculum.* Willowdale, ON: Author.

Amin Anjomshoaa, S. K. (2006). Exploitation of Semantic Web technology in ERP systems. *IFIP TC8 International Conference on Research and Practical Issues of Enterprise Information Systems* (pp. 417-427). Vienna, Austria: IFIP International Federation for Information Processing.

Anderson, M., Banker, R. D., Menon, N. M., & Romero, J. A. (2011). Implementing enterprise resource planning systems: Organizational performance and the duration of the implementation. *Information Technology Management, 12*(3), 197–212. doi:10.1007/s10799-011-0102-9

Andersson, A., & Linderoth, H. (2008). An explorative study of ERP-projects learn not to learn – A way of keeping budgets and deadlines in ERP-projects? *Journal of Enterprise Information Systems, 2*(1), 77–95. doi:10.1080/17517570701793830

Annus, T. (2004). *Identification of transversal competences and qualifications*. Office for Official Publications of the European Communities. Cedefop Reference series, 52. Retrieved from http://www.cedefop.europa.eu/EN/Files/3037_EN27.pdf

Anupama Mallik, P. P. (2008). *Multimedia ontology learning for automatic annotation and video browsing*. ACM International Conference on Multimedia Information Retrieval.

Aronson, J. Z. (1996). How schools can recruit hard-to-reach parents. *Educational Leadership, 53*(7), 58–60.

Assumpció Estivill, E. A. (2005). Use of Dublin Core metadata for describing and retrieving digital journals. *Proceedings of the 2005 International Conference on Dublin Core and Metadata Applications.*

В: Образовательные технологии. 1. Полат, Е., Бухаркина, М., & Моисеева М. (2004). *Теория и практика дистанционного обучения* (Theory and practice of distance learning). Москва: Академия.

Bailey, C. (2006). *What is open access*. Retrieved from http://www.digital-scholarship.com/cwb/WhatIsOA.pdf

Bandecchi, M., Melton, B., Gardini, B., & Ongaro, F. (2000). The ESA/ESTEC concurrent design facility. *Proceedings of 2nd European Systems Engineering Conference* (EuSEC 2000).

Banker, R. D., Chang, H., & Majumdar, S. K. (1996). A framework for analyzing changes in strategic performance. *Strategic Management Journal, 17*, 693–712. doi:10.1002/(SICI)1097-0266(199611)17:9<693::AID-SMJ847>3.0.CO;2-W

Bannon, L., & Bødker, S. (1997). Constructing common information spaces. *Proceedings of the Fifth European Conference on Computer-Supported Cooperative Work.*

Barak, M., & Yehudit, J. D. (2004). *Enhancing undergraduate students' chemistry understanding through project-based learning in an IT environment*, (pp. 118-139). Wiley InterScience. Retrieved June 31, 2011, from www.interscience.wiley.com

Barjis, J. (2010). The relevance of modeling and simulation in enterprise and organizational study and organizational modeling and simulation. *Lecture Notes in Business Information Processing, 63*, 15–26. doi:10.1007/978-3-642-15723-3_2

Basoglu, N., Daim, T., & Kerimoglu, O. (2007). Organizational adoption of enterprise resource planning systems: A conceptual framework. *The Journal of High Technology Management Research, 18*(1), 73–97. doi:10.1016/j.hitech.2007.03.005

Baum, J. R. (2000). A longitudinal study of the causes of technology adoption and its effects upon new venture growth. *Frontiers of Entrepreneurship Research,* 1-12.

Baum, J. R., & Wally, S. (2003). Strategic decision speed and firm performance. *Strategic Management Journal, 24*(11), 1107–1129. doi:10.1002/smj.343

Bazeley, P. (2007). *Qualitative data analysis with NVivo.* Sage Publications Ltd.

Becerra-Fernandez, I., Murphy, K., & Simon, S. (2000). Enterprise resource planning: Integrating ERP in the business school curriculum. *Communications of the ACM, 43*(4), 39–41. doi:10.1145/332051.332066

Becker, J., Kugeler, M., & Roseman, M. (2003). *Process management: A guide for the design of business processes.* Heidelberg, Germany: Springer.

BECTA. (2003). *What the research says about using ICT in maths*. British Educational Communications and Technology Agency. Retrieved from http://partners.becta.org.uk/page_documents/research/wtrs_maths.pdf

Bellier, S. (2004). *Le savoir-être dans l'entreprise: Utilité en gestion des ressources humaines.* Paris, France: Vuibert.

Bendoly, E., & Cotteleer, M. (2008). Understanding Behavioral sources of process variation following enterprise system deployment. *Journal of Operations Management, 26*(1), 23–44. doi:10.1016/j.jom.2007.03.002

Beneitone, P., & Meer, I. V. D. (2000). *Tuning educational structures in Europe*. University of Deusto, University of Groningen. Retrieved from http://tuning.unideusto.org/tuningeu

Berners-Lee, T. (1999). *Weaving the Web: The original design and ultimate destiny of the World Wide Web by its inventor*. San Francisco, CA: Harper.

Berry, L. L. (1983). Relationship marketing. In Berry, L., Shostack, G., & Upah, G. (Eds.), *Emerging perspectives on services marketing* (pp. 25–28). Chicago, IL: American Marketing Association.

Bingimlas, K. A. (2009). Barriers to the successful integration of ICT in teaching and learning: A review of the literature. *Eurasia Journal of Mathematics. Science and Technology Education, 5*(3), 235–245.

Bíró, A., & Tomcsányi, R. (2006). *SAP bevezetés az ELTE-n informatikus szemmel*. Networkshop 2006.

Bloom, B. S. (1981). *All our children learning: a primer for parents, teachers, and other educators*. New York, NY: McGraw-Hill.

Bojars, U. (2001). *Extending FOAF with Resume Information*. Retrieved from http://www.w3.org/2001/sw/Europe/events/foaf-galway/papers/pp/extending_foaf_with_resume/

Borbásné Szabó, I. (2006). *Educational ontology for transparency and student mobility between universities*. 28th International Conference on Information Technology Interfaces; ITI 2006, Cavtat, Croatia.

Boyce, S., & Pahl, C. (2007). Developing domain ontologies for course content. *Journal of Educational Technology & Society, 10*(3), 275–288.

Bradley, P., Browne, J., Jackson, S., & Jagdev, H. (1995). Business process re-engineering (BPR) - A study of the software tools currently available. *Computers in Industry, 25*, 309–330. doi:10.1016/0166-3615(94)00044-Q

Brickley, D., & Guha, R. (2004. 02 10). *RDF vocabulary description language 1.0: RDF schema*. Retrieved from http://www.w3.org/TR/rdf-schema/

Brinkkemper, S. (1996). Method engineering: Engineering of information systems development methods and tools. *Information and Software Technology, 38*(4), 275–280. doi:10.1016/0950-5849(95)01059-9

Brown, J. S., Collins, A., & Duguid, S. (1989). Situated cognition and the culture of learning. *Educational Researcher, 18*(1), 32–42.

Carlile, P. R. (2002). A pragmatic view of knowledge and boundaries: Boundary objects in new product development. *Organization Science, 13*(4), 442–455. doi:10.1287/orsc.13.4.442.2953

Carr, N. (2003). IT doesn't matter. *Harvard Business Review, 81*(5), 41–49.

Catts, H., & Kamhi, A. (2005). Excerpt from language and reading disabilities. Retrieved from http://www.education.com/reference/article/metacognitive-process-text-comprehension/

Chang, G.-C. (2008). *Strategic planning in education: Some concepts and methods, directions in educational planning*. Symposium to Honour the Work of Francoise Caillods, 3-4 July, 2008.

Chapman, D. W., & Mahlk, L. O. (Eds.). (2004). *Adapting technology for school improvement: A global perspective*. Paris, France: UNESCO and International Institute for Educational Planning.

Chen, I. A. (2003). Understanding customer relationship management (CRM): People, process and technology. *Business Process Management Journal, 9*(5), 672–688. doi:10.1108/14637150310496758

Chen, M., & Hambrick, D. (1995). Speed, stealth and selective attack: How small firms differ. *Academy of Management Journal, 38*, 453–483. doi:10.2307/256688

Chigona, A., & Dagada, R. (2011). Adoption and use of e-learning at tertiary level in South Africa: A qualitative analysis. *Proceedings of the Global Conference on Learning and Technology*, Melbourne, 27th March – 1st April 2011, (pp. 93-101).

Chou, D., Tripuramallu, H., & Chou, A. (2005). BI and ERP integration. *Information Management & Computer Security, 13*(5), 340–349. doi:10.1108/09685220510627241

Cirrus Shakeri, D. F. (2011). *Semantic technologies at SAP – A strategic perspective*. Semantic Technology Conference, San Francisco.

Clemons, E., & Row, M. (1991). Sustaining IT advantage: The role of structural differences. *Management Information Systems Quarterly, 15*(3), 275–292. doi:10.2307/249639

College of Family Physicians of Canada. Section of Teachers of Family Medicine. (2011). *'Triple C' + CanMeds-FM*. Retrieved from http://www.cfpc.ca/triple_C/

Criswell, E. (1989). *The design of computer-based instruction*. New York, NY: Macmillan Publishing Company.

Cronan, T., Douglas, D., Alnuaimi, O., & Schmidt, P. (2011). Decision making in an integrated business process context: Learning using an ERP simulation game. *Decision Sciences Journal of Innovative Education, 9*(2), 227–234. doi:10.1111/j.1540-4609.2011.00303.x

Crow, R. (2004, August). *A guide to institutional repository software*. Open Society Institute. Retrieved from http://www.soros.org/openaccess/pdf/OSI_Guide_to_IR_Software_v3.pdf.

Cruz, J. L., López, D., Sánchez, F., & Fernández, A. (2008). Evaluación de competencias transversales mediante un examen no presencial (A take-home exam to assess transversal competences). *Proceedings of the V Congreso Internacional de Docencia Universitaria e Innovación* (pp. 1-25). Lleida, Spain.

Cyganiak, R. (2011). *The linking open data cloud diagram*. Retrieved from http://richard.cyganiak.de/2007/10/lod/

Das, A. K., Sen, B. K., & Dutta, C. (2005). *Digitization of scholarly materials in India*. ICDE Conference 2005, Tokyo.

Dau, F. (n.d.). *SAP community network*. Semantic Technologies for Enterprises. Retrieved from http://www.sdn.sap.com/irj/scn/go/portal/prtroot/docs/library/uuid/10e372a0-7258-2e10-2a85-c894c6340b61?QuickLink=index&overridelayout=true

Davenport, T. H. (1998). Putting the enterprise into the enterprise system. *Harvard Business Review*, (July-August): 121–131.

David, P. (2005). *Fulfilling the promise of scholarly publishing: Can open access deliver?* IFLA 2005 Satellite Meeting No 17, Oslo, Norway. Retrieved from http://www.ub.uio.no/konferanser/ifla/IFLA_open_access/programme_abstracts.htm.

Davidson, A., & Näckros, K. (2007). Practical assignments in IT security for contemporary higher education. In the *Proceedings of World Conference on Information Security Education 2007*, (pp. 25-32).

Davidson-Shivers, A. G. V., & Rasmussen, K. L. (2006). *Web-based learning: Design, implementation, and evaluation*. Upper Saddle River, NJ: Pearson.

Davis, D. (1988). Professionalism means putting your profession first. *Journal of Legal Ethics, 2*(1), 341.

Dechow, N., & Mouritsen, J. (2005). Enterprise resource planning systems, management control and the quest for integration. *Accounting, Organizations and Society, 30*, 691–733. doi:10.1016/j.aos.2004.11.004

Deng, Q., Jin, X., Yin, A., & Tu, B. (2010). Design of teaching system of compound ERP talents. In The *Proceedings of the International Conference on Computer Application and System Modeling (ICCASM 2010)*, (pp. 340-343).

Deng, Q., Yin, A., & Tu, B. (2009). Design and application of practical teaching framework of ERP course. In The *Proceedings of the 4th International Conference on Computer Science & Education, ICCSE '09*, 25-28 July 2009, (pp. 1346-1348).

Dey, P. K., & Cheffi, W. (in press). Risk management in enterprise resource planning projects: Case study of an UK-based organization. [in press]. *International Journal of Production Economics*.

Dodge, H. R., Fullerton, S., & Robbins, J. E. (1994). Stage of the organizational life-cycle and competition as mediators of problem perception for small businesses. *Strategic Management Journal, 15*(2), 121–134. doi:10.1002/smj.4250150204

Dublin Core Ontology. (n.d.). Retrieved from http://dublincore.org

Duffy, T., & Jonassen, D. (1992). *Constructivism and the technology of instruction: A conversation*. USA: Lawrence Erlbaum Associated.

Du, W., Shang, M., & Xu, H. (2006). A novel approach for computer security education using Minix instructional operating system. *Computers & Security, 25*(3), 190–200. doi:10.1016/j.cose.2005.09.011

Edwards, S., & Hepner, M. (2010). Providing ERP resources for the classroom. *Proceedings of the Association of Business Information Systems,* Dallas, Texas.

Eisenhardt, K. M. (1989). Making fast strategic decisions in high-velocity environments. *Academy of Management Journal, 27*, 299–343.

Ekstedt, E., Lundin, R. A., Söderholm, A., & Wirdenius, H. (1999). *Neo-industrial organizing*. New York, NY: Routledge.

Elliot, A. (2010). Equity, pedagogy and inclusion. Harnessing digital technologies to support students from low socio-economic backgrounds in higher education. *The Journal of Community Informatics, 6*(3).

Enterprise Content Management-ERP & ECM. (n.d.). Retrieved June 14, 2011, from http://www.ademero.com/resources/learning-center/enterprise-content-management/erp-and-ecm.php

Esteves, J., & Pastor, J. (2001). Enterprise resource planning systems research: An annotated bibliography. *Communications of the Association for Information System, 7*(8).

European Communities. (2008). *Statistical Classification of Economic Activities in the European Community, Rev. 2*. Retrieved from from: Eurostat's Metadata Server: http://ec.europa.eu/eurostat/ramon/nomenclatures/index.cfm?TargetUrl=LST_NOM_DTL&StrNom=NACE_RE V2&StrLanguageCode=EN&IntPcKey=&StrLayoutCod e=HIERARCHIC

European Ministers for Higher Education. (2001). *Towards the European higher education area*. Communiqué of the meeting of European Ministers in charge of Higher Education in Praga. Retrieved from http://www.bologna-bergen2005.no/Docs/00Main_doc/010519prague_communique.pdf

European Ministers for Higher Education. (2003). *Realising the European higher education area*. Communiqué of the Conference of Ministers responsible for Higher Education in Berlin. Retrieved from http://www.bologna-bergen2005.no/Docs/00-Main_doc/030919Berlin_Communique.PDF

European Ministers for Higher Education. (2005). *The European higher education area -Achieving the goals*. Communiqué of the Conference of European Ministers Responsible for Higher Education in Bergen. Retrieved from http://www.bologna-bergen2005.no/Docs/00-Main_doc/050520_Bergen_Communique.pdf

European Ministers for Higher Education. (2007). *Towards the European higher education area: Responding to challenges in a globalised world*. London Communiqué. Retrieved from http://webarchive.nationalarchives.gov.uk/20100202100434/dcsf.gov.uk/londonbologna/uploads/documents/londoncommuniquefinalwithlon-donlogo.pdf

European Ministers for Higher Education. (2009). *The Bologna Process 2020. The European higher education area in the new decade*. Communiqué of the Conference of European Ministers Responsible for Higher Education, Leuven and Louvain-la-Neuve. Retrieved from http://www.ond.vlaanderen.be/hogeronderwijs/bologna/conference/documents/Leuven_Louvain-la-Neuve_Communiqu%C3%A9_April_2009.pdf

Fan, C., Zhang, P., Liu, Q., Yang, J., & Xi, W. (2011). Research on ERP teaching model reform for application-oriented talents education. *International Education Studies, 4*(2), 25–30. doi:10.5539/ies.v4n2p25

Ferdig, R. E. (2006). Assessing technologies for teaching and learning: Understanding the importance of technological pedagogical content knowledge. *British Journal of Educational Technology, 37*(5), 749–760. doi:10.1111/j.1467-8535.2006.00559.x

Fishman, B., & Davis, E. (2006). Teacher learning research and the learning sciences. In Sawyer, R. K. (Ed.), *Cambridge handbook of the learning sciences* (pp. 535–550). Cambridge, UK: Cambridge University Press. doi:10.1017/CBO9780511816833.033

FOAF Project. (n.d.). Retrieved from http://www.foaf-project.org/

Forbes, D. (2005). Managerial determinants of decision speed in new ventures. *Strategic Management Journal, 26*, 355–366. doi:10.1002/smj.451

Frank, J. R. (Ed.). (2005). *The CanMEDS physician competency framework. Better standards. Better physicians. Better care*. Ottawa, Canada: The Royal College of Physicians and Surgeons of Canada. Retrieved from http://rcpsc.medical.org/canmeds/index.php

Frisch, S. R., & Talbot, Y. (1984). Faculty development in family medicine: A survey of needs and resources. *Journal of Medical Education, 59*(10), 831–833.

Frumkes, L. (1996). *Design and materials for an electronic textbook for first-year Russian*. Ph.D. dissertation, University of Washington.

Gagné, R. M., Wager, W. W., Golas, K. C., & Keller, J. M. (2005). *Principles of instructional design*. Thomson/Wadsworth.

García, L. A., & Díaz, C. (2008). *Las competencias para el empleo en los titulados universitarios. Observatorio permanente para el seguimiento de la inserción laboral*. Ed. Sedicana.

Gasper, D. (2002). Is Sen's capability approach an adequate basis for considering human development? *Review of Political Economy*, *14*(4), 435–461. doi:10.1080/0953825022000009898

Gattiker, T., & Goodhue, D. (2005). What happens after ERP implementation: Understanding the impact of inter-dependence and differentiation on plant-level outcomes. *Management Information Systems Quarterly*, *29*(3), 559–585.

Gaurav Harit, S. C. (2006). Using multimedia ontology for generating conceptual annotations and hyperlinks in video collections. *Proceedings of the 2006 IEEE/WIC/ACM International Conference on Web Intelligence*.

General Medical Council. (2001). *Good medical practice*. London, UK: General Medical council.

Gérard, F., & Roegiers, X. (2009). *Des manuels scolaires pour apprendre: Concevoir, évaluer, utiliser*. Editons De Boeck Universite, Groupe De Boeck.

Gilbreth, L. (1921). *The psychology of management*. The Macmillan Company. Retrieved August 16, 2010, from http://www.gutenberg.org/files/16256/16256-h/16256-h.htm

Gold, R. L. (1958). Roles in sociological fieldwork. *Social Forces*, *36*, 217–223. doi:10.2307/2573808

Grabski, S., Leech, S., & Schmidt, P. (2011). A review of ERP research: A Future agenda for accounting information systems. *Journal of Information Systems*, *25*(1), 37–78. doi:10.2308/jis.2011.25.1.37

Greenberg, P. (2010). *CRM at spped of light* (4th ed.). Mcgraw Hill.

Gupta, M., & Kohli, A. (2006). Enterprise resource planning systems and its implications for operations function. *Technovation*, *26*(5-6), 687–696. doi:10.1016/j.technovation.2004.10.005

Gururao, K. (n.d.). *ERP 4 educational institutes*. Retrieved from www.advisor2u.com

Guthrie, R., & Guthrie, R. (2000). Integration of enterprise system software in the undergraduate curriculum. In The *Proceedings of the Information Systems Education Conference 2000*, Vol. 17.

Hamid Nach, A. L. (2008). *Implementing ERP in SMEs: Towards an ontology supporting managerial decisions*. International MCETECH Conference on e-Technologies.

Hamilton, S. (2004). *Justification of ERP investments part 4: Replacing or re-implementing an ERP system*. Retrieved February 1, 2012, from http://www.technologyevaluation.com/Research/ResearchHighlights/Erp/2004/02/research_notes/TU_ER_XSH_02_13_04_1.asp

Hardiono, A. D. R., & Tintri, D. (2009). ERP analysis and implementation module of sale & distribution by tiny ERP. *Proceedings PESAT (Psikologi, Ekonomi, Sastra, Arsitektur & Sipil)* Universitas Gunadarma – Depok. ISSN 1858-2559

Haug, G., Kirstein, J., & Knudsen, I. (1999). *Trends in learning structures in higher education*. Copenhague, Denmark: Danish Rectors' Conference Secretariat.

Hawking, P., McCarthy, B., & Stein, A. (2005) Integrating ERP's second wave into higher education curriculum. In The *Proceedings of the PACIS 2005*, (pp. 1001-1008).

Hayes, H. (2005, August). *Digital repositories helping universities and colleges*. JISC Briefing Paper - High Education Sector. Retrieved from http://ww.jisc.ac.uk/uploaded_documents/HE_repositories_briefing_paper_2005.pdf

Hayes, G., & McGilsky, D. (2007). Integrating ERP into BSBA curriculum of Central Michigan University. *International Journal of Quality and Productivity Management*, *7*(1), 12–27.

Heflin, J., Hendler, J., Luke, S., Gasarch, C., Zhendong, Q., Spector, L., et al. (2000. 04). *University ontology*. Retrieved from http://www.cs.umd.edu/projects/plus/SHOE/onts/univ1.0.html

Hendrawirawan, D., Tanriverdi, H., Zetterlund, C., Hakam, H., Kim, H., Paik, H., & Yoon, Y. (2007). ERP security and segregation of duties audit: A framework for building an automated solution. *Information Systems Control Journal, 2,* 1–4.

Hennig-Thurau, L. M. (2011). Modeling and managing student loyalty: An approach based on the concept of relationship quality. *Journal of Service Research, 3*(4), 331–344. doi:10.1177/109467050134006

Henninger, M., & Kutter, A. (2010). Integration of education and technology – A Long-term study about possibilities and adequacy of a learning management system for education. *Journal on Systemics, Cybernetics, and Informatics, 8*(3).

Higgins, S. (2003). *Does ICT improve learning and teaching in schools?* Nottingham, UK: British Educational Research Association.

Hobby, J. (1999). Looking after the one who matters. *Accountancy Age, 28,* 28–30.

Holsapple, C. W., & Sena, M. P. (2005). ERP plans and decision-support benefits. *Decision Support Systems, 38*(4), 575–590. doi:10.1016/j.dss.2003.07.001

Hong Kong Education and Manpower Bureau. (1998). *Information technology for learning in a new era: Five-year strategy 1998-99 to 2002-03.*

Hsu, K., Sylvestre, J., & Sayed, E. (2006). Avoiding ERP pitfalls. *Journal of Corporate Accounting & Finance,* (May/June): 67–74. doi:10.1002/jcaf.20217

Huang, S., Chang, I., Li, S., & Lin, M. (2004). Assessing risk in ERP projects: Identify and prioritize the factors. *Industrial Management & Data Systems, 104*(8), 681–688. doi:10.1108/02635570410561672

Hughes, J., & Beer, R. (2007). A security checklist for ERP Implementations. *EDUCAUSE Quarterly, 30*(4), 7–10.

Hunton, J., Lippincott, B., & Reck, J. (2003). Enterprise resource planning systems: Comparing firm performance of adopters and non-adopters. *International Journal of Accounting Information Systems, 4,* 165–184. doi:10.1016/S1467-0895(03)00008-3

Hussein, H. B. (2011). Attitudes of Saudi universities faculty members towards using learning management system (JUSUR). *The Turkish Online Journal of Educational Technology, 10*(2), 43–53.

Huynh, M., & Chu, H. (2011). Open-source ERP: Is it ripe for use in teaching supply chain management? *Journal of Information Technology Education, 10,* 181–194.

Hyo-Jeong, S., & Bosung, K. (2009). Learning about problem based learning: Student teachers integrating technology, pedagogy and content knowledge. *Australasian Journal of Educational Technology, 25*(1), 101–116.

Iasi, Romania: Polirom. Беспалько, В. (2007). Параметры и критерии диагностической цели (The parameters and criterions for diagnostic aim).

Ifinedo, P. (2007). An empirical study of ERP success evaluations by business and IT managers. *Information Management & Computer Security, 15*(4), 270–282. doi:10.1108/09685220710817798

Jansen-Vullers, M. H., & Netjes, M. (2006). Business process simulation - A tool survey. In K. Jensen (Ed.), *Seventh Workshop and Tutorial on the Practical Use of Coloured Petri Nets and the CPN Tools (pp. 77-96).* Aarhus, Denmark: University of Aarhus Press.

Johnson, L., Smith, R., Willis, H., Levine, A., & Haywood, K. (2011). *The 2011 horizon report.* Austin, TX: The New Media Consortium.

Johnstone, J. (2007). Technology as empowerment: A capability approach to computer ethics. *Ethics and Information Technology, 9,* 73–87. doi:10.1007/s10676-006-9127-x

Joint Quality Initiative Group. (2004). *Shared Dublin descriptors for short cycle, first cycle, second cycle and third cycle awards.* Retrieved from http://www.jointquality.org/content/descriptors/CompletesetDublinDescriptors.doc

Jones, G. K., Lanctot, A., & Teegen, H. J. (2001). Determinants and performance impacts of external technology acquisition. *Journal of Business Venturing, 16,* 255–283. doi:10.1016/S0883-9026(99)00048-8

Joseph, G., & George, A. (2002). ERP, learning communities, and curriculum integration. *Journal of Information Systems Education, 13*(1), 51–58.

Judge, W. Q., & Miller, A. (1991). Antecedents and outcomes of decision speed in different environmental contexts. *Academy of Management Journal, 34,* 449–463. doi:10.2307/256451

Jung, I. (2005). ICT-pedagogy integration in teacher training: Application cases worldwide. *Journal of Educational Technology & Society, 8*(2), 94–101.

Karthik Thatipamula, S. C. (2005). Specifying spatio temporal relations for multimedia ontologies. *PReMI 2005. Lecture Notes in Computer Science, 3776,* 527–532. doi:10.1007/11590316_83

Katzenbach, J. R., & Smith, D. K. (1993). *The wisdom of teams.* London, UK: McGraw-Hill.

Kerimoglu, O., Basoglu, N., & Daim, T. (2008). Organizational adoption of information technologies: Case of enterprise resource planning systems. *The Journal of High Technology Management Research, 19,* 21–35. doi:10.1016/j.hitech.2008.06.002

Kiepuszewski, B. (2003). *Expressiveness and suitability of languages for control flow modelling in workflows.* PhD thesis, Queensland University of Technology, Brisbane, Australia.

Kiesler, J., & McGuire, H. (1987). Aspects of computer-mediated communication. *International Psychologist, 32*(10), 45–67.

Kim, H. S. (2010). An assessment model and practical rubric design for thesis assessment. *Proceedings of the International Conference on Engineering Education,* Gliwice, Poland.

Kirschner, P., van Merrienboer, J., Sloep, P., & Carr, C. (2002). How expert designers design. *Performance Improvement Quarterly, 15*(4), 86–104. doi:10.1111/j.1937-8327.2002.tb00267.x

Kirstin Dougan, T. D. (2007). *Bibliographic/multimedia database model documentation.* University of Wisconsin. *MINDS@UW HOME.* (n.d.). Retrieved from http://minds.wisconsin.edu

Klahr, D., & Simon, H. A. (1999). Studies of scientific discovery: Complementary approaches and convergent findings. *Psychological Bulletin, 125*(5), 524–543. doi:10.1037/0033-2909.125.5.524

Kocher, M., & Sutter, M. (2006). Time is money-Time pressure, incentives, and the quality of decision-making. *Journal of Economic Behavior & Organization, 61,* 375–392. doi:10.1016/j.jebo.2004.11.013

Koulopoulos, T., & Frappaolo, C. (2000). *Smart things to know about knowledge management.* Cornwall, UK: T. J. International Ltd.

Lavanya. (Mar. 2011). Customer relationship management and higher education: A vision. *Advances in Management, 4*(3), 18-22.

Lave, J. (1988). *Cognition in practice: Mind, mathematics, and culture in everyday life.* Cambridge, UK: Cambridge University Press. doi:10.1017/CBO9780511609268

Lave, J., & Wenger, E. (1990). *Situated learning: Legitimate peripheral participation.* Cambridge, UK: Cambridge University Press.

Law, A. M., & Kelton, W. D. (1991). *Simulation modeling and analysis* (3rd ed.). New York, NY: McGraw-Hill.

Leach, D. (2004). Professionalism: The formation of physicians. *The American Journal of Bioethics, 4*(2). doi:10.1162/152651604323097619

Linderoth, H., & Lundqvist, A. (2004). Learn not to learn: Paradoxical knowledge creation and learning in ERP-projects. In *Proceedings IRNOP VI, 2004,* (pp. 409-422). Turku, Finland: Academy University Press.

Linderoth, H., & Lundqvist, A. (2004). Learn not to learn: Paradoxical knowledge creation and learning in ERP-projects. In *Proceedings IRNOP VI, 2004,* (pp. 409-422). Turku, Finland: Academy University Press.

Lonchamp, J. (2000). *A generic computer support for concurrent design.* Advances in Concurrent Engineering: Presented at Seventh ISPE International Conference on Concurrent Engineering: Research and Applications, Lyon Cluade Bernard University, France, July 17-20, 2000. CRC Press.

Lundin, R. A., & Söderholm, A. (1995). A theory of the temporary organization. *Scandinavian Journal of Management, 11*(4), 437–455. doi:10.1016/0956-5221(95)00036-U

Lynch, C. (2003). *Institutional repositories - Essential infrastructure for scholarship in the digital age.* ARL Bimonthly report 226. Retrieved from http://www.arl.org/newsltr/226/ir.html

Madiba, M. (2009). *Investigating design issues in e-learning.* Unpublished PhD Thesis, University of the Western Cape.

Madon, S. (2004). Evaluating the impact of e-governance initiative: An exploratory framework. *Electronic Journal on Information Systems in Developing Countries, 20*(5), 1–13.

Mager, R. (1997). *Preparing instructional objectives.* CEP Press.

Mager, R. (2011). *Preparing instructional objectives. A critical tool in the development of effective instruction.* Atlanta, GA: CEP Press, The Center for Effective Performance, Inc.

Magnusson, J., Oskarsson, B., Gidlund, A., & Wetterberg, A. (2009). Process methodology in ERP-related education: A case from Swedish higher education. In The *Proceedings of the BIS 2009 Workshop, LNBIP 37,* (pp. 214–219).

Mahadevan, S., & Rahman, S. (2002). *Modern profile of a digital library and the associated learning object model for posting, meta-tagging and integrating content into digital libraries.* 32nd ASEE/IEEE Frontiers in Education Conference, November 6-9, 2002, Boston, MA.

Makadok, R. (1998). Can first-mover and early-mover advantages be sustained in an industry with low barriers to entry/imitation? *Strategic Management Journal, 19*(7), 683–696. doi:10.1002/(SICI)1097-0266(199807)19:7<683::AID-SMJ965>3.0.CO;2-T

Marnewick, C., & Labuschagne, L. (2005). A conceptual model for enterprise resource planning (ERP). *Information Management & Computer Security, 13*(2), 144–155. doi:10.1108/09685220510589325

Márquez, R. D., Moreno, R. A., González, C., Espejo, R., & Herruzo, E. (2009). An experience to define the enterprising attitude as a transversal competence in the European higher education area. In Mendez-Vilas, A. (Eds.), *Research, reflections and innovations in integrating ICT in education (Vol. 1,* pp. 3–677). Badajoz, Spain: Ed. Formatex.

Martin, R. (2010). The age of customer capitalism. *Havard Business Review,* January.

May, C. (2008). Approaches to user education. *Network Security,* (9): 15–17. doi:10.1016/S1353-4858(08)70109-0

Mcknight, S. (2007). *A futuristic view of knowledge and information management.* Retrieved October 18, 2011, from http://www.ub.edu/bid/19mcknig.htm

Mergel, B. (2007). Contemporary learning theories, instructional design and leadership. *Studies in Educational Leadership, 6,* 67–98. doi:10.1007/978-1-4020-6022-9_5

Mérida, R., Angulo, J., Jurado, M., & Diaz, J. (2011). Student training in transversal competences at the University of Cordoba. *European Educational Research Journal, 10*(1), 34–52. doi:10.2304/eerj.2011.10.1.34

Mintzberg, H., Raisinghani, D., & Theoret, A. (1976). The structure of 'unstructured' decision processes. *Administrative Science Quarterly, 21,* 246–275. doi:10.2307/2392045

Mishra, P., & Koehler, M. J. (2006). Technological pedagogical content knowledge: A framework for teacher knowledge. *Teachers College Record, 108*(6), 1017–1054. doi:10.1111/j.1467-9620.2006.00684.x

Mohamed, S., & McLaren, T. S. (2009). Probing the gaps between ERP education and ERP implementation success factors. *AIS Transactions on Enterprise Systems, 1,* 8-14. Retrieved from http://enterprise-systems.net

Montes-Berges, B., Castillo-Mayén, M. R., Rodríguez-Espartal, N., López-Zafra, E., & Augusto, J. M. (2011). Transversal competence for nursing and physiotherapy students. *Proceedings of the 5th International Technology, Education and Development Conference* (pp. 3345-3351). Valencia, Spain.

Moon, Y. B. (2007). Enterprise resource planning (ERP): A review of the literature. *International Journal of Management and Enterprise Development, 4*(3), 235–264. doi:10.1504/IJMED.2007.012679

Moshe, T. (1998). Primary and secondary school teachers' perceptions and actions regarding their pupils' emotional lives. *School Psychology International, 19,* 151–168. doi:10.1177/0143034398192004

Mumtaz, S. (2000). Factors affecting teachers' use of information and communications technology: A review of the literature. *Technology, Pedagogy and Education, 9*(3), 319–342. doi:10.1080/14759390000200098

Murray-John, D. P. (2008). *Keyword domainizer review.* Retrieved from http://www.patrickgmj.net/project/university-ontology

Muthu, S., Whitman, L., & Cheraghi, S. H. (2006). *Business process reengineering: A consolidated methodology.* Paper presented at the 4th Annual International Conference on Industrial Engineering Theory, Applications and Practice. San Antonio, Texas.

Ngai, E. W. T., Law, C. C. H., & Wat, F. K. T. (2008). Examining the critical success factors in the adoption of enterprise resource planning. *Computers in Industry, 59*(6), 548–564. doi:10.1016/j.compind.2007.12.001

Njenga, J. K. (2011). *eLearning adoption in Eastern and Southern Africa higher education institutions.* Unpublished PhD Thesis, University of the Western Cape.

Nonaka, I. (1997). *Organizational knowledge creation.* Knowledge Advantage Conference.

Nonaka, I. (1994). A dynamic theory of organizational knowledge creation. *Organization Science, 5*(1), 14–37. doi:10.1287/orsc.5.1.14

Nonaka, I., & von Krogh, G. (2009). Tacit knowledge and knowledge conversion: Controversy and advancement in organizational knowledge creation theory. *Organization Science, 20*(3), 635–652. doi:10.1287/orsc.1080.0412

Ojala, M., Vilpola, I., & Kouri, I. (2006). Risks in ERP project – Case study of IS/ICT management capability maturity level and risk assessment. In The *Proceedings of the Frontiers of eBusiness Research.*

Okada, A. (2005). The collective building of knowledge in collaborative learning environments. In Roberts, T. (Ed.), *Computer–supported collaborative learning in higher education.* Hershey, PA: Idea Group Publishing. doi:10.4018/978-1-59140-408-8.ch004

OPSIL Project. (2010). *Observatorio Permanente para el Seguimiento de la Inserción Laboral.* Retrieved from http://www.feu.ull.es/es/proyecto/opsil/28/

Order 2514/2007. (2007). Retrieved from http://www.boe.es/boe/dias/2007/08/21/pdfs/A35424-35431.pdf

Osburg, J., & Mavris, D. (2005). A collaborative design environment to support multidisciplinary conceptual systems design. *SAE Transactions, 114*, 1508–1516.

Ottar, B., Anita, R., & Erlend, A. (2007). Holistic ERP selection methodology. In *Proceedings of the 14th International EurOMA Conference: Managing Operations in an Expanding Europe,* Ankara, Turkey.

OWL Working Group. (2007). *Web Ontology Language (OWL).* Retrieved from http://www.w3.org/2004/OWL/

Paquette, G. (2004). Instructional engineering for learning objects repositories networks. *Proceedings of International Conference on Computer Aided Learning in Engineering Education* (CALIE 04).

Parker, D. (1992). Teaching the ethical use of information assets. *Information Security Journal: A Global Perspective, 1*(1), 13-16.

Parker, A. (1997). A distance education how-to manual: Recommendations from the field. *Educational Technology Review, 8*, 7–10.

Parker, A. (1999). Interaction in distance education: The critical conversation. *Educational Technology Review, 12*, 13–17.

Payne, J. W., Bettman, J. R., & Luce, M. F. (1996). When time is money: Decision behavior under opportunity-cost time pressure. *Organizational Behavior and Human Decision Processes, 66*, 131–152. doi:10.1006/obhd.1996.0044

Peltier, T. (2005). Implementing an information security awareness program. *Information Security Journal: A Global Perspective, 14*(2), 37-49.

Peng, G., & Nunes, M. (2009). Identification and assessment of risks associated with ERP post-implementation in China. *Journal of Enterprise Information Management, 22*(5), 587–614. doi:10.1108/17410390910993554

Penman, S. (2003). *Financial statement analysis and security valuation* (2nd ed.). McGraw-Hill/Irwin.

Perlow, L., Okhuysen, G., & Reppening, N. (2002). The speed trap: Exploring the relationship between decision making and temporal context. *Academy of Management Journal, 45*, 931–955. doi:10.2307/3069323

Peterson, C. (2003). Bringing ADDIE to life: Instructional design at its best. *Journal of Educational Multimedia and Hypermedia, 12*(3), 227–242.

PISA project. (1997). *OECD Programme for International Student Assessment (PISA project).* Retrieved from http://www.pisa.oecd.org/pages/0,3417, en_32252351_32235731_1_1_1_1_1,00.html

Plevyak, H. (2001). Communication triangle for parents, school administration and teachers: A workshop model. *Education, 121*(4), 768–773.

Pollack, T. (2002). Educational opportunities in enterprise resource planning (ERP). In *Proceedings of the 2002 ASCUE Conference*, June 9 – 13, 2002, Myrtle Beach, South Carolina, (pp. 191-197).

Polyakov, A., & Medvedovskiy, I. (2010). ERP security. Myths, problems, solutions. Source Barcelona 2010. Retrieved October 1, 2011, from http://dsecrg.com/files/pub/pdf/ERP%20Security.%20Myths,%20Problems,%20Solutions.pdf

Popescu, M., & Popescu, E. (2010). *A human resource ontology for recruitment* (pp. 896–900). Annals Economic Science Series.

Porter, P. (2010). *Effectiveness of electronic textbooks with embedded activities on student learning.* Ph.D. dissertation, Capella University.

Poston, R., & Grabski, S. (2001). Financial impacts of enterprise resource planning implementations. *International Journal of Accounting Information Systems, 2*, 271–294. doi:10.1016/S1467-0895(01)00024-0

Protege Home Page. (n.d.). Retrieved from http://protege.stanford.edu/

Railean E. (2008) Aspects of teaching and learning processes in the closed and open didactical systems. *Learning Technology Newsletter, 10*(4).

Railean, E. (2006). Concept mapping in instructional design of educational software. *Proceedings of 8th International Conference on Development and Application Systems.*

Railean, E. (2010). *A new didactical model for elaboration the electronic textbooks.* ICVL 2010.

Railean, E. (2010). Metasystems approach to research the globalised pedagogical processes. *Annals of Spiru Haret University Mathematics – Informatics Series, Special Issue New Results on E - Learning Methodologies, 31 – 50.*

Railean, E. (2012). Issues and challenges associated with the design of electronic textbook. In Khan, B. H. (Ed.), *User interface design for virtual environments: Challenges and advances* (pp. 238–256). Hershey, PA: IGI Global. doi:10.4018/978-1-61350-516-8.ch015

Rajshekhar, T. B. (2003). *Improving the visibility of indian research - An institutional open access model.* Indo-US Workshop on Open Digital Libraries and Interoperability.

Ralevich, V., & Martinovic, D. (2010). Designing and implementing an undergraduate program in information systems security. *Education and Information Technologies, 15*(4). doi:10.1007/s10639-010-9123-y

Rao, S. S. (2000). Enterprise resource planning: Business needs and technologies. *Industrial Management & Data Systems, 100*(2), 81–88. doi:10.1108/02635570010286078

Ravesteyn, P., & Köhler, A. (2009). Industry participation in educating ERP. *Communications of the IIMA, 9*(2), 45–56.

RDF Working Group. (2004. 02 10). *Resource description framework (RDF).* Retrieved from http://www.w3.org/RDF/

Reavy, A. (2011). *Schools looking forward to future with electronic textbooks.* Retrieved from http://www.sj-r.com/top-stories/x767223962/Schools-looking-forward-to-future-with-electronic-textbooks.

Reck, J. (2004). Discussion of firm performance effects in relation to the implementation and use of enterprise resource planning systems. *Journal of Information Systems, 18*(2), 107–110. doi:10.2308/jis.2004.18.2.107

Reeves, T. C., Herrington, J., & Oliver, R. (2005). Design research: A socially responsible approach to instructional technology research in higher education. *Journal of Computing in Higher Education, 16*(2), 96–115. doi:10.1007/BF02961476

Reinertsen, D., & Smith, P. (1991). The strategist's role in shortening product development cycles. *The Journal of Business Strategy, 12*(4), 18–22. doi:10.1108/eb039425

Rezgui, Y., & Marks, A. (2008). Information security awareness in higher education: An exploratory study. *Computers & Security, 27*(7-8), 241–253. doi:10.1016/j.cose.2008.07.008

Rienzo, T., & Han, B. (2011). Does ERP hands-on experience help students learning business process concepts? *Decision Sciences Journal of Innovative Education, 9*(2), 177–207. doi:10.1111/j.1540-4609.2011.00300.x

Roberts, T. (2006). *Self, peer, and group assessment in e-learning*. Hershey, PA: Idea Group Publishing. doi:10.4018/978-1-59140-965-6

Robeyns, I. (2005). The capability approach: A theoretical survey. *Journal of Human Development, 6*(1), 93–114. doi:10.1080/146498805200034266

Romero, J. A., Menon, N., Banker, R. D., & Anderson, M. (2010). ERP: Drilling for profit in the oil and gas industry. *Communications of the ACM, 53*(7), 118–121. doi:10.1145/1785414.1785448

Roth, W.-M., & Van Eijck, M. (2010). *Fullness of life as minimal unit: Science, technology, engineering and mathematics (STEM) learning across the life span* (pp. 1027–1048). Siley Periodicals, Inc., Science Education. doi:10.1002/sce.20401

Royal Decree 1125/2003. (2003). Retrieved from http://www.boe.es/boe/dias/2003/09/18/pdfs/A34355-34356.pdf

Royal Decree 1393/2007. (2007). Available at; http://www.boe.es/boe/dias/2007/10/30/pdfs/A44037-44048.pdf

Royal Decree 1509/2005. (2005). Available at; http://www.boe.es/boe/dias/2005/12/20/pdfs/A41455-41457.pdf.

Rudic, G. (2011). *Center for Modern Pedagogy blog*. Retrieved from http://www.pedagogiemoderne.com/blog

Russell, R. (2006). A framework for analyzing ERP security threats. *In Proceedings of the Euro-Atlantic Symposium on Critical Information Infrastructure Assurance*, March 23-34 2006, Switzerland

Saldaña, J. (2009). *The coding manual for qualitative researchers*. Sage.

Sawhney, M. S. (2004, January 15). Creating growth with services. *MIT Sloan Management Review*, 45.

Schmidt, K., & Bannon, L. (1992). Taking CSCW seriously. *Computer Supported Cooperative Work, 1*(1), 7–40. doi:10.1007/BF00752449

Schmidt, K., & Simone, C. (1996). Coordination mechanisms: Towards a conceptual foundation of CSCW systems design. *Computer Supported Cooperative Work, 5*(2), 155–200. doi:10.1007/BF00133655

Schnitzer, D. (2003). *What is quantum psychology?* Retrieved from http://users.skynet.be/sky52523/en/peronal_development/quantum_psychology.htm

Schütt, P. (2003). The post-Nonaka knowledge management. *Journal of Universal Computer Science, 9*(6), 451–462.

Scott, J. E., & Vessey, I. (2000). Implementing enterprise resource planning systems: The role of learning from failure. *Information Systems Frontiers*, (August): 213–232. doi:10.1023/A:1026504325010

Sen, A. K. (1999). *Development as freedom*. Oxford, UK: Oxford University Press.

Shakleton, P., Ramp, A., & Hawking, P. (2001). IS '97 model curriculum: Where do enterprise resource planning systems fit. *Business Process Management Journal, 7*(3), 225–233. doi:10.1108/14637150110392700

Sharma, S., & Sefchek, J. (2007). Teaching information systems security courses: A hands-on approach. *Computers & Security, 26*(4), 290–299. doi:10.1016/j.cose.2006.11.005

Sicilia, M. A. (2009). How should transversal competence be introduced in computing education? *ACM SIGCSE Bulletin Archive, 41*(4).

Smith, W., & Moore, J. (2004). *Programmed learning: Theory and research. An enduring problem in psychology*. Princeton, NJ: D. Van Nostrand company, Inc.

Smith, B., & MacGregor, J. (1992). What is collaborative learning? In Goodsell, A. S., Maher, M. R., & Tinto, V. (Eds.), *Collaborative learning: A sourcebook for higher education. National Center on Postsecondary Teaching, Learning, & Assessment.* Syracuse University.

Smith, K. G., Grimm, C. M., Gannon, M. J., & Chen, M. (1991). Organization information processing, competitive responses, and performance in the US domestic airline industry. *Academy of Management Journal, 34*, 60–85. doi:10.2307/256302

Smith, P., & Reinertsen, D. (1992). *Shortening the product development cycle. Research Technology Management.* May-June.

Somers, T. M., & Nelson, K. G. (2003). The impact of strategy and integration mechanisms on enterprise system value: Empirical evidence from manufacturing firms. *European Journal of Operational Research, 146*, 315–338. doi:10.1016/S0377-2217(02)00552-0

Sosnovsky, S., & Tatiana, G. (2005). *Development of educational ontology for C-programming.* 11th International Conference Knowledge-Dialogue-Solution, Varna, Bulgaria.

Spanish Ministry of Education. Culture and Sport. (2003). *La integracion del sistema universitario español en el espacio europeo de enseñanza superior.* Retrieved from http://www.uab.es/iDocument/IntegracioSistemaUniversitariEspanyolEnEEES,0.pdf

Stalk, G. (1988). Time – The next source of competitive advantage. *Harvard Business Review, 66*(4), 41–51.

Standish Group. (2006). *Chaos report 2006.* Retrieved from http://www.standishgroup.com/chaos/beacon_243.php-2006-11-07-14.59

Stevenson, H., & Gumpert, D. (1985). The heart of entrepreneurship. *Harvard Business Review, 63*(2), 85–94.

Stewart, T. (1997). *Intellectual capital.* DoubleDay Business.

Stoffa, V. (2007). *Modelling, simulation, animation in e-learning courses.* Retrieved from http://www.ittk.hu/netis/doc/textbook/stoffa_animation_eng.pdf

Strand, K. A., & Hjeltnes, T. A. (2009). Design of customized corporate e-learning. *International Journal of Media. Technology and Lifelong Learning, 5*(2), 14.

Strand, K. A., & Staupe, A. (2010). The concurrent e-learning design method. In Abas, Z. (Eds.), *Proceedings of Global Learn Asia Pacific 2010* (pp. 4067–4076).

Strand, K. A., & Staupe, A. (2010). *Action research based instructional design improvements. NOKOBIT 2010, Norsk konferanse for organisasjoners bruk av informasjonsteknologi* (pp. 25–38). Tapir Akademisk Forlag.

Stratman, J. (2007). Realizing benefits from enterprise resource planning: does strategic focus matter? *Production and Operations Management, 16*(2), 203–216. doi:10.1111/j.1937-5956.2007.tb00176.x

Styles, R., & Shabir, N. (2008). *Academic institution internal structure ontology (AIISO).* Retrieved from http://vocab.org/aiiso/schema

Suber, P. (2007, June). *Open access overview.* Retrieved from http://www.earlham.edu/~peters/fos/overview.htm

Tannenbaum, D., et al. (2009). *CanMEDS-FM.* Working Group on Curriculum Review. Retrieved from http://www.cfpc.ca/uploadedFiles/Education/CanMeds%20FM%20Eng.pdf

Tannenbaum, D., Konkin, J., Parsons, E., Saucier, D., Shaw, L., & Walsh, A. (2011). *Triple C competency-based curriculum: Report of the working group on postgraduate curriculum review – Part 1.* Mississauga, Canada: College of Family Physicians of Canada.

Tarcsi, A. (2005). *Oktatási információs rendszerek Magyarországon* [in Hungarian]. 3th International Conference on Management, Enterprise and Benchmarking, Budapest.

Tarcsi, A. (2005). *Learner's data description in Educational Information System.* 5th International Conference of PhD Students, Miskolc.

Taylor, F. (1911). *The principles of scientific management,* (pp. 5 – 29). New York, NY: Harper Bros. Retrieved August 16, 2010, from http://www.fordham.edu/halsall/mod/1911taylor.html

Teo, Y., & Ho, D. J. (1998). A systematic approach to the implementation of final year project in an electrical engineering undergraduate course. *IEEE Transactions on Education, 41*(1), 25–30. doi:10.1109/13.660783

Thamisgith. (2011). *Electronic textbooks - Better for students, better for the environment.* Retrieved from http://thamisgith.hubpages.com/hub/Electronic-Textbooks---Better-For-Students--Better-For-The-Environment

The official Bologna Process website. (2007). Retrieved from http://www.ond.vlaanderen.be/hogeronderwijs/bologna

Tiwana, A. (1997). *The knowledge management toolkit - Practical techniques for building a KM system.* Pearson Education.

Tserng, H. P., Yin, S. Y., Dzeng, R., Woud, B., Tsai, M., & Chen, W. (2009). A study of ontology-based risk management framework of construction projects. *Automation in Construction, 18*(7), 994–1008. doi:10.1016/j.autcon.2009.05.005

Uluoglu, B. (2006). *Declarative / procedural knowledge.* Retrieved from http://www.designophy.com/designpedia/design-term-1000000001-declarative-.-procedural-knowledge.htm

Umble, E. J., Haft, R. R., & Umble, M. M. (2003). Enterprise resource planning: Implementation procedures and critical success factors. *European Journal of Operational Research, 146*(2), 241–257. doi:10.1016/S0377-2217(02)00547-7

United Nations Development Programme (UNDP). (1990). *Human development report 1990.* New York, NY: Author. Retrieved from http://hdr.undp.org/en/report/global/hdr1990

Valderrama, E., Rullán, M., Sánchez, F., Pons, J., Mans, C., & Giné, F. ... Peig, E. (2009). Guidelines for the final year project assessment in engineering. *Proceedings of the 39th ASEE/IEEE Frontiers in Education Conference,* M2J-1. San Antonio, Texas.

Van Holsbeck, M., & Jeffrey, Z. (2004). *Security in an ERP world.* IT Toolbox Security. Retrieved December 12, 2004, from http://hosteddocs.ittoolbox.com/MH043004.pdf

Vance, A. (2008). ERP security tools: Data mining and analysis software can help auditors test access controls for key enterprise resource planning systems. *Internal Auditor, 65*(1), 25–27.

Vas, R. (2007). *Tudásfelmérést támogató oktatási ontológia szerepe és alkalmazási lehetőségei* [in Hungarian]. Doctoral dissertation, Corvinus University, Budapest.

Visscher-Voerman, I., & Gustafson, K. (2004). Paradigms in the theory and practice of education and training design. *Educational Technology Research and Development, 52*(2), 69–89. doi:10.1007/BF02504840

Vluggen, M., & Bollen, L. (2005). Teaching enterprise resource planning in a business curriculum. *International Journal of Information and Operations Management Education, 1*(1), 44–57. doi:10.1504/IJIOME.2005.007447

von Solms, H., & Hertenberger, M. (2004). A case for information ownership in ERP systems, security and protection. In *Proceedings of the Information Processing Systems, IFIP 18th World Computer Congress TC1119th International Information Security Conference 22–27 August 2004 Toulouse, France.*

Walden, J. (2008). Integrating web application security into the IT curriculum. In the *Proceedings of the 9th ACM SIGITE conference on Information technology education (SIGITE '08).* ACM.

Wally, S., & Baum, J. R. (1994). Personal and structural determinants of the pace of strategic decision making. *Academy of Management Journal, 37,* 932–956. doi:10.2307/256605

Wang, M.-L., & Yang, F. F. (2010). How does CRM create better customer outcomes for small deucational institutions? *African Journal of Business Management, 4*(16), 3541–3549.

Wikipedia. (n.d.). *Open access.* Retrieved June 1, 2011, from http://en.wikipedia.org/wiki/Open_access

Wilson, H. (2010). Factors for success in CRM systems. *Journal of Marketing Management, 18,* 193–219. doi:10.1362/0267257022775918

Wilson, J., & Lindoo, E. (2011). Using SAP ERP software in online distance education. *Journal of Computing Sciences in Colleges, 26*(5), 218–222.

Winer, R. (2001). A framework for customer relationship management. *California Management Review*, *43*(4), 89–105.

Wood, T., & Caldas, M. P. (2001). Reductionism and complex thinking during ERP implementations. *Business Process Management Journal*, *7*(5), 387–393. doi:10.1108/14637150110406777

Wu, J., & Wang, Y. (2006). Measuring ERP success: The ultimate users' view. *International Journal of Operations & Production Management*, *26*(8), 882–903. doi:10.1108/01443570610678657

Wynn, M., Dumas, M., & Fidge, C. (2007). Business process simulation for operational decision support. *Lecture Notes in Computer Science*, *4928*, 66–77. doi:10.1007/978-3-540-78238-4_8

Yang, J., & Jiang, H. (2009). Research of ERP practice teaching system of the economics and management majors of independent institutes. In the *Proceedings of the Second International Conference on Education Technology and Training*, (pp. 56-59).

Young, M. (2007). Enterprise resource planning (ERP): A review of the literature. *International Journal Management and Enterprise Development*, *4*(3), 235–264. doi:10.1504/IJMED.2007.012679

Уилсон Р. Квантовая психология. Киев: Янус. (1998). 304 с.

Zeleny, M. (2012). *Knowledge-information circulation through the enterprise: Forward to the roots of knowledge management*. Retrieved from http://www.bnet.fordham.edu/zeleny/pdf/kn_infor_cir.pdf

Zheng, Y. (2009). Different spaces for e-development. What can we learn from the capability approach? *Information Technology for Development*, *15*(2), 66–82. doi:10.1002/itdj.20115

Zheng, Y., & Walsham, G. (2008). Inequality of what? Social exclusion in the e-society as capability deprivation. *Information Technology & People*, *21*(3), 222–243. doi:10.1108/09593840810896000

Zlate, M. (1999). *Psihologia mecanismelor cognitive* (The psychology of cognitive mechanisms).

About the Contributors

Kanubhai K. Patel is Assistant Professor of Computer Science at Ahmedabad University. He previously worked as faculty member at Gujarat University. He completed his MCA from Gujarat Vidyapith, Ahmedabad in June 1997. Areas of research interest for Patel include assistive technology, virtual learning environments, computer networks, and enterprise resource planning. He has authored over fifteen publications, including two refereed journal papers and three book chapters. He is reviewer in couple of peer reviewed journals.

Sanjay K. Vij received his PhD degree from IIT, Bombay, in 1974. He is currently a Director in the Department of CE-IT-MCA, Sardar Vallabhbhai Patel Institute of Technology (SVIT), Vasad. His research interests include text mining, knowledge management, and NLP. He has authored over twenty publications, including over seven refereed journal papers and two book chapters. He is a registered PhD guide with Dharmsinh Desai University, Nadiad. He is Member Board of Studies at MS University, Baroda and Dharmsinh Desai University, Nadiad. He had been a panel of experts/advisor in GSLET and GPSC. He is reviewer in couple of peer reviewed journals. He has been Chairman of Computer Society of India, Vadodara Chapter.

* * *

Rosa Mª Aguilar is a Permanent Lecturer at the University of La Laguna. She teaches simulation techniques and intelligent control within the Advanced Computer Engineering and Industrial Automatic and Electronic Engineering degree courses. Her research interests focus on the modelling and simulation of systems, as well as on the use of artificial intelligence techniques in decision making processes within complex systems. She defended her doctoral thesis in 1998 and she has participated in 25 research projects, acting as principal researcher in ten of them. She has around 60 conference publications to her name and has supervised a total of 4 doctoral theses.

Silvia Alayón is Assistant Professor at University of La Laguna (Spain). Her PhD has been developed in the Computer Science field. Her research areas are focused on machine learning, classification and medical image processing. In the educational field she is working on the design of the technical and legal procedures needed for the development of the final year project by engineering students in enterprises.

Annika Andersson is a coordinator for "ERP-systems as a pedagogical tool" in US.B.E - Umea School of Business and Economics in Sweden. She has experiences from ERP-systems in education since 2006. Her research since 2003 has been in the area of Management-Project management focusing learning in contracted ERP-projects. As a project manager for ERP-education her tasks are coordination, integration of methods, content knowledge, PBL, and cases.

Douglas Archibald is the educational researcher scientist at the C.T. Lamont Centre for Research in Primary Care, Bruyère Research Institute and the Department of Family Medicine, University of Ottawa. Dr. Archibald has a PhD in Education (University of Ottawa) and a Masters of Arts in Education (Ontario Institute for Studies in Education). His program of research incorporates various facets of medical education which include interprofessional education, research methodology, and eLearning. Some recent projects have included the assessment of an online training program involving simulation to improve medical residents' knowledge and skills to manage patients with inflammatory arthritis and the development and validation of assessment instruments for interprofessional education. Doug has recent publications in the fields of eLearning and health care education.

Yeray Callero was born in Haría, Lanzarote and attended the University of La Laguna, where he studied Computer Science and obtained his degree in 2008. He is currently working on his PhD with the Department of Systems Engineering and Automation at the same university. His PhD research is focused on health monitoring via mobile phones and ultra-low energy body area networks. In addition, he has experience in another research fields like simulation of business processes and business processes reengineering.

Agnes Chigona holds a Doctorate Degree in Education. She is currently employed by Cape Peninsula University of Technology to teach Research Methods, and supervise postgraduate students in the Faculty of Education and Social Sciences. Her current research interests are in area of adoption and use of Information Communication Technologies in teacher education as well as the domestication of the technology in institution of higher learning for teaching and learning.

Rabelani Dagada is a Lecturer of Information and Communications Technology, and Knowledge Management at the Wits Business School of the University of the Witwatersrand, Johannesburg. Dagada has over 16 years experience in the field of ICT and knowledge management. His role in academia is a departure from successful career in the industry. Actually, he still serves as a consultant in corporate South Africa. Dagada was the Winner of 2008 ICT Visionary Award. He was honoured by the Computer Society of South Africa (CSSA) and the IT Web during the 2008 CSSA Annual President's Awards Banquet which took place in Montecasino on 5th November 2008. He received the Award "in recognition of foresight and achievement in transforming business by adopting and implementing leading-edge technology." Dagada is the President of the CSSA and a member of its Board of Directors.

Krishma Desai has been working as an Assistant Professor in the Department of Textile Technology. Prof. Desai has also started her career with the industry where she had worked for over 1 year before joining an academic institution. She has over 14 years of experience and actively involved in the areas of technical textiles, development of fabric structures, CAD/CAM in textiles, et cetera. She has published and/ or presented over 15 papers in national as well as international journals and conferences.

Gayatri Doctor is currently an Associate Professor at the Faculty of Technology Management, CEPT University, Ahmedabad, India. She graduated with BSc in Mathematics, Computer Science and Physics from Jadavpur University Calcutta. Did her Masters in Computer Applications (MCA) from MS University, Baroda, MPhil in Information Technology from Gujarat Vidyapith and a PhD in Information Technology from DharamSinh Desai University, Nadiad. She started her career with corporate experience at WIPRO Infotech, then research experience at the INFLIBNET Programme of University Grants Commission. She then moved to academics, having been at Faculty at the ICFAI Business School, a visiting faculty at different institutions like Gujarat Vidyapith, Gujarat University. Her areas of interest are Digital Repositories and Knowledge Management.

Carina Gonzalez is Assistant Professor at University of La Laguna (Spain). She has done her PhD in Computer Science. Her research interests are focused on the application of Artificial Intelligence techniques, multimedia adaptive interfaces, and social videogames in Education. Currently she is working on the evaluation of learning communities in virtual environments of CSCL and 3D games. Carina has written widely in the field of computer science applied to the educational field.

Michael Hirsh, M.D., C.C.F.P, F.C.F.P., a family physician currently practicing in Ottawa, is a preceptor for medical students and is the Director of Undergraduate Medical Education for the Department of Family Medicine at the University of Ottawa. Trained in Montreal, he joined the Family Medicine Unit at the Queen Elizabeth Hospital in 1985, where he developed an interest in medical education, as well as rural, becoming the Director of the Family Medicine Rural Program at McGill University. After moving to Ottawa in 1993, he joined the University of Ottawa's Family Medicine Department as the Director of Community Teaching Practices. In 2005, he became the Distributed Medical Education Director at The Faculty of Medicine expanding his role to working with learners in both Family Medicine and Specialty disciplines. In 2010, after completing a term as Faculty Distributed Medical Education Director, Dr. Hirsh returned to the Department of Family Medicine to assume the position of Undergraduate Medical Education Director, a position he continues to lead today.

Tor Atle Hjeltnes received an MS degree in Industrial Economics and Technology Management from the Norwegian University of Science and Technology, in 2002. He is currently a Business Developer at the TISIP Research Foundation, Principal at TISIP Vocational College, and Assistant Professor at the Faculty of Informatics and E-Learning at Sør-Trøndelag University College. Since 2002, Tor Atle has worked on several national and international research e-learning projects. Relevant focus areas have been development and delivery of tailor made e-learning courses with credits for the public and private sector and projects focusing on models for cost effective and cost efficient e-learning. Tor Atle lectures in both online and on campus courses in sales, marketing management, economics, multidisciplinary collaboration, and entrepreneurship (www.itfag.hist.no).

Rebecca J. Hogue is pursuing a PhD in Education at the University of Ottawa. Her professional background is in instructional design and software quality assurance. She holds a Master of Arts Degree in Distributed Learning (Distance Education), and a Bachelor of Science Degree in Computer Science. Her passion is for teaching learning professionals how to integrate technology into their teaching practice. Her research involves creating faculty development resources for integrating mobile technology into university teaching.

Theodoros Kargidis is a Professor in the Department of Marketing, of ATEI of Thessaloniki. He graduated from Aristotle University of Thessaloniki Greece with a diploma in Economics, while obtained his Master's (D.E.S.S.) from Universite Paris I Pantheon Sorbonne and PhD in E-Leaning from the department of Applied Informatics, of the University of Macedonia. Currently remains active in the area of accounting information systems, management, and entrepreneurship. He has published several articles in international scientific journals and conferences.

Prakashchandra Khatwani holds the position of Head, Department of Textile Technology and also worked for about 4 years as the Head of Institution. He has over 26 years of experience which includes 7 years with the industries. At present also, he has been actively associated with the industries by way of setting-up of textile units, design and development of machinery components/parts/textile products, providing technical know-how to the technocrats- particularly, in the areas of technical textiles, training to man power from industries. His present area of work is automation in weaving industries – the project is supported by Department of Science and Technology, New Delhi. He has published / presented over 90 papers in national/international journals / conferences.

Donna Leith-Gubranson is the Manager of Special Projects at the Department of Family Medicine, University of Ottawa. In this capacity, she plans, manages, and implements numerous projects including the DFM's recent awarding of full accreditation from the College of Family Physicians of Canada, the implementation of the DFM's three-year strategic plan, the redevelopment of the postgraduate curriculum, the design and implementation of the DFM's faculty development program and the establishment of a departmental communications plan. She oversees and monitors overall project status including schedules, progress, coordination, deliverable, milestones, and financial reports.

Colla MacDonald is a Full Professor in the Faculty of Education, cross appointed with the Faculty of Medicine, and a Senior Researcher at the Élisabeth Bruyère Research Institute. Her research concentrates on curriculum design, evaluation, and eLearning. She has published over 80 refereed articles, book chapters, and conference proceedings. Colla has been principal investigator of SSHRC, Ministry of Health and Long-Term Care, Inukshuk Wireless, Canadian Foundation for Innovation, Office of Learning Technologies and CIHR funded research projects. Currently, seven PhD students work with her to conduct research on various aspects of emerging technologies. She published the Demand-Driven Learning Model and W(e)Learn framework, which have been as quality standards to design, delivery, and assess programs. Colla has won the International WebCt Exemplary Course Award (twice) the Business/ Professional 2010 International e-Learning Award, and the Faculty of Education's top researcher award. She is on an advisory committee with the World Health Organization and has two eBooks accepted for publication by Bentham Science Publishers.

Martha McKeen is a PhD student in the Faculty of Education at the University of Ottawa. She is also the Coordinator of Special Projects at the Department of Family Medicine and has worked on several high profile portfolios including the redevelopment of the postgraduate curriculum, the development of a faculty development program and also provides support to community and rural faculty members. Martha has represented her work at several local and national conferences including the 2011 Family Medicine Forum in Montreal, the 2011 Academy for Innovation in Medical Education (AIME) Day in Ottawa, and most recently at the 2012 Jean-Paul Dionne Symposium in Ottawa.

Madeleine Montpetit is an Assistant Professor at the University of Ottawa and a practicing family physician at the Riverside Family Health Team where she supervises residents and is the Unit Postgraduate program director. She is presently the Physician Lead for Faculty Development at the Department of Family Medicine and her interests include Curriculum Design, Remediation and The Struggling Learner and Innovations in Medical Education. She is a cofounder of the Academic Support Process website which is an open access online resource for medical teachers. Her list of awards include the Andre Peloquin Memorial Award for Excellence in Medical Education (2011), The University of Ottawa Award of Excellence in Innovation in Postgraduate Medical Education (2010), The Ottawa Hospital Physician Clinician Recognition Award (2010) and Teacher of the Year (2007). She has been the recipient of multiple funding offerings for Faculty Development Projects. Her significant role in this project spanned from conception, through development to implementation phases of the initiative.

Vanesa Muñoz received her MS degree in Computer science in 2001 and her PhD degree in Computer Science in 2007 from the University of La Laguna. She is assistant professor in the Department of Systems Engineering and Control and Computer Architecture at the University of La Laguna, Spain. Her current research interests are decision-making, discrete event simulation, human computer interaction, artificial intelligence, intelligent agents, and intelligent tutorial systems. She has participated in a total of 9 research projects and she has published 12 papers in journals and around 30 papers in conferences.

Viral Nagori is working as an Asst. Professor in GLS Institute of Computer Technology (MCA) in Ahmedabad from last 7 years and in total having 8 years of experience in academic. He has done BBA, MCA and currently pursuing PhD in Computer Science in the area of "Design of Expert system prototype for analysis and implementation of motivational strategies on ICT Human Resources." He has published 8 papers in national and international conferences and journals. Other areas of interest include delivering talks on time management, stress management, motivation, leadership, and soft skills.

Colla MacDonald is a Full Professor in the Faculty of Education, cross appointed with the Faculty of Medicine, and a senior researcher at the Élisabeth Bruyère Research Institute. Her research concentrates on curriculum design, evaluation, and eLearning. She has published over 80 refereed articles, book chapters, and conference proceedings. Colla has been principal investigator of SSHRC, Ministry of Health and Long-Term Care, Inukshuk Wireless, Canadian Foundation for Innovation, Office of Learning Technologies and CIHR funded research projects. Currently, seven PhD students work with her to conduct research on various aspects of emerging technologies. She published the Demand-Driven Learning Model and W(e)Learn framework, which have been as quality standards to design, delivery, and assess programs. Colla has won the International WebCt Exemplary Course Award (twice) the Business/

Professional 2010 International e-Learning Award, and the Faculty of Education's top researcher award. She is on an advisory committee with the World Health Organization and has two eBooks accepted for publication by Bentham Science Publishers.

Martha McKeen is a Ph.D. student in the Faculty of Education at the University of Ottawa. She is also the Coordinator of Special Projects at the Department of Family Medicine and has worked on several high profile portfolios including the redevelopment of the postgraduate curriculum, the development of a faculty development program and also provides support to community and rural faculty members. Martha has represented her work at several local and national conferences including the 2011 Family Medicine Forum in Montreal, the 2011 Academy for Innovation in Medical Education (AIME) Day in Ottawa, and most recently at the 2012 Jean-Paul Dionne Symposium in Ottawa.

Erika Nyitrai received a MSc teaching degree of Mathematics and Informatics at Eötvös Loránd University Faculty of Science in 2006. Since 2004, she works for the Faculty of Informatics as a demonstrator. In 2006, she became an Assistant Professor there, at Department of Algorithms and their Applications. Now she teaches algorithms, data structures, programming for beginners, and graphics. In 2006, she started doctoral studies at PhD School of Computer Science of Eötvös Loránd University. Her topic is XML databases, Semantic Web, ontologies, and conclusions. She is interested in creating, searching, and sharing educational materials, and the possibilities of describing the knowledge of training and the structure of a university, with using ontologies.

Srinivas Subbarao Pasumarti is Professor and Head, Department of Management Studies, Commerce and HRM of Maharajahs Post Graduate College, Vizianagaram. Presently he is working as Director, Center for Management Research and Chief Coordinator, Center for Entrepreneurship Development. He obtained MBA (IB), MBA (Fin), M.Com. M.H.R.M., MA, M.Phil, B.L., Ph.D. PGDCS., P.G.D.Ex.M.M., PGD T, and T.M from various universities. Recently Berhampur University awarded D.Litt (Post Doctoral research) on his thesis on FDI in Tourism. He is the first person in the faculty of Commerce & Management studies of Andhra University area who received the D.Litt. He is an alumnus of IIM, Ahmedabad. He is an approved research guide of various universities Ph.D. students. He authored and edited 21 books in the area of finance, tourism, and cases in management. Besides a list (90) of articles, book chapters, case studies, book reviews and research papers were published in various national and international journals. He presented papers in various international conferences held at Singapore, Malaysia, Thailand, Australia, Srilanka, Turkey, China, and Japan.

Elena Railean is a researcher at the Academy of Science of Moldova. She was written the book "Methodology of Educational Software" and over 53 articles in theory and practice of pedagogy and educational technology. She writes at the intersection of philosophy of learning, cybernetic pedagogy, competence pedagogy, quantum psychology, and knowledge management. The focus of her research is to investigate the metasystems approach of learning processes, knowledge based design, principles of writing, and assessment in digital semantic workspaces. Elena is author of new didactical model for electronic textbook development, which affordance is to develop the core structure of competence through dynamic and flexible instructional strategy.

Suseela Rani is a Post Graduate in Commerce, Business Management (HRM) and also holds a Diploma in Computer Science obtained from Andhra University. She is pursuing her PhD on Industrial Relations in Indian Jute Industry in post liberalization. She is having 4 years teaching experience besides 14 years of IT industry experience (educational software development). At present she is working as Associate Professor, Department of MBA, TRR College of Engineering & Technology, Patancheru, Medak (Dt.), A.P., India. She presented papers in various national seminars held in different parts of the country. She published around 10 articles on different areas of HRM and finance in various national and international journals.

Christine Rivet is an Associate Professor at the Department of Family Medicine at the University of Ottawa. She is also a practicing family physician at the Melrose Family Health Centre at the Civic Campus of the Ottawa hospital where she supervises residents. Dr. Rivet completed her Medical degree at McGill University. She has also completed Master's level courses in Evidence-Based Medicine at Oxford University and is a graduate of the University of Western Ontario's Masters of Clinical Science in Family Medicine program. She recently completed a Diploma in Practical Dermatology from Cardiff University in Wales. Dr. Rivet was instrumental in the design and facilitation of the Essential Teaching Skills course. She is an experienced faculty development educator who brings relevance and practicality to physician learning.

Jorge A. Romero has a PhD in Management Science and also holds an MBA from The University of Texas at Dallas. He has expertise in market measures of firm performance, and accounting information systems. He currently works as Assistant Professor in the Accounting Department at Towson University. Also, he has industry experience in the United States and Latin America.

José Luis Sánchez is Professor at University of La Laguna (Spain). He has done his PhD about mathematical methods and programming to study the EEG evolution. His research areas are mainly focused on signal processing and medical image processing. Currently, he is working on nevus segmentation and applications of fractional calculus to control and image processing. In the educational field, he is working on the evaluation of transversal competences in higher education in engineering and in knowledge representation.

Arvid Staupe holds an MS degree in Computer Science from the Norwegian Institute of Technology (NTH). Currently Associate Professor of Computer Science in the Department of Computer and Information Science at Norwegian University of Science and Technology, he served previously as principal of Trondheim Technical University College. Arvid has considerable experience with online distance learning and computers in education, and has held several key positions with Norwegian and Nordic governmental authorities in relation to the use of computers in education. He has been the director of a Research and Development division in the Norwegian Ministry of Education and Research, an adviser in the Research Council of Norway, a member of the Nordic Council for introducing computers into schools, and a member of the Norwegian government's advisory group on computers in education. Further, he has participated in several Norwegian and European R&D projects within the field of e-learning.

Knut Arne Strand received an MS degree in Informatics from the University of Trondheim, Norway, in 1994. He worked in the IT industry in the Nordic region for 13 years before joining Sør-Trøndelag University College as an Assistant Professor in 2007. He is currently a PhD candidate in the field of customized e-learning for corporate clients, with a particular focus on interdisciplinary involvement of relevant stakeholders in the design and development of new e-learning deliveries. Knut Arne is enrolled in the doctoral program in the Department of Computer and Information Science at Norwegian University of Science and Technology, and is employed as a PhD candidate at the Faculty of Informatics and E-Learning at Sør-Trøndelag University College.

Adam Tarcsi received an MSc teaching degree of Informatics at Eötvös Loránd University Faculty of Informatics in 2004. In 2004, he started doctoral studies at PhD School of Computer Science of Eötvös Loránd University. His research is based in Web Information Systems. He has experience in SAP and Web development and in business analytics. In 2008 he became an Assistant Professor at the Department of Media and Educational Informatics. Now he teaches SAP Development, Enterprise Resource Planning, Services-Oriented Architectures, and Web Engineering. He is the Leader of the Web Engineering Research Team and the ERP Research Team at Eötvös Loránd University Faculty of Informatics. He is also the principal researcher of ERP and Enterprise Application Development research projects there.

Theodosios Tsiakis is a Lecturer in the Department of Marketing, of ATEI of Thessaloniki. He belongs in the Division of Organization and Management, expert in economics and specialized in Management of Information Systems. He graduated from the department of International and European Economic and Political Studies from the University of Macedonia and received his Ph.D. in Information Security Economics from the department of Applied Informatics, of the University of Macedonia. His research interests are security economics, e-business, risk management, trust, and Information Systems Management. He has published several articles in international scientific journals and conferences.

Balázs Varga received a MSC teaching degree of Mathematics and Physics at Eötvös Loránd University Faculty of Science in 2001, and a MSC teaching degree of informatics at Eötvös Loránd University Faculty of Informatics in 2004. Since 1999 he works for the Faculty of Informatics as a demonstrator. He became an Assistant Professor at Department of Algorithms and their Applications in 2001. Now he teaches algorithms, data structures, formal languages, and graphics. He started doctoral studies at PhD School of Computer Science of Eötvös Loránd University in 2001. His topic is indexing of multimedia materials, Semantic Web, and ontologies.

Index